T0102741

Spirituality and Human Psyche

Spirituality and Human Psyche

Nandita Chaube

ISBN:	Softcover	978-1-4828-6759-6
	eBook	978-1-4828-6758-9

Print information available on the last page.

To order additional copies of this book, contact
Partridge India
000 800 10062 62
orders.india@partridgepublishing.com

www.partridgepublishing.com/india

Contents

Section B

Preface

This book *"**Spirituality and Human Psyche**"* is a compilation of the original thoughts and empirical work done in the area of spirituality, well-being, unusual experiences, and mental health etc. It can be clearly seen that the human psyche is a very complex phenomenon which is very difficult to interpret and understand. A number of studies have been conducted on the various aspects of human psyche but it is still an unresolved mystery and probably this is the reason why Psychology doesn't have any clear explanation for these phenomenons. Moreover it will not be unrelated to state that human nature has a tendency of attributions. Hence in such situations when there is a lack of the evidences people tend to use their hunch to explain such phenomenon and they become more spiritual and attribute God for these occurrences.

The present book is an effort to solve this mystery in special connection with spiritual powers. It is an attempt to provide logical interpretations and connections between various psychic phenomenon and spirituality via various concepts of spirituality, psychic experiences and other pseudo sciences. This book will be of great interest and concern to the people who experience extra sensory perceptions and have interest in the study of spiritualism.

Needless to say that in the contemporary era of science and logic where no solid evidence for the explanation of the phenomenon like unusual experiences, extra sensory perceptions in connection with spirituality is present, the occurrences of such phenomenon are still widely seen and therefore it is receiving immense attention of the readers in general. The book reflects as an addition to the persistent efforts of the researchers towards the interpretation and causal factors of such phenomenon.

The exceptional feature of the current book is that it focuses upon spirituality in relation to the human psyche which contributes as a distinctive feature of this book. The current book is a compilation of the thoughts of various researchers who view spirituality in connection with the human psychic experiences. The available books in the market are basically concerned with the subject matter of spirituality but the current book is a collection of versatile thoughts of various researchers on spirituality in association with psychic phenomenon. Hence the book justifies its title and it is assumed that because of this feature the book will be successful to draw the attention of the readers.

Acknowledgements

I show my reverence to the supreme divinity God whose gracious blessings gave me the required devotion for the compilation of this work.

I am highly indebted to my father Mr. Ashutosh Chaube and mother Dr. Abha Sharma for their constant motivation and unconditional support. Without their invaluable contributions it would never have been possible to present this book in its present form. I am grateful and express my thanks to my grandparents who have been an inspiration to me.

I owe my special thanks to Prof. K. Ramakrishana Rao, Chancellor, GITAM University, Visakhapatnam for providing me all his precious time and sharing his valuable knowledge and ideas.

I express my thanks to Prof. S.K. Dubey, Vice-chancellor Amity University Rajasthan for providing the necessary work environment to complete this work and giving support by his knowledgeable ideas.

With deep sense of gratitude I acknowledge Prof. S.L. Kothari, Pro-Vice-Chancellor f Amity University Rajasthan for providing me enormous support and motivation to produce quality work.

I would be failing my duty if I fail to express my inexplicable gratitude Dr. G.K. Aseri for motivating me throughout my work and helping me to continue my struggle towards academic achievements.

Last but not the least I express my sincere thanks to all the contributors of this book, for being patient and showing trust.

List of Contributors

Dr. Nandita Chaube
Assistant Professor, Amity Institute of Behavioral and Allied Sciences, Amity University Rajasthan, INDIA

Ms. Caroline Fernandes
Certified Holistic Wellness Life Coach, Innervision Wellness LLC Georgia, UNITED STATES

Aneesh Kumar P
Department of Psychology
Christ University, Bangalore, India

Chitrankana Bandyopadhyay
Department of Psychology
Christ University, Bangalore, India

Mr. Boban Eranimos,
Research Scholar, School of Behavioural Sciences, Mahatama Gandhi University, Kottayam, Kerala, INDIA

Mr. Shuvabrata Poddar
Assistant Professor, Department of Clinical Psychology, Central Institute of Psychiatry (CIP), Ranchi, INDIA

Dr. Arthur Funkhouser
Instructor,* C. G. Jung Institute, Küsnacht, *SWITZERLAND

Dr. Dharmendra Sharma
Counselor, Fiji National University, Suva, FIJI

Ms Bosky Sharma
Research Officer, Fiji National University, Suva, FIJI

Dr. Meeta Malhotra
Assistant Professor, Amity Institute of Behavioral and Allied Sciences, Amity University Haryana, Gurgaon, INDIA

Mr. Prateek Kumar Singh
Assistant Professor, Maharani Laxmi Bai Government College of Excellence, Gwalior, Madhya Pradesh, INDIA

Prof. Akbar Husain
Professor, Department of Psychology, Aligarh Muslim University, Uttar Pradesh, INDIA

Fauzia Nazam
Research Scholar, Department of Psychology, Aligarh Muslim University, Uttar Pradesh, INDIA

Dr. Nudrat Jahan
Assistant Professor, Department of Clinical Psychology, Faculty of Behavioural and Health Sciences, SGT University, Gurgaon, Haryana, INDIA

Dr. Zar Nigar
Guest Lecturer,
Centre for Study of Comparative religions and Civilizations, Jamia Millia Islamia, New Delhi, INDIA

Dr. Anita Chauhan
Assistant Professor (Psychology), L.L.R. Institute of Legal Studies, Solan HP, INDIA

Ms Tara Overzat
MS, LAPC, NCC, Mercer University, University of North Georgia, UNITED STATES

Ms Annie Singh
Research Scholar
Department of Psychology and Wellbeing, School of Humanities and Social Sciences, Gautam Buddha University, Greater NOIDA, Uttar Pradesh, INDIA

Dr. Subhasis Bhadra
Assistant Professor and Head, Department of Social Work, Gautam Buddha University, Greater Noida, Uttar Pradesh, INDIA

Satchit Prasun Mandal
Department of Psychology, Banaras Hindu University, Varanasi (UP), INDIA

Yogesh Kumar Arya
Department of Psychology, Banaras Hindu University, Varanasi (UP), INDIA

Rakesh Pandey
Department of Psychology, Banaras Hindu University, Varanasi (UP), INDIA

Dr. Anurag Upadhyay
Lecturer, Government Collage, Uttar Pradesh, INDIA

Dr. Rejani.TG.
Faculty, Institute of Behavioural Sciences, Gujarat Forensic Sciences University, Gujarat, INDIA

Vaishali Mardhekar
Visiting Faculty, Modern College of Arts, Science and Commerce, Pune, INDIA

Neha Vartak
Remedial Teacher, Prasanna Autism Centre, Pune, Maharashtra, INDIA

Dr. P.Vijayalakshmi Anbu
Senior Lecturer in Psychology, Faculty of Allied Health Science, Sri Ramachandra University, Chennai, INDIA

Ms Aanchal Sharda
PG Student University of Delhi, INDIA

Mr. Subhash Meena
Research Scholar, Department of Psychology, Jai Narain Vyas University, Jodhpur, Rajasthan, INDIA

Dr. Nadeem Luqman
Assistant Professor, Amity Institute of Behavioral and Allied Sciences, Amity University Haryana, INDIA

Dr. Supriya Srivastava
Assistant Professor, Amity Institute of Behavioral and Allied Sciences,
Amity University Haryana, INDIA

Dr. Amita Puri
Associate Professor, Amity Institute of Behavioral and Allied Sciences,
Amity University Haryana, INDIA

Dr. Debjani Mukhrerjee
Head, Department. of Psychology, St. Thomas College, Bhilai CG, INDIA

Rashmi Singh
Assistant Professor,
Department of Psychology, Mahatma Gandhi. Kashi Vidyapith University, Varanasi, U.P., INDIA

Interpretation of Sleep Paralysis as a Paranormal Experience: Indian Perspective

Nandita Chaube

Abstract: The present study aims to explain the paranormal view of sleep paralysis prevailing in India. Sleep Paralysis is associated with a hypnogogic or hypnopompic state in which the sufferer feels inability to move, speak or react. It is a intermediary state between wakefulness and sleep that consequentially leads to complete muscle atonia (muscle weakness). Scientific explanations describes this state as a hypervigilant state of amygdala during sleep but some researches explain it in terms of paranormal happenings like demonic attacks on the individual. Indian view of sleep paralysis explains it under three clusters. The first cluster takes into account high prevalence of sleep paralysis among young adults and negative give and take accounts with ghost or ancestor in *Pataal* (Hell). The second cluster is based upon the sleeping position. It is observed that mostly sleep paralysis is likely to occur while the sleeper is lying in supine position. In this position *Kundalini*, a spiritual energy that regulates the healthy functioning of body organs is less active and hence the flow of energy is reduced and it is easier to immobilize the motor system of the sleeper. The third cluster explains the time of occurrence of sleep paralysis. Some spiritual findings are in contrast with the scientific findings that sleep paralysis occurs in deep sleep when the negative energies are to put least efforts to carry out their desires. The present paper throws light on the controversy between spiritual and scientific interpretations of sleep paralysis in specific reference to Indian explanations.

Introduction

Sleep Paralysis is a state in which the individual suffers from temporary inability to move, speak, react, cry out or opening eyes etc. This state occurs either when falling asleep or waking up. The sufferer of sleep paralysis reports being conscious about his/her surroundings but inability to perform voluntary functions. In the writings of Samuel Johnson sleep paralysis is considered to be the effort of demons, which sit on the chests of sleepers and molest them. Sometimes this demon may do some strangling acts like exerting pressure on the chest. Sufferers of sleep paralysis may also report floating sensations, out-of-body experiences and and other types of hallucinations (Hufford, 1982). These unusual sensory experiences are called hypnagogic and hypnopompic experiences. Most often the sufferer is released from this state within few seconds or minutes but a persistant anxiety continues as an after affect of Sleep Paralysis. Excessive effort to move the body may result in intense pain in the limbs when trying to move them.

Sleep Paralysis is most likely to occur when someone is lying in a supine position. This state may last for seconds to minutes and rarely longer for about an hour too. People frequently report sense of presence which they perceive as threatening. An extreme sense of fear is common in such experiences. The sense of this felt presence is very vague and difficult to describe. Sufferer may feel to be on vigilance of the demon and also being monitored by it.

Sleep Paralysis is most often associated with narcolepsy which is a neurological condition where people experience irresistible sleep attacks that can occur anytime during the day such as while driving, eating, working, talking etc. This state lasts for about 10-20 minutes after which the person feels so refreshed. A study reports that 60% of the non-narcoleptic population experiences sleep paralysis at least once in their lives (French & Santomauro, 2007). Another related concern is cataplexy which is characterized by a sudden loss of muscle tone during the states of extreme excitement. This loss of muscle tone may be partial or complete. In the complete loss of muscle tone the person may simply collapse. Although the sufferers remain conscious during the episode of cataplexy and they may also experience hallucinations during prolonged attacks and subsequently fall asleep.

However, Sleep Paralysis is a condition not necessarily associated with narcolepsy always and vice versa. Studies suggest that the prevalence of sleep paralysis among people suffering from narcolepsy is not static and in the range of 40% to 60% (Hishikawa, 1976).

Symptoms

Cheyne et al. (2000) have observed some of the prominent symptoms of Sleep Paralysis -

1. It occurs frequently among 3-6% of the world population.
2. It is more likely to happen to young adults. About 30% of young adults experience Sleep paralysis at least once in their lives.
3. It can last from a few minutes to a few hours at a time.
4. People also experience, sense a presence during the state of paralysis. Fear grips them and some of them have said that a demonic force was out to possess their soul or was trying to crush or smother them.
5. In some cases, people feel pressure or a choking sensation. This is accompanied by breathing difficulties. In few instances, this escalates into sexual molestation or assault.
6. A foul smell has been perceived at times during the paralytic attack.
7. It is more likely to happen when sleeping on one's back (supine position).
8. People who go through it are embarrassed by the event thinking that something must be wrong with them mentally.

Classification

There are two main categorizations of sleep paralysis, isolated sleep paralysis, isolated sleep paralysis and recurrent isolated sleep paralysis. Of these two types, isolated sleep paralysis is much more common than recurrent isolated sleep paralysis. Isolated sleep paralysis episodes are most likely to occur at the time sleep onset and sleep offset. Evidences suggest that the sleep paralysis occurs more often when the sleeper is lying in a supine position but the mechanism for this is not known (McCarty & Chesson, 2009). Episodes of isolated sleep paralysis are usually not very frequent and they occur for a short period, roughly about a minute or so. One time occurrence of sleep paralysis in an individual's lifetime is also evident. On the other hand recurrent isolated sleep paralysis is a chronic condition in which the sufferer encounters frequent episodes of sleep paralysis throughout their lifetime. One of the major differences between isolated sleep paralysis and recurrent isolated sleep paralysis is duration. Episodes of recurrent isolated sleep paralysis can persist for about an hour or so, and the sufferer is more likely to experience perceived out of body experiences. Whereas isolated sleep paralysis episodes are generally short (hardly of a minute) and are particularly occur with the intruder and incubus hallucinations. In isolated sleep paralysis the sufferer will never have more than one episode but it is likely to happen in recurrent isolated sleep paralysis.

Prevalence

Sleep paralysis can be seen in about 6.2% of the general population. It is more common with the patients of narcolepsy. Evidences suggest that about 30-40 % of narcoleptic population has sleep paralysis as a comorbid symptom. It has been noticed that majority of the sufferers of sleep paralysis suffer from irregular episodes once in a month or once in a year. In case of recurrent isolated sleep paralysis only 3% of the population has been seen to suffering from it. Sleep paralysis is common among both males and females irrespective of gender, however 36% of the general population within the age range of 25-44 years is found to be more vulnerable to develop sleep paralysis.

Causes of Sleep paralysis

There are various factors that can play a very important role in the occurrence of sleep paralysis. Some of them are sleep disruptions like insomnia which is very common in shift workers. Other factors that may increase the risk of sleep paralysis may include depression, anxiety, stress, traumatic life events etc. A number of studies have been conducted concerning the factors working behind the onset or aggravation of sleep paralysis. A study by Hinton, Pich, Chhean, Pollack and McNally (2005) that finds a positive correlation between PTSD and sleep paralysis indicates an increased risk of sleep paralysis attacks with an increase in traumatic life events.

Another study indicates that sleep paralysis is more common in African American than white American populations. It is associated with trauma, stress and depression but not to any psychiatric disorders but substance abuse. They also suggested that sleep disruption has also a role in the sleep paralysis which is an outcome of alcohol and substance abuse which severely disrupts REM sleep (Mellman, Aigbogun, Graves, Lawson & Alim, 2008). There are other evidences too which are suggestive of such associations between sleep paralysis and anxiety. (Otto, Simon, Powers, Hinton, Zalta & Pollack, 2006).

Researches establishing a relationship between the distress caused by a sleep paralysis and social anxiety reveals that distress levels are associated with dysfunctional social imagery, extreme anxiety and fear of death in non-threatening situations as well as feelings of being observed which is likely to provoke feelings of sensed presence (Solomonova, Nielsen, Stenstrom, Simard, Frantova & Donderi, 2008).

Simard and Nielsen (2005) also found a higher level of social anxiety in the sufferers of sleep paralysis who report a feeling of sensed presence as compared to those having no such feelings. They concluded that people with socially anxiety create a frightening hallucination of an evil presence during REM sleep which continues in sleep paralysis. These hallucinations may reflect the image of prior traumatic social events.

The relation of sleep paralysis with depression is also evident in some researches. A study reveals a strong association between sleep paralysis and depression which is not explained by anxiety as a comorbidity of depression but an independent condition for the onset of sleep paralysis. Moreover there are other factors also that increase the chances of sleep paralysis such as stressful life events, sleep disturbances, victims of sexual abuse, sleep deprivation, and genetic link etc. that contribute to sleep paralysis (Szklo-Coxe, Young, Finn & Mignot, 2007).

Sleep Paralysis and unusual experiences: Succubus and Incubus

In the western folklore there is a concept of succubus and incubus that are the types of demons which harass the humans for the satisfaction. An incubus is said to be a male demon that prays on women's chest at night. The aim of incubus is to mate with the female to produce a child. Though this notion is rejected by some scholars who believe that these are the stories made up by the human women to explain pregnancy outside of marriage. However, it is also said that this demon sometimes continues to assault the woman it may eventually result in death. On the other hand a Succubus is a female demon that attacks human males. Many countries on the globe support this notion in different manner. Mesopotamia (2400bc) is the first country which has the first documented evidence of sleep paralysis. Sleep paralysis with hypnagogic and hypnopompic hallucinations have not only been associated with alien abductions, but also with the otherworldly creatures. Over a long period emerged many interpretations and different names for the Demons. In Greece it is Greek ephialtes (one who leaps upon) and mora (the night "mare" or monster, ogre, spirit, etc.), Roman incubus (one who presses or crushes), German mar/mare, nachtmahr, Hexendrücken (witch pressing), and Alpdruck (elf pressure); Czech muera, Polish zmora, Russian Kikimora, French cauchmar (trampling ogre), Old English maere (mab, mair, mare-hag), hagge, (evil spirit or the night-mare--also hegge, haegtesse, haehtisse, haegte); Old Norse mara, Old Irish mar/more, Newfoundland Ag Rog (Old Hag), and the Spanish pesadilla (Hufford, 1982; Sebald, 1978). Greeks had the pnigalion (the choker) and the barychnas (the heavy breather) troubling the sleepers (Keissling, 1977). These creatures not only attacked the humans at night but also were able to change their shapes while attacking. (Keissling, 1977).

Sleep paralysis is usually misinterpreted as nightmare. Kirby (1901) identifies nightmare as the foundation of all mythology. Although some scholars have a very strong view that the occurrence of nocturnal attack in mythology, religion, and legend is very unusual. Ardat lili (Lilitu) was a wicked Sumerian spirit which is said to be the most primitive old hag demon who was capable of flying preferably at night. She very often used to attack sleeping men. She constituted an example of Hebrew Lilith and the Roman Lamia (Russell, 1995). The female demons were known for the nocturnal attacks. In the tradition of Middle East and Europe there are further more related spirits are identified with the prominent wicked behaviours like leaping upon, oppressing, or crushing, supine individuals as they attempt to sleep at night.

Other possible interpretations of sleep paralysis based upon paranormal occurrences

Following are the **possible explanations of** sleep paralysis that are based upon the findings of Spiritual Science Research Foundation (SSRF) which asserts that sufferers of Sleep paralysis can experience or encounter a presence around them during the episode of sleep paralysis because it occurs as a result of the attacks by ghosts (demons, devils, negative energies etc.). This felt presence is experienced due to sixth sense.

Vulnerable young adults

Sleep paralysis is more common in young adults. Spiritual interpretations explain the occurrence of sleep paralysis in young adults in terms of negative give-and-take account with a ghost or ancestor in the subtle regions of the Nether world or Hell (*Paataal*). Moreover higher levels of worldly desires make the young adults prone to be a victim of sleep paralysis because ghosts having predominant worldly desires fulfill their own by possessing the body of such individuals. On the other hand the elderly people who have less of such desires and they are more likely to have a completed give and take account are less likely to have sleep paralysis.

Sleepingbposition

While talking about sleeping position it would be significant to mention about *Kundalini which is a spiritual energy* flowing to the various systems and of the body and is significant for their functioning. While lying on the either side one of the two main channels of the *Kundalini* is active. However in the supine position both the channels flow a much reduced amount of energy and hence the *Kundalini* is least active in supine position which results in reduced or immobilized motor system of the sufferer. This is the reason why most cases of sleep paralysis report the attack to occur while sleeping in the supine position.

Onset and offset of sleep

The spiritual research in contrast to the scientific research says that only 10% of cases experience sleep paralysis while onset of offset of sleep. In 90% of cases it occurs during the sleep. Hence the affected person is not aware of it or semi-aware of it. Spiritual Science Research Foundation while studying the sleep patterns during the sleep paralysis found that the sufferers appeared to be immobile or unconscious at night during the sleep. They were found to be immobile to the efforts of waking them up. Hence it is the most suitable time for the ghosts or negative energies to attack and occupy the human body when they have less energy to resist.

Hallucination

There is a spiritual interpretation of hallucinations that occur during sleep paralysis. A folklore explains that the hallucinations that occur during the sleep paralysis are the outcome of the evil practices of demons and the negative energies. It happens because of the aliens abductions and the demons that sit on your chest in the night. There are many other spiritual interpretations explaining the causes of hallucinations during sleep paralysis but are the most common ones.

Scientific interpretations of sleep paralysis

At night our body releases a chemical that stops us from sleep walking and keeps our brain aligned with your body. During the states of stress, the chemicals in our brain deviate from this norm that results in a partial woke up state. But these chemicals are partially active in the body because the brain is not fully asleep. If all our brain is woke up then the chemicals will dissipate. The reason behind the hallucination during the sleep paralysis is that we dream while in a semi wakeful state. Therefore the hallucination reflects off of our retina and makes us believe that we are seeing an alien etc.

The chemistry of sleep

The mechanism behind the paralysis of muscles has been a mystery though. Early researches pointed out a neurotransmitter called glycine as a responsible factor for the occurrence of sleep paralysis but there are still some researches that prove the occurrence of sleep paralysis even in the absence or blockage of glycine. Hence the researchers of University of Toronto focused upon two different nerve receptors in the voluntary muscles which are metabotropic and ionotropic. Ionotropic responds to both glycine and GABA, while metabotropic responds to GABA and not glycine.

Prevention

There are a number of conditions which are identified to be associated with an increased risk of sleep paralysis such as, sleep deprivation, an erratic sleep schedule, insomnia, stress, sleeping in the supine position, overuse of stimulants, physical fatigue, and few psychiatric medications. Researches also indicate a possibility of genetic component in the occurrence of sleep paralysis in monozygotic twins. Moreover sleeping in the supine position is also considered to be a very prominent factor of sleep paralysis because in this position an obstruction in the sirway may be caused idue to thecollapse of the soft palate. Hence making small body movements, mental movements, eye movements, imagining yourself moving, taking proper sleep, sleeping regularly, sleeping on your side, identifying the triggers, etc can be of a big help in treating sleep paralysis.

Conclusion: Sleep paralysis is a very common phenomenon which is considered to be a scientific in nature but in certain aspects science also fails to explain the factors working behind it. A number of researches have been conducted in this area but there is always found a gap in the information which gives rise to the paranormal explanations of sleep paralysis. Though sleep paralysis is not a dangerous or life threatening phenomenon but it appears to be very dangerous to the sufferer especially in its active phase. It can be dealt by some spiritual practices like chanting, meditation, prayers and by changing the sleeping positions.

References

Baker, R. A. (1992). Alien abductions or alien production? Some not so unusual personal experiences. Lexington, KY: October 1992. Retrieved from: http://www.ufobbs.com/txt4/3057.ufo

Blackmore, S. (1998). Abduction by aliens or sleep paralysis? *Skeptical Inquirer,* 22, 23-28.

Cheyne, J. A. (2000b). Effects of Body Position on Sleep Paralysis and Hypnagogic and Hypnopompic Hallucinations. In preparation.

Solomonova, E., Nielsen, T., Stenstrom, P., Simard, V., Frantova, E. & DonDeri, D. (2008). Sensed presence as a correlate of sleep paralysis distress, social anxiety and waking state social imagery. *Consciousness and Cognition* 17*(1)*49-63.

French, C.C. & Santomauro, J. (2007). Something wicked this way comes: Causes and interpretations of sleep paralysis. In S. Della Sala (Ed.) Tall tales about the mind and brain: Separating fact from fiction (pp.380–398). Oxford: Oxford University Press.

Hinton, D.E., Pich, V., Chhean, D., Pollack, M.H., & McNally RJ. (2005). Sleep paralysis among Cambodian refugees: association with PTSD diagnosis and severity. *Depression and Anxiety,* 22*(2)*47-51.

Hishikawa, Y. (1976). Sleep paralysis. In C. Guilleminault, W. C. Dement & P. Passouant (Eds.) Advances in sleep research. Vol. 3. (pp.97–124). New York: Spectrum.

Hufford, D. J. (1982), The terror that comes in the Night: An experience-centered study of supernatural assault traditions. Philadelphia: University of Pennsylvania Press.

Kiessling, N. (1977). The incubus in English literature: Provenance and progeny. Seattle: Washington State University Press.

McCarty, D.E., Chesson, & A.L. Jr. (2009). A case of sleep paralysis with hypnopompic hallucinations. Recurrent isolated sleep paralysis associated with hypnopompic hallucinations, precipitated by behaviorally induced insufficient sleep syndrome. *Journal of Clinical Sleep Medicine.* 15,5*(1)*83-4.

Mellman, T.A., Aigbogun, N., Graves, R.E., Lawson, W.B., & Alim, T.N. (2008). Sleep paralysis and trauma, psychiatric symptoms and disorders in an adult African American population attending primary medical care. *Depression and Anxiety,* 25*(5)*435-40.

Otto, M.W., Simon, N.M., Powers, M., Hinton, D., Zalta, A.K., & Pollack, M.H. (2006). Rates of isolated sleep paralysis in outpatients with anxiety disorders. *Journal of Anxiety Disorders,* 20*(5)*687-93.

Ramsawh, H.J., Raffa, S.D., White, K.S., & Barlow, D.H. (2008). Risk factors for isolated sleep paralysis in an African American sample: a preliminary study. *Behaviour Therapy*, 39,386-97.

Russell, J. B. (1995). A history of witchcraft: Sorcerers, heretics, and pagans. London: Thames and Hudson.

Sebald, H. (1978). Witchcraft: the heritage of heresy. New York: Elsevier North Holland, Inc.

Simard, V. & Nielsen, T.A. (2005). Sleep paralysis-associated sensed presence as a possible manifestation of social anxiety. *Dreaming*,15, 245-260.

Spanos, N. P. (1996). Multiple identities and false memories: A sociocognitive perspective. Washington, DC: American Psychological Association.

Szklo-Coxe, M., Young, T., Finn, L., & Mignot, E. (2007). Depression: relationships to sleep paralysis and other sleep disturbances in a community sample. *Journal of Sleep Researches, 16(3) 297–312.*

Reiki

M. Caroline Fernandes

Abstract: This article describes Reiki (pronounced Ray -Key) an ancient Japanese art of healing modality which is growing in popularity in the West. This healing modality has three levels of attunements, of which level one is for self-care, level two is for distance and level three is for mastery. Reiki, also known as 'Ki' or 'Chi', is an electrical field of energy that flows through the body, and determines the state of health (Stein, 1995). Using this concept, this article will present three case studies and discuss how Reiki, which is a spiritual practice, is used in hospitals and psychotherapies with much success. Finally, this article concludes with the importance of Reiki practitioner's competency and responsibility towards clients by safeguarding their privacy and rights.

Introduction

Maria sat in her arm chair, cushioned up for her back to relax, feet up to release the aches in her legs. She sat shivering, wondering and occasionally shedding a tear or two thinking how she will be able to face the challenges ahead of her. The second round of chemotherapy started taking its toll. The symptoms were keeping up with the list her doctor had provided. However prepared one might be for the ordeal a breast cancer patient has to undergo, one is never quite prepared to face it. As she sat weak and absorbed in self-pity, Maria did not hear the front door open. When she saw her best friend walk in with a woman she was annoyed, mainly because she didn't want anyone to see her as a vulnerable cancer patient. Being too weak to protest Maria let

Mrs. Braganza, the woman her friend brought along, hold her hand. Maria wanted to protest that it was not a good time but before she uttered the words she felt a surge of energy escaping from her hand that was being held by Mrs. Braganza. Breathing hard and drifting in and out as if in a trance, that is all Maria remembered the next day when she was once again visited by Mrs. Braganza. This time, she had many questions and Mrs. Braganza had all the answers as she placed her hands on Maria's shoulders. Maria's body felt light as it tingled all over. Forty five minutes passed by and all Maria could think was how peaceful she felt. Three months later Mrs. Braganza got a phone call. It was Maria. Maria was excited and full of gratitude as she informed Mrs. Braganza she had returned to work and that her life and her attitude towards chemotherapy and her battle against cancer had changed since the last time she saw her.

Mrs. Braganza is an energy healer. She channels healing energy and transmits it through the palm of her hands into the client's body to restore a normal energy balance and, therefore, health. Bioenergy healing therapy has been used to treat a wide variety of ailments and health problems, and is often used in conjunction with other alternative and conventional medical treatments.

Reiki (pronounced Ray – Key)

The living body, human or animal, radiates warmth and bioenergy. This energy is the life force itself, and has as many names as there are human civilizations. Reiki, also known as 'Ki' or 'Chi', is an electrical field of energy that flows through the body, and determines the state of health. When 'Ki' or 'Chi' departs the living organism, life has departed (Stein, 1995).

The act of laying hands on the human or animal body to comfort and relieve pain is as old as instinct. When experiencing pain, the first thing most people do is put their hands on it. When a child falls and scrapes the knee, the mother instantly touches it (or at times kisses it) and makes it feel better. A mother's instinct when a child is feverish or ill directs her to place her hands on the child's forehead. Human touch conveys warmth, serenity, and healing. It also conveys caring and loving. The same goes for animals. Instead of their hands they use their tongues. This simple act is the basis for all touch healing techniques (Stein, 1995).

Reiki is an ancient Japanese art of healing. In the 1800's Reiki was re-discovered by Mikao Usui as he sought the healing methods used by Buddha and Christ. Today, reiki is widely used in western european and eastern countries. The process of attunement or initiation is what sets reiki apart from every other form of laying on of hands or touch healing modalities. In reiki only a Master/Teacher is able to pass on the attunement to a student. A person who is attuned as a reiki healer has had the body's energy channels opened and cleared of obstructions by the reiki attunements. The student now not only receives an increase in the life energy or 'Ki' for personal healing, but gets connected to the source or all Universal or God.

Reiki is learned in three sequential levels. The first level of initiation, or attunement, is where a reiki master passes on reiki vibration energy to the student. This is believed to make the student more sensitive to bioenergy field variations; it is relevant to basic self-care and easily incorporated into one's lifestyle. The second level enables the reiki student to balance the bioenergy field of the recipient. The third level is the mastery level where a student becomes a teacher (Brathovde, 2006). Reiki healing energy is transfer through laying of hands and distance, meaning a practitioner can be in the same room or physically away from the recipient such as being in a different state or even a different country.

Reiki is an experiential practice and in order to be a skilled reiki practitioner one has to personally practice reiki as self-care. Using reiki on a regular basis helps practitioners to be more connected and in tuned to "inner wisdom" which in turn makes them a good listener. This deeper connection allows practitioners to better understand the process of healing and the frequency of the subtle energy flow from self to recipients. Reiki level one helps with self-care and self-awareness. Reiki level two helps with aiding others through ailments and self-care. Reiki level three supports the practitioner in training reiki level one and reiki level two.

Some of the benefits a reiki session provides includes stress and anxiety reduction, deep relaxation, improved sleep patterns, pain reduction, promotes natural healing, enhances immune system functions, wound healing, supports healthy eating habits, supports pharmaceutical and herbal supplements, reduces side effects of pharmaceutical or herbal supplements, brings mental clarity, and enhances spiritual awareness.

Reiki in Hospitals

Reiki is growing in popularity in hospitals in the UK, USA and Canada. According to Rand (2014) reiki is gaining wider acceptance in the medical establishment. Hospitals are incorporating reiki by training their physicians, nurses and support staff. Additionally, there has been an increase in reiki volunteer in hospitals, hospice and medical centers.

Case Study #1

Samantha is a 48 year old Hispanic female who was receiving chemotherapy for breast cancer. After researching the benefits of Reiki she added it as a complementary and alternative medicine (CAM) to her traditional treatments in order to help her body heal. Samantha mostly scheduled her reiki treatment the day after she received chemotherapy. She firmly believed that reiki reduced the symptoms of chemotherapy when compared to the days she did not receive reiki treatments. During the reiki treatment, Samantha felt a surge of energy in the areas where her breast tissues were healing after the mastectomy. She stated she felt 'hot hands' and a buzzing sensation while the reiki practitioner placed her hands over her chest. Before the reiki treatment, Samantha was not able to lift both of her arms due to the pain and tightness in her chest muscles. After each reiki treatment she was able to comfortably lift her arms up and down. During one of her scheduled reiki treatment the practitioner noticed her right leg felt a 'little off' since on that particular day Samantha's right leg had an extreme surge of bioenergy flow. As a routine after treatment the practitioner shares her general intuitive observations. This time she shared her concerns over the right leg at which Samantha passed off as the side effects to the radiation due to chemotherapy. Nevertheless, her reiki practitioner insisted she check her right leg. During the visit to her oncologist Samantha mentioned the concerns stated by her reiki practitioners. Being a skeptic of holistic healing her oncologist shrugged the information off. However, on Samantha's persistence a series of tests were carried out which resulted as negative. Several weeks later, Samantha called her reiki practitioner to inform her that was in the intensive care unit due to pulmonary embolism during which test results confirmed there were several deep vein thrombosis (DVT) formed in her right leg vein. Her oncologist was speechless. Now the same oncologist has introduced reiki healing as part of a wellness program in the hospital for cancer patients. Until today Samantha continues with her reiki treatments. She is now declared cancer free.

Reiki and Religion

Often Reiki is mistaken to be a religious believe system but it is not a religion and it does not have affiliations to any religion, past or present. Reiki is spiritual in nature and is often known as a 'spiritual practice' mainly since it does not require the practitioner to guide it nor to believe in it. Reiki purely flows with intention. Since Reiki is not faith based, one is free to learn and apply it to their personal belief system. However, there are some reiki practitioners who have developed an understanding to integrate reiki into their religious belief with great success, Dr. Ruth Allen is one of them. In her book 'The Holy Spirit and the Spirit of Reiki', Dr. Ruth who is a scientist, a researcher and a reiki master writes, "Christians are taught or encouraged to pray before a session and to call on God, Jesus Christ, and the Holy Spirit to work directly through them and to achieve the healing for them." (Ruth, 2011).

Case Study #2

Kesha is a 28 year old white Christian female who was diagnosed with dysmenorrhea, a form of severe menstrual cramps and nausea, since she was a teenager. For years she suffered. The medications prescribed by her physician would only give her temporary relief. Her dysmenorrhea was acute with extreme symptoms which forced Kesha to plan her lifestyle around her menstrual cycle. Kesha was very religious and she did not believe in alternative treatments such as meditation and energy work. Most of the time during her menstrual cycle she would take prescription medications to help her manage the symptoms of dysmenorrhea. During one of her painful menstrual circle, Kesha who ran out of the prescription medications desperately called her friend who is a reiki practitioner. Her friend sent Keisha distance reiki to soothe her cramps. To Keisha's astonishment within 5 minutes of sending distance reiki she felt a release from her abdomen and no longer felt any pain. In fact she claimed she felt light headed and calm. Needless to say, this experience has changed Keisha's lifestyle. Today Keisha is a reiki level one student who only drinks a warm cup of herbal tea to soothe her menstrual pain. She no longer takes prescription medications as she gives herself a self reiki treatment whenever needed. Keisha plans to continue with the reiki levels training in order to educate and heal individuals to better manage chronic pain without excessive pain medication.

Reiki in Psychotherapy

As humanistically oriented therapies are on the rise, reiki has begun to play a prominent part in strengthening, centering and remodeling emotional expressions by integrating mind and body (LaTorre, 2005). Supported by research, many therapists have added CAM therapies to their traditional psychotherapies. Additionally, therapist are offered continues educational credits in the form of CAM therapies such as reiki. Therapists who incorporate reiki in their sessions agree that the success rates are higher and that client's achieve their goals quicker as opposed to sessions without reiki or CAM therapies. The American Psychological Association (APA) lists Reiki under the acceptable CAM therapies for continued education stating that Reiki has shown to help with stress and pain management, as well as promote relaxation (APA, 2015)

Case Study #3

Jason is a 34 year old African American who visited a reiki master due to panic attacks and depression. After years of psychotherapy, his psychiatrist referred him to a reiki master to help Jason find inner balance before recalibrating his medication. During treatment when the reiki practitioner laid her hands on Jason he began to enter a deep state of relaxation. After about twenty minutes into the session Jason's body began to shiver and he asked the practitioner for a blanket to cover himself. Few minutes later, Jason began to tremble and complained that he could not breathe. Knowing he was entering a stage of 'deep release' the reiki practitioner verbally calmed Jason down and continued with her work. After the session, Jason cried as he told the reiki practitioner, "I was swept by a gigantic wave which pulled me into the water. I didn't know how to swim. I struggled to catch my breath and tried to catch some air. I fought and fought until I felt a sharp pain in my chest… then everything went blank… and there was silence…" A month later, Jason's psychiatrist called the reiki practitioner to inform her that he was very pleased with Jason's progress and he added name to his CAM practitioner's referral list for future reference.

Fortunately, there are many like Maria, Samantha, Kesha and Jason who have benefited from reiki treatments. Overall reiki has been gaining popularity in the west since there is an increase in individuals making the spiritual connection to mind and body. Although research indicates there are many chronically ill who opt for CAM therapy treatments such as reiki nevertheless there are those individuals who are healthy and opt for reiki treatments on a regular basis in order to live a healthier and well balanced lifestyle. Since reiki is not a religious practice there has been a great surge in the numbers of individual from diverse religious background getting attuned to reiki healing energy modality. More so, some practice reiki for personal application and some for professional applications such as nurses, massage therapists, doctors and psychotherapists. In addition to benefiting adults, reiki energy also benefits children, animals and plants. Since reiki is non-invasive and spiritual in nature, some parents allow their children to be attuned to reiki level one and reiki level two.

Since Reiki is growing in popularity there are several ongoing researches carried out in universities and hospitals throughout the world in order to establish a concrete link between bioenergy and biopsychology. Therefore, in order to achieve maximum benefits of reiki one needs to be an active practitioner. It is believed that practicing Reiki on a daily basis not only magnifies the healing energy but it also enhances the healing process with a much higher frequency. Subsequently Reiki is utilized in therapies and treatments by professionals such as counselors, nurses, doctors, and psychologist therefore it is important for the practitioners to be competent in the efficacy of Reiki. If used within a session, the practitioner should undertake ongoing efforts to develop and maintain competency. Lastly, it is imminent that Reiki practitioners provide services with integrity, honesty and responsibility towards their clients by safeguarding their privacy and rights and also by providing informed consent prior to Reiki treatments.

Acknowledgements

These case studies were independently conducted by InnerVision Wellness LLC, a holistic wellness center in Georgia, USA.

Reference

Allen, R. M. (2011). *The Holy Spirit and the Spirit of Reiki: One Source, One Spirit.* Tennessee: North Bluff Publishing

American Psychological Association (2015). Alternative Techniques: Welcome to 'CE Corner'. Retrieved from http://www.apa.org/monitor/2013/04/ce-corner.aspx

Brathovde, A. (2006). A pilot study: Reiki for self-care of nurses and healthcare providers. *Holistic Nursing,* 20(2): 95-101, 2006. In Center for Reiki Research, Retrieved from http://www.centerforreikiresearch.org/

LaTorre, M. (2005). Integrative perspectives. The use of Reiki in psychotherapy. *Perspectives In Psychiatric Care, 41*(4), 184-187.

Rand, W. L. (2014). *Reiki in Hospitals.* The International Center of Reiki Training. Retrieved from http://www.reiki.org/reikinews/reiki_in_hospitals.html

Stein, D. (1995). Essential Reiki: A Complete Guide to an Ancient Healing Art. California: Crossing Press.

Children's Perceptions of Death and Dying: Role of Indian Culture, Religion and Spirituality

Aneesh Kumar P & ChitrankanaBandyopadhyay

Abstract: Death and dying does not simply pertain to related physiological processes and the eventual end of life, rather it is considered to be a focal conceptof every culture and religion. The meanings, symbols and understanding associated with death and dying impacts every individual within the culture. The present secondary review based article with 'death' as its primary theme aims to resort to Indian culture and spirituality, in providing a rich base with respect to the beliefs and perceptions in children. In close relevance, a mention of mythology associated with the ideology of death will be touched upon. Hindu philosophy provides a treasure trove of insight into what death particularly entails. Contrary to colloquial belief, it is far from the termination of life as we know it. It is however, a cyclic, everlasting journey that the immortal soul has to traverse across space and time, only using the replaceable, temporary body as a mere vessel in context to a particular epoch or with relevance to the extent to which one attains his/her purpose in one's previous life. In other words, death is not the end, but the absolution of life. Therefore, 'Karma', 'Reincarnation', 'Moksha' and other related gems of Indian Shastrasare an integral part of our culture. In addition, global psycho-developmental research shows a specific existential pattern in how children, being relatively ignorant of the concept of death, tend to perceive death, depending upon their personal experiences of loss and bereavement. The article would help in developing indigenous models of working with children and also help develop research insights.

Key words: Death, Children's Perception, Indian Culture, Spirituality, Hindu Philosophy

Introduction

"Though the ordinary man looks upon death with dread and sadness, those who have gone before know it as a wondrous experience of peace and freedom." – ParamahansaYogananda

It is this universal apprehension for deathperhaps that in its own paradoxical garb unites us all into society as we know it. It is safe to say that most of us are plagued by consensual concerns regarding the meaning of the physical life, how to best live in the light of inevitability of death, how to cope with grief of loss and bereavement andfor those of us who believe in the elusive afterlife, the path towards the attainment of a "good death". It is this urgent need of a good death that keeps us all duty-bound, staunchly being lead by a magnanimous list of socio-normative doctrines and commandments. What results is cohesion, morale and all things that constitute the mortar required for civilization. This however rests on the ideology of dualism, such that the mind and the body are predisposed to be independent of each other, predetermined with their own courses. Substituting the concept of 'soul' with that of 'mind' here, Descarte's philosophy unknowingly provides a subtle base for Hindu beliefs of the transmigration of the soul as a distinctive entity that is capable of attaining ultimate nirvana once it has vacated its bodily vessel. Death, thus also brings to light an element of free-will as opposed to determinism that exists in our life and living, which is prophesised by Hindu scriptures as the freedom to choose our respective morality-bound paths towards salvation, or otherwise.

Objective of the Article

The broad objective of the article is to throw light upon how culture influences children's perceptions of death and dying. Therefore, the article aims to explore the understanding of death and dying within the Indian Hindu culture and also how children perceive death and dying.

Method

This review-based article generated evidence from national and international journals, periodicals, religious texts, philosophical writings and books. The article also includes information collected from interviews with various experts and also from few children.

Death and Culture

Culture may be broadly defined as the cumulative deposit of knowledge, experience, beliefs, values, attitudes, meanings, hierarchies, religion, notions of time, roles, spatial relations, concepts of the universe, and material objects and possessions acquired by a group of people in the course of generations through individual and group striving. Death is something which is inevitable and a part of life. In certain non- western cultures including India, death is defined as being good or bad. (Emanuel & Emanuel, 1998; Firth., 1989; Thomas & Chambers, 1989; Westerhof, Katzko, Dittmann- Kohli&Hayship, 2001). The term culture loosely culminates from the Roman phrase "culturaamini" that directly translates into "cultivation of the soul". And where there is conjuring of the soul, there is the resultant death of it or the physicality that contains it. Cultural viewpoints regarding this very cessation of existence may vary across a spectrum, ranging from Individualism to Collectivism. As such, Individualistic cultures, the reigning mascot of which has been and is, the United States of America, has a death-denying attitude with a marked essence of stoicism to it, otherwise known as the "Jackie Kennedy Syndrome", focuses on the role of the following:

Urbanization: that estranges the individual from nature and the life/ death cycle that characterizes it,
Seclusion of the aged and the dying: from the mainstream society making death a foreign experience inducing the fear of loneliness,
Nuclear families: resulting in lesser access to extended, aged family members and lack of opportunities to experience death first-hand,
Advances in medical technology: giving the illusion of having a certain degree of control over death and its prevention,

Mass death: what with nuclear destructions, wars and terrorist attacks, the status of the individual death has been desensitised against.

Lack of emotions: while dealing with bereavement and grief that is supposedly implicative of good coping styles and emotional strength, whereas, the Freudian concept of inability to 'decathect' from the relationship with the deceased leads to pathological grief or 'disenfranchised' grief (Doka, 1989).

In sharp contrast, Collectivist cultures like that of our very own nation, stress on:

Familism: such that a single family member is responsible for not only the aged and the dying, but also for all the other grieving family members,

Ancestor worship: which maintains a sense of contact with us and with those who have expired,

Rituals: which are carried out as a characteristic of the community to which one belongs. Also, rituals induce a sense of support and we-feeling from all those who are part of it in times of sorrow and bereavement,

Philosophising death: with the aid of religion and spirituality rather than subjecting it to Freudian ego defence mechanisms such as that of 'isolation' or 'intellectualization',

Social status: Death of a family member directly colours society's perception of an individual. For instance, the status of the widow though having seemingly risen from the period of "Sati DahaPratha", still seems to be one that is subjected to pity and societal hardships.

Death and Spirituality

According to Burkhardt (1989), "spirituality is that which gives meaning to one's life and draws one to transcend oneself. Spirituality is a broader concept than religion, although that is one expression of spirituality. Other expressions include prayer, meditation, interactions with others or nature, and relationship with God or a higher power."

Spirituality, in close collaboration to Hindu convictions of soul-body dualism, has been somewhat associated with Jung's psychodynamic perspective of "ego death", which is a pantheistic phenomenon of sorts, where the individual renounces his need for a separate self-centred existence. Spiritual crisis or spiritual emergency, on the other hand, is recognized by the American Psychiatric Association as a distinct psychological disorder that involves a person's pathological and somewhat delusional relationship with a transcendent being or force. The disorder may be accompanied by any combination of symptoms such as feelings of depression, despair, loneliness; loss of energy or chronic exhaustion not linked to a physical disorder; loss of control over one's personal and/or professional life; unusual sensitivity to light, sound, and other environmental factors; anger, frustration, lack of patience; loss of identity, purpose, and meaning; withdrawal from life's everyday routines; a sense of abandonment by God; feelings of inadequacy; estrangement from family and friends; loss of attention span, self-confidence, and self-esteem; so on and so forth. Spirituality, however, when not predisposing to psychiatric ailments, could be an aid to coping with grief and bereavement.

Death and Hinduism

"*vasamsijirnaniyathavihayanavanigrhnatinaro'parani tathasariranivihayajirnanyanyanisamyatinavanidehi*" – Srimad Bhagavad Gita

The above quotation directly translates into "As a person gives up old and worn out garments and accepts new apparel, similarly the embodied soul giving up old and worn out bodies verily accepts new bodies."

The Upanishads constitutes the basic foundation of certain elements of Indian philosophy, which in turn advocate spiritual monism and mysticism. Thus, Indian philosophy is mostly spiritual in essence and is based on rational speculation in harmony with the Vedas. One of the most prominent pearls of philosophy in this respect is the act of consciously aiming at achieving the highest possible state of perfection, otherwise known as 'moksha', in human life. The culture of India says that the wishes of a dying person must be respected. Hindus have always been reluctant to take up techniques to prolong one's life (Deshpande et al., 2005).

All schools of Indian philosophy recognize the reality of the world, which is believed to be spatio-temporal and causal in order. As such, every finite, positive entity is produced and destroyed. From the point of view of the physical sciences, atoms are indivisible and eternal. Hence, the reality of the permanent self is wholesomely acknowledged in Hindu scriptures(Doorenbos, 2003).

"As we sow, so we reap"- as is the Law of 'Karma'- provides the backbone of the Hindu concept of afterlife, such that the individual is bound to make payments for or reap the benefits of his sins or his virtues respectively, in his successive life. Performance of a duty or a prescribed action leads to merit ('punya') or virtue ('dharma') with respect to one's soul. Violation of a duty or the commission of a forbidden action, on the other hand, taboos the soul with a label of demerit ('papa') or vice ('adharma'). Merits and demerits thus are unseen agencies which mature in the course of time and bear fruits in one's future lives, if not in his current one itself. Either way, there is no escape from the consequences of one's actions such that the Law of 'Karma' is the single most inexorable law governing moral causation.

Hindu mythology provides an abundance of insight into this concept. The great Epic, Mahabharata, delineates upon a similar perspective through the demise of Bhishma, the valiant Kuru warrior-prince. In the splendour of his youth, Bhishma had been the object of desire of princess Amba of Kashi. However, Bhishma himself was a sworn celibate who had received the boon of death at will from Lord Brahma, such that he would only lay his weapons down and succumb to death either in front of a woman or a eunuch. Having been rejected by Bhishma when asked for his hand in marriage, Amba put an end to her own life out of a broken heart and bruised pride – only to swear in vengeance, to return in the following life and be the cause of Bhishma's subsequent death. Amba thus, was originally reincarnated as Shikhandini, King Dhrupad's daughter, but was later transformed through austerities into Shikhandi, who some believe was a male, while others debate was a eunuch. The battle of Hastinapur between the Kauravas and the Pandavas held witness to this, as the Pandavas on Lord Krishna's advice, appointed Shikhandi as the lead charioteer, such that Bhishma leading the Kauravas could no longer defend or arm himself against the shower of arrows that rained over him from the opposing army. This excerpt, hence, not only brings to light the Hindu philosophy of afterlife, but also emphasizes on the Law of Karma, such that Bhishma paid his debts of unrightfully rejecting and in the process, humiliating Amba in her previous life.

The transmigration of the soul may be considered to be the corollary of the Law of 'Karma'. The souls, much like energy, are eternal and can neither be born or destroyed, consistent with the second law of Thermodynamics. Their birth is association with bodies, while theirdeath is nothing more than dissociation from the same. They survive the death of their bodies and simply acquire another, as a vessel or attire: superhuman, human or subhuman as they may be, that is appropriate to the moral deserts acquired by them in the present life.

Taking a minor detour into Buddhism, one may find very close resemblance with this concept and with that of 'reincarnation' in the Jataka Tales, folklore based on Buddha's various lives across the dimensions of time and space. As per Buddha's four noble truths, encircled around the perpetual existence of suffering in the mortal world, there is a noble eight-fold path to salvation from the shackles of suffering, which frees the soul from its vicious, cyclical journey of a plethora of life-forms, each with its characteristic but inevitable share of suffering. Death, in this process simply acts as a bodily stop-gap between any two successive births as the soul continues to strive for its aforementioned, ultimate goal. In this context, the same soul thus continues through a cyclical journey of births such that 'Samsara' is a relatively beginning less series of births and deaths. It is a bondage to one's embodied life in this spatio-temporal world. It is thus the imprisonment of a pure spirit in a destructible impure body.

In conclusion, the Indian philosophical perspective of death is far from that of the ultimate end, but a never-ending journey from this to that life, eternally, till the soul attains pantheistic liberation.

Children and their perception of death

"I think death is a window to another life. I would like to be reborn as a human again. Death is never in our control. I know this because of stories my grandma keeps telling me of how Lord Shiva with the beating of his 'dumru' maintains all life forms on the planet and we would all die the moment the beating stops. Also, when my great grandmother passed away, I realized how much I loved her and how I didn't spend enough time with her when she was around. I keep thinking what could have been if I was nicer to her. I never thought of all this when she was alive, it was only when she died." -a 12 year old Bengalifemale school student on being asked, "What does death mean to you?" (Anonymity preserved on parental request)

Death in children is most prevalent in the first two months after birth because of their underdeveloped immunity system. Older infants in comparison to adolescents who are generally more cautious, preoccupied with the self, conscious and inactive are more vulnerable to fatal accidents rather than debilitating physical illnesses because of a wide range of vaccinations available now. "Crib deaths" – the unexpected demise of seemingly normal, healthy children also occur more often than not.

The perception of death in children, however, takes longer to mature than their conception of life. This is because of their comparatively lesser number of intimate experiences with the former. Children's meaning of death flourishes shortly after their understanding of the animate and the inanimate. Initially, death is mostly impersonal (except in the cases of a family member, friend, a pet etc) and external (unless the child himself is experiencing some sort of chronic illness). Also, they typically tend to associate death with old age and the elderly. By ages 3 to 6, theyengage in 'magical thinking' (believes that words, thoughts or actions can cause death and that death is reversible and is mostly a punishment for bad behaviour.)Between the ages of 5 to 9, concepts of death in children are concretely established such that children believe that death is a spirit that "takes you away" and is potentially contagious. 9-13 year olds worry about how their worlds are going to change because of the deceased, grow interest in death related religious rituals and are self-conscious about their fears. Adolescents of the age range 13-18 years tend to view death as an interruption or an enemy, tend to romanticise or intellectualise death, may resort to escapism or repression to cope, and are more concerned about the future with respect to death. Some of the factors influencing the way infants perceive death are:

- First-hand experiences with the death of one or more loved ones brings children closer to the element of finality of death and sometimes to physical distortions that accompany death.
- Second-hand contact through mass media (pictures of dying people, battle-grounds, mass murders, terrorism aftermaths, burials etc in newspapers and magazines, scenes of death and grief shown in movies and television shows, so on and so forth.)
- Adult's reactions to death who may end up ignoring the child in order to overprotect him from the grief of loss of a loved one. As Barclay had

explained, "surrounded by gaunt-eyed adults who do not see or hear a word that you say can magnify the idea of death's enormity almost beyond belief."

- Religious teachings at home or at school (concepts of heaven and hell in relation to living a moral, dutiful life, concepts of afterlife, etc). The more religious the background of a child, the more specific are his concepts of death.

In general, children are not very much concerned about what happens after death unless religious instruction emphasizes otherwise. For example: if taught about the Law of Karma, children are bound to think of life after death as pleasant or punishing in relevance to the actions one indulge in, in one's present birth – which is simultaneously aided by their parallel maturation of Causality Perception(Coward and Sidhu, 2000; Easwaran, 2007). These concepts formed in early childhood remain more or less constant with minor modifications and sometimes are subjected to absolute rejections during adolescence – mostly when they learn to radically question the logic and reasonability in the religious teachings. Children who receive little or no religious instruction about life after death seldom wonder about it or build up any conception of it.

However, as reported by Dr.Olson (Associate Professor of Psychology and Cognitive Science, Yale University) in an article in Psychology Today, case studies have shown that children ranging from ages 5-12 are innate advocates of the concept of dualism, or in Paul Bloom's terms, are "natural born dualists". They have an intrinsic understanding of how the mind lives on even after the body has died, i.e. of the soul-body dichotomy, as is evident in studies conducted by Bering and Bjorkland (2004; 2005). Children tend to conceptualise that feelings, desires, emotions and the cognitive abilities of a dead organism (say, a cat or a mouse, as has been used in most of the studies) persist, even though they believe that the brain as such is no longer of physical functionality. This trend has been found regardless of the religious background of the child, the presence or the absence of it, which as Bering suggests, implies that children have a predisposition to acknowledge religious beliefs about afterlife. In close context could be Hindu philosophical gems that preach transmigration of the soul as a phenomenon independent of bodily decay.

A very recent study done by Anglin (2014), involved 348 Undergraduates of a mean age of 18 years. It has been found with the help of the Implicit

Association Test that religious beliefs about death and afterlife taught in childhood (at around 10 years of age) persist implicitly; even though one's explicit beliefs may seem to be in contrast with them. These results held true for both religious and non-religious students, once again pointing towards an innate predisposition towards conceptualisations of afterlife, with or without extraneous religious reinforcements.

With respect to adolescents, Chin-Chin Gan and Jin-KuanKok in a cross-cultural study of colour identification and death perception of teenagers, reported that Indian adolescents tend to associate death with the colours black (symbolising fear and ignorance of death) and red (symbolising anger and hatred). A rationale for this maybe the limited exposure of the Indian adolescents to Hindu beliefs of the cyclical journey of the soul, such that death is not literally death of the self, which lead them to view the phenomenon in such a negative light. In contrast, the Chinese sample seemed to associate death with peace because of their reported Taoist backgrounds that instilled in them the belief of death being the catalyst in one's transformation from being a biological propagator to a spiritual benefactor. However, the Indian sample was relatively small due to which the results cannot be generalised.

In a comparative study done between Hindu and Christian participants, (young children of 6-8 years, older children of 10-12 years and adults), it was found that Hindu participants of all age groups were comparatively more consistent in their accurate conceptualisations of life, death, afterlife, reincarnation, heaven and hell of animals, trees, humans and inanimate objects such as rocks.

In a paper on content analysis of children's literature on death (PolingandHupp, 2008) three components were found to be the core theme, such that 12% of the books analyzed, contained all biological components (such as irreversibility, non-functionality, causality and universality) while75% of the books contained socio-cultural elements of death rituals and perceptions of heaven. For emotional components, sadness was the most frequently cited emotion (90% of books), followed by anger (65% of books) and longing (63% of books). Such literature not only acts as an aid to children's coping styles to grief and bereavement (Johnson, 1999; Polak, 2007) but also fuels children's conceptualization of death (Guy 1993; Klingman, 1980). Biological components were found to be most prevalent among picture books for younger children than in story books for older ones probably because toddlers need to inculcate a basic perception of physical features of death and dying before they realize the necessity of learning to cope with personal, subjective experiences of death. Moreover, socio-cultural aspects mentioned in books emphasize on the spiritual existence of the soul even after the biological death of the being, which may seem contradictory to biological components such as that of irreversibility, but have been consciously incorporated by the authors because of the psychological benefits they provide to children in grief. (Benore& Park, 2004) The emotional functions that death literature serves for younger and older children only vary in quality. For infants, it is the interaction between the adult story-teller and themselves that lead to rapport building and provide a sense of support and consolation during hard times of death in the family(Guy, 1993). Also, older children find solace in story books regarding death where the characters are identifiable with those in their own family, especially when other family members are unsure of how to sensitively approach the topic (Corr, 2004). Western society encourages expression of grief in private (solitary) for recouping good mental health (kangawa- Singer and Blackhall, 2001; Shapiro, 1995). But for the Hindus, expression of grief is 'public'.

Through a qualitative analysis of images of heaven and the spiritual afterlife as provided in children's storybooks, Malcolm (2011) explores the therapeutic contributions of the same in the lives of bereaved children. Such literature through concepts of a virtual afterlife, symbolize the persistence of bonds with the deceased, such that most books state that heaven allows for the same lifestyle as the person had as a mortal back in his previous life. This as such portrays death as just another phase on a continuum rather than an ultimatum, such that, pet cats continue to lay comfortably on someone's lap devouring tuna, children engage in play with their heavenly peers, and grandmothers continue to bake cookies for their beloved grandchildren. Also, there is a tone of certainty in such heaven-centric stories where those who are more vulnerable and dependantin reality such as children and pets, are conceptualized as being taken care of even in their afterlives, making death seem less threatening, confusing, distressing and anxiety-causing as an unavoidable phenomenon.

Moreover, a paper titled as "Spirituality and coping among grieving children: A preliminary study" (Andrews and Marotta, 2005), elucidates upon the role of the child's relationship with God, his family and peer groups and secondary attachments with pets and familiar objects as the most significant contributors to effective coping. It also seems that it is the inability of the infant, unlike adults, to individuate and separate the self from the being of the deceased family member that hinders overcoming a sense of an irreversible loss. This in turn makes a controversial turn towards assessing, perhaps, the efficacy in an ambiguous or even an anxious parent-child relationship, which later as a boon in disguise of a curse may buffer the child from the suffering that accompanies bereavement. Children additionally seem to find maximum solace in factual explanations of death provided by adults and have been typically known to dream during REM sleep about the expired (Stickgold, 2002), mostly because of marked neuronal plasticity of the developing brain (Seigal, 2002), that is slowly learning to integrate the emotional components of the right hemisphere with the cognitive prowess of conceptualization, representation and understanding, of the left hemisphere.

Conclusion

In order to summarize thus, it seems that the development of an understanding of death could well be explained with a life-span approach, such that sophistication for abstractions and philosophising from a Hindu point of view, stems at the age of 9-13 years and is more or less innate among children. Also, childhood religious internalizations of death and afterlife tend to persist throughout one's life. Studies also indicate that lack of exposure to Hindu preaching may result in a fearful schematic ideation of death and a less accurate conceptualization of death and dying.

As quoted by Carl Jung (1995), "for most people it means a great deal to assume that their lives will have an indefinite continuity beyond their present existence. They live more sensibly, feel better and are more at peace." This almost provides an existential justification for the presence of and the eventual need for embracing Hindu concepts such as that of afterlife. However, Freud, by definition has termed the belief in death and afterlife to be "patently infantile" in nature, on grounds of it being "so foreign to reality, that to anyone with a friendly attitude to humanity it is painful to think that the great majority of mortals will never be able to rise above this view of life." (Sigmund Freud, 1961) Infantile as it may be, this may provide the rationale for a sort of instinctual, primal need for such a Hindu view on death (or the lack of it), that exist in children and persist in later developmental years, as has been concluded from the prior mentioned studies.

Recommendations and Implications

Death constitutes of one of the harshest elements of reality. When exposed abruptly to it at the closest interpersonal level, it is immediately followed by an existential crisis that the child invariably goes through. Developmentally not equipped to indulge in abstractions of what does or does not pertain to death, it is the lookout of the clinician to sensitively introduce the child to biological perspectives of universality and irreversibility of death before he could inculcate the emotional sophistication of philosophising about death with the aid of religion and spirituality. Physical concepts of death being a unidirectional phenomenon may be distressing to the child at first, but factual, honest information regarding all life culminating into death, the absence of any sort of bias in nature regarding senescence, might be reassuring to the child eventually, as he comes to realize that his grief is shared and far from exclusive. It must also be ensured that the multitude of questions that rises in the child's mind immediately after are patiently addressed, additionally helping him accept the lack of human answers to somepara-psychological mysteries of death. This in turn may prove to be beneficial in coping with bereavement. The clinician additionally may incorporate family members with marked spiritual inclinations in family/group therapy for grief management of the child, who through religious folklores and interactive story-telling may provide solace to the child regarding a peaceful afterlife of the deceased with concepts of a good death, karma and existence of heaven as delineated upon, previously. As such, clinical practice must loosen its water-tight scientific psychotherapeutic boundaries in order to make way for religious and spiritual belief systems in providing adaptive relief to children struggling to cope with the death of a loved one.

References

Andrews, C. R., & Marotta, S. A. (2005). Spirituality and coping among grieving children: A preliminary study. Counseling and Values, *50*(1), 38-50.

Bharati, P., &Tyagi, G. (2014). Reincarnation: Truth or Lie. Innovative Journal Of Medical And Health Science, *4*(4), 120-127

Branson K. (2014, November 3). Beliefs about the soul and afterlife that we acquire as children stick with us. Retrieved from http://news.rutgers.edu/news/beliefs-about-soul-and-afterlife-we-acquire-children-stick-us/20141102#.VT5HosazPf5

Bryce. N.S. (2007, April). Hindu and Christian children's concepts of life, death, and afterwards. (Honours Thesis), Retrieved from http://download38.jointbooks.org/pdf/death-and-afterwards- 4oem9.pdf

Childers, P., &Wimmer, M. (1971). The concept of death in early childhood. *Child Development,42*, 1299-1301.

Doka, J.K. (2011, March 26). Helping children spiritually cope with dying and death. Retrieved fromhttp://www.huffingtonpost.com/kenneth-j-doka/helping-children-spiritua b 839764.html?ir=India

Edmunds. D.L. (2012, November 23). From Spiritual Crisis to Spiritual Awakening. Retrieved from https://www.psychologytoday.com/blog/extreme-states-mind/201211/spiritual-crisis-spiritual-awakening

Gamliel, T. (2003). The Macabre Style: Death Attitudes of Old-Age Home Residents in Israel. *Ethos, 31*(4), 495-512.

Gartley, W., &Bernasconi, M. (1967). The concept of death in children. *The Journal of genetic psychology, 110*(1), 71-85.

Gould, G. M. (1891). Immortality. *The Monist, 1*(3),372-392.

Graham. A. J. (2013, January 17). How Do Children Comprehend the Concept of Death? Retrieved from https://www.psychologytoday.com/blog/hard-realities/201301/how-do-children-comprehend-the-concept-death

Gupta, R. (2011). Death beliefs and practices from an Asian Indian American Hindu perspective. *Death studies, 35*(3), 244-266.

Hood Jr, R. W., & Morris, R. J. (1983). Toward a theory of death transcendence. *Journal for the Scientific study of Religion,22*(4), 353-365.

Hurlock, E. B. (2008). Child Development (6th ed.). N.p.: McGraw-Hill.

Malcolm, N. L. (2011). Images of heaven and the spiritual afterlife: Qualitative analysis of children's storybooks about death, dying, grief, and bereavement. The Journal of Genetic Psychology, 62(1), 51-76.

Motto, A. L. (1955). Seneca on death and immortality. *Classical Journal*, 187-189.

Olson, K. R. (2013, December 12). Children's' understanding of death and the afterlife. Psychology Today. Retrieved from https://www.psychologytoday.com/blog/developing-minds/201312/children-s-understanding-death-and-the-afterlife

Poling, D. A., &Hupp, J. M. (2008). Death sentences: A content analysis of children's death literature. The Journal of Genetic Psychology, 169(2), 165-176.

Radhakrishnan, S. (2009). Indian Philosophy (2nd ed., Vol. 1). N.p.: Oxford University Press.

Salek. E.C. (2014, October 9). How Children Understand Death & What You Should Say. Retrieved from http://www.healthychildren.org/English/healthy-living/emotional-wellness/Building-Resilience/Pages/How-Children-Understand-Death-What-You-Should-Say.aspx

Sharma, C. (2009). A critical survey of Indian Philosophy. N.p.: MotiLalBanarasiDass.

White, E., Elsom, B., &Prawat, R. (1978). Children's conceptions of death. *Child Development*, *49*(2),307-310.

Déjà Vu Experiences in Different Psychiatric Populations: An Overview

[1]Mr. Boban Eranimos,
[2]Mr. Shuvabrata Poddar,
[3]Dr. Arthur Funkhouser PhD

Abstract: Déjà vu is defined as "subjectively inappropriate impressions of familiarity of the present with an undefined past". It is a strange, fascinating and mysterious human experience observed in 70% to 80% of the general, non-clinical population. The present article discusses the déjà vu experience in different psychiatric populations. Studies have found that déjà vu experiences are more common among neurotic populations as compared to psychotic populations. With respect to organic conditions déjà vu experiences are encountered in those suffering from temporal lobe epilepsy. Medical and non-medical explanations are not fully able to explain this strange phenomenon. Additional work is still needed in order to elucidate the many aspects of these intriguing experiences.

1 Trainee in Clinical Psychology, Central Institute of Psychiatry (CIP), Ranchi, India.

2 Assistant Professor in Clinical Psychology, Central Institute of Psychiatry (CIP), Ranchi, India.

3 Instructor, C. G. Jung Institute, Küsnacht, Switzerland.

INTRODUCTION

Among the epics, India's Yoga Vasistha has a story about a king named Lavana. He was a well-known ruler in ancient times and was renowned for his magnanimity. One day a juggler came from a distant place to his court with a certain horse and presented it to him, as the king was particularly interested and skilled in hunting. As a part of the royal routine, the King headed off faraway with all his acquaintances and the royal knights for hunting. Being an enthusiastic hunter, he paid little attention to the sunset. Unfortunately, the King became very anxious when he realized that he was separated from his knights. He was helpless in the dense forest where the darkness covered the trees, evoking the horrors of wild nature. As time went on, the day dawned, the sun rose, and he grew thirsty and hungry. Unexpectedly a certain woman passed near the king; she was in a hurry to deliver food for her father on time. The king, when she was close, begged for some food to allay his hunger. She replied, "I shall give you food if you consent to marry me". The king declared himself ready to marry her; she gave him food, and they got married. She gave birth to two sons and two daughters, and lived there for sixty years. Once, a big famine and drought hit their area and the children began to cry for food with their empty stomachs. At last, Lavana sacrificed himself by jumping into a burning fire, as he himself became the food for his children. Suddenly, the king woke up from his sleep, He was sure that it was a dream, but he became very nervous. The king set out the next day with his ministers to find the place he had seen in his dream. He discovered the exact place in the forest. He found an old woman there who told him that a king had come, married her daughter, and then there was a famine and everyone had died. He returned to his palace. The king was aware about the plight of her husband, but he could not explain how it could have happened.

Going through the Vedas, Upanishads and Epics in India, we can read about these kinds of experiences and incidents. This concept of past lives can be traced as far back as the times of ancient Egypt, India, Greece, and Rome (Head& Cranston, 2000; McClelland, 2010). Eastern philosophical, religious and spiritual doctrines such as Buddhism, Hinduism, Jainism, and Taoism are closely related with the concept of reincarnation and rebirth (Knapp, 2005; Obeyeskere, 2002; Sharma, 1990, 2001; Vincanne, 2001). Indian philosophy can provide many ideas about spirituality, reincarnation, consciousness and dream-related studies to the World. However, it is true that Indians have hardly attempted studying déjà vu experiences or taking them as subjects of scientific enquiry, as Indians have understood these experiences within spiritual and religious frameworks. In the past, the western world had also viewed these experiences as paranormal, but now they have changed their view and tend to see them as symptomatic of psychopathology. Many studies have been made in this area but researchers were not able to find conclusive evidence mainly due to the complexity and ineffability of these experiences.

DÉJÀ VU: FLEETING FEELING OF FAMILIARITY

Déjà vu is a widespread, fascinating, and the mysterious human experience. For over a century, the phenomenon of déjà vu has attracted much interest, and in recent times, researchers in various scientific fields (Sno & Linszen, 1990; Brown, 2004) have studied it. Whereas research on the déja vu experience has a long history reaching back into the mid-1800s, it has struggled for serious consideration by the scientific community. The French psychiatrist Emile Boirac first coined the term déjà vu, meaning, "already seen," in 1879. Déjà vu experiences, defined as *subjectively inappropriate impressions of familiarity of the present with an undefined past* (Neppe, 1983a), are observed in 70% to 80% of the nonclinical general population (Adachi et al., 2003). Déjà vu is thus a common experience, with a majority of the population having experienced it at least once in their lifetimes (Brown, 2003).

TYPES OF DÉJÀ VU

There are several subtypes of déjà vu mentioned in the literature. Art Funkhouser (1995) wrote about three main forms of déjà vu. He classified them as déjà vécu (already experienced or lived through), déjà senti (already felt) and déjà visité (already visited). In the technical sense, what is normally called "déjà vu" is more accurately termed "déjà vécu". This is the feeling that one has already experienced something before or lived through it. The déjà senti experience is not recalled later and is mostly seen in the seizure aura of temporal lobe epilepsy. With "déjà visité", one recognizes a location or landscape even though never having been there before.

VARIOUS SUB TYPES OF DÉJÀ VU EXPERIENCE

In the literature, many other subtypes of déjà vu have been mentioned. Table 1 below lists many of them. "Déjà vu" is often used as an umbrella term for all of them, including all sensory modalities.

Deja arrive	happened	Déjà pressenti:	sensed
Déjà connu:	known (personal)	Déjà raconté:	told
Déjà dit:	said (spoken)	Déjà recontré:	encountered
Déjà entendu:	heard	Déjà rêvé:	dreamed
Déjà eprouvé:	experienced	Déjà senti:	felt, smelt
Déjà gôuté:	tasted	Déjà su:	known (intellectually)
Déjà fait:	done	Déjà trouvé:	found (met)
Déjà lu:	read	Déjà vécu:	lived
Déjà parlé:	spoken	Déjà visité:	visited
Déjà pensé:	thought	Déjà voulu:	desired

Table 1: 1 Different subtypes of déjà vu (Neppe, 1983a)

One can assume that most people are familiar with these experiences. Today scientific researchers in the fields of neuroscience and neuropsychology have come up with explanations based on theoretical reasoning and some empirical evidence. As more scientists have begun studying this phenomenon in recent years, many hypotheses about causes of déjà vu have been proposed. Scientific explanations of déjà can be mainly divided into four categories: dual–processing explanations (two cognitive functions that are shortly out of synchrony), neurological explanations (brief dysfunction in the brain), memory explanations, and double perception explanations (a brief break in one's on-going perceptual processing) (Brown, 2004). Early researchers tried to establish a link between déjà vu and serious psychopathology with hopes of finding the some diagnostic value in the experience.

NON–MEDICAL EXPLANATIONS OF DÉJÀ VU EXPERIENCE

Many explanations have been put forward based psychodynamic points of view. Most psychodynamic explanations consider déjà vu as an ego defense mechanism, which helps us to allay fears resulting from unexpected or direct confrontation with anxiety-provoking situations (anxiety that comes from repressed memories or intrapsychic conflicts among id, ego and super ego). The sudden block of emotional stimulus from external present experience leads to a distorted consciousness thereby creating an artificial, fleeting feeling of familiarity. Some other researchers have explained déjà vu as a reflection of unfulfilled wishes or dissolving boundaries of various parts of the psyche or of the self and the environment. On the contrary, some explanations see déjà vu is as a positive effort to fulfill an unconscious desire. Initially Freud suggested that déjà vu represented a recollection of unconscious fantasies coupled with a desire to improve the present situation (Freud, 1901/1960). Later he explained déjà vu as a positive counter-part of depersonalization and derealization.

PARAPSYCHOLOGICAL EXPLANATIONS OF DÉJÀ VU

The strange natures of déjà vu experiences have occupied parapsychologists for more than a century. The sense of familiarity was explained as resulting from precognitive experience: persons who have experienced déjà vu often say they were able to predict what happened next or the present familiarity was foreshadowed by their dreams. Another conjecture suggests that in a present situation telepathic awareness is used to tap into the mind of someone else in the past or the future time (de Lamartine, 1835; Lalande, 1893). Still others claim such experiences may come from an out-of-body experience or the present familiarity is derived from a past life (reincarnation). According to hereditary transmission, explanations past life memories are mainly acquired through genetically transmitted information from one generation to another. The Jungian idea of synchronicity (Carl Jung, 1951/1972) has been brought in when these experiences are meaningful and Jungians point out that individuals are interconnected with symbols and themes. Rosen (1991) has suggested the Jungian concept of the collective unconsciousness is behind the déjà vu phenomenon. Due to the subjective nature of such experiences, parapsychological explanations of déjà vu are difficult to test and prove empirically.

MEDICAL EXPLANATIONS OF DÉJÀ VU

Déjà vu experiences are common in the general, population, but the earliest studies were constructed on the assumption that a déjà vu experience is a symptom of psychopathology and it was attributed to mental illness. Many researchers found that an increased incidence of déjà vu experiences is more common in patients with psychiatric illnesses (Richardson and Winokur, 1968, Lewis et al,1984, Kirshner, 1973). According to Pickford (1944), déjà vu can be considered as an incidental symptom in a variety of psychotic conditions. Over the past few years, researchers have conducted many studies of déjà vu as linked with neurotic, psychotic and other pathophysiological conditions.

PSYCHOTIC CONDITIONS

Schizophrenia is one of the most debilitating psychiatric disorders. Marked by symptoms such as delusion, hallucination and gross disturbances in behavior, many attempts have been made in the last few years to determine the link between déjà vu and schizophrenia. It is difficult to identify déjà vu experience in schizophrenia, because it is very hard to extricate déjà vu experiences from the patient's chronic psychopathological symptoms: some patients adopt such experiences in creating their delusional systems. Déjà vu experiences are often good ingredients for this purpose, so some patients said they had delusional déjà vu experiences (Kirshner, 1973; Sno, 1994). Earlier, many studies were conducted to learn about the quantitative and qualitative nature of déjà vu. Some researchers suggest that the difference is more qualitative than quantitative (Arnaud, 1896; Sno & Linszen, 1990; Sno et al., 1992) but others argue for a definite qualitative difference (Berndt-Larsson, 1931; Chari, 1964; Harper, 1969). Richardson and Winokur conducted a study among 301 inpatients in 1968 and found that among psychiatric schizophrenics, the incidence of déjà vu (54%) was not much higher than within other psychiatric subgroup categories. Greyson (1977) conducted a study among schizophrenics at the University of Virginia hospital and found a higher incidence (65%) of déjà vu experience in the schizophrenic population compared to the non-schizophrenic population

(51%). Likewise, Neppe's (1983b) study found little difference in the déjà vu incidence between schizophrenics (65%) and normal (69%) samples.

Adachi etal. (2006) conducted a study with 113 patients and 386 non-clinical controlled subjects. They found that the déjà vu experiences among schizophrenics were less frequent (53.1%) than in the control group of non-clinical subjects (76.2%). All the subjects reported they were distressed by the experience. Adachi et al. (2007) conducted a study among schizophrenic patient in relation to psychopathologies and antipsychotic medications. Their study found that among 113 schizophrenic subjects 53.1% had déjà vu experiences. Patients with negative symptoms do not frequently experience déjà vu; the frequency of approximately 70% was similar to that in the nonclinical population (Adachi et al., 2001, Adachi et al., 2003). This finding shows that brain dysfunction is increased with the onset of negative symptoms there by hindering the development of déjà vu experiences. Studies have shown that negative symptoms could create a broad variety of cognitive dysfunctions, which include memory disturbances, (Basso et al., 1998) but memory dysfunction can often give rise to déjà vu experiences (Krishner, 1973).

NEUROTIC CONDITIONS

Déjà vu is more common among neurotic patients. It has been shown to be common among patients with mood fluctuations (Heymans, 1904, 1906), bipolar mood disorders (Lewis et al., 1984) psychasthenia (Gordon, 1921; Kinnier Wilson, 1929). Richardson and Winokur (1968) conducted a study in which the déjà vu experiences of 301 psychiatric patients were evaluated in 10 different subgroups. They broke down the psychoneurotic group into three categories. The incidence of déjà vu among anxiety neurotics (58%) and hysterics (57%) are higher compared to those suffering from depressive reactions (38%). In personality disorders, déjà vu experiences have been reported to be higher than in other groups. Harper (1969), in his study, found no relationship between déjà vu and neurosis.

Some researchers have expressed doubt as to whether or not déjà vu is a dissociative experience. Irwin (1996) found that there is little relationship between déjà vu and dissociative tendencies. Sno et al. (1994) found a significant positive relationship between déjà vu and DES (Dissociative Experience Scale) scores. Adachi et al. (2008) conducted a study to investigate the relation between déjà vu and dissociative experiences in 227 non-clinical subjects who were evaluated using the inventory of déjà vu experience assessment scale and the dissociative experience scale (DES). Out of 227 subjects, déjà vu experiences occurred in 162 (71.4%) of the individuals.

In addition, researchers have investigated the link between depersonalization and déjà vu. Some have asserted that the two terms could be used interchangeably; they ascertain that depersonalization and derealization refer to a similar phenomenon (Brauer et al., 1970; McKellar, 1978). Freud (1914/1955) proposed that déjà vu is a positive counter-part of depersonalization and derealization phenomena. According to Heyman's (1904, 1906) studies, it was found that 82% of the patients with depersonalization had déjà vu and only 48 % of patients who had not experienced depersonalization had déjà vu experiences. Mayers and Grant (1972) suggest that déjà vu creates a fear response, and this may lead to panic attacks. Brauer et al. (1970) found that déjà vu is significantly correlated with depersonalization (0.32) and not with derealization (0.18) but Adachi et al. (2003) found an on-significant correlation between déjà vu and depersonalization.

ORGANIC CONDITIONS

Déjà vu experiences are more common in various organic conditions. The link between déjà vu and epilepsy is stronger than in any other organic condition, especially more associated with seizure activity in temporal lobe epilepsy (TLE). People had often given retrospective anecdotal accounts and personal experiential reports regarding the occurrence of déjà vu just prior to temporal lobe epileptic seizures or during the seizure between convulsions. The nature of the déjà vu for TLEs may differ from those experienced by non-epileptics in that it is slightly protracted and the same déjà vu experience may be duplicated. Mullan and Penfield (1959) recreated déjà vu–like experiences in a laboratory setting. They electrically stimulated the cortical surface of the brain and duplicated the pre-seizure aura in 10 of 217 TLEs, and déjà vu-like phenomena occurred in 6 of these 10 patients in the temporal area. Three sites where seizures associated with déjà vu-like familiarity have been shown to originate are the mesial temporallobe (Jackson, 1888; Halgren et al., 1978; Weinand et al., 1994), the superior lateral temporal cortex (Penfield & Perot, 1963), and a network involving both lateral and medial aspects of the temporal lobe (Bancaudet al., 1994; Gloor, 1990). Most research relating déjà vu to physical pathology has focused on persons with TLE, but several investigations have addressed the question as to whether déjà vu is differentially associated with other types of neurological disorders. Richardson and Winokur (1968) conducted one study among seven different neurosurgical patient categories on the incidence of déjà vu.

Diagnostic Group	No. of Cases	Incidence
General (Parkinsonism, MS, seizure)	54%	54%
Brain (concussion, subdural, tumor)	44	45
Spinal cord/nerve roots (HNP)	39	33
Peripheral nerves (carpal tunnel, tic)	23	22
Meninges	4	0
Cerebral vessels	16	31

Table.1.2 Déjà Vu incidence in various neurological conditions (Brown, 2004)

They found no important differences across the groups with sufficient sample sizes, but did note that those groups with brain dysfunctions (the first two listed above) show a higher incidence of déjà vu. They then recombined their neurosurgery and psychiatric patients into three different groups and found a relatively comparable déjà vu incidence across those groups with cerebral pathology only (42%; N = 47), psychiatric illness only (48%; N = 289), and no cerebral or psychiatric illness (39%; N = 73). Weinstein (1969) noted that déjà vu may occur in a transient fashion during the recovery phase following brain trauma with disturbances of consciousness (i.e., closed head injuries). However, the rest of the literature on various neurological disorders does not point to a clear association of déjà vu with any particular neurological dysfunction.

CONCLUSION

Early researchers elucidated déjà vu within the parapsychological realm. However, later researchers made an effort to establish a connection between déjà vu and serious psychopathology in order to find the diagnostic value to déjà vu. They found déjà vu experiences are less common in different psychiatric populations but there does not seem to be any special association between déjà vu and psychotic or neurotic conditions. Some studies found déjà vu experience is associated with temporal lobe epilepsy. Déjà vu is still under-investigated and is an unexplored subject area in clinical and in general populations. The Diagnostic and Statistical Manual (DSM) of the American Psychiatric Association (APA) considered déjà vu to be due to pathology of the mind. More systematic and scientific studies are needed in order to establish what links there may be between déjà vu and different psychiatric disorders.

REFERENCES

Adachi, N., Adachi, T., Akanuma, N., Matsubara, R., Ito, M., Takekawa, Y., & Arai, H. (2007). Déjà vu experiences in schizophrenia: relations with psychopathology and antipsychotic medication. *Comprehensive psychiatry*, 48 (6), 592-596.

Adachi, N., Adachi, T., Kimura, M., Akanuma, N., & Kato, M. (2001). Development of the Japanese version of the Inventory of Déjà vu Experiences Assessment (IDEA). *Seishin Igaku (Clinical Psychiatry)*, 43, 1223–1231.

Adachi, N., Adachi, T., Kimura, M., Akanuma, N., Takekawa, Y., & Kato, M. (2003). Demo -graphic and psychological features of déjà vu experiences in a nonclinical Japanese population. *Journal of Nervous and Mental Disease*, 191, 242–247.

Adachi, N., Akanuma, N., Adachi, T., Takekawa, Y., Adachi, Y., Ito, M., et al. (2008). Déjà vu experiences are rarely associated with pathological dissociation. *Journal of Nervous and Mental Disease*, 196, 417–419.

Adachi, T., Adachi, N., Takekawa, Y. et al,(2006). Déjà vu experiences in patients with schizophrenia. *Comprehensive Psychiatry*, 47, 389–393.

Arnaud, F. L. (1896). Un cas d'illusion du'déjà vu'ou de'fausse mémoire'. *In Annals Médico-Psychologiques*, 3, 455-471.

Bancaud, J., Brunet-Bourgin, F., Chauvel, P., & Halgren, E. (1994). Anatomical origin of déjà vu and vivid "memories" in human temporal lobe epilepsy. *Brain*, 117, 71–90.

Basso, M. R., Nasrallah, H. A., Olson, S. C., Bornstein, R. A. (1998). Neuropsychological correlates of negative, disorganized and psychotic symptoms in schizophrenia. *Schizophrenia Research*, 31, 99-111.

Berndt-Larsson, H. (1931). Ueber das déjà vu und andere Täuschungen des Bekanntheistgefühls. *Zeitschrift für Gesamte Neurologie*, 133, 521–543.

Brauer, R., Harrow, M., & Tucker, G. J. (1970). Depersonalization phenomena in psychiatric patients. *British Journal of Psychiatry*, 117, 509–515.

Brown, A. S. (2003). A review of the déjà vu experience. *Psychological Bulletin*, 129, 394–413.

Brown, A.S. (2004). *The déjà vu experience*. New York: Psychology Press.

Chari, C. T. K. (1964). On some types of déjà vu experiences. *Journal of the American Society of Psychical Research*, 58, 186–203.

de Lamartine, M. A. (1835). Souvenirs, impressions pensées et paysages pendant un voyage en orient 1832–1834. Oeuvre Complètes, 5, Paris: Charles Gosselin.

Freud, S. (1901/1960). Psychopathology of everyday life. Standard Edition, 6. London: Hogarth Press.

Freud, S. (1914/1955). Fausse reconnaissance (déjà raconté) in psycho-analytic treatment. *Standard Edition*, 13. London: Hogarth Press.

Funkhouser, A. (1995). Three types of déjà vu. *Scientific and Medical Network Review*, 57:20 - 22.

Gloor, P. (1990). Experiential phenomena of temporal lobe epilepsy: Facts and hypotheses. *Brain*, 113, 1673–1694.

Gordon, A. (1921). Illusion of "the already seen" (paramnesia) and of "the never seen" (agnosia). *Journal of Abnormal Psychology*, 15, 187–192.

Greyson, B. (1977). Telepathy in mental illness: Deluge or delusion? *Journal of Nervous and Mental Disease*, 165, 184–200.

Halgren, E., Walter, R. D., Cherlow, D. G., & Crandall, P. H. (1978). Mental phenomena evoked by electrical stimulation of the human hippocampal formation and amygdala. *Brain*, 101, 83–117.

Harper, M. A. (1969). Déjà vu and depersonalization in normal subjects. *Australian and New Zealand Journal of Psychiatry*, 3, 67–74.

Head, J., & Cranston, S. L. (2000). *Reincarnation: An East-West anthology*. New York, NY: Aeon.

Heymans, G. (1904). Eine enquete und depersonalisation und 'fausse reconnaissance.'*Zeitschrift fur Psychologie*, 36, 321–343.

Heymans, G. (1906). Weitere daten uber depersonalisation und'fausse reconnaissance.' *Zeitschrift fur psychologie*, 43, 1–17.

Irwin, H. J. (1996). Childhood antecedents of out-of-body and déjà vu experiences. *Journal of the American Society for Psychical Research*, 90, 157–173.

Jacoby, L. L. (1988). Memory observed and memory unobserved. In U. Neisser & E. Wino- grad (Eds.), *Remembering reconsidered ecological and traditional approaches to the study of memory* Cambridge: Cambridge University Press, 45–177.

Jung, C. G. (1951/1972). *On Synchronicity*. In: The Collected Works of C. G. Jung, Princeton, NJ: Princeton University Press, 8, 520–531.

Kinnier Wilson, S. A. (1929). *Modern problems in neurology*. New York: William Wood.

Kirshner, L. A. (1973). The mechanism of déjà vu. *Diseases of the nervous system*, 34, 246–249.

Knapp, S. (2005). *Reincarnation and karma: How they really affect us*. Lincoln, NE: iUniverse.

Lalande, A. (1893). Des paramnesies. Revue Philosophique, 36, 485–497.

Lewis, D. O., Feldman, M., Greene, M., & Martinez-Mustardo, Y. (1984). Psychomotor epileptic symptoms in six patients with bipolar mood disorders. *American Journal of Psychiatry*, 141, 1583-1586.

McClelland, N. C. (2010). *Encyclopedia of reincarnation and karma*. Jefferson, NC: McFarland & Co.Inc

McKellar, A. (1978). Depersonalization in a 16-year-old boy. *Southern Medical Journal*, 71, 1580–1581.

Mullan, S., & Penfield, W. (1959). Illusions of comparative interpretation and emotion. *Archives of Neurology and Psychiatry*, 81, 269–284.

Myers, D. H., & Grant, G. (1972). A study of depersonalization in students. *British Journal of Psychiatry*, 121, 59–65.

Neppe, V. M. (1983a). The causes of déjà vu. *Parapsychological Journal of South Africa*, 4, 25–35.

Neppe, V. M. (1983b). The concept of déjà vu. *Parapsychological Journal of South Africa*, 4, 1–10.

Obeyesekere, G. (2002). *Imagining Karma. Ethical Transformation in Amerindian, Buddhist, and Greek Rebirth*. Berkeley, CA: University of California Press.

Penfield, W., & Perot, P. (1963). The brain's record of auditory and visual experience. *Brain*, 86, 596–695.

Pickford, R. W. (1944). Déjà vu in Proust and Tolstoy. *International Journal of Psycho-Analysis*, 25, 155-165.

Richardson, T. F. & Winokur, G. (1968). Déjà vu—As related to diagnostic categories in psychiatric and neurosurgical patients. *Journal of Nervous and Mental Disease*, 146, 161–164.

Rosen, D. S. (1991). The déjà vu experience: Remembrance of things past?. *American Journal of Psychiatry*, 148, 1418.

Sharma, A. (1990). Karma and reincarnation in Advaita Vedanta. *Journal of Indian Philosophy*, 18(3), 219-236.

Sharma, A. (2001). *A Jaina perspective on the philosophy of religion: Lal Sundarlal Jain research series XVI*.Delhi, India: Motilal Banarsidass.

Sno, H. N. (1994). A continuum of misidentification symptoms. *Psychopathology*, 27(3-5), 144-147.

Sno, H. N., & Linszen, D. H. (1990). The déjà vu experience: Remembrance of things past? *The American journal of psychiatry*.147, 1587–1595.

Sno, H. N., Linszen, D. H., & de Jonghe, F. (1992). Déjà vu experiences and reduplicative paramnesia. *British Journal of Psychiatry*, 161, 565–568.

Sno, H. N., Schalken, H. F. A., de Jonghe, F., & Koeter, M. W. J. (1994). The inventory for déjà vu experiences assessment. *The Journal of Nervous and Mental Disease*, 182, 27–33.

Vincanne, A. (2001). The sacred in the scientific: Ambiguous practices of science in Tibetan medicine. *Cultural Anthropology*, 16(4), 542-575.

Weinand, M. E., Hermann, B., Wyler, A. R., Carter, L. P., Oommen, K. J., Labiner, D., Ahern, G., & Herring, A. (1994). Long-term subdural strip electrocorticographic monitoring of ictal déjà vu. *Epilepsia*, 35, 1054–1059.

Weinstein, E. A. (1969). Patterns of reduplication in organic brain disease. In Vinken, P. J. & G. W. Bruyn (Eds.), *Handbook of Clinical Neurology*, Vol. 3. Amsterdam: North-Holland. 251–257.

Lucid Dreaming & Yognidra

Dharmendra Sharma
Bosky Sharma

Abstract: In Eastern and Western cultures both, the concept of conscious dreaming is widely accepted. Scientists only really became paid attention in proving the existence of lucid dreaming in the last couple of years but prior to that, there were still lots of fascinating references to lucid dreams throughout history. Tracing back, over the centuries, personal records of philosophers, artists and authors have talked about the concept of self-awareness in dreams. For example, the French philosopher Rene Descartes explained his lucid dreaming as illusions and hence not relevant. Tibetan Buddhist monks have integrated heightened self-awareness and dream control in their path to enlightenment. Ancient Indian Saints, Yogis in India, practice yogic sleep, also known as Yoga Nidra -Lucid sleeping. It is a full conscious state in which one can b deeply relaxed and this is the state where lucid dreaming state can be generated and hence, leads to easily confusion of the two seperate experiences of its kind. The present paper is an attempt to understand the frameworks of the experience of two states having relatively differences in the degree on the dimensions of the consciousness Flanagan (1991) and Hence, in distinguishing the difference between the two it's the degree to which one is aware of the physical environment as compared to the dream environment or has no awareness of the actual environment. Janakanda (1992), Ballantyne & Deva (1990).

Introduction

'Dreaming' is common across the globe among all humans irrespective of race or culture and have been experienced several times in life. Blackmore (1984). Since ancient times in varied cultures, 'dreams' have been regarded as a source of inspiration, mystery, messages & healing source Kilborne (1987).

'Dreams' are said to be nightly miracle wherein, all the things in the state seems 'real' along-with the experiences, sensations and feelings of dreamer of being a part of it. The seemingly objective universe is a creation of the dreamer's mind, a subjective, illusionary, transient production that creates and controls the dreamer's mind and on being awake the dreamer feels like "it was only a dream" suggesting that it was not "real". We generally don't question the reality of our dreams until after we have awakened. At this time the dreamer is said to be "lucid" i.e. dreaming and being aware that he/she is dreaming and the consciousness seems to be quiet wakeful F. Van Eden (1931).

The concept of conscious dreaming is widely accepted in both Eastern and Western cultures. Tracing back, over the centuries, personal records of philosophers, artists and authors have talked about the concept of self-awareness in dreams. For example, the French philosopher Rene Descartes found his lucid dreams so vivid, he concluded that our waking senses are illusory and not to be trusted. Tibetan Buddhist monks have integrated heightened self-awareness and dream control in their path to enlightenment. Ancient Indian Saints, Yogis in India, practice yogic sleep. i.e. a state of deep sleep wherein the meditative state one remains in the waking state of consciousness, gently focusing on the mind, allowing thought patterns, emotions, sensations, and images to come and go, also known as Yoga Nidra - Lucid sleeping. It is among the deepest possible states of relaxation while still maintaining full consciousness and the practices of which generate lucid dreaming and hence, leads to easily confusion of the two separate experiences of its kind.

The present piece of work is an effort and attempt to understand the frameworks of the experience of two states having relatively differences in the degree on the dimensions of the consciousness Flanagan (1991) and hence, it is imperative that for understanding the frameworks of the experience of lucid dreaming, we need to understand the psychological approach that takes an information processing view of lucid dreaming while other sees lucidity in sleep as a cognitive tool while still few others emphasis more on self-awareness.

Physiological approaches show that lucidity is significantly more aroused REM sleep experience than no lucid REM sleep. This sleep experience in EEG and lucidity work is based on the association of lucidity to meditation Gackenbach (1991).

UNDERSTANDING SLEEP & LUCID DREAMING

Sleep and especially restful and sound sleep is very significant for the body to restore energy for efficient functioning and getting refreshed. Each and every night, brain passes through four stages of sleep which takes about 90-110 minutes and marks one full sleep cycle i.e. Sound sleep with five full sleep cycles for eight hours per night. LaBerge et al. (1981), proved, lucid dreaming emerging during uninterrupted REM sleep in support to the past studies too. The four Stages of Sleep are as follows:

NREM Stage 1 is a light sleep and one is easily woken. One begins to loose muscle tone, causing twitches and jerks. Have hypnagogic hallucinations, swirling light and color patterns which hypnotize the mind into a restful sleep. Here in, stage 1, loss of self-awareness and most sensory attachment to the physical world is seen. The brainwave frequencies descend from Alpha through Theta state (4-7 Hz). During this stage mixed but slow low voltage EEG pattern emerges.

NREM Stage 2 loss of nearly all muscle tone, the physical body cannot workout the approaching dreams. However, the brainwave slows down furthermore and they do show brief bursts of higher brainwave activity what is called as sleep spindles and K-complexes. Half of all the sleep of a person is spent around in Stage 2; a light dreamless sleep. Here the person is harder to awake.

NREM Stage 3 & 4, has slow sleep waves (SWS) having high voltage brain waves, that consists of unconscious delta activity. Here most stimuli cause no reactions and the sleeper seems to be less responsive to the environment. On being awakened, one will feel especially dopey and confused for a couple of minutes. Another dreamless stage of sleep, wherein sleepwalking most likely is to occur.

REM, stage is the onset of dreaming. During this stage, the activity of brain changes rapidly, Delta waves disappear, fast, low- voltage activity returns. The person begins moving eye lids, rapidly. There is almost suppression of activity in body muscles. Indeed muscle relaxation is so great that a state bordering on paralysis seems to exist. The duration is variable, but the REM periods tend to increase in the length toward morning. The respiration patterns are found to become irregular in this phase. Breathing might even stop for few seconds, but soon regains the normal place. The temperature of the brain fluctuates and so does the flow of blood in the cerebrum. The expression of the brain and the mind suggests that the mind is not asleep in this period. This stage is also known as paradoxical sleep because the sleeper, though showing more active and high voltage brainwaves than before, is harder to awake.

Longest and most memorable lucid dreams usually occur in the fourth and fifth sleep cycles, during phases of REM sleep. Indeed, the more chances one has to sleep in, the better it allows extended REM time in the morning, more vivid dreams, and more chances to become lucid.

UNDERRSTANDING SLEEP & YOG NIDRA

Yognidra, also known as state of dynamic sleep, is also characterized as a relaxation technique and is said to be equivalent to over 4 hours of sleep. It's more effective and efficient form of psychic and rejuvenation than conventional sleep. It's a conscious way of deep body and mind relaxation. Yoga Nidra was taught by the ancient sages for the purpose of exploring the deep impressions or samskaras, which drive our actions or karma. They taught this so that sincere seekers can purify the deeper aspect of the mind-field, which is accessed in the formless state of conscious Deep Sleep.

According to the Swami Jyaneshwara, the goal of Yoga Nidra is spiritual insight and experience, not just to change the physical brain activity, there is some correlation with the brain wave patterns.

Beta level is typically the level of 'awake' working state.ie. Daily mental activity, alert, active. It is also the level of activity associated with tension or stress. Alpha level is a state of relaxed, passive attention, reverie, often considered the goal of relaxation exercises. While this is a very relaxing state and useful to be practiced, it is sometimes incorrectly thought to be the goal of yoga nidra.

Theta level, normally considered to be unconscious, possibly drowsy, or half asleep. This level is also sometimes incorrectly considered to be the level of yog nidra, where there is still the experience of Images and steams of thoughts.

Delta level, considered to be unconscious, dreamless, deep sleep (Prajna). In yoga nidra the brain waves are at this level, as the particular is in conscious deep sleep, beyond the activity experienced at the other levels. Theta, sometimes may exhibit delta in deep sleep Mangalteertham (1998).

Yoga Nidra is the intermediate stage of awakened and sleep and it is the stage of the brain when it produces Alpha waves. As S.M.Roney – Dougal (2001) observed in a study, initial EEG showed Beta activity prominently with intermittent Alpha activity. With the advancement of Yoga Nidra Beta activity was slowly replaced by Alpha activity and still further by smooth well-formed Alpha activity. Yoga Nidra gained alpha activity and with further advancement gradually Theta activity was noted intermixed with alpha activity suggestive of deep state of relaxation.

Corby, James C., Walton T. Roth, Vincent P. Zarcone, Jr., and Bert S. Kopell (1978) studied Autonomic and electroencephalographic (EEG) correlates of Tantric Yoga meditation and found that unlike most previously reported meditation studies, proficient meditators demonstrated increased autonomic activation, increased alpha and theta power, minimal evidence of EEG- defined sleep, and decreased autonomic orienting to external stimulation during meditation while unexperienced meditators demonstrated autonomic relaxation. An episode of sudden autonomic activation was observed that was characterized by the meditator as an approach to the Yogic ecstatic state of intense concentration.

In yoga, a fourth state of consciousness *Turiya*, a continuous 24-hour-a-day "ever present wakefulness," by Plotinus, is beyond the usual three of waking, dreaming, and nondream sleep Feuerstein (1996). According to C. Alexander & Langer, (1990); Walsh & Vaughan (1993) uninterrupted lucidity throughout sleep is recognized in yoga and Christian meditation, is a goal of Tibetan dream yoga too. In Transcendental Meditation it marks the maturation of sporadic "transcendental consciousness" into unbroken "cosmic consciousness" and as per Maslow (1971; Wilber (2000) in western terms, this is the transition from a peak to a plateau experience and from an altered state to an altered trait. Transcendental Meditation practitioners have yielded sleep EEG profiles consistent with alert awareness throughout sleep Mason, Alexander, Travis, Marsh, Orme-Johnson, & Gackenbach, (1997). Alike, for Freud, dreams were a royal road to the unconscious So as for meditative traditions, lucid dream and non dream sleep are a royal road to consciousness, allowing meditation and maturation to continue throughout the night.

Dreams are reflections of memory and express the inner tendencies, conflicts, aspirations, desires and motives of the unconscious mind. Unconscious mind works beyond the space and time. It reflects past buried memories as well as past lives and the present experiences too. Dreams are subjective experience of our neural activity representing thinking patterns and thought processes that are ongoing. Dreams, in many cultures, are source, to attain higher level of consciousness and increase one's self-awareness. The nature of sleep and dreams, they may give clues to the nature of consciousness itself.

Scientists only really became interested in proving the existence of lucid dreaming in the last couple of years but prior to that, there were still lots of fascinating references to lucid dreams throughout history. However, it has until recently evoked a lot interest in cross cultural studies, studies over various variables related to paranormal, psychical, religious & spirituality and other fields of psychology like parapsychology, transpersonal psychology, neuro-cognitive psychology etc. to name a few. Having known to have significant transpersonal implications of Lucid dreaming rigorous and extensive investigations are being carried out to further investigate higher advanced forms of lucidity, finding technological means to enhance it, observation of physiological correlates, using lucid dreaming as a spiritual practice, also building conceptual bridges to ancient techniques such as Yog Nidra and Tibetan dream yoga as well as demonstrating transpersonal implications of lucidity research and finding, links, connection, disconnection between the two fields. However, very few investigations have been carried out to establish cause and effect relationship of Yog nidra and various transcendental meditation practices alongwith lucid dreaming, because of the nature of the phenomenons' and its practice to attain it. Hence, in the present research an attempt is made by the researchers to shed some light on the two phenomena's as well as it opens the doors to further investigative advancement in the direction.

UNDERSTANDING DREAM & LUCID DREAMING

As mentioned above the longest and most memorable lucid dreams usually occur in the fourth and fifth sleep cycles, during phases of REM sleep. Indeed, the more chances one has to sleep in, the better it allows extended REM time in the morning, more vivid dreams, and more chances to become lucid. Hearne (1978) in a study proved, Lucid dreaming as a phenomenon occurring during sleep. Other Researchers too suggests that in the lucid dream, there is higher arousal, sufficient to build up an enhanced self in the wakeful sleeping, what makes the dream seem more real on waking up is because the 'self' seen and remembered in the dream is more similar to the one who is dreaming. However, because the one seen is similar to the one dreaming, therefore the dreamer is more conscious of it and remembers vividly. Lucid dreams proposes novel outlook for research in consciouness and especially for understanding self-consciousness. Hobson (2009) showed that nonlucid dreams show primary consciousness, including sensory imagery and the experience of a self interacting with the dream world and is not specific to the wake state. However, it can be distinguised from sensory inputs and motor outputs. Lucid dreams also provides rich examples of secondary consciousness, and specifically of more sophisticated cognitive and metacognitive processes occurring in sleep.

According to many western psychologists and meditation traditions' clear awareness in a long run can be sustained through lucid dreaming; dreams and even non dream sleep; non dream lucidity, possibilities are asserted until recently. Metzinger, (2004, 2009); Windt & Metzinger, (2007). The differences between lucid and non-lucid dreams is by relating them to different levels of self-related processing. Metzinger, 2004, 2009; Revonsuo, 2006; Ichikawa, 2009). As per some of the contemporary philosophers working on dreams, non-lucid dreams are conscious experiences as they are phenomenal states and there is something like to dream, and (contra Malcolm 1956, 1959; Dennett, 1976) dreams give rise to consciously experienced imagery during sleep. According to (Metzinger, 2004), however, most non-lucid dreams lack important layers of waking self-consciousness and hence, are said to be subjective experience in a conceptually weak sense.

Lucid Dream studies, suggests to witnessing dreaming, somatic arousal decrease, and the consciousness in sleep to the states desired by the practice of meditation becomes stable Gackenbach et al (1987).

Acc.to Sufi philosopher, Ibn Arabi, lucid dreaming has been mentioned as "providing great benefits" Shah (1971). A number of explorers and spiritual masters such as Sri Aurobindo (1970) and Rudolf Steiner (1947) also reported success with lucid dreaming.

According to the Dalai Lama (1983), Tibetan yogis are taught to develop lucidity, first in their dreams, and then in their nondream sleep, so as to remain continuously aware twenty-four hours a day. Meanwhile, during daylight hours they cultivate the awareness that their waking experience is also a dream. The ideal result is unbroken awareness, the sense that all experience is a dream, and ultimately "the Great Realization."

UNDERSTANDING DREAM & YOGNIDRA

Dreams, in many cultures, are source, to attain higher level of consciousness and increase one's self-awareness. The nature of sleep and dreams, they may give clues to the nature of consciousness itself. In yog nindra, there is no dream sequence, thoughts are found to be in a formless form, visual awareness and physical awareness along with body awareness is absent. This is known as Prajna, and is truer, deeper knowledge store.

Acc. to the Ogilvie, Hunt & et.al (1982) there is connection in lucidity-meditation as inferred from alpha waves in lucid and nonlucid REM.

Ogilvie, Hunt, Tyson, Lucescu, & Jeakins, D. (1982), observed increase of alpha in prelucid REM stage and early in lucidity and have associated this to the entrance, phases of waking meditation.

Similarly, West (1980) and Teneli & Krahne (1987) are of similar opinion that increase in alpha is observed at the beginning and at the end of meditation.

Researches shows that regular practice of meditation stabilizes the thought and the meditator is conscious of his true state that is, he is aware that he is sleeping and sometimes dreaming during the entire night, known as 'witnessing sleep' Alexander, Boyer & Johnson, (1985).

Past studies with meditation and EEG shows a fair consistent association of alpha with meditation. Gackenbach & Bosveld (1989).

Mangalteerthan(1998), concluded that practice of yognidra brings alpha dominance in the brain, which is characterized by mental relaxation.

Gackenbach, Cranson & Alexander, (1986) was of the opinion that, on several levels of analyses dream lucidity parallels waking meditation. However, the occurrence of lucidity can be spontaneous in non-meditating populations, but the average frequency of such experiences is considerably less than that in meditating adults. Gackenbach (1989).

Ballantyne & Deva, (1990) He experiences the loss of conscious control and an enhancement of sensory quality Janakanda (1992).

Thus, Yoga nidra is a state between sleep & Samadhi, Half sleep and Half waking state, useful and a simple practice said to be the art of yogis, known as psychic sleep. It is imperative to understand that Dreaming and Not-Dreaming (Deep Sleep) are two different processes or levels of consciousness. Some phases of meditation deal with those Dreaming level images, but Yoga Nidra relates to conscious Deep Sleep. Yoga Nidra means Yogic Sleep, not Yogic Dreaming. The real significance of lucid dreams is that they guide us to higher levels of consciousness, for they suggest what it would be like to discover that we are not yet fully awake.

CONCLUSION

Hence, Lucid dreaming and transpersonal studies are two vigorous and important fields with overlapping interests and much to contribute to one another. Unfortunately, they have remained largely isolated and ignorant of each other, in spite of the fact that lucid dreaming research has significant transpersonal implications and from the above paper it can be concluded that using lucid dreaming as a spiritual practice, and building conceptual bridges to ancient techniques such as Yog Nidra or Tibetan dream yoga, the two are easily confused though they aren't similar as the two separate experiences of its kind are the two states having relatively differences in the degree on the dimensions of the consciousness. Flanagan (1991) and as discussed above, in distinguishing the difference between the two it's the degree to which one is aware of the physical environment as compared to the dream environment or has no awareness of the actual environment. Janakanda (1992), Ballantyne & Deva (1990).

REFERRENCES

Alexander, C., & Langer, E. (Eds.). (1990). Higher stages of human development. New York: Oxford University Press.

Alexander, C.N., Boyer, R. & Orme-Johnson, D. (1985). Distinguishing between transcendental consciousness and lucidity. *Lucidity Letter*, 4(2), 68-85.

Aurobindo (1970). Thelifedivine,5th ed, Pondicherry, India:Ashram Publications Department.

Ballantyne, J.R., Govind Sastry Deva. 1990. Yoga-sutras of Patanjali. Delhi: Parimal, p 48–87

Blackmore S. (1984). A Psychological Theory of the Out of Bosy Experience. *Journal of Parapsychology,* Vol. 48.

Corby, James C., Walton T. Roth, Vincent P. Zarcone, Jr., and Bert S. Kopell (1978). Psychophysiological correlates of the practice of Tantric Yoga meditation. Archives of General Psychiatry, 35(5):571- 580. Also in D. H. Shapiro, and R. N. Walsh, eds., Meditation: Classic and Contemporary Perspectives. New York: Aldine Publishing, 1984, pp. 440- 464. PMID: 365124.

Dalai Lama (1983). Talk given at the International TranspersonalAssociation. Daves, Switzerland.

Dennett, D. C. (1976). Are dreams experiences? Philosophical Review, LXXIII, 151-171.

Feuerstein, G. (1996). The Shambhala guide to yoga. Boston: Shambhala.

Flanagan O. (1991). Consciousness reconsidered. Cambridge, Mass MIT, p 109, 215.

F. van Eeden (1931) "A Study of Dreams," *Proceedings of the Society for Psychical Research 26: 439.*

Gackenbach, J., & Bosveld, J. (1989). Control your dreams, New York, Harper & Row.

Gackenbach, Jayne. (1991). Dreaming, Frameworks for understanding lucid dreaming, 1(2), 109-128.

Gackenbach, J., Cranson, R., & Alexander, C, (1986). Lucid dreaming, witnessing and the Transcendental meditation: A developmental relationship. Lucidity Letter, s5, 34-41.

Hearne, K. (1978). Unpublished doctoral dissertation, University of Liverpool. Lucid dreams: An electrophysiological and psychological study.

Hobson, A. (2009). The neurobiology of consciousness: lucid dreaming wakes up. International Journal of Dream Research, 2, 41-44.

Ichikawa, J. (2009). Dreaming and imagination. Mind and Language, 24, 103-121.

Janakanda S. 1992. Yoga, tantra and meditation in daily life. London:Rider, p 99.

Kilborne, B. (1987). "Moroccan Dream Interpretation and Culturally Constituted Defense Mechanisms." *Ethos* 9 (4): 294-311.

LaBerge, S., Nagel, L., Dement, W. and Zarcone, V. (1981). Lucid dreaming verified by volitional communication during REM sleep. Perceptual and Motor Skills, 5: 727-732. *LaBerge, op. cit., 156.*

Malcolm, N. (1956). Dreaming and skepticism. The Philosophical Review, LXV: 14-37.

Malcolm, N. (1959). Dreaming. New York: Humanities Press.

Mangalteertham, Sannyasi (Dr A.K Ghosh), (1998). Yoga Nidra - Altered State of Consciousness 1n Swami Satyananda's Yoga Nidra. Bihar School of Yolta, Munger, 6th edition.

Maslow, A. (1971). The farther reaches of human nature. New York: Viking

Mason, L., Alexander, C., Travis, F., Marsh, G., Orme-Johnson, D., & Gackenbach, J. (1997). Electrophysiological correlates of higher states of consciousness during sleep in long term practitioners of the Transcendental Meditation program. Sleep, 20,101–110.

Metzinger, T. (2004). Being no one. The self-model theory of subjectivity (2nd ed.). Cambridge, MA: MIT Press.

Metzinger, T. (2009). The ego tunnel. The science of the mind and the myth of the self. New York: Basic Books.

Ogilvie, R., Hunt, H., Tyson, P., Lucescu, M. & Jeakins, D. (1982). Lucid dreaming and alpha activity: A preliminary report. *Perceptual and Motor Skills*, 55, 795-808.

Revonsuo, A. (2006). Inner presence: consciousness as a biological phenomenon. Cambridge: The MIT Press.

SM Roney – Dougal (2001). Altered States of Consciousness and Yogic Attainment inRelation to Awareness of Precognitive and Clairvoyant Targets; Psi Research Centre Saraswati, Sw. Satyananda; Yoga nidra; Yoga Publication Trust, Munger, Bihar;2001.

Shah, I. (1971). The Sufis. New York: Anchor/Doubleday

Steiner.R, (G, Metaxa, transl). (1947). Knowledge of the higher worlds anditsattainment,3rd ed. NewYork: Anthroposophic Press.

Teneli, B. & Krahne, W. (1987). EEG changes of Transcendental Meditation practitioners. A*dvances in Biological Psychiatry.* 16, 41-71.

Walsh, R., & Vaughan, F. (Eds.). (1993). Paths beyond ego. Los Angeles: J. Tarcher.

West, M.A. (1980). Meditation and the EEG. *Psychological Medicine*, 10, 369-375.

Wilber, K. (2000). The eye of spirit: An integral vision for a world gone slightly mad. Vol. 7. The collected works of Ken Wilber. Boston: Shambhala

Windt, J. M., & Metzinger, T. (2007). The philosophy of dreaming and self-consciousness: what happens to the experiential subject during the dream state? In D. Barrett & P. McNamara (Eds.), The new science of dreaming (Vol. III, pp. 193-247). Westport, CT: Praeger.

Religious Coping and Caregiving Stress

Meeta Malhotra

Abstract: Religious beliefs and practices constitute one of the most frequently used methods of coping in times of crisis. Family caregivers of persons with serious mental illness often turn to spirituality for support, and religiosity may be an important contributor to caregiver adjustment. Review of papers revealed high level of religious beliefs and religious coping among caregivers and some association with improved mental and spiritual health. Positive caregivers experience is also reported. The purpose of the current paper is to present insights in how caregiving is experienced by family caregivers, and the religious coping strategies utilised by them. A lot of studies have shown that caregivers try faith healing at one time or the other. It can be concluded that religion may serve as a potentially effective method of coping for and so the need is to integrate it into psychiatric and psychological practice. Moreover, collaborative partnerships between mental health professionals and religious communities represent a powerful resource for meeting the support needs of caregivers of persons with serious mental illness.

Key words: Caregiving; Burden; Coping; Religious coping strategies

Introduction

The caregiving experience has been extensively investigated in some chronic/severe mental illnesses. It is evident that relatives of patients with mental illness are likely to experience considerable stress as a result of the caregiving role. The coping strategies adopted by them may influence their response to the complex set of demands placed upon them when a close member of the family suffers from severe mental illness. Coping influences adjustment and the use of effective coping strategies have consistently been linked with higher levels of well-being (McCrae & Costa, 1986).

Caring for a family member with mental illness is a challenging task. It requires time, patience and energy and may cause frustration among caregivers. To minimize disruptions within the family and individual suffering, caregivers must adapt to their new role by learning successful coping strategies.

Coping is defined as a set of concrete response to a stressful situation or event that is intended to resolve the problem or reduce distress. Coping does not imply success, but efforts to resolve a stressful situation. Several factors influence the stress-coping response. Some factors are related to the stressor such as; intensity, scope, duration, number and nature of concurrent stressors and predictability. Those related to the individual experiencing the stressor include level of personal control, feeling of competence, availability of social support, information and guidance, and access to resources (equipment and supplies). Others are age at the time of stress and cognitive appraisal. Positive coping mechanisms include, looking to God for strength and help, working with God as a partner, and thinking of oneself as part of a larger spiritual force. In contrast, negative coping mechanisms include viewing life challenges and personal difficulties as punishment from God, feeling abandoned by or alienated from God in the face of life challenges, and attributing negative circumstances to the Devil. Whereas positive religious coping is linked with psychosocial well-being, negative religious coping is associated with maladaptation (e.g., Herrera et al., 2009).

Religious beliefs and practices constitute one of the most frequently used methods of coping in times of crisis. This is particularly so in case of chronic stress and adjustment to changed life circumstances such as prolonged illness (Ellison 1991; Stanton Staton, Danoff- Burg, Cameron, Bishops, Collins, Kirk, Sworowski & Twillman, 2001). According to Pargament (1996) religion acts as an orienting system, a general way of perceiving and dealing with the world. It acts as a frame of reference for interpreting and evaluating events, as well as a resource to fall back upon in times of crisis. It also helps in providing a sense of comfort and closeness with God (Pargament & Park, 1995). Prayer is often thought of as the most distinctive characteristic or behaviour associated with religion and is the most frequently mentioned religious coping (Cinnirella & Loewenthal, 1999).

Though some researchers have viewed religious coping as an emotion focused strategy, others like Pargament (1996) view it as being both problem focused as well as emotion focused. Pargament, Smith, Koenig and Perez (1998) identified three forms of religious coping with stress: the self-directing, collaborative and the deferring style. The self-directing style lays emphasis on the individual's own responsibility and active role in solving the problem. The deferring style places the responsibility of solving problems on God, with the individual playing a passive role. The collaborative style involves a sharing of responsibility for solving the problem on God as well as the individual. The self-directing and collaborative styles have been linked with higher levels of psychological competence, while the reverse is true for the deferring style.

In a study Pargament, Ensing, Falgout, Olsen, Reilly, van Haitsma & Warren (1990) found that the most strongly endorsed approaches to negative events was that the individual had to accept the situation and that the event represented God's will. Belief in a just world, the experience of God as a supportive partner in the coping process, search for spiritual support through religion and involvement in religious rituals were related to positive outcome.

The caregiving wives used belief in God, prayer and forgiveness as coping mechanisms. Caregivers also engaged in private prayer, and sought spiritual guidance in making daily life decisions more frequently than non-caregivers (Kaye & Robinson, 1994).

The prevalence of religious coping and its relationship with symptom severity and over all functioning was examined by Tepper, Rogers, Colemon and Maloney (2001). Overall, 325 (80%) of the participants reported using some type of religious activity or had some type of religious belief that helped them cope with symptoms. Specific strategies like prayer or reading the Bible were more likely to be used by patients with greater symptoms and poorer level of functioning. It was concluded that religious beliefs and activities serve as important coping strategies, warranting their integrations to interventions for these patients.

Loewenthal, Cinnirella, Evoixa and Murphy (2001) in a study reported that religious coping activities were seen as relatively ineffective in comparison with social and cognitive forms of coping, such as community support and having goals to aim for. For individuals who used religious coping, religious faith and the use of prayer were found to be most effective strategy.

The role of religion and spirituality in dealing with the caregiving situation was evaluated by Chang, Noonan and Tenenstedt (1998). Results indicated that caregivers who made greater use of religious coping were more likely to have a good quality relationship with the elderly care recipient, and this in turn was associated with lower levels of psychological distress as well as role distress.

The studies reviewed indicate that religious beliefs and practices are an important part of the coping process for an individual stressful situation like caregiving. Some studies on caregivers also highlight the fact that the religious or spiritual dimension facilitates adjustment to the caregiving role. Not all religious coping is positive, and some forms of religious coping which are maladaptive have also been identified. Religious beliefs and practices have been found to be useful in providing a sense of control, hope and better adjustment, and common practices like prayer and seeking support and reassurance from God have emerged as the most frequently used religious coping strategies.

A substational body of research has suggested that there is positive link between religious and spiritual involvement and fewer depressive symptoms, higher positive affect and life satisfaction, lower levels of morbidity, and increased longevity (e.g., Chatters, 2000; Koenignig et al., 1999; Miller & Thoresen, 1999; Pargament, 1997; Patrick & Kinney, 2003).

Caregivers used belief in God and prayer as a coping mechanism. Moreover, belief in a just world, and the experience of God as a supportive partner in coping process was related to positive outcome (Kaye, & Robinson, 1994; Pargament, et. al., 1990; Loewenthal, et. al., 2001).

Religious beliefs and practices influence both appraisals as well as coping with stress as is evident from Western as well as Indian studies. Caregivers sought consolation and solace in their religion and spirituality. Infact, it was consistently found that some aspects of spirituality allowed these caregivers to survive the severe stress experienced as a result of their caregiving responsibilities.

It was observed from the reviews religious help seeking formed an important part of psychiatric help seeking, with traditional healers often given preference over medical or psychological treatment' as observed by a number of researchers (Chaddha, Agarwal, Singh, & Raheja, 2001; Chandrashekhar, 1981; Kakar, 1982).

One of the important ways of dealing with stressors of caregiving in Indian context is reliance on 'Karma theory'. Caregivers used it to explain their problems. The doctrine of 'karma' deserves special attention. It is roughly translated as 'destiny' or fate, against which all human efforts are seen to be of no avail (Rao, 2001). The theory of karma enables the acceptance of present suffering as unavoidable, and gives hope that one can avoid suffering in future, through performance of righteous deeds (Dalal & Misra, 1999).

Many of the caregivers saw the illness as an affliction given by God and they felt that only God could provide a solution. This belief helped caregivers to cope with their problems especially when the illness had been continuing for years and no mode of treatment either medical or traditional worked. Moreover, when attribution to an external cause was made it absolved the individual of personal responsibility resulting in better coping and emotional well being. Lam and Palsane (1997) also observed that in Indian settings low stress is associated with external control such as God or fate as this reduces the individual sense of personal responsibility. When caregivers accept the illness and disability resulting from the illness, as a karmic fall out, this help in reducing emotional distress, and act as a mechanism of rationalization and coping with the stress of caregiving. A deferring style of coping where the caregiver placed the responsibility on God, with the individual playing a passive role was identified by Pargament (1996). When caregivers saw God as the cause then they also believed that one day God will provide the solution.

Many times caregivers offered supernatural explanations such as black magic or possession by a spirit. In such cases, they often visited faith healers or adopted other forms of religious coping. It appears as if there is a parallel system run by faith healers to the medical system. This is because folk traditions often emphasize supernatural causes, as well as astrology and karma (Ng, 1997). When they consider cause of illness beyond their control then they feel solution is also beyond them. This feeling helped in reducing their stress.

Not all forms of religious coping, however, are beneficial to the individual. Some of them can be harmful and lead to negative outcomes. Some of the negative forms of religious coping include spiritual discomfort, appraisal of events as a punishment from God, and interpersonal religious discontent (Pargament, Koening & Perez, 2000). Individuals who express dissatisfaction with the church or God, or feelings of abandonment or anger at God experience poorer mental health status, negative mood state, poor conflict resolution and also feelings of despair, hopelessness and resentment (Pargament et. al., 1998). Religious coping thus takes diverse forms and method and can have both positive as well as negative outcome for the individual.

To conclude

The stress buffering effect of religious coping is evident. Acceptance is an often used strategy. This helped caregivers to deal with the distress associated with caregiving. Moreover, it provided caregivers a frame work with the help of which they were able to make sense of what was happening to them. Religion acted as an orienting system, a general way of perceiving and dealing with the world. It is a frame of reference for interpreting and evaluating events as well as a resource to fall back upon, in time of crisis. It also helped them, in providing a sense of comfort and closeness with God (Pargament & Park, 1995). Calling upon their spirituality proved to be comforting for many caregivers as they sought to deal with essential issues related to their relative's illness.

In research literature religious beliefs were found to facilitate coping with the stressors of caregiving (RamMohan, et. al., 2002a), and it has also been recommended that they may be incorporated in therapeutic programs (Sharma et. al., 1995). People take comfort in the concept of karmaphala. This finding is similar to the ones obtained in earlier studies (Agarwal & Dalal, 1993; Dalal & Pande, 1998; Dalal & Singh, 1992; Joshi, 1995).

Family intervention programs, for chronic mentally ill need to be culturally sensitive and flexible as observed by Kapur (1992). Moreover, as observed in this paper, certain themes need to be incorporated when designing interventions for families. These include providing information that is compatible with the educational and religious background of the caregivers. Thus, it could be concluded that the religious and spiritual dimension facilitated caregiver adjustment. Religious belief and practices have been found to be useful in providing a sense of control, hope and better adjustment. Common practices such as prayer and reposing trust in God have emerged as the most frequently used religious coping strategy.

The present paper has several noteworthy implications for social service delivery and policy making. It is imperative for service provider to ask caregivers if and how they use religion to help them to cope. Simply acknowledging and respecting caregivers' religious belief can be very helpful. The need is to identify and support caregivers' religious involvement. Social workers could ask caregivers about religious practices (e.g. scripture reading, prayer) that have been meaningful to them and discuss how they may be relevant to their ability to cope with the stress of caregiving. the need is to make caregivers to be aware of their own religious beliefs to with difficult situations in caregiving. Policy makers could advocate for improving caregiver support by providing faith-based programs and interventions.

Future research will need to incorporate the important issues of religious coping that influence caregiving outcomes for families dealing with mental illness and might compare motivation for caregiving, coping processes and spiritual and religious perspective of different ethnic groups. Qualitative research could provide a deeper understanding of how racially diverse group of caregivers use religion to cope with caregiving burden differently. The findings suggest that religiosity plays an important role in decreasing caregiver burden. It is also important for agencies or hospitals to provide services and training for caregivers that include the components of religiosity and its impact on the caregivers' perception of burden and depression.

References

Agarwal, M., & Dalal, A. K. (1993). Beliefs about the world and recovery from myocardial infraction. *Journal of Social Psychology, 133(3),* 385-394.

Chaddha, R. K., Agarwal, V., Singh, M., & Raheja, D. (2001). Help seeking behaviour of psychiatric patients before seeking care at a mental hospital. *International Journal of Social Psychiatry, 47,* 471-478.

Chandrasekhar, C. R., Issac, M. K., Kapur, R. L., & Parthasarthy, R. (1981). Measurement of priority mental disorders in the community. *Indian Journal of Psychiatry, 23,* 173-178.

Chang, B. H., Noonan, A. E., & Tennstedt, S. L. (1998). The role of religion/ spirituality in coping with caregiving for disabled elders. *The Gerontologist, 3,* 463-70.

Chatters, L. M. (2000). Religion and health: Public Health research and practice. *Annual Review of Public Health, 21,* 335–367.

Cinnirella, M., & Loewenthal, K. M. (1999). Religious and ethnic group influences on beliefs about mental illness: A qualitative interview study. *British Journal of Medical Psychology, 72,* 505-524.

Dalal, A. K., & Misra, G. (1999). Emerging perspectives in stress and health. In G. Misra (Ed.), *Psychological Perspectives on Stress and Health.* New Delhi: Concept Publishing Company.

Dalal, A. K., & Pande, N. (1988). Psychological recovery of the accident victims with temporary and permanent disability. *International Journal of Psychology, 23,* 25-40.

Dalal, A. K., & Singh, A. K. (1992). Role of causal and recovery beliefs in the psychological adjustment to a chronic disease. *Psychology and Health, 2,* 193-203.

Ellison, C. G. (1991). Religious involvement and subjective well-being. *Journal of Health and Social Behaviour, 32,* 80-99.

Herrera, A. P., Lee, J. W., Nanyonjo, R. D., Laufman, L. E., & Torres-Vigil, I. (2009). Religious coping and caregiver well-being in Mexican-American families. *Aging & Mental Health, 13,* 84–91.

Joshi, M. S. (1995). Lay explanations as causes of diabetes in India and the UK. In I. Markova and R.M. Farr (Eds.), *Representations of Health Illness and Handicap.* Switzerland: Harwood Academic Publishers.

Kakar, S. (1982). *Shamans, Mystics, and Doctors.* New Delhi: Oxford University Press.

Kapur, R. L. (1992). The family and schizophrenia: Priority areas for intervention research In India. *Indian Journal of Psychiatry, 34,* 3-7.

Kaye J., & Robinson, K. M., (1994). Spirituality among caregivers. *Image: The Journal of Nursing Scholarship, 26,* 218-221.

Koenig, H. G., Hays, J. C., Larson, D. B., George, L. K., Cohen, J. H., McCullough, M. E., Blazer, D. G. (1999). Does religious attendance prolong survival? A six-year follow-up study of 3,968 older adults. *Journals of Gerontology: Medical Sciences, 54*A, M370–376.

Lam, D. J., & Palsane, M. N. (1997). Research on stress and-coping: Contemporary Asian perspectives. In S. R. H. Kao and D. Sinha (Eds.), *Asian Perspectives on Psychology.* New Delhi: Sage Publications.

Lazarus, R. S. & Folkman, S. (1984). Coping and adaptation. In W.G. Gentry (Ed.), *Handbook of Behavioural Medicine,* 13A, 105-12.

Loewenthal, K. M., Cinnire!la. M., Evoixa, G., & Murphy, P. (2001). Faith conquers all Beliefs about the role of religious factors in coping with depression among different cultural-religious in the UK. *British Journal of Medical Psychology, 74,* 293-303.

McCrae, R. R., & Costa, P. T. (1986). Personality, coping and coping effectiveness in an adult sample. *Journal of Personality, 54,* 385-405.

Miller, W. R., & Thoresen, C. E. (1999). Spirituality and health. In W. R. Miller (Ed.). *Integrating spirituality into treatment: Resources for practitioners*(pp. 3–18). Washington, DC: American Psychological Association. doi:10.1037/10327-001

Ng, C. H. (1997). The stigma of mental illness in Asian cultures. *Australian and New Zealand Journal of Psychiatry, 31,* 382-390.

Pargament, K. I. (1996). Religious methods of coping: Resources for the conservation and transformation of significance. In E. P. Shafranske (Ed.), *Relation and the Clinical Practice of Psychology.* Washington DC: APA Press.

Pargament, K. I., & Park, C. L. (1995). Merely a defence? The variety of religious means and ends. *Journal of Social Issues, 5,* 13-32.

Pargament, K. I., Ensing, D. S., Falgout, K., Olsen, H., Reilly, B., van Haitsma, K., & Warren, R. (1990). God help me: Religious coping efforts as predictors of the outcomes to significant negative life events. *American Journal of Community Psychology, 18,* 793-823.

Pargament, K. I., Koenig, H. G., & Perez, L. M (2000). The many methods of religious coping: Development and initial validation of the RCOPE. *Journal of Clinical Psychology, 56,* 519-543.

Pargament, K. I., Smith, B., Koenig, H. G., & Perez, L. M. (1998). Patterns of positive and negative religious coping with major life stressors. *Journal for the Scientific Study of Religion, 37,* 710-724.

Pargament, K. I. (1997). *The psychology of religion and coping: Theory, research, and practice.* New York, NY: Guilford

Patrick, J. H., & Kinney, J. M. (2003). Why believe? The effects of religious beliefs on emotional well being. *Journal of Religious Gerontology, 14,* 153–170.

Rammohan, A., Rao, K., & Subbakrishna, D. K. (2002a). Religious coping and psychological well being in carers of relatives with schizophrenia. *Acta Psychiatric Scandinavia,* 105, 356-362.

Rao, A. V. (2001). The karma theory and psychiatry. *Indian Journal of Psychiatry, 43,* 112-117.

Sharma, I. Azar, M. Z., & Varma, S. L. (1995). Religious psychotherapy: A cross-cultural perspective. *Indian Journal of Social Psychiatry, 11,* 53-55.

Staton, A. L., Danoff- Burg, S., Cameron, C. L., Bishops, M., Collins, C. A., Kirk, S. B., Sworowski, L. A., & Twillman, R. (2001). Emotionally expressive coping predicts psychological and physical adjustment to breast cancer. *Journal of Consulting and Clinical Psychology, 68,* 875-882.

Tepper, L., Rogers, S. A., Coleman, E. M., & Maloney, H. M. (2001). The prevalence of religious coping among persons with persistent mental illness. *Psychiatric Services, 52,* 660-665.

Breakwell, G. M. (1995). Interviewing. In G.M. Breakwell, S. Hammond and C. Fife Schaw (Eds.), *Research Methods in Psychology* (pp. 230-242). London: Sage.

Paranormal Belief and Spiritual Experience in College Students

Prateek Kumar Singh
Bosky Sharma
Dharmendra Sharma

Abstract: Throughout the history almost every culture has reported experiences and beliefs' in paranormal phenomenon. According to Tobayck, (1988), paranormal beliefs & psi phenomenon's are strange, uncommon events accompanying with myths & rituals, perceived to be in contradict to scientific laws and principles. With the growing interest of parapsychology, the varied paranormal or psi phenomenon are being taken up as a research area to be explored with a scientific perspective over the cultural beliefs. This study was designed to measure paranormal belief and spiritual belief in college students, wherein, randomly 88 students of age group 16-26 years, with average age of 19.49 years, 47 male (53.4 %) participants and 41 female (46.6 %) participants were selected from educational institute in Gwalior. Results suggest that both gender hold same level of belief on paranormal activities. Both male and female have equal level of spiritual experience. However, on one of the factor of paranormal belief scale i.e. extraordinary life forms male hold stronger belief on extraordinary life form in comparison to females and on other factors of paranormal belief scale – traditionally religious belief, psi, witchcraft, superstition, spiritualism and precognition male and female hold same level of belief.

Key Words: *Paranormal belief, Spiritual experience*

INTRODUCTION

'Paranormal' the word in itself, seems as if it has a lot to reveal and unfold. It strikes a mark in the mind and creates lot of querries, questions and inquisitiveness. To believe or not to believe in the paranoraml phenomenon is yet another issue to address. Gallup (1997) found that ninety percent of the americans believe in atleast one paranoramal phenomenon, though having no substantial proof in its existence. In the developing nations, the paranormal beliefs are felt to be more integrated in the societies and hence, challenging the beliefs is a hard task.

India is a nation with diverse culture and with most deeply religious societies wherein religion, plays a central and a definitive role in the life of most of the people. In a multi-cultural and polytheistic society like India, ritualistic behaviors and paranormal belief is ingrained in the general psyche of the individuals. At early age children are reminded of their roles and places in society. This is reinforced by the fact many believe in gods and spirits and have an integral and functional role in determining their life (Eugene M. Makar, 2008).

Lot have been talked, published, read and discussed about it and its related variables. Around 1960, it was at its peak as massive parapsychology books and games were sold (Trussi,1972). Hence, it has been a key area of interest to try and understand the increasing beliefs in paranoramal phenomenons. Blackmore (1997), in his research concluded that 59% were believers in paranormal. Many researches have attempted to distinguish believers from non-believers of paranoramal (Kennedy, 2005).

Paranoramal phenomenons are described as the ones whose occurrence cannot be explained with the help of common scientific principles and are not understood by human mind and therefore is said to be unnatural. (Brugger & Mohr, 2008). According to Broad (1949); Tobayck, (1995) the term explains phenomena, that are –if real- supposed to be violating basic limits and principles of science. Huntly & Peeters (2005), believed that paranormal activites has association with prophets & Saints. They are historically said to be centre of spiritual powers and people connect them with possibiltiy of supernatural on an emotional level Hart (2008).

The word 'spiritual' comes from Latin spiritus, in turn from spirare - to breathe (Wulff, 1997). Shafranske and Gorsuch (1984) defined spirituality, broadly, as "a transcendent dimension within human experience, discovered in moments in which the individual questions the meaning of personal existence and attempts to place the self within a broader ontological context". Vaughan (1991) defined it as "a subjective experience of the sacred". Definitions of spirituality usually put more emphasis on the individual and on subjective experience. Often, spirituality is allied to religiosity; also its most commonly held view considers spirituality may or may not be taking its expression in a religious context. Pargament, (1999) Saroglou & Mun˜oz-Garcı´a (2008), Saucier & Skrzypinska,(2006) Zinnbauer et al., (1997).

However, distinguishing ones identifying as spiritual people but not religious from the ones being spiritual and religious too is not clear. Koeing (2008). Nevertheless, what unites spirituality and religiosity is a belief in supernatural spirits. In religions, this belief takes the form of doctrines about issues like God, the Holy Spirit, Heaven, and Hell, whereas nonreligious spirituality is not tied to religious doctrines. Beck & Miller (2001) Religiosity was not significantly correlated with belief in paranormal However; negative affect over the preceding year was positively correlated to beliefs in paranormal.

Kuzendorf, Tassone, Gauthier, Monroe, McArdle, Watson & Papoutsak is (2007), studied archiach's spiritual beliefs and proved that half of their subjects in the study believed that non-humans can literallly meet them in their dreams. The two thirds of the ghost believers claim to have seen ghost and two thirds of the lord believers reported to have experienced the Lord. Lastly, one tenth of the extraterrestrial believers said they have met extaterrastrials.

Thus, being vigorously researched by few inorder to quench their thirst of knowledge and to have definite proof in its existence. It is evident that the large number of newspaper articles, books, televison propgrams, movies and groups that focus on such topics, Scheidt (1973).

Research Studies in India, have reported the prevalence of superstitious beliefs. In a sample of 1600 high school pupils belonging to 13 schools in Kerala, Thimotheose (1973) examined the nature and extent of superstitious beliefs prevalent among high school pupils, Out of the 60 superstitious beliefs given in the inventory, more than 42 were supported by above 50% of the participating pupils.

Santhi (1982) found that, in India, superstitious beliefs are prevalent among people belonging to all strata of society and among people of all levels of formal education. Similarly, Patel (1984) has pointed out that majority of Indians had belief in superstitions.

In another study prevalence of superstitious beliefs were found among first year college female students, while intelligence, creativity, and academic ability were found inversely related to the superstitious beliefs (Sumaranjitha & Sreedhar, 1992).

Gupta (1999) found the prevalence of superstitious behaviour among male and female students of different professional courses.

George and Sreedhar (2006) found that students coming from urban area believe more in superstition than those from rural area. They also found that females have more irrational beliefs than males.

Psi experiences are sometimes presented as associated with an advanced state of consciousness or spiritual development Grosso (1992); Murphy (1992); Ring (1984). Traditional yoga writings similarly proposed that paranormal abilities are associated with developing spirituality Prabhavananda & Isherwood, (1981). Mystical or transcendent experiences are widely interpreted as evidence of high spirituality and are sought through practices such as yoga meditation (Kornfield, 2000). As noted above, psi experiences are frequently reported as a form of mystical experience. The occurrence of these experiences is taken as a sign of spiritual superiority by some people (usually males) and is widely recognized that the occurrence of transcendent experiences does not necessarily indicate ethical behavior, compassion, wisdom, integration, or other characteristics normally associated with spirituality (Kornfield, 2000; Zweig, 2003) in both eastern and western spiritual organizations Gonsiorek (1995); Kornfield (2000); Neimark(1998); Roemischer (2004); Zweig (2003).

Tobacyk (1988) compared university students and foud that Finland yield lower score on paranormal belief for traditional religious concepts, witchcraft, superstitions but had higher scores for belief in extraordinary life forms Tobacyk & Pirttila Backman (1992).

Davis (1988) found lower scores in college studetns for traditioal religious belief, superstitions, extraordinary life forms and precogniton whereas higher in spiritualist belief.

Irwin (1991) found stronger belief in spiritualism and precognition compared to traditional religious belief.

To understand how people believe in its possibility has been a prominent aveneu of psychological enquiries and the present study is an attempt to measure the paranormal belief and spiritual belief in college students hpothesising that :

1. There exists no difference between male and female subjects on spiritual experience scale.
2. There exists no difference between male and female subjects on paranormal belief scale.
3. There exists no difference between male and female subjects on traditionally religious belief factor of paranormal belief scale.
4. There exists no difference between male and female subjects on psi factor of paranormal belief scale.
5. There exists no difference between male and female subjects on witchcraft factor of paranormal belief scale.
6. There exists no difference between male and female subjects on superstition factor of paranormal belief scale.
7. There exists no difference between male and female subjects on spiritualism factor of paranormal belief scale.
8. There exists no difference between male and female subjects on extraordinary life form factor of paranormal belief scale.
9. There exists no difference between male and female subjects on precognition factor of paranormal belief scale.

METHOD

Participants: Sample consists of randomly selected 88 students of age group 16-26 years, with average age of 19.49 years, selected from educational institute in Gwalior. Sample consists of 47 male (53.4 %) participants and 41 female (46.6 %) participants.

Measures Used:

Paranormal belief scale (revised – 26 item) developed by Jerome J. Tobacyk is a seven-point rating scale was used as tool to measure paranormal belief in sample. This scale provides a separate score on each of seven factorially derived subscales with each subscale reflecting a major dimension of paranormal belief.

These subscales are Traditional Religious Belief, Psi, Witchcraft, Superstition, Spiritualism, Extraordinary Life Forms, and Precognition. The four-week test-retest reliability for full scale is 0.92. This scale appears to be a conceptually and psychometrically satisfactory measure of paranormal beliefs (Tobacyk, 2004).

Daily Spiritual experience scale (DSES – 16 item) developed by Dr Lynn Underwood was used as a tool to measure spiritual experience in sample.

RESULTS

On spiritual experience scale at 0.05 level of significance and 86 degree of freedom t-value is 1.56, this difference is considered to be not statistically significant and our null hypothesis stands correct. This means though male and female sample group means differ by 5.39 level, this difference is by chance and both male and female have same level of spiritual experience.

Mean and t-values of Male & Female on Spiritual Experience scale and Paranormal Belief Scale

PBS factors	***M***	***SD***	***t-value***
Spiritual Experience			
Male (n = 47)	52.32	14.03	1.56
Female (n = 41)	57.71	18.29	
Paranormal Belief			
Male (n = 47)	104.43	25.58	0.4118
Female (n = 41)	106.76	27.49	

$^{*}p < .05$

On paranormal belief scale at 0.05 level of significance and 86 degree of freedom t-value is 0.41, this difference is considered to be not statistically significant and our null hypothesis stands correct. This means, though, male and female sample group means differ by 2.33 level, this difference is by chance and both male and female have same level of paranormal belief.

Thus it can be concluded that both male and female hold same level on paranormal belief and spiritual experience. Neither of the gender holds high or low level at paranormal belief and at spiritual experience, and the difference in means could be reasonably attributed to chance.

Following chart shows mean values of male and females on paranormal belief and spiritual experience.

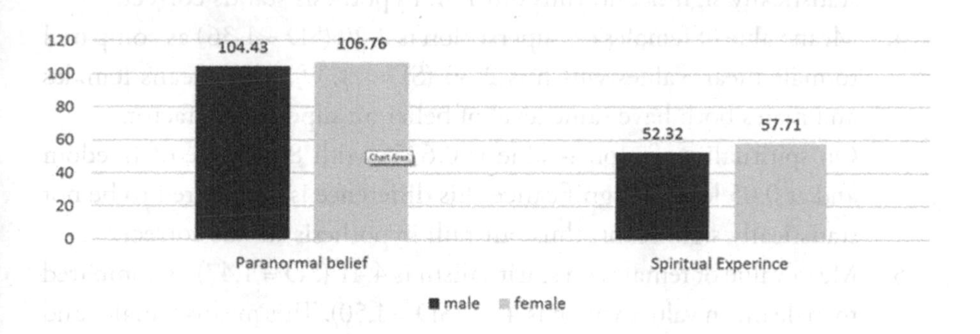

As Paranormal belief scale also provides a separate score on each of the seven factorially derived subscales with each subscales reflecting a major dimension of paranormal belief. Gender difference on each factor were also explored.

On traditionally religious belief factor, t-value is 0.8917 with 86 degree of freedom and at 0.05 level of significance this difference is considered to be not statistically significant, thus our null hypothesis stands correct.

1. Mean value of females on traditionally religious belief is 5.24 (SD = 1.39) as compared to male mean values which is 4.98 (SD = 1.39). This means females and males both have same level of traditionally religious belief.

   On Psi factor, t-value is 1.2978 with 86 degree of freedom and at 0.05 level of significance this difference is considered to be not statistically significant, thus our null hypothesis stands correct.
2. Mean value of females on Psi is 4.63 (SD = 1.34) as compared to male mean values which is 4.26 (SD = 1.39). This means females and males both have same level of belief on Psi factor.

   On Witchcraft factor, t-value is 0.4900 with 86 degree of freedom and at 0.05 level of significance this difference is considered to be not statistically significant, thus our null hypothesis stands correct.
3. Mean value of females on Witchcraft is 4.24 (SD = 1.73) as compared to male mean values which is 4.06 (SD = 1.71). This means females and males both have same level of belief on Witchcraft factor.

On superstition factor, t-value is 0.5657 with 86 degree of freedom and at 0.05 level of significance this difference is considered to be not statistically significant, thus our null hypothesis stands correct.

4. Mean value of females on superstition is 2.20 (SD = 1.36) as compared to male mean values which is 2.36 (SD = 1.39). This means females and males both have same level of belief on superstition factor.

   On spiritualism factor, t-value is 0.6358 with 86 degree of freedom and at 0.05 level of significance this difference is considered to be not statistically significant, thus our null hypothesis stands correct.

5. Mean value of females on spiritualism is 4.41 (SD = 1.47) as compared to male mean values which is 4.21 (SD = 1.50). This means females and males both have same level of belief on spiritualism factor.

   On extraordinary life form factor, t-value is 2.0871 with 86 degree of freedom and at 0.05 level of significance this difference is considered to be statistically significant. Our null hypothesis that there exist no difference between male and female subjects on traditionally religious belief factor of paranormal belief scale is rejected.

6. Mean value of females on extraordinary life form is 3.88 (SD = 1.17) as compared to male mean values which is 4.40 (SD = 1.19). On this factor male have scored high in comparison to females, thus male belief strongly on existence of extraordinary life form in comparison to females.

   On precognition factor, t-value is 0.3614 with 86 degree of freedom and at 0.05 level of significance this difference is considered to be not statistically significant, thus our null hypothesis stands correct.

7. Mean value of females on precognition is 4.24 (SD = 1.43) as compared to male mean values which is 4.13 (SD = 1.57). This means females and males both have same level of belief on precognition factor.

***t*-values of Male & Female on Sub Factors of Paranormal Belief Scale**

PBS factors	*M*	*SD*	*t-value*
Traditionally religious belief			
Male (n = 47)	4.98	1.39	0.89
Female (n = 41)	5.24	1.39	
Psi			
Male (n = 47)	4.26	1.39	1.29
Female (n = 41)	4.63	1.34	
Witchcraft			
Male (n = 47)	4.06	1.71	0.49
Female (n = 41)	4.24	1.73	
Superstition			
Male (n = 47)	2.36	1.39	0.57
Female (n = 41)	2.20	1.36	
Spiritualism			
Male (n = 47)	4.21	1.50	0.63
Female (n = 41)	4.41	1.47	
Extraordinary life form			
Male (n = 47)	4.40	1.19	2.08*
Female (n = 41)	3.88	1.17	
Precognition			
Male (n = 47)	4.13	1.57	0.36
Female (n = 41)	4.24	1.43	

*$p < .05$

Following graph shows the mean values of female and male on all sub factor of paranormal belief scale.

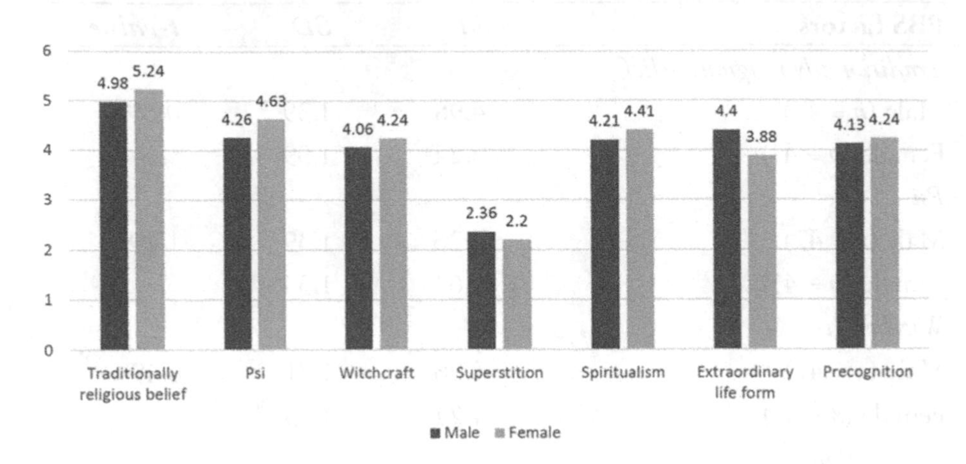

DISCUSSION & CONCLUSION

In spite of education and living in technologically advanced and developing society new generation college going students have strong paranormal belief Jahoda (1968), Salter & Rouetledge (1971) and have spiritual experience. 71% of sample holds average and above level of paranormal belief. College students strongly believe that Psi phenomena, witchcraft, superstition, extraordinary life form and precognition are real process. No gender difference exist, except in extra ordinary life form, on above factors and both male and female college students believe this phenomena to be true Emmons & Sobal (1981); Haraldson (1985),;Tobayck & Milford (1983). On extra ordinary life form males strongly believe in existence of life on other planet, such as the Loch Ness Monster and abdominal snowman of Tibet in comparison (Tobayck and Milford (1983) ;Tobayck & Pritila –Backman (1992) to female found similar results in which male significantly scored high on believing in extra ordinary life form than women. Lewis C (2002) similarly college students report to have spirituality. Majority of students hold moderate level of spiritual experience, and both male and female have similar level of spiritual experience.

In our efforts to find out the difference in paranormal belief scale and spiritual experience scale in adolescence and adults we have reached to some interesting conclusion.

Results suggest that both gender hold same level of belief on paranormal activities.

1. Further result suggests that both male and female have equal level of spiritual experience.
2. On one of the factor of paranormal belief scale i.e. extraordinary life forms male hold stronger belief on extraordinary life form in comparison to females.
3. On other factors of paranormal belief scale – traditionally religious belief, psi, witchcraft, superstition, spiritualism and precognition male and female hold same level of belief.

REFERRRENCES

Beck. R., & Miller. J. P. (2001). Erosion of belief and disbelief: Effects of religiosity and negative affect on beliefs in the paranormal and supernatural. *The Journal of Social Psychology*, 14, 277-287.

Blackmore.S. (1997). Parapsychology:Sex Differences. *British Jounal of Psychology*, 88,683-694.

Broad. C.D. (1949). The relevance of psychical research to philosophy. *Philosophy*, 24, 291-309.

Brugger. P., Mohr. C. (2008). The paranormal mind: How the study of anomalous experiences and beliefs may inform cognitive neuroscience. *Cortex, 44, 1291-1298.*

Davies. M. F. & Kirkby. H. E. (1985). Multidimensionality of the relationship between perceived control and belief in the paranormal: spheres of control and types of paranormal phenomena. *Personality and Individual Differences*, 6, 661-663.

Emmons, C.E & Sobal J (1981). Paranormal beliefs: Testing the marginality hypothesis. Sociological Focus,14, 49-56.

Eugene M. Makar (2008). *An American's Guide to Doing Business in India.* ISBN 1-59869-211-9.

Gallup.G. (1997). The Gallup poll: Public opinion. Willington: Scholarly Resources.

George.S & Sreedhar.K.P (2006). Globalisation and the Prevalence of Superstitious Beliefs. *Journal of the Indian Academy of Applied Psychology*, 32, 3, 241-247.

Grosso. M. (1992) Frontiers of the soul: Exploring psychic evolution. Wheaton, IL: QuestBooks

Gonsiorek. J.C. (1995). (Ed.) Breach of trust: Sexual exploitation by health care professionals and clergy. Thousand Oaks, CA: Sage.

Gupta. N. K. (1999). Superstitious behaviour amongst Professional Graduates. *Praachi Journal of Psycho-cultural Dimensions*, 15, 75-77.

Haraldscon, E (1985). Representative national surveys of psychic phenomenona Iceland, Great Britain, Sweden, USA and Gallup's multinational survey. Journal of the society for Psychichal Research,53,145-158.

Hart. T. (2008). Head vs. Heart: Dissection of Paranormal Beliefs. *36th Annual Western Pennslvania Undergraduate Psychology Conference.* 1-4. Eric, PA.

Huntley. C., Peeters. P. (2005). Paranormal Beliefs, Religious Beliefs and Personality Correlates. *Manchester Metropoltan University.*

Irwin. H. J. (1991a). A study of paranormal belief, psychological adjustment, and fantasy proneness. *Journal of the American Society for Psychical Research*, 85, 317-331.

Jahoda G. (1968). Scientific training and the persistence of traditional beliefs among West African University Students. Nature, 220, 1356.

Kennedy.J. (2005) Personality and Motivations to believe, Misbelieve, And Disbelieve I Paranormal Phenomena. *Journal of parapsychology*, 69, 263-292.

Koenig. HG (2008). Concerns about measuring 'spirituality' in research. *J Nerv Ment Dis.* 196:349Y355.

Kornfield, J. (2000). After the ecstasy, the laundry. New York: Bantam Books.

Kunzendorf. R.G., Tassone, Sarah, Gauthier, Allyson, Monroe, Linda, McArdle, Erin, Watson, Gloria, Papoutsakis, Eena. (2007). The Archaic Belief in Dream Visitations as it Relates to "Seeing Ghosts," "Meeting the Lord," As well as "Encountering Extraterrestrials". *Imagination, Cognition and Personality*, 27,1, 71-85.

Lewis, C. M. (2002). Investigating student's belief in the paranormal.

Murphy. M. (1992). The Future of the Body: Explorations into the Future Evolution of Human Nature. Los Angeles, CA: Jeremy P. Tarcher.

Neimark, J. (1998). Crimes of the soul. Psychology Today, Retrieved November 2, 2005, from http://cms.psychologytoday.com/articles/index.php?term=pto-19980301-000043.xml.

Patel, Sumitra, L. (1984) Superstitions among school children. *Educational Review*,90,74-76.

Pargament KI (1999). The psychology of religion and spirituality? Yes and no. *Int J Psychol Relig*, 9:3Y16.

Prabhavananda, & Isherwood, J. (1981). How to know God: The yoga aphorisms of Patanjali. Hollywood, CA: The Vedanta Society of Southern California

Ring, K. (1984). Heading Toward Omega: In Search of the Meaning of Near-Death Experiences. New York: William Morrow.

Roemischer, J. (2004). Women who sleep with their gurus – and why they love it. What is Enlightenment, Issue 26. Retrieved October 20, 2005, from http://www.wie.org/i26/women-who-sleep.asp.

Salter, C.A., & Routledge L.M (1971). Supernatural Beliefs among graduate students at the University of Pennsylvania. Nature, 232, 278-279.

Santhi, G. (1982). Some aspects of Tamil folklore: A note on superstition beliefs. *Folklore*, 23,189-193.

Saroglou V, Mun˜oz-Garcı´a A (2008) Individual differences in religion and spirituality: An issue of personality traits and/or values. *J Sci Stud Relig.* 47:83.

Saucier G, Skrzypinska K (2006) Spiritual but not religious? Evidence for two independent dispositions. *J Pers.* 74:1257Y1292.

Scheidt, R. (1973). Belief in supernatural phenomena and locus of control. *Psychological Report, 32, 1159-1162.*

Shafranske, E. P., & Gorsuch, R. L. (1984). Factors associated with the perception of spirituality in psychotherapy. *Journal of Transpersonal Psychology*,16, 231–241.

Sumaranjitha, L. & Sreedhar, K.P. (1992). Unsubstantiated Beliefs in Adolescent Girls. *The Creative Psychologist,* 4, 35-40.

Thimotheose, K.G. (1973). An investigation into the relationship between Superstitious beliefs and Family background among the High school pupils. *Ph.D. Thesis,* Kerala University.

Tobacyk, J. (1988). A revised paranormal belief scale. *Unpublished manuscript.* Ruston: Louisiana Tech University.

Tobacyk, J.J & Pirttila-Backman(1992). Paranormal Beliefs and their Implications in University Students from Finland and the United States. *Journal of Cross-Cultural Psychology,* 23, 1, 59-71.

Tobayck, J. J. (1995). Final thoughts on issues in the measurement of paranormal belief. *The Journal of Parapsychology,* 59, 141-145.

Tobacyk, J. J. (2004). A Revised Paranormal Belief Scale. *The International Journal of Transpersonal Studies, 23, 94-98.*

Tobacyk, J. J.& Milford (1983). Belief in paranormal phenomena: Assesment instrument development and implications for personality functioning. Journal of Personality and Social Psychology, 44,1029-1037.

Truzzi, M. (1972). The occult revival as popular culture: some random observations on the old and the nouveau witch. *The Socilogical Quarterly,* 13, 16-36.

Vaughan, F. (1991). Spiritual issues in psychotherapy. *Journal of Transpersonal Psychology,* 23, 105–119.

Wulff, D. M. (1997). Psychology of religion: Classic and contemporary (2nd ed.). New York: Wiley.

Zinnbauer BJ, Pargament KI, Cole B, Rye MS, Butter EM, Belavich TG, Hipp KM, Scott AB, Kadar JL (1997) Religion and spirituality: Unfuzzying the fuzzy. *J Sci Stud Relig.* 36:549Y564.

Zweig, C. (2003) The holy longing: The hidden power of spiritual yearning. New York: Tarcher/Putnam.

Psychotherapy and Tantric Rituals

Nudrat jahan

Abstract: Since ancient time, all over the world, Mental illness is perceived as possession of a demon or evil spirit. Most favorite method of elimination of such b*ezier* behavior had been *exorcism*. Even the development of modern clinical psychology and effectiveness of psychotherapeutic method could not stop people of following such practices. Due to lack of education and awareness about mental illness it is not amazing that people are still approaching those methods, but, it is interesting and surprising that sometimes they get benefitted by such *Tantric* or healers. Places where e*xorcism* is well practiced are also indicating toward the history of success of these rituals in dealing with mental illnesses. Without tracing the cause of effectiveness of these traditional methods our knowledge of psychotherapy seems incomplete. To understand the effectiveness of these rituals, we carefully examine the method or some common practices of performing these rituals. Common practices includes chanting of *Mantras,* tying the patient with chain, beating the patient, Keeping or tying lucky charms, hanging something in home wearing bracelets, rings of different stones or thread, metals and chains, etc. Present writ-up is an effort to discover psychotherapeutic element in these rituals. It may help to understand element of psychotherapy concealed in such healing approaches.

Key Word: ***Bezier, Exorcism, Tantric, Mantras***

In the morning of a busy day, I heard a loud voice of an old lady in the Psychiatric OPD. She was angry and shouting on the Psychiatrist "You told me my ward is suffering from depression, you stopped me to bring him to *Baba* deliberately. He took medication for days, but not recovered. I bring him to Baba and now he is fine, relaxed and eating well. He is in good health now. You are cheater and making money from us, we will never bring him to you!" Old lady left with the patient, everybody including psychiatrist was morn. She was an illiterate villager of Haryana.

Since ancient time, in Asia and many other continents of the world, Mental illness is often perceived as possession of a demon. Even the development of modern clinical psychology and effectiveness of psychotherapeutic method are unable to completely erase the traces of practicing traditional rituals from the mind of our society. *Bezier* behaviour at first hand, taken as possession of an evil spirit and tried to treat through *exorcism*. It reflects a collective unconscious of our society about Mental illness, which has its root in demonological or dark era of clinical psychology. In India and most other countries of all over the world such rituals have always been first choice for the public to treat the strange behaviour. Literature of the places, well known for the *Exorcism,* like Balaji temple in Mahndipur, Rajasthan indicates toward the history of success of these rituals in dealing with odd behaviour/mental illnesses. Though researchers also criticized its effectiveness (Dwyer,2003), a great Psychotherapist can't refuse it completely. Without tracing the cause of effectiveness of these traditional methods our knowledge of psychotherapy seems paralyzed. Present writ-up is an effort to discover psychotherapeutic element in these rituals.

My frequent meetings with Indian patients and their families revealed that in majority of the cases first remedy for is to approach an exorcist and then a Temple or shrine, as sufferer believed to be possessed primarily. Few researchers also studied and reported neuroticism in the induction of "trance" in these patients (Satija et. al, 1982). People has strong social network of information of easily accessible people and places that practice these rituals and offer's such services. Due to lake of education and awareness about mental illness in these countries it is not amazing that people are still approaching those methods. We hold our interest, when they report benefit, even if for hours or few days. As it become very relevant to understand the effectiveness of these rituals, we carefully examine the method or some common practices of performing these rituals, of treat strange behaviour. It may help to understand element of psychotherapy concealed in such healing approaches. Common practices in exorcism for removal of evil spirit include chanting of *Mantras*. Mantras are the words of different religious books. It means a sacred utterance, a sound, or a syllable, word, phonemes, or group of words believed by some to have psychological and spiritual power. Earliest, at least 3000 year back it was composed by Vedic times by Hindus in india. Now it is found in various religions Buddhism, Jainism and Sikhism. Mantra serves a central role in the tantric school of Hinduism. There is strong belief that repetitive chanting of these mantras by sufferer himself or by family member will resolve all kind of problem. Few researchers also searched the linguistic view of mantras (Harvey, 1989). Keeping or tying lucky charms, hanging something in home is also suggested by the *tantric* to remove the evil spirit. These are the things like bracelets, rings of different stones or metals and chains. Sometime, a priest gives at the end of a ceremony. Lucky charm is believed to bring good luck for wearer. People wear it with the intention of attracting good luck, wealth or health or strong belief that it's effect will solve the problem of life. Sometime it includes hanging something in home. It includes different kinds of faces or posters or wall decors recommended by priests. These things are placed on the door, room and balcony to prevent the entry of negative energy or eliminate it from the house. Some researchers also proved that lucky charm actually works (Bates, 2010). Sometime to completely remove the effect of possession and keep other members of the family safe people in India perform different kind of Puja: another kind of spritual activity. It is a prayer ritual performed by Hindus to host, honor and worship one or more deities, or to spiritually celebrate an event. It may be perform in home or in a garden, temple or bank of river. Zimmer (1984) relates puja to yantras, with the rituals helping the devotee focus on the spiritual concepts. Puja in Hinduism, claims Zimmer, is a path and process of alteration of consciousness, where the devotee and the spiritual significance of the deity are brought together. This ritual puja process, in different parts of India, is considered to be liberating, releasing, purifying and a form of yoga of spirit and emotions. (Rodrigues,2003; Pintchman, 2008). *Puja* himself include one or all above mentioned methods of eliminating odd behaviour in a systematic manner. Similarly like Puja's, *exorcism* it is also a set of rituals. In this process it is beliefs that the negative energy is removed, shifted or tied with something. Betting the patient and tying with the chains during performing special ritual may typically see in this process. An impression of these rituals gives us a clear picture to inspect the elements of psychotherapy and get understanding about the effectiveness of above methods in treating odd behaviour.

Elements of psychotherapy in tantric rituals

Change in Schema: Schemas are the cognitive frame work which helps to define world around us. As dirty mirror can't present a clear view, faulty schema can't correctly define the events of our life. Inspite of advancement of medical sciences, mostly in such cases where there is strong oddity in behaviour it is found that search of cause of long lasting troubles or illnesses end-up with the conclusion of black magic done by a witch or *Dayan*. Black magic has traditionally referred to the use of supernatural powers or magic for evil and selfish purposes (Melton, 2001). This belief also resulted as frequent murder of suspected women in villages of India. According to the National Crime Records Bureau (NCRB) data, 54 women were murdered in Jharkhand alone in 2013, the highest in the country, with witch-hunting as motive (Das, 2014). As Wagener stated on the basis of their study of major depression patients changes in Early Maladaptive Schema (EMS) are highly relevant for changes in symptom distress and EMS can not only be changed by schema therapy but also by other approaches, like psychodynamic therapy (Wegwner, Alfter, Geiser, Leidtke, & Conrad, 2013). Link of strange behaviour with black magic change the view of a person about the illness and troubles of life, when narrated by a priest. Patient and family perform several rituals and try hard to overcome the effect of such magic. This ritual can be chanting Mantras, offering Puja to any specific place, hanging something in the home or wearing lucky charms. It changes the patients Schema about the illness and sometime this result as relief from illness for short or long duration.

Perception of shift of responsibility: Literature of cognitive behaviour therapy also supports the effect of perception of shift of responsibility on decreasing distress and anxiety among the patients of different mental disorder. When the patient suffering from the depression or elevated state of mood approaches to a priest he/ she immediately consol that he himself is not responsible for his behaviour and it is because of possession of evil spirit. This approach decreases the stress of patient's mind, as he has already heard tales about possession of spirit and removal of evil spirit with exorcism. Now onward patient and his family took it only as a matter of searching and approaching a right person who can perform such rituals efficiently. It gains the family support and empathy for the patient ultimately.

Catharsis: Catharsis is originated from the Greek word katharsis meaning "purification" or "cleansing". it is the purification and purgation of emotions—especially pity and fear—through art (Merriam & Webester, 1995). As described by the Freud's psychoanalytic school of psychology catharsis of repressed material have high level of therapeutic value, if done in front of the trained or experienced one. Concept of confession also reports the reduction of stress caused by wrong deeds, after confession in front of a priest. Confession has been described as "a pillar of mental health" because of its ability to relieve anxieties associated with keeping secrets (Wilkes, 2012). The concept of confession in religion varies extensively across various belief systems, and is usually more similar to a ritual by which the person acknowledges thoughts or actions considered sinful or morally wrong within the confines of the confessor's religion (Rogers, 1998). Similar to confession elevated state of a mental illness some time gives an opportunity to the patient to release his pent-up emotion or feelings. It decreases the severity of illness.

Family support: Family expectations can impact one's recovery (Tartakovsky, 2011). Due to collective effort of the patient family proper attention is pays to the patient's health and diet, patient feels himself safe and being cared by the family. In disorder where lack of family support and empathy has been the maintaining factor, family support during these rituals work well. Sometime the patient gradually show benefit from these rituals.

State of trance and suggestibility: Trance- a state of focused concentration is a state of increased suggestibility, during which critical faculties are reduced and subjects are more prone to accept the commands and suggestions. It is subjective and varies from person to person and from one trance experience to the next. Trance can be experienced on a continuum from light to very deep. Profound level of trance, called by many names. One name is the Esdaile State. In this trance state, under the guidance of a trained hypnotherapist, people can undergo surgery without anesthesia. They feel no pain. People in this state can turn off sensation in all or any part of the body. If worded properly and very concisely, direct suggestions to the subconscious may be effective here. Sometimes the person will remember what occurred during hypnosis, and sometimes not. Similarly, in the exorcism the patient may achieve the deepest level of trance and gets direct suggestion to the sub-conscious. It helps him to reduce the oddity of their behaviour.

As study done by Satija (1982) advocates the need to understand the psychotherapeutic elements in these rituals over view of psychotherapeutic value of tantric rituals suggests the immense need of work in the field of Cultural responsive cognitive behaviour therapy concealed in tantric rituals by recent researchers.

Conclusion

During the exploration of Tantric rituals (chanting Mantras, Beating and tying the patient, hanging lucky charms or wearing something to prevent negative energy) by psychological perspective we found that these practices have very high psychotherapeutic value. It gives an opportunity to restore and balance psyche to some patients. By this way they do catharsis to release their emotions and pent-up feelings. In some cases perception of shift of responsibility reduce anxiety of being responsible for some negative outcomes of life. It helps to change patient's schema about the problem faced in their life. In some sever cases of Bezier behavior State of trance: a high suggestibility state gives opportunity to a tantric to influence the patient psyche. Most importantly, family support received by the patient plays a crucial role in effectiveness of traditional healing techniques. At the end we can say that complete rejection of such approaches seems not relevant, instead of that, a careful research on such techniques can broad the spectrum of cultural responsive psychotherapy.

References

Bates, D. (2010). New research proves that lucky charm do actually work. http://www.redicecreations.com/article.php?id=10888

Das, M. (2014). *India's own witch-hunt- 160 women killed in 2013.* The News Minute; http://www.thenewsminute.com/news_sections/683.

Dwyer, G. (2003). Healing and transformation of self in *Divine and Demonic: Supernatural affliction and its treatment in North India*, NY, RoutledgeCurzon. p.n. 83

Harvey Alper (1989). *Understanding Mantras*, State University of New York, page 10-14. Retrieved from http://en.wikipedia.org/wiki/Special:BookSources/8120807464

Rodrigues, H.P. (2003). *Ritual Worship of the Great Goddess*, McGill Studies in the History of Religions, State University of New York Press. Retrieved from http://en.wikipedia.org/wiki/Special:BookSources/0791453995

Melton, J. G. (2001). *Black magic, Encyclopedia of occultism & Parapsychology*. vol.1. No.5. Gale research inc. A-L

Merriam, & Webester. (1995). *Merriam-Webster encyclopedia of literature.* USA: Merriam-WebesterInc. 217

Rogers, W. S. (1998). *The language of confession, interrogation, and deception.* 2-10

Tartakovsky, M. (2011). 15 ways to support a loved one with serious mental illness. *psychcentral.* Retrieved from http://psychcentral.com/lib/15-ways-to-support-a-loved-one-with-serious-mental-illness/0007039

Pintchman, T. (2008). "Raising Krishna with Love: Maternal devotion as a form of yoga in a women's ritual tradition", in *Theory and Practice of Yog.*, Knut Joacobsen.

Satija, D.G., Nathawat, S.S., Singh, D., Sharma, A. (1982). A study of patient attending Mahandipur Balaji tample: psychiatric and psychodynamic aspects. *Indian Journal of Psychiatry, 24 (4)*, 375-379.

Wegwner, I., Alfter, S., Geiser, F., Leidtke, R., & Conrad, R. (2013). Schema change without schema therapy: the role of early maladaptive schemata for a successful treatment of major depression. *Psychiatry, 1* (76), 1-17, doi: 10.1521/psyc.2013.76.1.1.

Wilkes, P. (2012). *The Art of Confession: Renewing Yourself Through the Practice of Honesty*, New York, Workman publishing company. P.n.- 9.

Zimmer, Heinrich. (1984). *Artistic Form and Yoga in the Sacred Images of India.* Translated by Gerald Chapple and James B. Lawson, Princeton University Press.

Para Psychology in Islamic Perspective

Zar Nigar

Abstract: Psychology is the study of behavior of all living organism and Para psychology is an important area of study which is concerned with the extra sensory perception of humans. This paper is an attempt to give a theoretical outline of psychology & some paranormal experiences in Islamic perspective with references of Quran.

Key Words: Islam, Para psychology, human beings, dreams & Jinn.

Introduction

Islamic Psychology: Islam is not only a religion that deals with some prayers and rituals, but it is also a system based on a set of rules by which any one can order his or her personal and social life. These specific rules and laws don't govern only faith but they govern each & every minute of personal as well as interpersonal functions of human beings.

The main source of Islamic teachings and laws is Quran. It deals with all branches of knowledge that a person needs in his daily life. It gives enough importance to psychology and mental health of a person. We can find Islamic perspectives on psychology and well-being in a number of verses about sensory perceptions of human beings, but it goes further and discusses the involvement of Jin and Satan in human personality – a new perspective of psychology. This raises relevant issues such as the goals of Satan, whispers, magic, possession and its signs, methods used by him as well as means of protection from him. The history of Islamic psychology begins with the history of mankind, from very beginning of the mistake of Adam and Eve in Haven by committing a sin against the command of Allah. That incident shows that human behavior is flexible and easy to be influenced. The Quranic statement about the above incident is:

> "Then did Satan make them slip from the haven, and get them out from the state in which they had been. We said: "Get you down all with enmity between yourselves. On earth will be your dwelling place and your means of livelihood for a time." Then learnt Adam from His Lord Words of inspiration, and his lord turned towards him, for He is Oft-Returning, Most Merciful." (Quran, 2:36-37)

Islamic Perspective on Parapsychology: Parapsychology is a branch of psychology. Some dreams, mental experiences at the time of death, existence of Jinn and all allied issues fall under the study of Parapsychology. Almost the one third of Quran concerns the above mentioned subjects.

The Quran points out many dreams of prophets (pbut); Dream of Prophet Abraham is one of the famous dreams in history about the sacrificing of his beloved son Ismael, is narrated in Quran (Quran, 37: 102). Prophet Joseph also saw a dream in his childhood about his Prophet ship and he was an expert in dream interpretation, Quran mentioned his interpretation and it's after effects on that society at more than one place (Quran, 12: 41, 43-49, 101). A dream played significant role in a great victory by its psychological support in the battle of Badr in the period of Prophet Muhammad (PBUH). The Quran says about it:

> "Remember! In your dream Allah showed them to you as few, if He had shown them to you as many, you would surely have been discouraged, and you would surely have disputed in (your) decision, but Allah saved you for He knows well the secrets of hearts." (Quran, 8: 43)

We can say some dreams truthful and inspiring are granted by Allah. They are shown to support or reassure a believer or warn them of some individuals, scolding them for some wrongdoings, foretell him of some good to anticipate or harm to beware of, and so on. Such dreams are attributed to Allah because of the truth and good they carry.

At times people do observe some dreams, false and unpleasant, mixed with truth and fabrication frightening them during sleep and even after waking up. Such dreams are whispered by a devil and are attributed to Satan. Once prophet Muhammad (PBUH) said that if anyone sees a good dream, it is from Allah, Let him pray Allah and speak about it. If any one sees a bad dream, it is from Satan. Let him seek refuge from Satan and not tell anybody about it. It will not then disturb him. (Bukhari)

As well as dreams there are a lot of verses in Quran utter about life, death and the mental experiences of a person at the time of death.

> It is He (Allah) Who gives life, and causes death, and to Him you (all) shall return. (Quran, 10: 56)
> He is the Irresistible, Supreme over His slaves, and He sends guardians (angels guarding and writing all of one's good and bad deeds) over you, until when death approaches one of you, Our Messengers take his soul, and they never neglect their duty. (Quran, 6: 61)
> Say: "The angel of death, who is set over you, will take your souls. Then you shall be brought to your Lord." (Quran, 32: 11)
> And the unconsciousness of death will come in truth. This is what you have been avoiding. (Quran, 50: 19)

Along with death, many verses in Quran authenticate the rebirth and the life hereafter. According to the Quran the present life is an assessment for the next life. All the Prophets of Allah called the people to worship and to believe in life after death. According to them Allah will raise all the dead and a day will come when the whole universe will be destroyed and then the dead will be resurrected to stand before Allah. But disbelievers always deny this concept on the basis of their assumption even they have no sound source for their denial of life after death. Quran exposed the weakness of their assumptions by advancing very logical and rational arguments in support of it:

> And he (i.e. man) presents for us an example and forgets his creation. He says, "Who will give life to bones while they are disintegrated?" Say, "He will give them life who produced them the first time; and He is, of all creation, Knowing." (Quran, 36:78-80)

> And they say there is not but our worldly life; we die and live and nothing destroys us except time. And they have of that no knowledge; they are only assuming. And when our verses are recited to them as clear evidences, their argument is only that they say, "Bring back our forefathers, if you should be truthful." Say, "God causes you to live, then causes you to die; then He will assemble you for the Day of Resurrection, about which there is no doubt," but most of the people do not know. (Quran, 45:24-26)

According to the Quran there will be a day for judgment after death of human beings and end of this world. That day will be the beginning of a life that will never end, and every person will be rewarded or punished by Allah for his or her good or bad deeds accordingly. The Quran very definitely states that the Day of Judgment must come and Allah will decide the fate of each soul according to his or her record of deeds:

> But those who disbelieve say, "The Hour (i.e. the Day of Judgment) will not come to us." Say, "Yes, by my Lord, it will surely come to you. God is the Knower of the unseen." Not absent from Him is an atom's weight within the heavens or within the earth or what is smaller than that or greater, except that it is in a clear register - That He may reward those who believe and do righteous deeds. Those will have forgiveness and noble provision. But those who strive against our verses seeking to cause failure - for them will be a painful punishment of foul nature. (Quran, 34: 3-5)

The belief in life after death not only ensures success in the Hereafter but also gives this world peace and happiness by making individuals most responsible for their duties, customs and commitments.

As far as all mentioned issues, the most discussed and controversial topic under the head of Parapsychology is the existence of Jinn around us. The big question is, do they exist or not? Allah replied in Quran:

> "And I have created the jinn and the mankind only that they should worship me." (Quran, 51: 56)

The Quran also affirms and makes it very clear that Muhammad (PBUH) was sent as a prophet to both communities of human beings and jinn. But like the human beings some of them (Jinn) believe in Allah and some of them don't do. Quran says:

> "Say: It has been revealed to me that a group of Jinn listened and said; 'Indeed we have heard the wonderful Quran. It guides unto right way so we believe in it, and we will not make partners with our Lord." (Quran, 72:1-2)

Like human beings, they can also be good, evil, or neutral. Humans cannot see them, but they can see humans. They eat and drink like humans. They are male and female who have children. The Jinn are frequently mentioned in Quran, especially a whole chapter is named 'al-Jinn' (Quran: 72). Jinn can possess humans, because they are able to easily go in and out of the human body, but still they are inferior to humans as Quran says:

> "Certainly We created humans in the best make." (Quran, 95: 4)

Prophet Muhammad (PBUH) provided us a set of instructions for getting protection from the evil of them (Jinn). The most effective forms are trying to stay clean, performing prayers and if someone is possessed by them then reciting by himself or another one some verses of second chapter (Quran, 2: 255 & 284-286) or last two chapters (Quran: 113 & 114) of Quran.

Conclusion: On the basis of the aforesaid, one may understand the brief concept of Parapsychology in Islamic perspective as expressed in the Holy Quran. This paper highlighted and pointed out the relevant verses of Quran on the above topic and one may go through them. The following books are suggested for further readings and explanations.

Suggested Books:

1. Abdur Rahman, Aysha. *Maqal fil Insan Dirasa Quraniyya*, Cairo, Egypt: Dar al Maarif, 1969.
2. Aisha. *Psychology from the Islamic perspective*, Riyadh: International Islamic Publishing House, 2011.

3. Ansari, Z.A. *Quranic Concepts of the Human Psyche,* Lahore: Institute of Islamic Thought, 1992.
4. Rizwi, S.A.A. *Muslim Tradition in Psychotherapy & Modern Trend,* Lahore: Combine Printer, 1989.
5. Sharif, Adnan. *Min Ilm el Nafs el Qurani*, Bairoot, Lebanon: Dar al Ilm lil Malayeen, 1987.
6. Vahab, A. A. *An Introduction to Islamic Psychology*, New Delhi: Institute of Objective Studies, 1996.

Reference:

The Holy Quran, Translation and Commentary by A.Y. Ali, Qatar: Publication of the Presidency of Islamic Courts & Affairs. 1948.

Mysticism

Anita Chauhan

Abstract: Mystical experience involves an expansion of consciousness beyond the conventional boundaries of organisms and correspond a large sense of identity and of contact with a universal being. All the mystics have expressed that we all are in essence, a drop of the Supreme Being. This drop is referred to as the Soul whereas the mind is a greater part of consciousness confined to the sensory processes; it is under the domain of attachment and aversion. They believe that there is a knot between the soul and mind which needs to be disentangled in order to transcend and have access to the mystical world. This knot can be disentangled through the practice of meditation. Meditation is the only technique through which a person can become healthy and attain permanent happiness by transcending oneself from the worldly affairs and can attain enlightenment or liberation from the transmigration cycle. Mystics believe that the karmas or our actions play an important role in getting access to the mystical world. The very cause of transmigration cycle is the karmas that are performed by the individual. The karmic cycle can be broken only by practising meditation. It helps in alleviating the root cause of the sufferings, thereby, providing with huge and incredible strength and constant source of spiritual, moral and emotional energy to deal with the adversities and resisting destructive attacks of the environment as well as social and mental disruption thereby leading to enhanced general well being.

Mysticism

Comprehending the basic essence and working of all the beings in the Universe has been a very intricate subject since the time immemorial. Many sages, saints, mystics, scientists have tried to resolve this riddle in their own ways. India is considered to be the birthplace of non-temporal values and attitudes like renunciation, meditation, the physic-psychic discipline of Yoga and the concept of non-violence (Jha, 2009). The spiritual movements like Ramakrishanan Mission, ISKON (International Society for Krishna Consciousness), Chinmaya Mission, Osho (Rajneesh), etc. have originated in India and later assumed international status. The mystical aspects of personality have been touched upon by the humanistic psychologists, such as, Adler who emphasized on striving for sincerity; Jung on wholeness or selfhood; Maslow and Rogers on self actualization; Victor Frankl on the search for meaning (Gupta, 2010). They advocated that the people are capable of expanding their consciousness, having control over their lives and circumstances integrating experience to drive a harmonious relationship between and within themselves, and their surroundings. Goleman (1978) said that the Tibetan wheel of life depicts realm of existence, which are metaphors for different states of mind, and planes of being (both of cosmological and psychological significance). The "Realm of the stupid Beats" shows the ideology of behaviorist school. "Hell Realms" of anger or anxiety depicts psychodynamic viewpoint. "Realm of Hungry ghosts" symbolizes insatiable craving as studied by Abraham Maslow, which he called "deprivation Motivation". "Heaven Realms" are blissful states of the highest order, which were termed "peak experiences" by Maslow. The realm of "Jealous gods" (who reached the bliss of heaven) depicted competitive attitude of the person. McClelland called this competitive human nature or need for achievement and power. "Human Realm" is the state where the person achieves spiritual progress. This can be equated with existentiality. The Buddha realm is the last realm of life shown in the Tibetan wheel. It depicted sainthood and cessation of sufferings. He said, the "Buddha realm" presents the greatest challenge to the western schools of psychology. Thus, the understanding of the coherent energy systems, its order and organization and adaptability of the living organisms comes from the eastern religious ideas (Davidson, 2008). The genesis of mysticism can be traced back to the ancient scriptures of Vedas and Upanishads (Sinha, 1985; Sinha, 1986). The ancient philosophy, religion, and folklore of India regard "oneness" of the mind, body and soul (Kapur, 2001; Sinha, 1986). Sankhya karika, an Indian scripture narrates three types of causality of illness and suffering, namely environmental, supernatural, and the self and that these causal factors are collectively responsible for most of the events in person's life (Dalal,2001). It has been advocated that a person can become healthy and attain permanent happiness by transcending oneself from the worldly affairs and can attain enlightenment or liberation from the transmigration cycle. Goleman (1978) propounded that Eastern countries have only one school of psychology: transpersonal school, wherein, meditation is the only technique, to explore the self and transcend oneself.

Mystical experience has been defined as the feeling of ecstasy and of contact with a universal being (Neher, 1980). This experience is conceived of as supernatural or paranormal and overwhelmed in nature. It is often accompanied by out-of-body experiences, intense absorption, body sensation, visions, automatisms and other transcendental feelings. The belief in gaining superhuman qualities through mystical experience is a matter of faith. Mystical experiences have been referred to as Samadhi, Nirvana, Cosmic consciousness, higher consciousness, peak experiences and so on by various cultures. The cosmic consciousness is related to contact with a universal God (James, 1902; Neher, 1980). In both the eastern and western spiritual writings, mystical experiences are reported and interpreted as evidence for a non-physical, transcendental bent of reality (McClenon, 1994; Woodward, 2000).

Gupta (2010) defined mysticism as a venture to an unspecified destination, experience of divine mysteries, that surpasses natural human apprehension, something of the occult or the metaphysical, a system of contemplative prayer and spirituality which is aimed at achieving direct intuitive experience of the divine. It is purely esoteric in nature. Mystical experience involves an expansion of consciousness beyond the conventional boundaries of organisms and correspond a large sense of identity, they also involve perception of the environment, transcending the usual limitations of sensory perceptions. Mysticism is more than a belief and a view. Mysticism is the basis of all religions, particularly as it appears in the lives of truly religious men. In the life of true mystics, beliefs exert a formative influence. They represent the dynamic the dominant tone of their personality as it develops and perfects itself. Thus, mysticism is a fundamentally active, formative, creative, transforming and ennobling principle of life. It is beyond the intellectual reason and scientific terms, but it means a spiritual group of the basic aim of life i.e. merger into god.

The eastern spiritual leaders or teachers/ masters often stress upon having the mystical experiences. In Christianity, various mystical effects were specifically described as having a distinctive role in convincing people that Jesus was a great or unique spiritual teacher. The advance of miracles in Latin countries had a key role in the proliferation of Christianity (Kennedy, 2010; McClenon, 1994; Woodward, 2000). McClenon (1994) argued that the formation and initial growth of religious group has centred on demonstration of paranormal effects that were more improved than those by competing religious groups. These findings suggest that the primary purpose of these experiences was perhaps transformative. These experiences are reported to be spontaneous which may be intended to be noticed as exceptional experiences that expands a person's sense of connectedness meaning in life, and spirituality. Belief on paranormal phenomenon is associated with spirituality, particularly for people with the strongest beliefs (Kennedy, 2003; 2010).

All the mystics have expressed that we all are in essence, a drop of the Divine Ocean, the Supreme Being, Universal consciousness, the Soul (Davidson, 2008). We travelled from this source outward entailing the quality and intricacy of vibration and manifestation. The soul became clothed in bodies of increasingly complex energy patterns and attention was laid outward. The soul became engrossed in the outward affairs and is oblivious of his ultimate reality. Davidson (2008) said the soul first encounters the universal, where the qualities and attributes of energy and matter as they appear in the familiar physical world are first manifested. The traditional (Sanskrit) and the modern mystical understanding, spoke of three sets of energy plexi related to qualities within the vibrational fields of existence. These qualities are also known as tattwas or elements: akash, air, fire, water and earth. These first arise in the casual region of the universal mind, where they are highly subtle in essence. The blueprint of these are found in the true astral regions or region of Sahan Dal Kanwal (Thousand petalled Lotus or Sahasra), the glittering and entraining powerhouse from which all creation below takes its existence and form. This region according to the mystics lie amidst the eye centre and it is believed that the creator of the universe resides here. A person physical form is thus made up of the five elements in both their gross and subtle aspects. According to Davidson (2008), all energy substance is of the tattwas, which we experience through our physical form, not only as the material phases of matter but also as the energetic substrate of our emotions, our sensory perception and our motor responses. Our living human form is constituted of an intricately woven fabric of the five tattwas in gross and subtle state. The weaver and integrator of this fabric is ultimately our soul, our consciousness or real life deep within, but in physical manifestation its cohering and life giving power flows out as the vibration that patterns and organizes these tattwas.

Kapur (2001) said that the Vedas and Upanishads advocate that the mind is a greater part of consciousness confined to the sensory processes. Rao (2010) said that the yoga tradition in the Indian subcontinent provides an apt explanation of the working of the mind. The mind is under the domain of attachment and aversion. It is a subservient to every situation, is engulfed in the whirlwind of desires, is fearful to come out of this whirlwind and thus, gets transient satisfaction (Encyclopedia of psychology, 1987). If the person is envisaged by delusion or ignorance, he can never understand his true nature and acquires only factual knowledge of the world or erroneous egoist self-concept, which is the foundation of pathology-inducing beliefs such as attachment, aversion and the need for defending self-image. The perception is distorted by attachment and aversion, which leads to unhealthy states and desires such as jealousy, fear, agitation and worry, which in turn act as mutual reinforces and help in the maintenance of the pathological state. This condition can be overcome only by mental training that would lead to recognition of the true self. Yoga provides unparalleled success in cultivating and controlling the human mind and achieving higher states of consciousness.

There is a knot between the soul and mind which needs to be disentangled in order to transcend and have access to the mystical world. Rama (1985) in his book perennial psychology of Bhagavad-Gita said The Bhagavad-Gita is the fountainhead of Eastern Psychology, in which psychological insights are intertwined with philosophical concepts. The purpose of Eastern religion, Philosophy, and psychology is to fulfill the goal of self-realization through a systematic way of directly experiencing the truth of existence, (spiritual) profits, which would lead the person to equanimity both in his internal and external life activities. In other words he can be liberated from the quagmire of emotionality, egotistical preoccupations and self-delusion and can action mental peace and happiness after exploring the person who makes sincere effects to self-actualization would be able to make a harmonious relationship between his internal and external self. He said, the psychology of the Bhagavad-Gita leads the students first to awareness of the center of consciousness, then to training that forces on the understanding and mastery of one's internal states and lastly to the skillful and selfless performance of actions in the external world.

Kinds of Mysticism

Gupta (2010) said mysticism can be divided into two categories:
1. Lower Mysticism 2. Higher Mysticism

1. **Lower Mysticism:** In this miraculous feat may be performed or physical disadvantages are gained such as departed spirits are made visible, fortune told, muscles developed, riches earned without effort, dangerous and incurable diseases cures by talismans, amulets or blessings, infallible prophecies are made, etc. These things whether occur or not they imply the belief that there are shortcuts to the attained of advantages through mysteries, supernatural or miraculous powers undiscoverable by reason. However, this kind of mysticism is inferior as it is meant solely to the attainment of inferior, worldly objects.
2. **Higher Mysticism:** This form of mysticism is superior. It implies the belief that the highest reality or the ultimate realization and fulfilment cannot be attained by reason alone. There are other avenues to them, namely the firm and steady control of will and its source the mind, the development of right emotions or both combined, together with the discovery of the higher reason. This kind of mysticism is considered superior as it is directed to the aberration of the spirit from the control of mind and body and the attainment of the highest bliss.

Meditation or Experiential Technique

The practice of meditation helps in transcending oneself to the higher realms of consciousness, and detachment from the everyday external world (Kakar,

1982; Kornfield, 2000). Mystical experiences gain strength from extremely strong psychological needs. Neher (1980) said the practice of Meditation could lead to increased response to habituation. He said the person who is deeply engrossed in his meditation practice becomes unaware of the external stimulus, and remains unresponsive to physiological and psychological stimuli. He said during meditation, when the body is quite and habituation and inhibitions are operating, the proprioreceptors (in the inner ear, muscles, tendons and joints) sometimes cease to supply sense of body locations. At this time the body may be perceived as expanding, becoming detached from the body, and having visionary states. The people who have transcended experiences often believes that there life is divided by some higher force or being (Kennedy & Kanthaman, 1995).

Theory of Karma

Mystics believe that the karmas or our actions play an important role in getting access to the mystical world. Daftaur and Sharma (1997) said the human beings posses reflective consciousness, and are capable of doing action (belongs to Karma Yoni) and transcending themselves from the bondages of sufferings and environmental forces. The sacred book Bhagavad-Gita enunciates three aspects of human life: past, present and future. Although, Gita says to every action there is equal and proportionate reaction or the person has to bear consequences of his actions. The Bhagavad-Gita rather advocates the performance of right and just actions that would negate or counter balance the effect of the past evil deeds. The Bhagavad-Gita emphasizes not on the renunciation of actions but on renunciation in actions, whereby meaning actions should be performed with the detached spirit, without, caring about the consequences (Sharma, 1976). However, it does not imply that the person should work like machine, without thinking of the probable consequences, it rather implies that the person must performs his duties after properly scrutinizing pros and cons of his actions, intelligently. The foremost desire of the person must be to experience ultimate truth and all his actions should be directed towards liberation from the transmigration cycle and all his suffering.

Nature of Mysticism

Mystical experiences are highly esoteric in nature. Kennedy (2010) has delineated certain characteristics of mystical experiences which are as follows:

Personality: People who were high scorers on absorption and fantasy proneness were reported to have mystical experiences (Kennedy, Kanthaman, & Palmer, 1994; Thalbourne, 1998, Lange, Thalbourne, Houran & Storm, 2000). The Myer-Briggs intuitive (N) and feeling (F) are all associated with belief in mysticism (Arcanpel, 1997; Gow, Lurie, 2001; Lister, Thinschmidt & Trautman, 1987; Murphy & Lester, 1976). Keirsey, 1998) stated that people with an NF personality type are mystical in outlook and often explore occultism, parapsychology and esoteric metaphysical systems.

Unconscious: Mystical experiences are thought to arise from an unconscious or higher realm of the mind and to be facilitated by efforts to still the conscious mind and reduce superficial unconscious activity. Both types of experiences are viewed as a link or doorway to a higher realm of interconnectedness. These experiences provide information above the higher realm of interconnectedness.

Lack of Control: Mystical experiences are spontaneous and normally outside of direct conscious control. One can create the conditions that are stages for the experience. However, direct substance and consistent control of mystical or transcendental experiences are very rare and very controversial (Kornfield, 2000).

Cause of mystical experiences

There are various circumstances that seem to induce mystical experience. A variety of physical conditions such as drugs, fasting, excitement, fatigue, and alterations in breathing can produce altered states of consciousness and allow unconscious ecstatic feeling to occur (Neher, 1980). Mystical experiences can also be evoked through connections with almost any stimulus such as art and music, religious ceremonies, and scenes in nature. This feeling can surface when ordinary conscious alter is superseded during reverse, fantasy, meditation, drowsiness or dreaming. Neher (1980) further said that depression and frustration are can generate mystical states. Gratification can be obtained through sublimation and fantasy. This route to mystical experience is much favored by many great religious mystic. These people deny intimacy with fellow human beings and consequently feel a close intimacy and identification with the spiritual world. Fulfillment of the needs after a long period of deprivation can also produce mystical feelings.

Effects of mystical experiences

People who were involved in yogic practices were found to have mystical experiences (Solfin, & Roney, 2010). Various studies have reported vivid effects on personality, sociability, health, and general well being and so on. People who have mystical experiences and practice meditation are found to be more sociable, less aggressive, less nervous and less irritable, more confident, more emotionally stable and more self-reliant than those who did not practice meditation (Janid, Vyas, & Shukla, 1988). Rao (2000) said the practice of yoga and asanas contribute to the health and vigour of the body. It also helps in overcoming tensions and restlessness; reduced anxiety, psychosomatic complaints, facilitating charge and formation of new and desirable patterns. Bhushan (2004) said the effectiveness of the yogic practices can be attributed to their psycho-somato-spiritual approach. It helps in alleviating the root cause of the sufferings through mental modifications that create problems and makes the mind disturbed. Yoga provides techniques and sadhanas that make the practioner master of his mind rather than victim of his emotions and desires. It emphasizes on non-attachment, as the path to enjoy lasting happiness and peace without being involved and disturbed by the attachment to the Worldly affairs. Engelman (1982) conducted a study that was designed o test the utility of yogic practices in increasing body and self-cathexis measures. The sample undertaken in the study comprised of subjects from the yogic practices and control group. They were administered Secord-Jourard Body Cathexis Scale as before and after measures. He found significant changes in self and body cathexis among the yoga group. This suggested that yoga is "intrapsychic system" of the therapy capable of producing desired results in changing feelings towards one's self and body. It has been revealed by various studies that devotion and obedience to the divine power and having mystical experiences provides with huge and incredible strength and constant source of spiritual, moral and emotional energy to deal with the adversities and resisting destructive attacks of the environment as well as social and mental disruption thereby leading to enhanced general well being (Kay, Gaucher, McGregor, & Nash, 2010; McCullough, & Willoughby, 2009; Pajević, Sinanović, & Hasanović, 2005). Lysne and Walchholtz (2011) in their review on religion, spirituality and mental health revealed that there was a positive relationship between religious beliefs and practices and greater life satisfaction, personal devotion produced the strongest positive correlations. Spiritual well being was a unique predictor of quality of life around three core domains, physical, social/family and emotional. The religious beliefs and practices may provide meaning and purpose to life thereby reducing anxiety and depression. It has been reported by various researches that the mystical experiences helps in gaining a broader and enhanced perspectives about life (Oner-Ozakan, 2007), and also promotes self-control or self-regulation (McCullough & Boker, 2007; McCullough, & Willoughby, 2009). The effect of mystical experiences has been found to have an effect on altering the person's world view and increasing the person sense of spirituality, connectedness and meaning in life (Kennedy & Kanthaman, 1995, McClenon, 1994, 2002; Palmer, 1979; Pamer, & Braud, 2002; White, 1997, Kennedy, 2010).

Kennedy (2010) opined that the human needs for superiority and efficiency appear to contaminate both science and spirituality. These motivations can act as an obstacle from being objective and rational for a proponent of science and for a proponent of spiritual from being compassionate and ethical. He thrusted that by setting aside the scientific parsimony, the most straight forward explanation may be a deep recognition that there is a spiritual realm which is the ultimate goal of fate and that may surprise the drives for reproductive and material success.

Reduction in Death Anxiety

Mystical experiences have also helped in reducing death anxiety. Death means cessation of life that is the life process come to a halt. Death is inevitable and biggest truth of life. Today, man boasts of his technological and scientific victories and advancements in almost every sphere of life. Deliberate actions have been adopted to safeguard interests of humankind and for promotion of health among the common people. However, he has been unable to conquer death. It is perceived as most dreadful truth of life by most of the people due to uncertainty and mystery associated with it (Broota and Midha, 2000). People fear death, as there would be abrupt ending to a continuous process of socialization. Mystics believe that there is life after death. The body dies but the soul is lives forever. This ideology might be helping in reducing death anxiety. Broota and Midha (2000) said religion, self- concept, and family values and concepts play an important part in shaping one's belief system and his/her meaning and perception of death. Death is inevitable for all beings. All the living beings are involved in the transmigration cycle and would remain in this cycle until and unless they realize themselves. In other words, they believe that soul is immortal and there is a possibility of life after death. The person must identify himself with God in order to get salvation from the cycle of life and death. The ancient Indian religious scriptures such as Samkhyan, Bhagavad-Gita, Upanishads and Samskara have propounded different stages of self-identification: body, mind, intellect, and spiritual (Daftuar and Sharma, 1997). The identification of the self with body produces the need for security. The threats related to body preservation, involved by impending disasters such as death leads to fear and thus anxiety. They said identification with body leads to physical desires, identification with mind to emotional desires, identification with intellect, leads to intellectual desires if we identify with spiritual aspect, we have no desires and thus attain self- or God-realization. Neher (1980) said, that the trauma of being near death probably after entailed psychological and physiological effects that can significantly alter consciousnesses. He said although the peripheral life-signs may be absent but there seems to be no evidence of all the parts of the brains being lifeless. It may be possible that the unconscious process that gives rise to vision will be operating. The cultural or religious beliefs regarding life after death help in alleviating death anxiety (Neher, 1980). He said that the mystical experiences during meditations helps dealing with the fear of death.

Conclusion

Mysticism is the basis of all religions. It is beyond the intellectual reason and scientific terms. A void is always felt by human beings at a certain time period of life despite his/her materialistic and worldly achievements. The yearning of the soul for its essence is always felt. Mystics advocate that through the practice of meditation, one can transcend his/her consciousness and realise oneself and become one with the universe i.e. the God. The eastern spiritual leaders or teachers/ masters often stress upon having the mystical experiences in order to free oneself from the transmigration cycle. These experiences are found to be spontaneous and intended to be noticed as exceptional experiences that expands a person's sense of connectedness, meaning in life, spirituality and helps in elevating death anxiety. Mystics advocate that a person must identify himself with God in order to get salvation from the cycle of life and death. The identification with body leads to physical desires, identification with mind to emotional desires, identification with intellect, leads to intellectual desires if we identify with spiritual aspect, we have no desires and thus attain self- or God-realization.

References

Archangel, D. (1997). Investigating the relations between Myers-Briggs type indicator and facilitated revision expenses. *Journal of the American Society for Physical Research, 91,* 82-95.

Bhushan, L.I. 2004. Yoga: An Instrument of Community Psychological transformation. *Indian Journal of Community Psychology,* 1(1), 11-24.

Broota, A. & Midha, A. 2000. Religiosity, Death Anxiety and self and family concept in conversion reaction. *Journal of Research and Application in Clinical Psychology.* Vol. III (1&2), 56-65.

Daftuar, C.N. & Sharma, R. (1997). Beyond Maslow – An Indian Perspective of Need-Hierarchy. *Journal of the Indian Academy of Applied Psychology,* 24, (1-2), 1-8.

Dalal, A.K. (2001). Health Psychology. In J. Pandey (Eds.), *Psychology in India revisited Developments in the Discipline.* Vol.2: Personality and health Psychology. New Delhi: Sage Publication.

Davidson J. (2008). *The web of life: Life force the energetic constitution of man and the neuro-endocrine connection.* New Delhi: New age books.

Engleman, S.R. 1982. Self and body cathexis change in Yogic Asana groups. *Indian Journal of Psychology,* 57, 97-103.

Goleman, D. (1978). The Impact of the new religions on Psychology. In J. Needleman & G. Baker (Eds.), *Understanding the New Religions* (pp. 113-12). New York: The Seabury Press.

Gupta, M.G. (2010). *Indian Mysticism: Rig Veda to Present Day.* Agra: M.G. Publishers

James, W. (1902). *The varieties of Religious Experience: A study in Human Nature.* New York: The modern library.

Janid, R.K. Vyas, J.N, & Shukla, T.R. (1988). The effect of the transcendental meditation Programme on the normal individuals. *Journal of Personality & Clinical studies,* 4(2), 145-149.

Jha, A. (2009). *Traditional Knowledge system in India.* New Delhi: Altantic

Kakar, S. (1982). *Shamans, Mystics and doctors: A Psychological enquiry In India and its Healing Traditions.* New Delhi: Oxford University Press.

Kakar, S. (1996). *The Indian Psyche.* Delhi: Oxford University Press.

Kapur M. (2001). Mental Health, Illness and Therapy. *Psychology in India revisited Developments in the Discipline.* Vol.2: Personality and health Psychology. New Delhi: Sage Publication.

Kay, A.C., Gaucher, D., Mcgregor, I., & Nash, K. (2010). Religious belief as compensatory control. *Personality and Social Psychology Review, 14*(1), 37-48.

Keirsey, D. (1998). *Please understand me II.* C.A.: Prometheus Neinesis Broks Company.

Kennedy, J.E. (2000). Do people guide psi or does psi guide people? Evidence and implication from life and lab. *Journal of the American Society for Physical Research, 94*, 130-180.

Kennedy, J.E. (2003). Content analysis of an anomalous experience collection: Evaluating perspective. *Journal of Parapsychology, 66*, 291-316.

Kennedy, J.E. (2010). Spirituality and the capricious, evasive nature of Psi. In K.R. Rao (Ed.), *Yoga and Parapsychology* (pp. 43-70). Delhi: Motilal Banarsidass Publishers.

Kennedy, J.E., & Kanthaman, H. (1998). An explanation study of the effects of paranormal and spiritual experiences on people's lives and well being. *Journal of the American Sciety for Psychical Research, 89*, 249-264.

Kennedy, J.E., Kanthaman, H, & Palmer, A. (1997). Psychic and spiritual experiences, health, well being and meaning in life. *Journal of Parapsychology, 58*, 353-383.

Kornfield, J. (2000). *After the ecstasy, the landing*. New York Bautam Books.

Lysne, C.J., & Wachholtz, A.B. (2011). Pain, Spirituality, and meaning making: what can we learn from the literature? *Religions, 2*, 1-16.

Lange, R., Thalbourne, M.A., Houran, J., & Storm, L. (2000). The Revised Transliminality Scale: Reliability and validity data from a Rasch top-down purification procedure. *Consciousness and cognition, 9*, 591-617.

McClenon, J. (1994). *Wondrous events: Foundation of religious beliefs*. Philadelphia: University of Pennsylvania Press.

McClenon, J. (2002) *Wondrous Healing: Shamanism, human evolution, and the origin of religion*. DeKalb, IL.: Northern Illinois University Press.

McCullough, M.E., & Boker, S.M. (2007). Dynamic modeling for studying self-regulatory processes: An example from the study of religious development over the life span. In A. D. Ong & M.V. Dulmen (Eds.), *Handbook of methods in positive psychology* (pp. 380-394). New York: Oxford University Press.

Murphy, K., & Lester, D. (1976). A search for correlates of belief in psi. *Psychological Reports, 38*, 82.

Oner-Ozkan, B. (2007). Future time orientation and religion. *Social Behavior and Personality, 35*, 51-62.

Pajević, I., Sinanović, O., & Hasanović, M. (2005). Religiosity and mental health. *Psychiatria Danubina, 17*, 84-89.

Palmer, J. (1979). A community mail survey of psychic experiences. *Journal of the American Society for Psychical Research, 73*, 221-251.

Palmer, G. & Braud, W. (2002). Exceptional human experiences, disclosure, and a more inclusive view of physical, psychological, and spiritual well being. *Journal of Transpersonal Psychology, 34*, 29-61.

Rama, S. (1985). *Perennial Psychology of the Bhagavad-Gita.* Pennsylvania: The Himalayan Institute of yoga Science and Philosophy of the U.S.A.

Rao, P.V.K. 2000. Yogasanas in Psychotherapy. *Journal of the Indian Academy of Applied Psychology,* 26 (1-2), 73-75.

Rao, K.R. (2010). *Yoga and Parapsychology.* Delhi: Motilal Banarsidass Publishers.

Sharma, C. 1976. Bhagavad-Gita. *A Critical Survey of Indian Philosophy.* Delhi: Motilal Banarsidas / Ideological Publishers & Booksellers. 32-39.

Sinha, D. (1986). *Psychology in a third World Country: The Indian Experience.* New Delhi: Sage Publications.

Sinha, J. (1985). *Indian Psychology: Cognition.* Vol.I. Delhi: Motilal Banarsidas.

Solfin, J., & Roney, S. (2010). A Re-analysis and summary of Data from a study of experienced versus novice yoga practitioners. In K.R. Rao (Ed.), *Yoga and Parapsychology: Empirical Research and Theoretical studies,* (pp. 351-371). Delhi: Motilal Banarsidass Publishers Private Limited.

Thalbourne, M.A. (1998) Transliminality: Further correlations and a short measure. *Sound of American Society for Psychical Research, 92,* 402-419.

White, R.A. (Ed.) (1997). Background Papers II. The NHE Network, 1995-1998: Progress and Possibilities. *Exceptional Human Experience, Special Issue, 15.*

Woodward, K.L. (2000). *The Book of Miracles: The meaning of the miracle stories in Christianity, Judaism, Buddhism, Hinduism, Islam.* New York: Simon and Schuster.

Past Lives' Blueprint on Present-Day Psychological Orientation - Therapeutic Analysis

ShaliniPurohit, Deepti Bhandari
Consultant Psychologist, Addresshealth &
Fortis Hospital, Bangalore, Karnatka
Consultant Psychologist & Past Life Regression
Therapist, 'Aastitva'-Being, Udaipur, Rajasthan

Abstract: Is our psychological orientation - composite of overt & covert behavior, personality, attitudes, emotions, thoughts / cognitive scripts etc., or merely a sum total of our prior learning, experiences, environmental conditions, society, norms etc.? As is the established fact and basis of almost all psychological studies or does our present day psychological orientation is 'much more' than this established fact. Does past life (lives) imprint our current psychological orientation? Past life regression is a general term for the ability of the unconscious mind to retrieve historical memories from previous lives, usually through hypnotic regression or altered state consciousness. Past Life Therapy searches emotionally or physically traumatic life memories for therapeutic purposes. The objective of this article is to explore the blueprints of the present-day psychological orientation in the distant past called past life, through the unconscious mind. The article also highlights the holistic resolution brought about by the Past Life Regression Therapy. Thus, in this article we will review the rationale of past lives' blueprint on present day psychological orientation and its applicability in clinical therapeutic analysis.

This article assembles a bibliographic survey of many research papers based on a Google Scholar and Pub Med search for "past life regression", "hypnosis" and "reincarnation".

Introduction

Chapter 2, verse 20 Srimad Bhagavad-Gita

najayatemriyatevakadacinnayambhutvabhavitavanabhuyah

ajonityahsasvato yam puranonahanyatehanyamane

"The soul never takes birth and never dies at any time nor does it come into being again when the body is created. The soul is birthless, eternal, imperishable and timeless and is never terminated when the body is terminated."

Srimad Bhagavad-Gita, chapter two is entitled: Sankhya Yoga: The Eternal Reality of the Souls Immortality. In this chapter of the Bhagavad-Gita are many verse references regarding the reality and science of reincarnation[1].

Eastern and Western thought differ greatly and are culturally driven. Although the general populace of Western countries does not talk about reincarnation much, it is studied in great detail by Western researchers. At the same time, Eastern cultures embrace the concept of reincarnation and embody it in their culture [2].

Past Life Research (PLR) invariably interweaves the concepts of Reincarnation, Rebirth, and Karma. It forms the bridge between the mind-body-soul triad[3]. PLR utilizes two types of approach: either practice based or evidence based. In practice based research, the results are obtained through pre-post therapy questionnaires, using large number of clients over a range of problems. The evidence based approach of research targets specific type of client problem using smaller number and a control group to demonstrate its effectiveness [4].

Past life therapy assumes the existence of the unconscious mind (Netherton&Shiffrin, 1978). Here mental processes take place without our awareness (Weiss, 1992). The unconscious operates as a tape recorder; it records and stores every experience, both positive and negative. Unlike the conscious mind, the unconscious never turns off; it can remember anything from anytime (Weiss; Netherton&Shiffrin). It is not bound by limits of time, logic, or space. It transports one back to those times before one's birth and regresses one to previous lifetimes.[3] During Past-Life-Regression the subject is helped to experience or relive past lives. In the process of regression the subject is first guided into deep states by giving constant suggestions. After reaching a 'satisfactory' level of altered state of consciousness, the subject is first regressed gradually down to the in-utero state (the time when subject was in the mother's womb). The subject is able to describe the experiences verbally.

Even in this New Age, Past-Life-Regression remains one of the best techniques to energize the spirit of individuals by making them to journey into their past lives. By exploring our past lives we can find the solutions for all present life problems[5]

Chapter 2, verse 22 Srimad Bhagavad-Gita

vasamsijirnaniyathavihayanavanigrhnatinaro'parani

tathasariranivihayajirnanyanyanisamyatinavanidehi

"As a person gives up old and worn out garments and accepts new apparel, similarly the embodied soul giving up old and worn out bodies verily accepts new bodies[1]."

The idea of reincarnation may contribute to an improved understanding of such diverse matters as: phobias and philias of childhood; skills not learned in early life; abnormalities of child-parent relationships; vendettas and bellicose nationalism; childhood sexuality and gender identity confusion; birthmarks, congenital deformities, and internal diseases; differences between members of monozygotic twin pairs; and abnormal appetites during pregnancy [6]. The reincarnation research efforts that we have studied fall generally into two categories. The first category being children who remember a past life or lives and the second category is of patients who have a past life or lives recall through hypnosis in regression therapy sessions[3].

Past Life Regression is done to identify why a person may be experiencing problems in the present. The reason for undertaking past-life-therapy is to improve the spiritual quality of our life, right now. Its chief objective is to make our life easier, better and more fulfilling, in this present moment. It directly addresses the internal cause. Past-life-regression-therapy is based on the principles of cause and effect (also known as law of karma). The word "karma" refers to the consequences of one's actions. Something that has been set in motion at some time in the past results in a corresponding effect on a person's present physical, emotional, mental or spiritual well-being, at this moment. This cause may be a past desire, a past thought, past feeling, a past emotion, a past vow, a past promise, a past decision, a past evasion or a past traumatic experience [5]. In Buddhism, karma is thought to directly impact future lifetimes either positively or negatively (Woolger, 1988). The word "karmic" is used to describe the patterns that we establish on our path towards wholeness (Lucas, 2001). The purpose of past life therapy is to identify established patterns and how they impact our growth. Although not consciously realized, throughout our various lifetimes we move towards karmic homeostasis as a result of our innate drive towards wholeness (Lucas, 2001). In India the psycho-physical practice of Yoga has long recognized past life patterns as a basic part of an individual's makeup (Woolger, 1988). Sarnskara is a term used to describe behaviors based on patterns developed in past lives. Woolger (1988) believes that specific patterns are inherited at birth. He identifies them as "psychic scar tissue" (p. 148). The purpose of these patterns is to learn[3].

History

Reincarnation and Past-Life-Regression are not modern concepts. People have believed in reincarnation since ancient times. There is sufficient evidence to show that the Hindus, Ancient Celts, the Egyptians, the Tibetans, and the Hebrew Cabalists etc. used past-life remembrance.

Freud can be considered as the grandfather of present day regression work. He came up with the idea that by making the unconscious conscious, one could restore choice and bring about healing. He discovered the link between past trauma and present symptoms and called it Psychic Determinism. He established that our past experiences determine our present behavior. This changed the face of psychotherapy forever and is the basis of regression work. Later, Jung postulated the concept of a Collective Unconscious and Archetypes (universal patterns). The ancient Indian sage PatanjaliMaharshi, has done extensive work on Past-Life-Regression. In his yoga sutras Patanjali Maharishi called this process of past-life-regression as ‹Prati-Prasav›. Prati-Prasav means you are born again in the memory; you go back to the very birth, the trauma when you were born, and you live it again. Buddha is said to have recounted thousands of his past-lives, of which around 550 have been narrated in the ‹Jataka› Tales. Mahavira called ‹Remembering past-lives› as ‹Jati-Smaran›. Early Tibetan history contains a wealth of literature on the subject of reincarnation and afterlife states. A lot of cases of Near Death Experiences are reported even in modern times where people are found to return to life after being pronounced dead. These experiences are very similar to early stages of death as described by the Tibetan sages. Many Christian mystics have stated that after death, the soul separates from the body and leaves. Ancient Egyptians believed in reincarnation. They believed that it took 3000 years to complete all lives that one had to live.

Though reincarnation has been studied scientifically only during recent times, the possibility that we live many lives has been accepted on faith since ancient times. It can be seen that evidence of the belief in reincarnation can be found in people of diverse cultures, from different parts of the world and even people from vastly different time periods (modern, medieval, ancient, prehistoric etc.)[5].

Research on Past Life Regression

"Past-life regression" in Western usage describes the emergence of impressions, images and sensations that seem to be memories of an earlier existence, usually occurring during special, evocative circumstances, such as psychotherapy. The term has evolved from a technology originated by Albert de Rochas, a French hypnotherapist at the turn of the century (Christie-Murray, 1981). Although the spontaneous recollection of apparent past-life memories by children is well documented in cultures that accept reincarnation (Stevenson,1975-80, 1980, 1987), most Western literature concerns recollections produced by adults in altered states of consciousness. The largest body comes from therapeutic modalities involving the deeper layers of the psyche, such as traditional psychoanalysis; Rolfing, acupressure and other body work; rebirthing; sensory isolation; controlled drug therapy; and hypnosis (Bache, 1990). Like age regression therapy, the systematic regressing of patients to produce past-life stories has proven unusually efficacious in the treatment of certain psychological and psychosomatic conditions (Carfaro, 1986; Cladder, 1986; Hull, 1984; Marriott, 1984; Nash, 1992; Netherton and Shiffrin, 1978; Schlotterbeck, 1987).

Therapeutic past-life regressions usually occur during nonordinary states featuring higher alpha electroencephalographic (EEG) activity and more right-hemisphere activity than normal waking consciousness, such as light trance, deep relaxation, or hypnosis, which are associated with greater visual imagery and a diminished or distorted sense of the passage of time, compared to ordinary (beta) awareness. Alterations in phenomenology during the regression, experienced by the subject as different modes of consciousness, are treated in relative terms as they differ from the baseline non ordinary state initiated to access the past life story [7].

As a traditional psychotherapist, Dr. Brian Weiss was astonished and skeptical when one of his patients began recalling past-life traumas that seemed to hold the key to her recurring nightmares and anxiety attacks. His skepticism was eroded, however, when she began to channel messages from "the space between lives," which contained remarkable revelations about Dr. Weiss's family and his dead son. Using past-life therapy, he was able to cure the patient and embark on a new, more meaningful phase of his own career. A graduate of Columbia University and Yale Medical School, Brian L.Weiss, M.D., is currently Chairman of Psychiatry at the Mount Sinai Medical Center in Miami[8].

Dr. Brian in his book talks about his patient Catherine who had come to his office seeking help for her anxiety, panic attacks, and phobias. Although these symptoms had been with her since childhood, in the recent past they had become much worse. Every day she found herself more emotionally paralyzed and less able to function. She was terrified and understandably depressed. In a series of trance states, Catherine recalled "past-life" memories that proved to be the causative factors of her symptoms. She also was able to act as a conduit for information from highly evolved "spirit entities," and through them she revealed many of the secrets of life and of death. In just a few short months, her symptoms disappeared, and she resumed her life, happier and more at peace than ever before[9].

Dr. Bryan Jameison had done similar research and conducted past-life therapy sessions since the late sixties. A book review of Dr. Jameison's books indicated that "during the course of his career he explored 73 of his own former lives. He stated, "Through regression one can see how much each incarnation is not merely an isolated event, but is rather an integral part of a much greater whole." Jameison experimented and found a method that allowed past life regression (PRL) through non-hypnotic past-life regression. It is where the patient induces his own state of tranquility that then allows for PRL. In his latest book, The Search for Past Lives: Exploring Reincarnations' Mysteries & the Amazing Healing Power of Past-life Therapy, Dr. Jameison presented 300 cases. Dr. Jameison discussed an interesting case about a woman called Nancy. Ever since she could remember, she had felt guilty in being alive, although her family life was pleasant and without many problems. She had attempted suicide three times, but all had failed. She agreed to past life regression therapy, though nothing significant was found during the first few sessions. Then, as expected, she finally found the cause for her depressive moods. She recalled her life during the World War II. She was sixteen years old and getting ready to have dinner with her family. She vividly could see the Gestapo breaking into her house ordering her family to go with them. Her father protested and was killed. She, her mother, and younger brother were dragged down the stairs and pulled out into the street. Then, they were pushed into a truck. Later on, they were cramped with others into a train. They ate, drank, soiled, vomited and urinated where they stood. After arriving at the train station, they were driven to a labor camp, like animals. A few days later, one Nazi took her and another girl to a big house next to the labor camp. The Nazi asked them to take a shower, put on makeup and dress up, which made them to look more presentable. They were then forced to prostitute for the Nazis. Under the guidance of Dr. Jameison, Nancy was able to let go of her guilt and come to peace. She no longer wanted to commit suicide. She also realized while listening to a replay of the particular regression therapy session that during this life, her younger brother from that life was her son and her mother was her daughter[2].

Similarly, Judy Hall is a counsellor and healer who has been running past-life exploration groups for more than twenty years. *Deja Who? A New Look at Past Lives* is described as the first book that accepts reincarnation and yet questions the validity of some recalled past lives. Many famous names appear time after time in past-life regressions, and the most useful part of this book is where Judy Hall explores in depth the possible alternative explanations to reincarnation which may explain such occurrences. These may be suggestion, paramnesia, cryptomnesia, false memory syndrome, possession, psychiatric illness, multiple personality disorder, and others. The validity and relevance of past lives are examined in the context of these alternative explanations [10].

Helen Wambach, a psychologist and clinical psychiatrist, developed a hypnotic technique by which she was able to regress her subjects back to previous lives. Over a period of 12 years, in a carefully-designed project, she regressed more than 1000 subjects. Each subject was given a post-hypnotic suggestion that enabled them to fill out a data sheet with precise details for each incarnation, following the session. When analysed and correlated these data sheets provided "... striking and extraordinary evidence of the existence of reincarnation." Numerous figures, tables and specimen data sheets included in the text provide much useful information about conditions of life throughout the overall period - information which it was possible to confirm in many instances [11].

The aim of the study by Hargun Ahluwalia & Jini K Gopinath was to examine the subjective experience of past life regression (PLR). 15 graduate students underwent PLR facilitated by a trained professional for this purpose. Using Interpretative Phenomenological Analysis (IPA), the data collected from the interviews with these individuals was analyzed. The participants were able to relate their experiences under trace with their present life scenarios and could find meaning in their experiences. Most participants reported positive effects of the experience and this may have implications for further research and therapy with non- clinical populations[12].

Research on Reincarnation/Rebirth

Although these terms are often used interchangeably, there is a significant conceptual difference between the two. On the whole, Buddhists believe in rebirth while Hindus, Jains, and some Christians believe in reincarnation. Strictly speaking, reincarnation means the assumption of another body by a permanent, eternal self (the Hindu notion of atman or the Christian notion ofsoul). Most Buddhists do not believe in a permanent self (anatman or anatta, without enduring self) but believe human consciousness (the "I" or self) dissolves at death and that only a subtle mindstream remains. The mindstream carries with it karmic imprints from prior lives and it is this subtle mind stream that conjoins with a new life-form after death. Thus, rebirth does not mean an identifiable human being assuming a new human body. Moreover, in Buddhism, rebirth is not always accomplished in human form. Depending on karmic circumstances, a human being can be reborn as an animal or as a being in any of the upper or lower realms[13].

For the last 40 years, researchers have collected cases of children who claim to remember previous lives. Subjects in these cases tend to make more verified statements about the previous life they claim to remember than do other subjects of reincarnationtype cases, and they tend to recall more names from that life. Analysis of reports from 35 Burmese subjects indicates that the intermission memories can be broken down into three parts: a transitional stage, a stable stage in a particular location, and a return stage involving choosing parents or conception. A comparison of these reports to reports of near-death experiences (NDEs) indicates that they show features similar to the transcendental component of Western NDEs and have significant areas of overlap with Asian NDEs[14].

Erlendur Haraldsson & Majd Abu-Izzeddin cites a case concerning a young boy in Baalchmay, Lebanon, who made specific statements before several family members asserting memories of a previous life, such as being a man who carried pistols and hand-grenades, having a mute friend, describing a house, having children, living in the village of Quaberchamoun, and being shot by armed people. The case is unusual because when the child was taken at age 7 to the village, a corresponding deceased person was identified by means of his claimed memories, and the widow and the man's brother became certain of the authenticity of the child's reincarnation through his correct answers to their questions, recognition of people and possessions, and his own knowledgeable questions to them[15].

In an article published in January 2004, Rivas T explored six cases of reincarnation type in Netherlands. According to her in the Netherlands one often encounters the almost untranslatable concept of 'nuchterheid', which partially overlaps with the English concepts of 'sobriety' and 'soberness'. 'Nuchterheid' in the relevant sense is an unwillingness to be overwhelmed by strong emotions and a resistance to any kind of 'superstitious', irrational or even religious beliefs. One of the cases is classical reincarnation case of a girl named Christina who recognized herself as a young girl who was caught in fire in previous lifetime. Her description was matched with the existing information and it turned out to be true. Her present lifetime was affected in the sense that she was frightened of going to the attic of her house [16].

A study was conducted by Davisdson JR et al. in which a survey was conducted about beliefs in karma and reincarnation among survivors of violent trauma. The results indicated five percent of the sample admitted strong agreement to a belief in karma and reincarnation (n=99), while 77% strongly disagreed with these beliefs (n=1,511). It was concluded few people subscribe strongly to a belief in karma and reincarnation in the US population, but personal experience of trauma may be associated with greater acceptance, as well as certain demographic and health-associated variables. The importance of holding such beliefs, which may represent an important way of coping following violent trauma, deserves further study [17].

Walter T et al, explored in a survey what reincarnation means to some of the westerners who believe in it, why they find it attractive, and how it relates to other aspects of their life, not least the religious organizations to which they belong but which do not teach it, They concluded that reincarnation is indeed for them a very private belief, detached from religious and other affiliations, from the New Age, from popular literature on the subject, and from everyday life [18]. In another study by Walter T, it was concluded that the understanding of *A* as the reincarnation of close family member *B*, found in several American and African tribes and in popular Hinduism, may be unusual in Britain; in so far as people play with past identities, this cannot easily be squared with postmodern theories of the self; the past identities constructed bear strong resemblance to current identities, and may be considered part of the modernist project of the self [19].

There also exists the monumental work of psychiatrist Dr. Ian Stevenson of the University of Virginia, an erstwhile president of the British Society for Psychical Research. For over 40 years Stevenson and his co-workers collected cases of spontaneous memories of "past lives" from many parts of the world, mostly from among children. His most recent book *Reincarnation and Biology*(Stevenson, 1997) was described by the reviewer for the British Scientific and Medical Network as "one of the great classics of twentieth century psi research" (Lorimer, 1997: 53). Nevertheless Stevenson's work continues to be ignored by mainstream psychology. Where the past life based approach to trauma and somaticized complexes differs from most conventional therapies--including the Reichian schools--is that it takes the position that the soul is much is greater than the ego-personality; a position to be found strongly in Jung, James Hillman (1977) and in the work of recent transpersonal psychologists. Thus the traumas that may surface during the therapeutic exploration of the current life may have other levels or deeper resonances to them. Often the releasing of trauma with this approach is like peeling skins from an onion. Compared to the great psycho-spiritual disciplines of the East, western psychotherapy is still in its infancy and is still learning to work with other dimensions of the soul such as residues of previous lives, ancestral memories or the influence of spiritual healing from other realms[20].

The aim of the article by Ukpokolo IE is to show that beyond the need for the justification of the belief in reincarnation, beyond the quest for evidences to prove its reality or otherwise, the idea of rebirth has a pragmatic role in the cultures where it is held. Using the theorization of rebirth among the Esan people of southern Nigeria as a pilot, it asserts that the idea of rebirth plays a psychosocial, therapeutic function of comfort and healing for those traumatized by the death of a loved one. This, it shall be seen, is similar to, even more reliable than, the role of photography in preserving cherished memories. The article attempts to establish the role of reincarnation, like photography, in bringing the past into the present[21].

According to Dr. Satwant Pasricha young children (subjects of cases of the reincarnation type) sometimes claim to have lived before and give specific details about those lives and display behavior that corresponds to the actual or expected behavior of the person (previous personality) whose life the subject claims to remember but the behavior is unusual for his present circumstances. The child may for example, show phobia of water if he remembered having been drowned in the previous life and has had no such traumatic experience or model available in the present life. Nearly 2600 reported cases of the reincarnation type have been scientifically investigated in several cultures over the past about five decades. In 64-80% cases a deceased person matching the statements of child was identified. Cross cultural comparisons have shown that certain features recur across cultures, which are: age of speaking about a previous life (between 2 and 4 years), age of discontinuation of talk about previous life (usually between 5 and 8 years), high incidence of violent death (63%) of the previous personality, far beyond the rate of violent death in the general populations of the respective countries, and high frequency of mention, by the subjects, of mode of death (78%) in the previous life, other features such as sex change and intermission between two lives vary between cultures [22].

As Mills and Lynn note the spontaneous cases of possible past-life memories that have been documented to date necessarily reflect a special subset of possible past-life memory, because the emphasis has been on "solvable cases" with a relatively short interval between the present and a previous reported life. Type B cases such as Ajendra Singh Chauhan's are especially useful in showing the accuracy of young children's statements and provide a check for the possibility of cultural elaboration based on acceptance of the case and information learned only after initial contact. Tucker's SOCS (2000) has been used to show how important parental questioning can be in eliciting the information necessary for solving a case. Indeed in this instance, the score for Ajendra's case would have been zero without the father's eventually asking his child for more information. The case suggests that Stevenson's vigilance in examining the accuracy of reported past-life statements made after the families have met minimizes the addition of further elements to such a case. The same care used in taking children's testimony about other issues than a past life (Bruck et al., 1998) needs to be exercised in assessing testimony some children give about apparent past-life memories. Finally, the principle of similarity of stimulus that impacts memory within one life seems to be active in Ajendra's case in his recall of memories from 8 months before his birth, of the violent death of another individual whose family Ajendra's did not know. Such cases definitely deserve careful consideration [23].

Past Lives' Blueprint and the Therapeutic Effects

The therapeutic effect of the Past Life Regression Therapy lies in the identification of the blueprint it lays on the current psychological make-up of the individual. The blueprint consists of the repeated behavioral patterns adopted by the individuals in order to learn and ascertain the wisdom of the lessons – yet to be learnt. This blueprint is the Karma of the individual. These blueprints have tendency to let us achieve the 'not yet learnt' lesson or the wisdom of life. According to Denning (in Lucas, 2001) each person chooses a specific lesson for each lifetime with specific settings andpersonalities which assists in attaining these lessons. The process of working through patterns takes many lifetimes (Lucas, 2001). In the life we are living today, we are making up for the mistakes. Individuals, who are karmically connected, reincarnate together. Gucciardi (1999) states, these individuals trigger each other continually so the issues that need to be addressed will come to surface[24].

Marquez (1999) found that remembering pre and prenatal experiences can significantly benefit one's life. The author conducted a study on 7 adults, in which some of the benefits experienced were changes in vision, healing of arthritis and relief from asthma. The subjects felt empowered and felt a greater control over their life [25].

Woolger (2002) throws light on how regression to past experiences, in the present or previous lives can have significant therapeutic benefit. He discusses the case of a woman who suffered from post traumatic stress disorder symptoms (PTSD) symptoms for 20 years since a car accident where she went through a NDE during subsequent surgery to save her life. When age regression was done on her to relive the incident, she described in detail watching her body being pulled from the wreckage, being taken to the hospital and then into surgery, ascending to a higher realm and meeting deceased members of her family who shone with very bright light. When she returned to her physical body, she found her pain coming back. Before this session of regression, she had not remembered these details and the session profoundly altered her outlook towards death and dying [26].

Zahi discusses 3 cases of therapeutic benefit from hypnotherapy. The first of these cases was that of a woman who complained of high levels of anxiety, pain and memory problems. Through hypnosis she regressed to the age of one year and found that the father was being hostile towards her and despite calls for her mother, she did not come to her rescue. For next few sessions she wanted her memory problems to be worked upon. She underwent past- life regression therapy. First she found herself in Egypt where her baby was killed and buried with the Pharaoh. She felt extremely guilty that she could not save her child. She also realized that her baby's soul was at peace and this brought her relief. In another PLR session she found herself as a mother during the holocaust that died but saved her son. This memory surprised her and she said that she had never saved anyone before. She said that this memory filled in the gaps in her memory that she was struggling with and she did not have memory problems again. Interestingly, Zahi proposes that benefit from therapy can also be felt by non- believers or those whose beliefs oppose that involving non- material elements such as the soul [27].

Woolgeralso reports the case of Heather, who came for therapy as she suffered from ulcerative colitis since early adolescence. When no significant conflict emerged through age regression, PLR was carried out. In the session she regressed to Holland during World War II at the time of the Nazi invasion. She found herself as an eight- year old girl in a Jewish family who while fleeing from an explosion was captured and subsequently killed. She described her bodily sensations as she awaited her turn to be in front of the machine gun fire and felt her stomach knotted in terror. For all this time, she had not been able to express the shock and trauma of having lost her parents, seeing mass slaughter and facing her own premature death, which may have resulted in bodily manifestations. In the session, she was allowed to release her anguish through cathartic sobbing, screaming, violent convulsions and dry vomiting. After the session her stomach problem improved significantly[4].

Past life research consists of practice and evidence based approaches. In practice based past life research, Hazel Denning studied the results by eight Regression Therapists with nearly 1000 clients between 1985 and 1992. Results were measured just after the therapy, after six months, one year, two years and five years. Of the 450 clients who could still be tracked after 5 years; 24% reported the symptoms had completely gone, 23% reported considerable or dramatic improvement, 17% reported noticeable improvement and 36% reported no improvement. (TanDam, 1990) [28].

In evidence based past life research, significant work has been done by Ron Van der Maesen. This was conducted using fifty-four clients who had reoccurring disturbing voices or thoughts. The Dutch Association of Reincarnation Therapists supplied the Past Life Therapists for the research. At a six month follow up after the therapy by an external Psychiatrist, the disturbing voices had disappeared in 25%, and a further 32% could now cope. Overall 80% had a positive subjective experience and would recommend this therapy for reoccurring problems like these in others.

Ron Van der Maesen also conducted past life research with Tourettes's syndrome. The work was conducted by 10 members of the Dutch Association of Reincarnation Therapists initially with 22 clients over the age range of 9 to 52 years old. Of the ten subjects who completed all the therapy and responded to the one-year follow-up questionnaire, 50% reported that their motor tics had for the most part largely disappeared or been greatly reduced in frequency.

The same also applied to their vocal tics. Five also reported that they were free of medication, in sharp contrast to the pre-study period [29].

Thus several cases point towards the likelihood of current pathologies in the present life arising from psychic residues of previous births. Such physical memories, that have nothing to account for them in the current life, turn out to be embedded in what is literally the subtle energy field that surrounds and penetrates the physical body. These old traumas, inherited though the subtle (energy) field, are consistently found in our work to re-imprint in the current body as rashes, birth marks weaknesses in certain limbs, organic problems such as a weak bladder, a weak heart and so on. (Woolger) In the field of PLR for non- pathological individuals, Woods and Baruss (2004) conducted a study with 24 students. Each of them participated in a single guided imagery session in which they were given either a pastlife or open suggestion. Participants who were given the past-life suggestion had better scores on measures of psychological well-being than those given the open suggestion[30].

However, the research on increased well- being and/or cathartic release as possible benefits of PLR on those who do not suffer from any somatic or psychological problem has not been explored abundantly. There is a need to explore the benefits of this therapy for the non- pathological population so as to extend psychotherapy to this majority population to enhance the quality of life.

In an article by Peres JF it is stressed upon that there is increasing recognition of the need to take into account the cultural environment and belief systems of psychotherapy patients because these values reflect basic assumptions about man's nature and the cognitive references used to cope with psychological difficulties. Currently accepted psychotherapeutic approaches take no account of the belief in life after death held by most of the world's population. Respect for patient opinions and subjective realities are a therapeutic need and an ethical duty, even though therapists may not share the same beliefs. Guidelines are suggested for professionals to develop collaborative models that help patients mobilize their intrinsic intelligence to find solutions to their complaints[31].

In 4 studies conducted by Spanos NP et al., subjects (Ss) received hypnotic suggestions to regress beyond birth to a previous life. In Study 1the development of a past-life identity was unrelated to indexes of psychopathology. Studies 2 and 3demonstrated that Ss developed past-life identities that reflected hypnotist-transmitted expectations. In Study 4 the credibility that Ss assigned to their past-life experiences was influenced bywhether the hypnotist defined such experiences as realor imagined. Combined data from the first 3studies indicated that hypnotizability predicted the subjective intensity of past-life experiences but not the credibility assigned to these experiences. Alternatively, beliefs, attitudes, and expectations concerning reincarnation predicted the degree of credibility assigned to these experiences. The finding that past-life responders had more favorable attitudes toward reincarnation and stronger expectations of developing past-life experiences than did no-past-life subjects supports the hypothesis that occurrences of secondary identity enactments are likely to be tied to situation-specific attitudes and expectations[32].

CONCLUSION

There is numerous data available, still not documented scientifically, which explicitly exhibits that the blueprints of our psychological make-up lies invariably in our past – the recent (current lifetime, conception onwards) and distant (past lives) both. The aim of Past Life Regression Therapy on exterior is to alleviate and relieving symptoms, exploring the fascinating past lives and the associated choices one made, which subsequently affect the present. On a deeper level, aim is to make our unconscious conscious and thereby balancing the both, to attain the holistic and integrated whole.

In his new book, Miracles Happen, Brian L. Weiss, MD, and his daughter, Amy, examine the physical, emotional, and spiritual healing that is possible when you freely accept and embrace the reality of reincarnation. In Miracles Happen, he and Amy share these remarkable real-life stories to reveal how past-life regression holds the keys to our spiritual purpose. The awareness that we have multiple lifetimes, separated by spiritual interludes on the other side, helps to dissolve the fear of death and bring more peace and joy into the present moment. Dr. Weiss's inspiring teachings, reveal how getting in touch with our past lives can profoundly and permanently heal mind and body. In the end, we come away inspired, renewed, and assured of the truth that we are eternal beings who are free to heal our current wounds by better understanding our past. [33].

The process of reincarnation, which Sri Aurobindo (the noted Indian spiritual teacher) accepts as a fact of life. However, he clarifies that it is not the outer personality that reincarnates, but rather the psychic being, whose aim is to grow through the process of evolution. In another letter to a disciple,

Sri Aurobindo commented on this in a somewhat humorous vein: "You must avoid a common popular blunder about reincarnation. The popular idea is that Titus Balbus is reborn again as John Smith, a man with the same personality, character, and attainments as he had in his former life with the sole difference that he wears coat and trousers instead of a toga and speaks cockney English instead of popular Latin. That is not the case. What would be the earthly use of repeating the same personality or character a million times from the beginning of time till its end? The soul comes into birth for experience, for growth, for evolution till it can bring the Divine into Matter. It is the central being that incarnates, not the outer personality—the personality is simply a mould that it creates for its figures of experience in that one life. In another birth it will create for itself a different personality, different capacities, a different life and career"[34].

Thus, for those who are open to it, this technique can provide a whole new perspective of life which enriches and strengthens the mind-body-soul connection. On the most superficial level, it is fascinating and adventurous to explore past lives, the choices made and the resultants experienced. On therapeutic level, life altering changes are made on physical (release of external, physical symptoms) level and emotional level (deeper associated emotions/cellular memories/energy knots) which results in new, adaptive, high functioning behavior out casting the old, malfunctioning behavior pattern. On transpersonal level an individual is able to explore the different planes of consciousness, thus obtaining greater understanding of purpose of life, the lessons learnt, the wisdom attained and its implication in daily life. When an individual is able to do so, (s) he attains the higher perspective of life on earth, a feeling of wholeness, a connection with The Source – Divine.

References

1. Bhagavad-Gita.org [Internet]. USA: Bhagavad –Gita Trust; [updated 2005 November 27; cited 2012 November 4]. Available from: http://www.bhagavad-gita.org/Articles/gita-reincarnation.html.
2. Pureinsight.org [Internet]. Zhengjian.org. [cited 2012 November 6]. Available from: http://pureinsight.org/node/219
3. Uwstout.edu [Internet]. Lightbourn C: Past Life Therapy: An Effective Psychotherapeutic Approach. [cited 2012 November 6]. Available from: http://www2.uwstout.edu/content/lib/thesis/2006/2006lightbournc.pdf
4. Regressionacademy.com [Internet]. **Past Life Regression Academy – PLRA [updated 2008; cited 2012 November 9]. Available from** http://www.regressionacademy.com/past-life-research.htm
5. Lifesearchacademy.com [Internet]. Hyderabad: Life Search Academy; [updated 2008; cited 2012 November 1]. Available from http://www.liferesearchacademy.com/regression/history-of-plr.html
6. Stevenson I. The explanatory value of the idea of reincarnation. J NervMent Dis 1977 ;164:305-26.
7. Wade J. The phenomenology of near-death consciousness in past-life regression therapy: a pilot study. Journal of Near death Studies 1998;17: 31-53.
8. Weiss, Brian L. Many lives, many masters: The true story of a prominent psychiatrist, his young patient, and the past-life therapy that changed both their lives. Touchstone, 1988. Available from http://xa.yimg.com/kq/groups/17588172/711574255/name/many-lives-many-masters-brian-weiss.pdf
9. Weiss, B. (1992). Through Time Into Healing. New York: Simon & Schuster
10. Ahluwalia H, Gopinath JK. Subjective Experience of Past – Life Regression. IOSR Journal of Humanities and Social Science (JHSS) 2012; 2:39-45.
11. Hall J. Howard Sasportas, editor. Principles of Past Life Therapy, 1st ed. Forres: Thorsons Publishers; 1996.
12. Wambach H. Reliving Past Lives. The evidence under hypnosis, 1st ed. London: Harper & Row Publishers; 1978.

13. Angelfire.com [Internet]. [cited November 1]. Available from: http://www.angelfire.com/yt/fairtibet/rebirth.html
14. Sharma P, Tucker JB. Cases of the Reincarnation Type with Memories from the Intermission Between Lives. Journal of Near-Death Studies 2004;23:101-18.
15. Davidson JR, Connor KM, Lee LC. Beliefs in karma and reincarnation among survivors of violent trauma--a community survey. Soc Psychiatry PsychiatrEpidemiol 2005;40:120-5.
16. Haraldsson E, Abu-izzeddin M. Development of Certainty About the Correct Deceased Person in a Case of the Reincarnation Type in Lebanon:The Case of Nazih Al-Danaf. Journal of scientific exploration 2002;16:363-80.
17. Walter T. Reincarnation, Modernity and Identity. Sociology 2001;35:21-38.
18. Walter T, Waterhouse H. A Very Private Belief: Reincarnation in Contemporary England. Sociology of Religion 1999; 60: 187-97.
19. Rivas T. Six cases of the reincarnation type in the netherlands. The Paranormal Review 2004; 29: 17-20.
20. Woogler RJ. Past Life Therapy, Trauma Release and the Body. Available from: http://www.rogerwoolger.com/pastlife.html
21. **Ukpokolo IE**. Memories in photography and rebirth: toward a psychosocial therapy of the metaphysics of reincarnation among traditional Esan people of Southern Nigeria. **J Black Stud.** 2012;43:289-302.
22. Pasricha SK. Relevance of para-psychology in psychiatric practice. Indian J Psychiatry 2011;53:4-8
23. Mills A. Inferences from the Case of Ajendra Singh Chauhan: The Effect of Parental Questioning, of Meeting the "Previous Life" Family, an Aborted Attempt to Quantify Probabilities, and the Impact on His Life as a Young Adult. Journal of Scientific Exploration 2004;18: 609–41.
24. Uwstout.edu [Internet]. Lightbourn C: Past Life Therapy: An Effective Psychotherapeutic Approach. [cited 2012 November 6]. Available from: **http://www2.uwstout.edu/content/lib/thesis/2006/2006lightbournc.pdf**

25. **Static.ning.com [Internet]. Marquez A. Healing Through the Remembrance of the Pre- and Perinatal: A Phenomenological Investigation [cited 2012 November 1]. Available from: http://static.ning.com/holotropicbreathwork/research/marquez1999.pdf**
26. Woogler RJ. Past Life Therapy, Trauma Release and the Body. Available from: http://www.childpastlives.org/library articles/woolger PLTherapy.htm
27. Zahi, A. Spiritual- Transpersonal Hypnosis. Contemporary Hypnosis. Available from :http://web.ebscohost.com/ehost/pdfviewer/pdfviewer?hid=22&sid=06f32b0c-6136-4b96-9867-6a36fbe85c44%40sessionmgr12&vid=1
28. Denning H. The Restoration of Health Through Hypnosis. Journal of Regression Therapy 1987; 2: 524.
29. Van der Maesen R. Past Life Therapy for People who Hallucinate Voices. The Journal of Regression Therapy 1999; 13.
30. Woods K, Baruss I. Experimental Test of Possible Psychological Benefits of Past-Life Regression. Journal of Scientific Exploration 2004; 18: 597–608.
31. **Peres JF**. Should psychotherapy consider reincarnation? **J NervMent Dis** 2012;200:174-9.
32. Spanos, Nicholas P., et al. Secondary identity enactments during hypnotic past-life regression: A sociocognitive perspective. Journal of Personality and Social Psychology 1991; 61: 308.
33. Brianweiss.com [Internet]. USA: The Weiss Institute; [updated 2010; cited October 25]. Available from: http://brianweiss.com/
34. Miovic, Michael, Newton W. Sri Aurobindo and Transpersonal Psychology. Journal of Transpersonal psychology 2004;36:111.

Is our psychological orientation - composite of overt & covert behavior, personality, attitudes, emotions, thoughts / cognitive scripts etc., or merely a sum total of our prior learning, experiences, environmental conditions, society, norms etc.? As is the established fact and basis of almost all psychological studies or does our present day psychological orientation is 'much more' than this established fact. Does past life (lives) imprint our current psychological orientation? Past life regression is a general term for the ability of the unconscious mind to retrieve historical memories from previous lives, usually through hypnotic regression or altered state consciousness. Past Life Therapy searches emotionally or physically traumatic life memories for therapeutic purposes. The objective of this article is to explore the blueprints of the present-day psychological orientation in the distant past called past life, through the unconscious mind. The article also highlights the holistic resolution brought about by the Past Life Regression Therapy. Thus, in this article we will review the rationale of past lives' blueprint on present day psychological orientation and its applicability in clinical therapeutic analysis. This article assembles a bibliographic survey of many research papers based on a Google Scholar and Pub Med search for "past life regression", "hypnosis" and "reincarnation".

Introduction

Chapter 2, verse 20 Srimad Bhagavad-Gita

najayatemriyatevakadacinnayambhutvabhavitavanabhuyah

ajonityahsasvato yam puranonahanyatehanyamane

"The soul never takes birth and never dies at any time nor does it come into being again when the body is created. The soul is birthless, eternal, imperishable and timeless and is never terminated when the body is terminated."

Srimad Bhagavad-Gita, chapter two is entitled: Sankhya Yoga: The Eternal Reality of the Souls Immortality. In this chapter of the Bhagavad-Gita are many verse references regarding the reality and science of reincarnation[1].

Eastern and Western thought differ greatly and are culturally driven. Although the general populace of Western countries does not talk about reincarnation much, it is studied in great detail by Western researchers. At the same time, Eastern cultures embrace the concept of reincarnation and embody it in their culture [2].

Past Life Research (PLR) invariably interweaves the concepts of Reincarnation, Rebirth, and Karma. It forms the bridge between the mind-body-soul triad[3]. PLR utilizes two types of approach: either practice based or evidence based. In practice based research, the results are obtained through pre-post therapy questionnaires, using large number of clients over a range of problems. The evidence based approach of research targets specific type of client problem using smaller number and a control group to demonstrate its effectiveness [4].

Past life therapy assumes the existence of the unconscious mind (Netherton&Shiffrin, 1978). Here mental processes take place without our awareness (Weiss, 1992). The unconscious operates as a tape recorder; it records and stores every experience, both positive and negative. Unlike the conscious mind, the unconscious never turns off; it can remember anything from anytime (Weiss; Netherton&Shiffrin). It is not bound by limits of time, logic, or space. It transports one back to those times before one's birth and regresses one to previous lifetimes.[3] During Past-Life-Regression the subject is helped to experience or relive past lives. In the process of regression the subject is first guided into deep states by giving constant suggestions. After reaching a 'satisfactory' level of altered state of consciousness, the subject is first regressed gradually down to the in-utero state (the time when subject was in the mother's womb). The subject is able to describe the experiences verbally.

Even in this New Age, Past-Life-Regression remains one of the best techniques to energize the spirit of individuals by making them to journey into their past lives. By exploring our past lives we can find the solutions for all present life problems[5]

Chapter 2, verse 22 Srimad Bhagavad-Gita

vasamsijirnaniyathavihayanavanigrhnatinaro'parani

tathasariranivihayajirnanyanyanisamyatinavanidehi

"As a person gives up old and worn out garments and accepts new apparel, similarly the embodied soul giving up old and worn out bodies verily accepts new bodies[1]."

The idea of reincarnation may contribute to an improved understanding of such diverse matters as: phobias and philias of childhood; skills not learned in early life; abnormalities of child-parent relationships; vendettas and bellicose nationalism; childhood sexuality and gender identity confusion; birthmarks, congenital deformities, and internal diseases; differences between members of monozygotic twin pairs; and abnormal appetites during pregnancy [6]. The reincarnation research efforts that we have studied fall generally into two categories. The first category being children who remember a past life or lives and the second category is of patients who have a past life or lives recall through hypnosis in regression therapy sessions[3].

Past Life Regression is done to identify why a person may be experiencing problems in the present. The reason for undertaking past-life-therapy is to improve the spiritual quality of our life, right now. Its chief objective is to make our life easier, better and more fulfilling, in this present moment. It directly addresses the internal cause. Past-life-regression-therapy is based on the principles of cause and effect (also known as law of karma). The word "karma" refers to the consequences of one's actions. Something that has been set in motion at some time in the past results in a corresponding effect on a person's present physical, emotional, mental or spiritual well-being, at this moment. This cause may be a past desire, a past thought, past feeling, a past emotion, a past vow, a past promise, a past decision, a past evasion or a past traumatic experience [5]. In Buddhism, karma is thought to directly impact future lifetimes either positively or negatively (Woolger, 1988). The word "karmic" is used to describe the patterns that we establish on our path towards wholeness (Lucas, 2001). The purpose of past life therapy is to identify established patterns and how they impact our growth. Although not consciously realized, throughout our various lifetimes we move towards karmic homeostasis as a result of our innate drive towards wholeness (Lucas, 2001). In India the psycho-physical practice of Yoga has long recognized past life patterns as a basic part of an individual's makeup (Woolger, 1988). Sarnskara is a term used to describe behaviors based on patterns developed in past lives. Woolger (1988) believes that specific patterns are inherited at birth. He identifies them as "psychic scar tissue" (p. 148). The purpose of these patterns is to learn[3].

History

Reincarnation and Past-Life-Regression are not modern concepts. People have believed in reincarnation since ancient times. There is sufficient evidence to show that the Hindus, Ancient Celts, the Egyptians, the Tibetans, and the Hebrew Cabalists etc. used past-life remembrance.

Freud can be considered as the grandfather of present day regression work. He came up with the idea that by making the unconscious conscious, one could restore choice and bring about healing. He discovered the link between past trauma and present symptoms and called it Psychic Determinism. He established that our past experiences determine our present behavior. This changed the face of psychotherapy forever and is the basis of regression work. Later, Jung postulated the concept of a Collective Unconscious and Archetypes (universal patterns). The ancient Indian sage PatanjaliMaharshi, has done extensive work on Past-Life-Regression. In his yoga sutras Patanjali Maharishi called this process of past-life-regression as 'Prati-Prasav'. Prati-Prasav means you are born again in the memory; you go back to the very birth, the trauma when you were born, and you live it again. Buddha is said to have recounted thousands of his past-lives, of which around 550 have been narrated in the 'Jataka' Tales. Mahavira called 'Remembering past-lives' as 'Jati-Smaran'. Early Tibetan history contains a wealth of literature on the subject of reincarnation and afterlife states. A lot of cases of Near Death Experiences are reported even in modern times where people are found to return to life after being pronounced dead. These experiences are very similar to early stages of death as described by the Tibetan sages. Many Christian mystics have stated that after death, the soul separates from the body and leaves. Ancient Egyptians believed in reincarnation. They believed that it took 3000 years to complete all lives that one had to live.

Though reincarnation has been studied scientifically only during recent times, the possibility that we live many lives has been accepted on faith since ancient times. It can be seen that evidence of the belief in reincarnation can be found in people of diverse cultures, from different parts of the world and even people from vastly different time periods (modern, medieval, ancient, prehistoric etc.)[5].

Research on Past Life Regression

"Past-life regression" in Western usage describes the emergence of impressions, images and sensations that seem to be memories of an earlier existence, usually occurring during special, evocative circumstances, such as psychotherapy. The term has evolved from a technology originated by Albert de Rochas, a French hypnotherapist at the turn of the century (Christie-Murray, 1981). Although the spontaneous recollection of apparent past-life memories by children is well documented in cultures that accept reincarnation (Stevenson,1975-80, 1980, 1987), most Western literature concerns recollections produced by adults in altered states of consciousness. The largest body comes from therapeutic modalities involving the deeper layers of the psyche, such as traditional psychoanalysis; Rolfing, acupressure and other body work; rebirthing; sensory isolation; controlled drug therapy; and hypnosis (Bache, 1990). Like age regression therapy, the systematic regressing of patients to produce past-life stories has proven unusually efficacious in the treatment of certain psychological and psychosomatic conditions (Carfaro, 1986; Cladder, 1986; Hull, 1984; Marriott, 1984; Nash, 1992; Netherton and Shiffrin, 1978; Schlotterbeck, 1987).

Therapeutic past-life regressions usually occur during nonordinary states featuring higher alpha electroencephalographic (EEG) activity and more right-hemisphere activity than normal waking consciousness, such as light trance, deep relaxation, or hypnosis, which are associated with greater visual imagery and a diminished or distorted sense of the passage of time, compared to ordinary (beta) awareness. Alterations in phenomenology during the regression, experienced by the subject as different modes of consciousness, are treated in relative terms as they differ from the baseline non ordinary state initiated to access the past life story [7].

As a traditional psychotherapist, Dr. Brian Weiss was astonished and skeptical when one of his patients began recalling past-life traumas that seemed to hold the key to her recurring nightmares and anxiety attacks. His skepticism was eroded, however, when she began to channel messages from "the space between lives," which contained remarkable revelations about Dr. Weiss's family and his dead son. Using past-life therapy, he was able to cure the patient and embark on a new, more meaningful phase of his own career. A graduate of Columbia University and Yale Medical School, Brian L.Weiss, M.D., is currently Chairman of Psychiatry at the Mount Sinai Medical Center in Miami[8].

Dr. Brian in his book talks about his patient Catherine who had come to his office seeking help for her anxiety, panic attacks, and phobias. Although these symptoms had been with her since childhood, in the recent past they had become much worse. Every day she found herself more emotionally paralyzed and less able to function. She was terrified and understandably depressed. In a series of trance states, Catherine recalled "past-life" memories that proved to be the causative factors of her symptoms. She also was able to act as a conduit for information from highly evolved "spirit entities," and through them she revealed many of the secrets of life and of death. In just a few short months, her symptoms disappeared, and she resumed her life, happier and more at peace than ever before[9].

Dr. Bryan Jameison had done similar research and conducted past-life therapy sessions since the late sixties. A book review of Dr. Jameison's books indicated that "during the course of his career he explored 73 of his own former lives. He stated, "Through regression one can see how much each incarnation is not merely an isolated event, but is rather an integral part of a much greater whole." Jameison experimented and found a method that allowed past life regression (PRL) through non-hypnotic past-life regression. It is where the patient induces his own state of tranquility that then allows for PRL. In his latest book, The Search for Past Lives: Exploring Reincarnations' Mysteries & the Amazing Healing Power of Past-life Therapy, Dr. Jameison presented 300 cases. Dr. Jameison discussed an interesting case about a woman called Nancy. Ever since she could remember, she had felt guilty in being alive, although her family life was pleasant and without many problems. She had attempted suicide three times, but all had failed. She agreed to past life regression therapy, though nothing significant was found during the first few sessions. Then, as expected, she finally found the cause for her depressive moods. She recalled her life during the World War II. She was sixteen years old and getting ready to have dinner with her family. She vividly could see the Gestapo breaking into her house ordering her family to go with them. Her father protested and was killed. She, her mother, and younger brother were dragged down the stairs and pulled out into the street. Then, they were pushed into a truck. Later on, they were cramped with others into a train. They ate, drank, soiled, vomited and urinated where they stood. After arriving at the train station, they were driven to a labor camp, like animals. A few days later, one Nazi took her and another girl to a big house next to the labor camp. The Nazi asked them to take a shower, put on makeup and dress up, which made them to look more presentable. They were then forced to prostitute for the Nazis. Under the guidance of Dr. Jameison, Nancy was able to let go of her guilt and come to peace. She no longer wanted to commit suicide. She also realized while listening to a replay of the particular regression therapy session that during this life, her younger brother from that life was her son and her mother was her daughter[2].

Similarly, Judy Hall is a counsellor and healer who has been running past-life exploration groups for more than twenty years. Deja Who? A New Look at Past Lives is described as the first book that accepts reincarnation and yet questions the validity of some recalled past lives. Many famous names appear time after time in past-life regressions, and the most useful part of this book is where Judy Hall explores in depth the possible alternative explanations to reincarnation which may explain such occurrences. These may be suggestion, paramnesia, cryptomnesia, false memory syndrome, possession, psychiatric illness, multiple personality disorder, and others. The validity and relevance of past lives are examined in the context of these alternative explanations [10].

Helen Wambach, a psychologist and clinical psychiatrist, developed a hypnotic technique by which she was able to regress her subjects back to previous lives. Over a period of 12 years, in a carefully-designed project, she regressed more than 1000 subjects. Each subject was given a post-hypnotic suggestion that enabled them to fill out a data sheet with precise details for each incarnation, following the session. When analysed and correlated these data sheets provided "... striking and extraordinary evidence of the existence of reincarnation." Numerous figures, tables and specimen data sheets included in the text provide much useful information about conditions of life throughout the overall period - information which it was possible to confirm in many instances [11].

The aim of the study by Hargun Ahluwalia & Jini K Gopinath was to examine the subjective experience of past life regression (PLR). 15 graduate students underwent PLR facilitated by a trained professional for this purpose. Using Interpretative Phenomenological Analysis (IPA), the data collected from the interviews with these individuals was analyzed. The participants were able to relate their experiences under trace with their present life scenarios and could find meaning in their experiences. Most participants reported positive effects of the experience and this may have implications for further research and therapy with non- clinical populations[12].

Research on Reincarnation/Rebirth

Although these terms are often used interchangeably, there is a significant conceptual difference between the two. On the whole, Buddhists believe in rebirth while Hindus, Jains, and some Christians believe in reincarnation. Strictly speaking, reincarnation means the assumption of another body by a permanent, eternal self (the Hindu notion of atman or the Christian notion ofsoul). Most Buddhists do not believe in a permanent self (anatman or anatta, without enduring self) but believe human consciousness (the "I" or self) dissolves at death and that only a subtle mindstream remains. The mindstream carries with it karmic imprints from prior lives and it is this subtle mind stream that conjoins with a new life-form after death. Thus, rebirth does not mean an identifiable human being assuming a new human body. Moreover, in Buddhism, rebirth is not always accomplished in human form. Depending on karmic circumstances, a human being can be reborn as an animal or as a being in any of the upper or lower realms[13].

For the last 40 years, researchers have collected cases of children who claim to remember previous lives. Subjects in these cases tend to make more verified statements about the previous life they claim to remember than do other subjects of reincarnationtype cases, and they tend to recall more names from that life. Analysis of reports from 35 Burmese subjects indicates that the intermission memories can be broken down into three parts: a transitional stage, a stable stage in a particular location, and a return stage involving choosing parents or conception. A comparison of these reports to reports of near-death experiences (NDEs) indicates that they show features similar to the transcendental component of Western NDEs and have significant areas of overlap with Asian NDEs[14].

Erlendur Haraldsson & Majd Abu-Izzeddin cites a case concerning a young boy in Baalchmay, Lebanon, who made specific statements before several family members asserting memories of a previous life, such as being a man who carried pistols and hand-grenades, having a mute friend, describing a house, having children, living in the village of Quaberchamoun, and being shot by armed people. The case is unusual because when the child was taken at age 7 to the village, a corresponding deceased person was identified by means of his claimed memories, and the widow and the man's brother became certain of the authenticity of the child's reincarnation through his correct answers to their questions, recognition of people and possessions, and his own knowledgeable questions to them[15].

In an article published in January 2004, Rivas T explored six cases of reincarnation type in Netherlands. According to her in the Netherlands one often encounters the almost untranslatable concept of 'nuchterheid', which partially overlaps with the English concepts of 'sobriety' and 'soberness'. 'Nuchterheid' in the relevant sense is an unwillingness to be overwhelmed by strong emotions and a resistance to any kind of 'superstitious', irrational or even religious beliefs. One of the cases is classical reincarnation case of a girl named Christina who recognized herself as a young girl who was caught in fire in previous lifetime. Her description was matched with the existing information and it turned out to be true. Her present lifetime was affected in the sense that she was frightened of going to the attic of her house [16].

A study was conducted by Davisdson JR et al. in which a survey was conducted about beliefs in karma and reincarnation among survivors of violent trauma. The results indicated five percent of the sample admitted strong agreement to a belief in karma and reincarnation (n=99), while 77% strongly disagreed with these beliefs (n=1,511). It was concluded few people subscribe strongly to a belief in karma and reincarnation in the US population, but personal experience of trauma may be associated with greater acceptance, as well as certain demographic and health-associated variables. The importance of holding such beliefs, which may represent an important way of coping following violent trauma, deserves further study [17].

Walter T et al, explored in a survey what reincarnation means to some of the westerners who believe in it, why they find it attractive, and how it relates to other aspects of their life, not least the religious organizations to which they belong but which do not teach it, They concluded that reincarnation is indeed for them a very private belief, detached from religious and other affiliations, from the New Age, from popular literature on the subject, and from everyday life [18]. In another study by Walter T, it was concluded that the understanding of A as the reincarnation of close family member B, found in several American and African tribes and in popular Hinduism, may be unusual in Britain; in so far as people play with past identities, this cannot easily be squared with postmodern theories of the self; the past identities constructed bear strong resemblance to current identities, and may be considered part of the modernist project of the self [19].

There also exists the monumental work of psychiatrist Dr. Ian Stevenson of the University of Virginia, an erstwhile president of the British Society for Psychical Research. For over 40 years Stevenson and his co-workers collected cases of spontaneous memories of "past lives" from many parts of the world, mostly from among children. His most recent book Reincarnation and Biology(Stevenson, 1997) was described by the reviewer for the British Scientific and Medical Network as "one of the great classics of twentieth century psi research" (Lorimer, 1997: 53). Nevertheless Stevenson's work continues to be ignored by mainstream psychology. Where the past life based approach to trauma and somaticized complexes differs from most conventional therapies--including the Reichian schools--is that it takes the position that the soul is much is greater than the ego-personality; a position to be found strongly in Jung, James Hillman (1977) and in the work of recent transpersonal psychologists. Thus the traumas that may surface during the therapeutic exploration of the current life may have other levels or deeper resonances to them. Often the releasing of trauma with this approach is like peeling skins from an onion. Compared to the great psycho-spiritual disciplines of the East, western psychotherapy is still in its infancy and is still learning to work with other dimensions of the soul such as residues of previous lives, ancestral memories or the influence of spiritual healing from other realms[20].

The aim of the article by Ukpokolo IE is to show that beyond the need for the justification of the belief in reincarnation, beyond the quest for evidences to prove its reality or otherwise, the idea of rebirth has a pragmatic role in the cultures where it is held. Using the theorization of rebirth among the Esan people of southern Nigeria as a pilot, it asserts that the idea of rebirth plays a psychosocial, therapeutic function of comfort and healing for those traumatized by the death of a loved one. This, it shall be seen, is similar to, even more reliable than, the role of photography in preserving cherished memories. The article attempts to establish the role of reincarnation, like photography, in bringing the past into the present[21].

According to Dr. Satwant Pasricha young children (subjects of cases of the reincarnation type) sometimes claim to have lived before and give specific details about those lives and display behavior that corresponds to the actual or expected behavior of the person (previous personality) whose life the subject claims to remember but the behavior is unusual for his present circumstances. The child may for example, show phobia of water if he remembered having been drowned in the previous life and has had no such traumatic experience or model available in the present life. Nearly 2600 reported cases of the reincarnation type have been scientifically investigated in several cultures over the past about five decades. In 64-80% cases a deceased person matching the statements of child was identified. Cross cultural comparisons have shown that certain features recur across cultures, which are: age of speaking about a previous life (between 2 and 4 years), age of discontinuation of talk about previous life (usually between 5 and 8 years), high incidence of violent death

(63%) of the previous personality, far beyond the rate of violent death in the general populations of the respective countries, and high frequency of mention, by the subjects, of mode of death (78%) in the previous life, other features such as sex change and intermission between two lives vary between cultures [22].

As Mills and Lynn note the spontaneous cases of possible past-life memories that have been documented to date necessarily reflect a special subset of possible past-life memory, because the emphasis has been on "solvable cases" with a relatively short interval between the present and a previous reported life. Type B cases such as Ajendra Singh Chauhan's are especially useful in showing the accuracy of young children's statements and provide a check for the possibility of cultural elaboration based on acceptance of the case and information learned only after initial contact. Tucker's SOCS (2000) has been used to show how important parental questioning can be in eliciting the information necessary for solving a case. Indeed in this instance, the score for Ajendra's case would have been zero without the father's eventually asking his child for more information. The case suggests that Stevenson's vigilance in examining the accuracy of reported past-life statements made after the families have met minimizes the addition of further elements to such a case. The same care used in taking children's testimony about other issues than a past life (Bruck et al., 1998) needs to be exercised in assessing testimony some children give about apparent past-life memories. Finally, the principle of similarity of stimulus that impacts memory within one life seems to be active in Ajendra's case in his recall of memories from 8 months before his birth, of the violent death of another individual whose family Ajendra's did not know. Such cases definitely deserve careful consideration [23].

Past Lives' Blueprint and the Therapeutic Effects

The therapeutic effect of the Past Life Regression Therapy lies in the identification of the blueprint it lays on the current psychological make-up of the individual. The blueprint consists of the repeated behavioral patterns adopted by the individuals in order to learn and ascertain the wisdom of the lessons – yet to be learnt. This blueprint is the Karma of the individual. These blueprints have tendency to let us achieve the 'not yet learnt' lesson or the wisdom of life. According to Denning (in Lucas, 2001) each person chooses a specific lesson for each lifetime with specific settings andpersonalities which assists in attaining these lessons. The process of working through patterns takes many lifetimes (Lucas, 2001). In the life we are living today, we are making up for the mistakes. Individuals, who are karmically connected, reincarnate together. Gucciardi (1999) states, these individuals trigger each other continually so the issues that need to be addressed will come to surface[24].

Marquez (1999) found that remembering pre and prenatal experiences can significantly benefit one's life. The author conducted a study on 7 adults, in which some of the benefits experienced were changes in vision, healing of arthritis and relief from asthma. The subjects felt empowered and felt a greater control over their life [25].

Woolger (2002) throws light on how regression to past experiences, in the present or previous lives can have significant therapeutic benefit. He discusses the case of a woman who suffered from post traumatic stress disorder symptoms (PTSD) symptoms for 20 years since a car accident where she went through a NDE during subsequent surgery to save her life. When age regression was done on her to relive the incident, she described in detail watching her body being pulled from the wreckage, being taken to the hospital and then into surgery, ascending to a higher realm and meeting deceased members of her family who shone with very bright light. When she returned to her physical body, she found her pain coming back. Before this session of regression, she had not remembered these details and the session profoundly altered her outlook towards death and dying [26].

Zahi discusses 3 cases of therapeutic benefit from hypnotherapy. The first of these cases was that of a woman who complained of high levels of anxiety, pain and memory problems. Through hypnosis she regressed to the age of one year and found that the father was being hostile towards her and despite calls for her mother, she did not come to her rescue. For next few sessions she wanted her memory problems to be worked upon. She underwent past- life regression therapy. First she found herself in Egypt where her baby was killed and buried with the Pharaoh. She felt extremely guilty that she could not save her child. She also realized that her baby's soul was at peace and this brought her relief. In another PLR session she found herself as a mother during the holocaust that died but saved her son. This memory surprised her and she said that she had never saved anyone before. She said that this memory filled in the gaps in her memory that she was struggling with and she did not have memory problems again. Interestingly, Zahi proposes that benefit from therapy can also be felt by non- believers or those whose beliefs oppose that involving non- material elements such as the soul [27].

Woolgeralso reports the case of Heather, who came for therapy as she suffered from ulcerative colitis since early adolescence. When no significant conflict emerged through age regression, PLR was carried out. In the session she regressed to Holland during World War II at the time of the Nazi invasion. She found herself as an eight- year old girl in a Jewish family who while fleeing from an explosion was captured and subsequently killed. She described her bodily sensations as she awaited her turn to be in front of the machine gun fire and felt her stomach knotted in terror. For all this time, she had not been able to express the shock and trauma of having lost her parents, seeing mass slaughter and facing her own premature death, which may have resulted in bodily manifestations. In the session, she was allowed to release her anguish through cathartic sobbing, screaming, violent convulsions and dry vomiting. After the session her stomach problem improved significantly[4].

Past life research consists of practice and evidence based approaches. In practice based past life research, Hazel Denning studied the results by eight Regression Therapists with nearly 1000 clients between 1985 and 1992. Results were measured just after the therapy, after six months, one year, two years and five years. Of the 450 clients who could still be tracked after 5 years; 24% reported the symptoms had completely gone, 23% reported considerable or dramatic improvement, 17% reported noticeable improvement and 36% reported no improvement. (TanDam, 1990) [28].

In evidence based past life research, significant work has been done by Ron Van der Maesen. This was conducted using fifty-four clients who had reoccurring disturbing voices or thoughts. The Dutch Association of Reincarnation Therapists supplied the Past Life Therapists for the research. At a six month follow up after the therapy by an external Psychiatrist, the disturbing voices had disappeared in 25%, and a further 32% could now cope. Overall 80% had a positive subjective experience and would recommend this therapy for reoccurring problems like these in others.

Ron Van der Maesen also conducted past life research with Tourettes's syndrome. The work was conducted by 10 members of the Dutch Association of Reincarnation Therapists initially with 22 clients over the age range of 9 to 52 years old. Of the ten subjects who completed all the therapy and responded to the one-year follow-up questionnaire, 50% reported that their motor tics had for the most part largely disappeared or been greatly reduced in frequency. The same also applied to their vocal tics. Five also reported that they were free of medication, in sharp contrast to the pre-study period [29].

Thus several cases point towards the likelihood of current pathologies in the present life arising from psychic residues of previous births. Such physical memories, that have nothing to account for them in the current life, turn out to be embedded in what is literally the subtle energy field that surrounds and penetrates the physical body. These old traumas, inherited though the subtle (energy) field, are consistently found in our work to re-imprint in the current body as rashes, birth marks weaknesses in certain limbs, organic problems such as a weak bladder, a weak heart and so on. (Woolger) In the field of PLR for non- pathological individuals, Woods and Baruss (2004) conducted a study with 24 students. Each of them participated in a single guided imagery session in which they were given either a pastlife or open suggestion. Participants who were given the past-life suggestion had better scores on measures of psychological well-being than those given the open suggestion[30].

However, the research on increased well- being and/or cathartic release as possible benefits of PLR on those who do not suffer from any somatic or psychological problem has not been explored abundantly. There is a need to explore the benefits of this therapy for the non- pathological population so as to extend psychotherapy to this majority population to enhance the quality of life.

In an article by Peres JF it is stressed upon that there is increasing recognition of the need to take into account the cultural environment and belief systems of psychotherapy patients because these values reflect basic assumptions about man's nature and the cognitive references used to cope with psychological difficulties. Currently accepted psychotherapeutic approaches take no account of the belief in life after death held by most of the world's population. Respect for patient opinions and subjective realities are a therapeutic need and an ethical duty, even though therapists may not share the same beliefs. Guidelines are suggested for professionals to develop collaborative models that help patients mobilize their intrinsic intelligence to find solutions to their complaints[31].

In 4 studies conducted by Spanos NP et al., subjects (Ss) received hypnotic suggestions to regress beyond birth to a previous life. In Study 1the development of a past-life identity was unrelated to indexes of psychopathology. Studies 2 and 3demonstrated that Ss developed past-life identities that reflected hypnotist-transmitted expectations. In Study 4 the credibility that Ss assigned to their past-life experiences was influenced bywhether the hypnotist defined such experiences as realor imagined. Combined data from the first 3studies indicated that hypnotizability predicted the subjective intensity of past-life experiences but not the credibility assigned to these experiences. Alternatively, beliefs, attitudes, and expectations concerning reincarnation predicted the degree of credibility assigned to these experiences. The finding that past-life responders had more favorable attitudes toward reincarnation and stronger expectations of developing past-life experiences than did no-past-life subjects supports the hypothesis that occurrences of secondary identity enactments are likely to be tied to situation-specific attitudes and expectations[32].

There is numerous data available, still not documented scientifically, which explicitly exhibits that the blueprints of our psychological make-up lies invariably in our past – the recent (current lifetime, conception onwards) and distant (past lives) both. The aim of Past Life Regression Therapy on exterior is to alleviate and relieving symptoms, exploring the fascinating past lives and the associated choices one made, which subsequently affect the present. On a deeper level, aim is to make our unconscious conscious and thereby balancing the both, to attain the holistic and integrated whole.

In his new book, Miracles Happen, Brian L. Weiss, MD, and his daughter, Amy, examine the physical, emotional, and spiritual healing that is possible when you freely accept and embrace the reality of reincarnation. In Miracles Happen, he and Amy share these remarkable real-life stories to reveal how past-life regression holds the keys to our spiritual purpose. The awareness that we have multiple lifetimes, separated by spiritual interludes on the other side, helps to dissolve the fear of death and bring more peace and joy into the present moment. Dr. Weiss's inspiring teachings, reveal how getting in touch with our past lives can profoundly and permanently heal mind and body. In the end, we come away inspired, renewed, and assured of the truth that we are eternal beings who are free to heal our current wounds by better understanding our past. [33].

The process of reincarnation, which Sri Aurobindo (the noted Indian spiritual teacher) accepts as a fact of life. However, he clarifies that it is not the outer personality that reincarnates, but rather the psychic being, whose aim is to grow through the process of evolution. In another letter to a disciple, Sri Aurobindo commented on this in a somewhat humorous vein: "You must avoid a common popular blunder about reincarnation. The popular idea is that

Titus Balbus is reborn again as John Smith, a man with the same personality, character, and attainments as he had in his former life with the sole difference that he wears coat and trousers instead of a toga and speaks cockney English instead of popular Latin. That is not the case. What would be the earthly use of repeating the same personality or character a million times from the beginning of time till its end? The soul comes into birth for experience, for growth, for evolution till it can bring the Divine into Matter. It is the central being that incarnates, not the outer personality—the personality is simply a mould that it creates for its figures of experience in that one life. In another birth it will create for itself a different personality, different capacities, a different life and career"[34].

Thus, for those who are open to it, this technique can provide a whole new perspective of life which enriches and strengthens the mind-body-soul connection. On the most superficial level, it is fascinating and adventurous to explore past lives, the choices made and the resultants experienced. On therapeutic level, life altering changes are made on physical (release of external, physical symptoms) level and emotional level (deeper associated emotions/cellular memories/energy knots) which results in new, adaptive, high functioning behavior out casting the old, malfunctioning behavior pattern. On transpersonal level an individual is able to explore the different planes of consciousness, thus obtaining greater understanding of purpose of life, the lessons learnt, the wisdom attained and its implication in daily life. When an individual is able to do so, (s) he attains the higher perspective of life on earth, a feeling of wholeness, a connection with The Source – Divine.

Section B

Written Emotional Disclosure and Spirituality: Why Both Matter

Tara Overzat

Abstract: Research suggests that written emotional disclosure has not only psychological and emotional benefits, but also physical health benefits. Spirituality, likewise, has been proven to help some individuals in their sense of well-being. There is a possibility of an overlap between the two concepts. Prayer, for example, may act as a form of emotional disclosure, which could explain some of its positive effects. Future implications of an intersection of these two interventions are discussed.

Keywords: written emotional disclosure, spirituality, prayer, health, well-being

Introduction

Written emotional disclosure has its origins in the work of James Pennebaker and his colleagues. Pennebaker initially created this low-cost intervention by asking participants to write for three to four days for approximately 20 to 30 minutes on a stressful event (Pennebaker & Beall, 1986). The positive results generated more research on the efficacy of written emotional disclosure, or expressive writing as it is sometimes called, by this researcher and many others, and with some researchers creating variations of the intervention. The differing interventions, however, generally utilize a similar writing prompt, which emphasizes that the participants write about difficult emotional topics, as follows in this partial example of a writing prompt: "For the next 3 days, I would like for you to write about your very deepest thoughts and feelings about an extremely important emotional issue that has affected you and your life." (Pennebaker, 1997).

Expressive writing differs from journaling in that journaling tends to take place over an extended period of time, is generally unstructured, and often involves keeping a diary or "journal" of the entries written. Previous research has evaluated the efficacy of journaling under this definition, with mixed results (e.g., Smith, Anderson-Hanley, Langrock, & Compas, 2005; Stone, 1998; Ullrich & Lutgendorf, 2002). Expressive writing is structured with a prompt and is intended to be a short-term activity, with recommendations of three to five sessions between 15 and 30 minutes in duration (Pennebaker, 1997), though there have been research designs as short as two 2-minute sessions (Burton & King, 2008).

As to why written emotional disclosure may work, Pennebaker and Beall (1986) noted that the act of not confiding about traumatic events correlated with greater occurrence of stress-related diseases. Pennebaker (1997) later clarified that not speaking about traumas was a constant low-level stressor—in short, that it takes effort to not disclose a disturbing event. As such, Pennebaker and Beall (1986) created an experiment to test if disclosing about such traumas through writing would have a short- or long-term impact on psychological and physical health. Their results were that participants experienced short-term negative effects (e.g., raised blood pressure and more negative mood) but were in need of fewer visits to the student health center in the six months following the intervention, suggesting that the short-term negative effects were temporary and that positive effects occurred long-term. The short-term versus long-term effect has been confirmed in other work as well (Francis & Pennebaker, 1992). In a follow-up study, Pennebaker, Hughes, and O'Heeron (1987) also found that "confessing" about traumas produced positive physical results. The researchers, however, performed their experiment by having students either disclose a traumatic event alone with a tape recorder, or having them perform this activity along with speaking about the trauma to an unseen "confessor" behind a curtain. They found that the participants disclosed more to the tape recorder than to the confessor. The researchers rationalized that this may be due to the participants feeling safer disclosing to the tape recorder than to an individual—even if that individual were unseen.

Qualitative research suggests that religious confession can also have positive psychological benefits depending on certain characteristics of the confessor and that confessor's beliefs. For individuals who believe in an all-loving and forgiving God, and who do not believe that their "sins" or misdeeds are an intrinsic part of themselves, confession seemed to give perceived positive psychological effects (McCormick & McMinn, 2012). Whereas confession can be one form of spiritually-accented emotional disclosure, prayer could be analyzed as another. Prayer has been reported to be an effective form of stress relief for certain individuals, though more research is needed to better understand the psychological constructs that may undergird the efficacy of prayer (Levine, 2008). It is possible that language that reflects positive emotions and adaptive personal observations are more frequent in prayer than in written emotional disclosures (VandeCreek, Janus, Pennebaker, & Binau, 2002). The research varies on this topic, however, with written prayer from a pediatric hospital showing unclear results of positive disclosure effects (Grossoehme et al., 2010).

Yet, various studies came to the conclusion that a strong sense of spirituality affected physical health. College students who, in one study, reported higher levels of spiritual well-being and involvement in spiritual activities also tended to report being in better physical health as well (Anye, Gallien, Bian, & Moulton, 2013). The terminally ill may be the most poignant and salient group to discuss the benefits of written emotional disclosure and of spirituality. Written emotional disclosure was found to help patients with terminal metastatic renal cell carcinoma sleep longer and have better sleep quality. These patients also functioned more effectively in the daytime (de Moor et al., 2002). In terms of spirituality, Dossey (2014) believes that to embrace the idea of a consciousness that dies with the body is to unnecessarily harm both the terminally ill and the surviving family and friends. It has been recommended that medical professionals engage clients in spiritually and culturally competent conversations around end-of-life issues, and a **prototype** distance-learning program on death and dying was found to help alleviate fears of death amongst the participants (Schlitz, Schooler, Pierce, Murphy, & Delorme, 2014).

As to how to interact with clients with varying views on spirituality and after-life issues, remaining open-minded is valuable (Schlitz et al., 2014). A clinician shared a case study of client who felt that he was having in-depth conversations with his deceased daughter following her sudden death. Rather than treat this as a clinical issue, say, of auditory hallucination, the clinician worked with the clients beliefs about death and the after-life, and the client experienced a healthy resolution, finding himself reconnecting to his wife, who was also grieving their daughter's death (Lomax, 2014).

Conclusion

More research may need to be done to determine how best to integrate the positive effects of written emotional disclosure and individual spiritual identities. There is a growing trend in psychotherapy in the United States towards understanding the spiritual issues of clients, and of responding in a way that is both ethical and empathic (Sperry, 2014). Helping clients with their emotional disclosure and positively utilizing disclosures that may already be occurring due to spiritual practice could become important parts of the counseling process and may inform future interventions.

References

Anye, E. T., Gallien, T. L., Bian, H., & Moulton, M. (2013). The relationship between spiritual well-being and health-related quality of life in college students. *Journal of American College Health, 61*(7), 414-421.

de Moor, C., Sterner, J., Hall, M., Warneke, C., Gilani, Z., Amato, R., & Cohen, L. (2002). A pilot study of the effects of expressive writing on psychological and behavioral adjustment in patients enrolled in a Phase II trial of vaccine therapy for metastatic renal cell carcinoma. *Health Psychology, 21*(6), 615-619.

Dossey, L. (2014). Should clinicians honor immortality? Reflections on the continuity of consciousness. *Spirituality in Clinical Practice, 1*(3), 184-188.

Francis, M. E., & Pennebaker, J. W. (1992). Putting stress into words: The impact of writing on physiological, absentee, and self-reported emotional well-being measures. *American Journal of Health Promotion, 6*(4), 280-287.

Grossoehme, D. H., VanDyke, R., Jacobson, C. J., Cotton, S., Ragsdale, J. R., & Seid, M.

(2010). Written prayers in a pediatric hospital: Linguistic analysis. *Psychology of Religion and Spirituality, 2*(4), 227-233.

Levine, M. (2008). Prayer as coping: A psychological analysis. *Journal of Health Care Chaplaincy, 15*(2), 80-98.

Lomax, J. W. (2014). Gaining perspective on death: Training program and language use outcomes assessment by Dr. Marilyn Schlitz et al. (2014). *Spirituality in Clinical Practice, 1*(3), 181-183.

McCormick, A. G., & McMinn, M. R. (2012). The intrapsychic and interpersonal effects of talking about guilt. *Journal of Psychology and Christianity, 31*(4), 354-365.

Pennebaker, J. W. (1997). Writing about emotional experiences as a therapeutic process. *Psychological Science, 8*(3), 162-166.

Pennebaker, J. W., & Beall, S. K. (1986). Confronting a traumatic event: toward an understanding of inhibition and disease. *Journal of Abnormal Psychology, 95*(3), 274–281.

Pennebaker, J. W., Hughes, C. F., & O'Heeron, R. C. (1987). The psychophysiology of confession: Linking inhibitory and psychosomatic processes. *Journal of Personality and Social Psychology, 52*(4), 781-793.

Schlitz, M., Schooler, J., Pierce, A., Murphy, A., & Delorme, A. (2014). Gaining perspective on death: Training program and language use outcomes assessment. *Spirituality in Clinical Practice, 1*(3), 169-180.

Smith, S., Anderson-Hanley, C., Langrock, A., & Compas, B. (2005). The effects of journaling for women with newly diagnosed breast cancer. *Psycho-Oncology, 14*(12), 1075-1082.

Sperry, L. (2014). Effective spiritually oriented psychotherapy practice is culturally sensitive practice. *Spirituality in Clinical Practice, 1*(3), 167-168.

Stone, M. (1998). Journaling with clients. *The Journal of Individual Psychology, 54*(4), 535-545.

Ullrich, P. M., & Lutgendorf, S. K. (2002). Journaling about stressful events: Effects of cognitive processing and emotional expression. *Annals of Behavioral Medicine, 24*(3), 244-250.

VandeCreek, L., Janus, M. D., Pennebaker, J. W., & Binau, B. (2002). Praying about difficult experiences as self-disclosure to God. *The International Journal for the Psychology of Religion, 12*(1), 29-39.

Health promotion for Juvenile Delinquents: Strengthening Spiritual wellness through Life Skills Education (LSE) interventions

Annie Singh and Subhasis Bhadra

Abstract: Mental Health and wellbeing of adolescent population holds great importance in present scenario of research. It is an established fact that mental wellbeing is a balanced state of mind in which an individual feels harmony within and around (Manjunath & Sahoo, 2011). Among the four dimensions of good mental health, spiritual aspect holds equal effectiveness in maintaining this balance. A disturbed and deviant personality is a result of disturbance between the four dimensions. Juvenile delinquency is one such problem behavior of adolescent population. Role of spiritual healing for juveniles can prove as an effective remedy for the deviations they reflect in their behavior. Life skills education training has proved its effectiveness worldwide as a promotional training and practicing method for maintaining good mental health and wellbeing. Spirituality as a part of life skills training module of juvenile delinquents can work wonders to promote mental wellbeing of juvenile delinquents in India and worldwide. Spiritual training through life skills will eradicate the Subjective deviant identity and faithlessness in Juveniles. Thus helping them to reason their decisions and actions and will prevent them from reentering into criminality and hopelessness.

Keywords-Mental Health, Life skills Education, Juvenile Delinquency, Spirituality, Religiosity

Introduction

Wellbeing can be defined with four interrelated dimensions. These dimensions in total are responsible for overall well-being, happiness, and life's satisfaction. WHO recognizes the four dimensions of wellbeing which are physical, mental, spiritual and social aspects (Parti, 2015). The first dimension of wellness includes all aspects of physical health. To have wellness in the first dimension, all of the physiological and mental systems should be working together naturally in an efficient manner. The mental well-being includes aspects related to beliefs, emotional health, outlook on the world and self-image of an individual. The third dimension of wellness is social well-being and it includes social relationships with family, friends, and social life of an individual. The social aspect related to persons happiness and health holds extreme importance for wellbeing. The fourth dimension of wellness is spiritual wellbeing that would relate to a person's sense of being connected to one's own self and the ideologies that a person looks upon and follows as a belief system and faith. Spirituality helps human beings to reason their existence and motivates them to live. It can be termed as GOD, or can be understood in terms of religion, it can be nature, universal love or justice. This sense of being connected to something larger than the practical aspects around us gives great meaning to life. Thus, spirituality promotes health and happiness. These four dimensions have different implications on an individual's life; lack of any one of these dimensions severely affects the normal existence that is needed for a healthy holistic, living. Human beings exist in unity of all these four dimensions and lack of wellness in any one dimension creates an imbalance in the entire system.

In 1948 WHO first introduced the concept of mental wellbeing. The concept since then has been presented in a wide range of disciplines with a variety of meanings attached to its practice in different set ups (UK Faculty of Public Health, 2010). Mental health is a state of well-being in which the individual realizes his or her own abilities, can cope with the normal stresses of life, can work productively and fruitfully, and is able to make a contribution to his or her community (WHO, 2010). Mental health can be defined through the broad dimensions that are related to the mental well-being component included in the WHO's definition of health, "A state of complete physical, mental and social well-being, and not merely the absence of disease". Diagram below relates to the promotion of well-being as it highlights all four dimensions of good health by WHO (World Health Organisation, 2015)

Diagram-1:

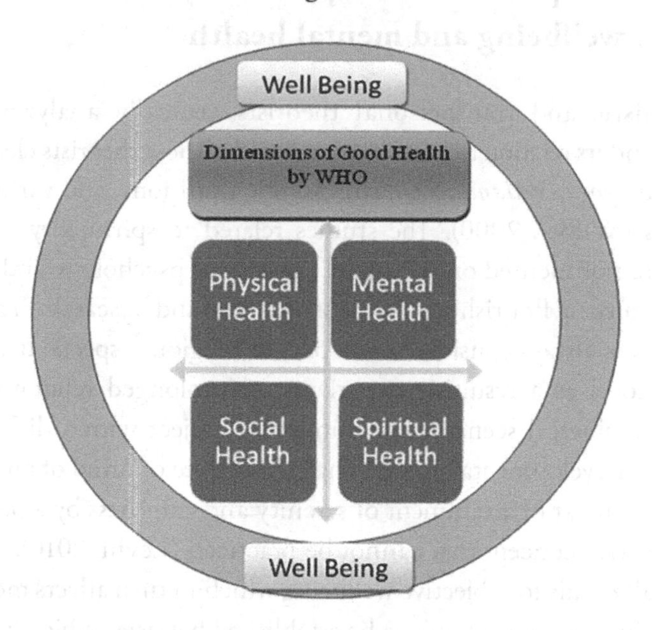

Spirituality as an essential feature of Mental Health

Spirituality as a term would relate to a concept that is core and center of every human being's thought process and personality. Spirituality brings a wholesomeness, energy, hope and serenity as its impression. It motivates and directs a person's behavior from deep within (Pulla, 2014). It defines quest for harmony and hope and helps an individual to relate to the fact that things exist beyond materialism. Looking into all the above mentioned factors, it can be maintained that mental health and spirituality are interrelated. Spirituality can be of immense help to people with mental health problems (Mental Health Foundation, 2015)

Mental wellbeing is essential for good physical health, as it helps in being focused on the goals that every individual sets in life (Pargament & Kenneth, 2013). Empirical studies have indicated that people in major life stresses like loss of a loved one, tragic deaths due to natural disaster, serious illness and broken relationships and divorce get healed and consoled through spirituality. Spiritual healing is one of the best ways of walking on the lines of coping and facing the most uncontrollable of problems with calmer attitude. Spiritual healing facilitates life transitions and helps a person to reframe stressful situations.

Theoretical implications on Spirituality connection to subjective wellbeing and mental health

Humanistic and transpersonal theorists critically analyzed issues of spirituality and its relation to good human health. These theorists clearly seemed influenced by *yoga, Vedanta, Zen*, the esoteric traditions, and various integral perspectives (Wilber, 2000). The studies related to spirituality and religion initially were not focused on the subject matter of psychology and psychiatry but did become a flourishing topic of debates and research. Traditionally spirituality was always considered as a part of religious aspects. It was defined and understood as a resulting experience of prolonged religious practices. Present psychological scenario looks into the subject with a different angle, stating it as a developmental process that affect state of mind of an individual. It holds the context of attainment of serenity and calmness by a person rather than a subjective concept that cannot be practiced (Levin, 2010).

Spiritually leads to subjective wellbeing which in turn affects mental health of an individual. A connection can be established between subjective wellbeing and spirituality on mental health. Durayappa (2010). The 3P model derives importance of global evaluation of subjective wellbeing on different states of a person's life. The Liking or Hedonic Happiness theory works on the principle of minimizing pain and extending life to a happier side to gain most out of it (Peterson, Ruch, Beermann, Park, & Seligman, 2007). Maslow has suggested a hierarchy of needs that suggests similar implications. The needing and wanting theory suggests similar aspects that an individual needs and likes wellbeing in life which relates to the satisfaction that one attains from accomplishments of goal in life. Mental Health Continuum Model This model describes the significance of subjective wellbeing in form of a process from ill-being to wellbeing. Keyes described individuals with good mental health as 'flourishing' in life and rank high on the factor of subjective wellbeing (Keyes, 2002). The social learning theory by Albert Bandura accounts the importance of spirituality by stating that social support decreases distress, despondency. There is an influential role of modeling in transmitting spiritual beliefs, values and spiritual lifestyle practices (Bandura, 2003). Theories like Social Selection also provide evidence of Spiritual training as an effective tool for decreasing deviant behavior (Mapp, 2009).

Importance of spirituality for mental health

Studies have shown spirituality as an important dimension in mental health recovery (Philips & Stein, 2007). Literature reflects that many people suffering serious mental illnesses want their spiritual beliefs, values and practices to be considered and included as a part of format of their treatment plans (Baetz, Griffin, Bowen, & Marcoux, 2004). Social workers and psychiatrists have highlighted that a person's religiosity or spirituality could affect the recovery process and this is consistent with current models that is focusing on wellness and recovery (Kruger, 2000). Psychiatrists and mental health workers should be trained on spiritual sensitivity, on the use of formal spiritual assessment tools for development of holistic theoretical frameworks which facilitate subjective wellbeing and quality of life (Metheany & Coholic, 2009).

Adolescent mental health and Spirituality

Adolescence can be considered as a time of defining and evaluating relationships with ones surroundings, parents and peers. It is important to understand adolescence in the continuum of the lifespan. The experiences of childhood have a significant impact on adolescence, while adolescence lays foundation for the experiences in adulthood.

On 8 December 2014, UNICEF declared 2014 a 'devastating' year for children. Looking at the ongoing conflicts in Syria, South Sudan, Iraq, Ukraine, the Palestinian territories, and the Central African Republic, UNICEF estimated that globally about 230 million children are currently residing in countries and regions affected by violent conflicts (UNICEF, 2014). The dimensions of physical, mental, social, moral and spiritual development of the children help them to understand their capabilities and aptitude. On the other hand ignoring their basic needs, harmful surroundings and wrong company may hinder their positive mental and spiritual health directly affecting their social and physical capabilities turning a child into a delinquent (Sahmey, 2013).

Mental health with its two dimensions of absence of mental illness and presence of a well-adjusted healthy personality fulfills all requirements of an ideal person who has high tolerance to frustrations and uncertainty (Verghese, 2008). Maintaining harmony with self essentially requires spiritual content in one's personality, which helps a person to relate to the right and wrong aspects of life and equally affects their decision making ability. Spirituality can provide an eminent baseline for cure and treatment of behavioral disturbances in adolescent populations like drug abused adolescents and juvenile delinquents.

Juvenile Delinquency

Juvenile delinquency poses as a big threat with firm roots in society. There is a need to deal with such population on a psychological and social level as well, where sensitive issues can be addressed with practical and sensible techniques that not only deal with behavioral health issues but also focus social upbringing of children who are delinquents. The study 'Root Causes of Juvenile Crimes', carried out in collaboration with the Department of Women and Child Development and the UNICEF, analyzed the cause for juvenile crimes. The study revealed that a majority i.e. 94 per cent of the boys were not under parental care. Also, about 89 per cent of them came from poor economic background. The study states that those facing economic stress in their day-to-day lives are forced to work at a young age where they get in touch with anti-social groups. Most of the juveniles are school dropouts and come from families below poverty line (Kulkarni, 2013).

An evaluation of Ohio's Behavioral Health/Juvenile Justice initiative in 11 counties found the various intervention program benefits young offenders diverted from detention centers to community-based agencies to treat mental health issues and drug abuse problems (Krestchmer, Butcher, Flannery, & Singer, 2014). Juvenile offenders can be benefitted from diversion or intervention programs through community agencies with services for mental health problems and substance abuse. It was evident that when schools, families and parents fail to meet the needs of children, they take up the contrasted path which eventually leads them to criminal world (Barnet, et al., 2015).

Theory and practice of religion, spirituality on Delinquency

Many theoretical arguments answer the question of involvement of religiosity and spirituality as beneficial in eradication of criminality from society. A criminologist, in the classic theory of social control states that delinquent acts are a result of an individual's weak and broken bond to society (Hrischi, 2002). Religious institutions instills normative beliefs, spirituality and foster commitment and involvement of an individual towards the society (Hrischi, 2002). Social Learning Theory accounts that a person is less prone to delinquent behavior if exposed to pro-social behavior mechanisms (Morgan, Cox, & Matthews, 2007). Arousal Theory with a socio-biological perspective connects criminal behavior to physical or neural arousal. It is for the adrenaline rush that a delinquent behavior is initiated. Spiritual healing through religion satisfies that need of stimulation, excitement and lessens the chances of engagement in criminal behavior (Baier, Colin, Bradely, & Wright, 2001).

Assessing mental health of juveniles

Mental health assessment of juvenile offenders helps to determine how the system can address their rehabilitation needs. A shortage of aftercare services and a lack of service coordination in the juvenile justice system, suggest the need to develop correctional models that integrate and coordinate multiple services for adolescent offenders, particularly community-based approaches, both during and after their justice system involvement. Interventions can facilitate the development of healthy interpersonal relationships and improve the participant ability to interact with family, peers, and others in the community. An absence of treatment may contribute to a path of behavior that includes continued delinquency and, eventually, adult criminality. The gross displacement of religiousness and spirituality leads to socially deviant behavior giving birth to antisocial personality. This happens due to lack of social support mechanisms, love and care from parents and faulty immediate social environment.

Problem behaviors and adjustment issues affect social life of an individual, thus increasing proneness to delinquency. Social support restores sense of being loved and cared for. Many studies rule out the benefits of social support in maintaining mental and spiritual wellbeing (Unchino, 2006). Social support enhances mental health by reducing stress and spiritual healing fosters a sense and meaning in life (Cohen, 2004). Through social support and spiritual wellbeing a person develops personal control. It helps an individual to develop insight into his own thought process, and enhancement in decision making ability which is good for wellbeing (Mirowsky & Ross, 2003). Many correctional approaches have been used widely for juvenile delinquents rehabilitation. Inclusion of spirituality with such approaches can be of immense benefit to delinquent children (Peggy, 2006).

Table 1: *The Available Therapeutic Techniques for Juvenile Delinquents Worldwide* (Singh & Bhadra, 2014)

Multisystemic therapy	**Functional Family therapy**	**Wrap Around Care**	**Cognitive behavior therapy**	**Multi-dimensional Treatment foster care**
MST was effective in decreasing recidivism during the follow-up period (Schaeffer, Bourduin, Cindy, & Charles, 2005)	FFT has reflected reductions in recidivism in out-of-home placements in as much as 55 percent cases (Alexander, Pugh, Parson, & Sexton, 2000)	Successful Implementation in child welfare, special education, mental health and juvenile justice set ups around the world (Flash, 2003)	Cognitive behavioural therapy has been found to be effective with offenders with substance abuse and extreme violent behaviours (Clark, 2010)	Includes treating and hospitalization MTFC is an approach that successfully deals with minor offenders in community set ups (Fisher & Chamberlain, 2000)
(Wig & Murthy, 2003) identify effective interventions for delinquency prevention	Ideal for adolescent population at risk of getting engaged into delinquency Low dropout rates and high completion rates (Alexander, Pugh, Parson, &Sexton, 2000)	Improved mental health of children and positive outcomes (Camey & Butell, 2003)	Reduces recidivism (Clark, 2010)	Reduction I n criminal activities More suitable and effective for girls (Chamberlain & Degarnos, 2007)

In the current scenario juvenile delinquency rises as a serious problem all over the world and considering the risk involved with the adolescent population, there is a need of targeted assessment of mental health involving spiritual healing along with skills training is need of the hour. It can help in checking the risk of their reentering into the cycle of crime, thus decreasing the problem of juvenile delinquency (Singh & Bhadra, 2014).

Juvenile delinquency in India

India is facing steadily a rise in juvenile crimes. There are various reasons like poverty, changing values, social pressures, economic differences that lead more than 50 percent of below poverty line adolescent population to engage into delinquent behaviors. (Singh & Bhadra, 2014)

According to Juvenile Justice (Care and Protection of Children) Act 2000 (Ministry of Law and Justice, 2000). 'Juvenile' is defined as a person who has not completed his/her 18th year of age. It outlines two target groups: Children in need of care and protection and Juveniles in conflict with law. This act calls for the establishment of Juvenile Justice Boards (JJBs) by the State Government. JJBs must contain a Metropolitan or Judicial magistrate and two social workers where one of the workers must be a woman. For the reception and rehabilitation of JCLs the state must set up Observation Homes and Special Homes in every district or group of districts. Observation homes are institutions for juveniles while their proceedings are underway. After the proceedings of a particular case are complete, the JJB may decide that the rehabilitation of the child is not complete and hence place them in a Special Home for no longer than three years.

Life skill education training, the concept and definition

There has been a growing interest of mental health professionals in the area of life skills. As the subject matter of life skills education training relates to facilitate the development of psychosocial skills. The life skills concept has always been reflected to be consistent in its application. It has the ability to comprise knowledge, attitude, and skills to sensibly sort problems of the social situation. It develops the preparedness for self-adjustment and helps the adolescents to deal with matters relating to sex, substance abuse, gender role, family life, health, media influence, environment, ethics, and social problems efficiently (Singh & Bhadra, 2014).

Life skills address multiple aspects like, promoting self-empowerment, develops coping abilities. It prevents indulgence in alcohol and drug abuse (Bhadra, 2011). An intervention model with life skills education training has shown potential of mainstreaming the delinquent children effectively (Singh & Bhadra, 2014). Spiritual healing if focused as a part of activity module in any intervention plan, it would affect the mental wellbeing and quality of life of delinquent children and would also decrease recidivism.

Future perspective of spiritual training as a part of an intervention module through life skills education for juvenile delinquents:

Life skills in its format of activities with spiritual healing would provide an excellent support system for individuals who face difficulties in coping with life's stresses. It would help an individual to identify strengths and weaknesses, which speed up the process of attaining self-esteem and confidence (Breath the Life healing center, 2015). Spiritual life skills through a variety of empowering tools and techniques teach an individual to embody the subjective aspect of one's personality.

Spirituality as a part of intervention of Juveniles

Effectiveness of spirituality can be analyzed and validated by applying professionally equipped methods like intervention and correctional methods. Spirituality helps inculcation of human values like peace, justice, love, right conduct and action, reflection of these values help a person to innate spiritual meaningfulness in their personality and lives (Pulla, 2014). Delinquent children in a way are deprived of basic human values, which can be inculcated in them through an applicable correctional measure. Spirituality has not been considered that specifically as a coping method and resilience factor in the lives of juvenile delinquents. Understanding of the role of Spirituality in the lives of juveniles can pave the way of developing an insight into the personal crisis, mental health issues and proneness of recidivism to delinquency (Wahl, Cotton, & Monore, 2008). Changed mindset can be achieved for the population like juvenile delinquents by making them responsible of their actions. Oneness of self and serenity cannot be achieved through a fragmented and delinquent personality. As stated in the paper it has been now an established fact that spiritual healing as a part of life skills education can work wonders for delinquent children. Disbelief and displacement of spirituality develops a sense of fearlessness in the child who takes up the path of delinquency. A strong subjective sense of negativity takes hold of them and their thought process concretely establishes a subjective deviant faith that shapes a subjective deviant identity. With this Subjective deviant identity, delinquent children reason their anti-social actions. An intervention should incorporate a factor that targets this lack of positive faith, spiritual awareness and religious aspect. Spiritual healing through life skills education training can serve as an answer to this problem. Activities based on life skills education training targeting life skills like, decisions making, and empathy building through spiritual healing and training should be devised and practiced. The spiritual serenity attained through such activities will help delinquent children to develop an insight into their subjective deviant identity and switch to a better thought process that helps them in developing coping measures and enhance their decisions making abilities.

Diagram 2: *Adaption of positive behavior through spirituality among Juvenile Delinquents*

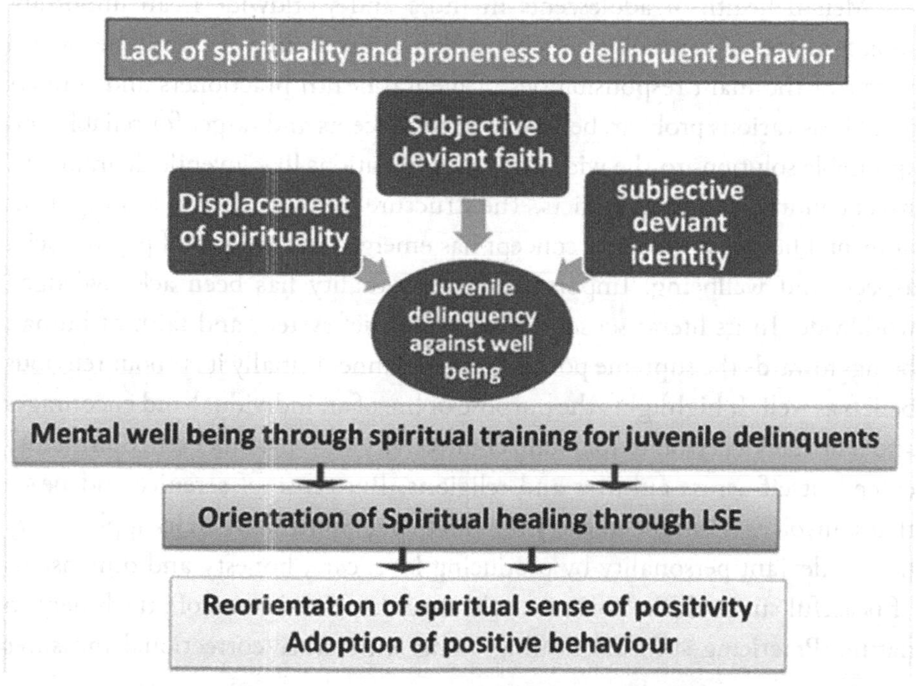

Table 2: *Format of Activities Conduced As Life Skills Education Module with Spiritual Healing For Juvenile Delinquents*

Life skills Activity	Objective of the session	Spiritual aspect
Meditation and relaxing	To help children develop rapport	Meditation the first step
Dream catching- Narration of dreams	Generate children's' interest.	Dream narration, acquaints children of their inner aspects
Question answer session	Discussion helps Children to analyze their thoughts	Open discussion with the facilitator enhanced the children's' self-esteem
Blue print of life focused their future, with a background of past	Children were able to look back and realize the wrong decisions	Life skills like Communication and interpersonal skills were targeted.

Mental health of adolescents in India and worldwide is an important subject matter of psychology, social work and psychiatry. It should be viewed as one of the main responsibilities of mental health practioners and trainers to address various problem behaviors of adolescents and target for reliable and applicable solutions to the wide array of populations like juvenile delinquents, street children and drug addicts. The structure of spirituality as a component of mental health studies as a concept has emerged in the light of psychosocial aspects and wellbeing. Importance of Spirituality has been acknowledged worldwide. In its literal sense it involves a belief system and faith of human beings towards the supreme power. In this manner initially it is about religious beliefs as well. It highlights the purpose of life of an individual and encourages and motivates a person to maintain connectivity with his inner self. Spirituality extends itself across cultures and religions. But sense of serenity and peace that it involves is unique to every human being. Spirituality in its applicability heals a deviant personality by producing love, care, honesty and dimensions of peaceful survival like patience, tolerance, hope and sense of attachment to nature. Practicing spiritual healing along with other correctional measures can help in establishing effective solutions for problems of vulnerable sections of society and maladjusted adolescent population like juvenile delinquents (Verghese, 2008).

Conclusion

It is evident with a large body of literature that spiritual healing is an eminent part of overall wellbeing. Eminent theorist like Albert Bandura has also stated that individuals are less likely to engage into delinquent behavior, if they are related and exposed to pro-social models. In this manner they are reinforced positively and spiritual healing starts with their engagement into pro-social behavior (Cox & Matthews, 2007). The spiritual component is necessary for young delinquents and it has been acknowledged by care takers that spirituality and religion based interventions and correction programs can establish a connectivity between society and the delinquent children. This would help in mainstreaming these children and would also decrease recidivism to delinquency (Larson, 2013). A module based on life skills training's has shown its competence as a flexible methodology that addresses the mental health issues of different populations in a successful manner. Spiritual healing if included as a part of life skills training intervention for juveniles can give excellent results as a corrective measure for mental health problems of juvenile delinquents worldwide.

Assessment of Spirituality

Akbar Husain and FauziaNazam

ASSESSMENT OF SPIRITUALITY

Akbar Husain* and FauziaNazam**
Department of Psychology
Aligarh Muslim University, India.

Abstract: Psychological assessment was considered as part of the scientific methodology applied to the study of mental and behavioural processes. In the last decade of the 20th century, psychologists became engaged in the assessment of spirituality. They needed to understand spiritual beliefs and motivation, spiritual behaviour and experiences of individuals. Types of assessment techniques such as spiritual well-being scales, spiritual fitness and wellness measures, spiritual intelligence measures, spiritual experiences measures, spiritual transcendent measures, spiritual orientation measures, spiritual personality measures, spiritual belief measures, and other assessment measures have been well described in this chapter. Empirical studies conducted in India in which these measures were used are also quoted here. This chapter is enriched with quantitative and qualitative approaches to spiritual assessment.

***Professor**
**** Research Scholar**

ASSESSMENT OF SPIRITUALITY

Since 1980s scholars have developed a multitude of instruments to assess various aspects of spirituality. In this chapter we review several quantitative measures that are particularly relevant for use in health settings, counselling, and therapy. Since spirituality is a multidimensional construct, so investigators need to be thoughtful about which facets they are interested in measuring; different dimension of spirituality seems to have distinct health and personality correlates. There has been a growing concern to move from a reliance on descriptive measures- which examine the practices and beliefs that people profess- to more functional measures, which highlight how individuals actually make use of their faith in their daily lives (Ellison & Levin, 1998; Gorsuch & Miller, 1999). The value of a particular instrument also depends on whether the items are confounded with the spiritual assessment one is interested in exploring and is appropriate for the purpose at hand. Measuresthat inquire if the respondent has ever had a particular type of spiritual experience may not be very sensitive in assessing changes over time (Gorsuch & Miller, 1999). In this review, we focus on standardized measures that are: (1) brief and practice for use with medical or psychiatric patients, (2) whose psychometric properties in health settings are established or at least promising, and we (3) emphasize instrument that are applicable to Hindu, Muslim as well as Christian individuals from varied age and ethnic and gender groups. Measures of spiritual coping, spiritual well-being, and other related constructs are discussed separately. Although most of these instruments are short questionnaires, in the final section we briefly note several alternate approaches to assessment.

Instruments that are most frequently used to assess the various domains of spirituality have been described here. Instruments described in this chapter are either original or revised. These measures assess religious or existential aspect of well-being. A number of investigators have argued that commonly used measures of health-related quality of life provide a narrow picture because they do not include a spiritual or existential dimension, which many patients report is important to them and which is conceptually distinct from other aspects of quality of life (Brady, Peterman, Fitchett, Mo, & Cella, 1999; Cohen, Mount, Strobel, & Bui, 1995). Measures of spiritual well-being were developed to fill this gap. Evidence supports the notion that spirituality is an important aspect of well-being. Spiritual well-being is best viewed as abroader quality of life. In our view, these measures provide information about the spiritual responses to illness i.e. religious/spiritual orientation to cope with it.

Spiritual Well-Being Measures

Human well-being and development has always been a central idea for the different branches of psychology including, health psychology, spiritual psychology, community psychology, geriatric psychology, guidance and counselling, positive psychology and personality assessment. Spiritual well-being is the inner coherence and self contentment that is obtained by the spiritual aspects of life such as connecting oneself with nature, with others in the society, maintaining unity and brotherhood, promoting growth of others. Scholars have studied different aspects of spiritual well-being including one's perceived relationship with God (Paloutzian & Ellison, 1982), purpose of life and life satisfaction (Paloutzian & Ellison, 1982), peace and faith (Peterman, Fitchett, Brady, Hrnandez, & Cella, 2002), and self-efficacy (Daleman & Frey, 2004).

Spiritual Well-Being Scale (SWBS)

This scale was developed by Paloutzian and Ellison (1982). It measures the perceived spiritual quality of life. The scale has two sub-scales, namely, *Religious Well-Being (RWB)*, and *Existential Well-Being (EWB)*. The RWBsub-scale measures one's perceived relationship with God, and the EWB sub-scale measures purpose of life and life-satisfaction. There are twenty items in SWBS, out of which ten items measures Religious Well-being, and ten items measures Existential Well-being. The SWBS can be self-administered as well as in group. The scale is paper-pencil type and it is available in two different languages (a) The English version, and (b) The Spanish version. The time taken by self administration of the scale is 10-15 minutes.

The SWBS has been popular, particularly in nursing research. It showed good internal consistency and test-retest reliability for the total score and subscales in multiple sample, mostly involving religious participants (Bufford, Paloutzian, & Ellison, 1991). Acceptable internal consistency also has been demonstrated among breast cancer patients (Mickley & Soeken, 1993; Mickley, Soeken, & Belcher, 1992) and family caregivers of hospice patients (Kirschling & Pittman, 1989). In medically healthy samples, constructive validity was supported by significant associations with meaning and purpose in life, emotional adjustment, marital adjustment, life satisfaction, self-concept, and physical health (Bufford, Paloutzian, & Ellison 1991). Studies with breast cancer patients have demonstrated significant associations between spiritual well-being scores and intrinsic religiosity (Mickley & Soeken, 1993; Mickley, Soeken, & Belcher, 1992). In some sample, scores were influenced by age and gender (Bufford, Paloutzian, & Ellison, 1991). A limitation of this instrument is a ceiling effect, so it is not useful for assessing highly religious individuals (Bufford, Paloutzian, & Ellison, 1991; Ledbetter, Smith, Vosler-Hunter, & Fischer, 1991). There has also been question about its factor structure.

These studies provide useful information about spiritual well-being scale. Spiritual Well-being Scale highlights interesting distinctions between religious and existential well-being through provision of separate subscales. This measure is an important because it assess aspects of quality of life that traditionally has been neglected in health research. However, because the items on these scales (particularly the existential or meaning subscales) seem to overlap with mood and psychological well-being, this measure may not be useful in predicting psychosocial outcome with which they are confounded.

According to Moberg (2005), the Spiritual Well-being Scale (Paloutzian & Ellison, 1982) is the most widely used instrument for the assessment of spirituality. However, it has been criticized for being biased toward Christian religiosity. Scott, Agresti, and Fitchett (1988) note that evangelical Christians often scored highest on the SWBS. Indeed, several items refer explicitly to an individual's relationship with God. Another metric that addresses this issue, and which is prototypical of how we defined the spiritual fitness domain, is Spiritual Involvement and Beliefs Scale (SIBS) (Hatch, et al., 1988), designed specifically to be inclusive of spirituality rather than religiosity. Maltby and Day (2001) argue that SIBS is indeed to reflect that "individuals can be very spiritual, without being religious." Another possible concern regarding SWBS as well as some other metrics (e.g., Fact-Sp [Functional Assessment of Chronic Illness Therapy- Spiritual Well-being) is that they describe constructs that may not necessarily be related to spirituality, such as sense of meaning and purpose, hope, or optimism. Koenig (2008) points out that these constructs are themselves often conceptualized as "well-being", which may render metrics such as the SWBS less useful for measuring spirituality. However, the SWBS is frequently used in spirituality research.

Shafi and Naseer (2014) conducted a comparative study to examine self-esteem and spiritual well-being among physically handicapped and normal adults by using Spiritual Well-being Scale (Paloutzian & Ellison, 1982) and Rosenberg's (1965) Self-Esteem Scale. Findings of their study revealed that there was no difference between the physically challenged and normal adults on spiritual well-being. However on self-esteem normal adults scored significantly higher than the physically challenged. However normal female adults scored higher than male adults on self-esteem and spiritual well-being though the difference was not significant.

Shaheen, Jahan, Shaheen, and Shaheen (2014) studied the impact of spirituality on suicidal ideation among university students by using Spiritual Well-being Scale (Paloutzian & Ellison, 1982) and Scale for Suicidal Ideation (Beck, Kovacs, & Weissman, 1979). They found that suicidal ideation was negatively correlated with spiritual well-being. Furthermore, spiritual well-being was found to be highly correlated with existential well-being and religious well-being.

The Functional Assessment of Chronic illness Therapy-Spiritual Well-being Scale (FACIT-Sp)

The FACIT-Sp was developed by Peterman, Fitchett, Brady, Hernandez, and Cella (2002). This scale was used to assess spiritual well-being. Although the measure originally assesses spiritual in cancer patients, a non-illness version created by modifying two items referring to illness. The revised scale has been used in research with non-cancer populations, including end-of-life caregivers (Desbiens & Fillion, 2007; Wasner, Longaker, Fegg, & Borasio, 2005). The FACIT-Sp consists of two subscales, measuring meaning/peace and faith, with 12 items such as: "I feel a sense of purpose in my life" and "I find strength in my faith or spiritual beliefs." Items are rated on a 5-point scale ranging from 0 (*not at all*) to 4 (*very much*). The FACIT-Sp demonstrates good internal consistency with Alpha of 0.87, 0.81, 0.88 for the full scale and for the meaning/ peace and faith subscales, respectively. The alphas for the present study were 0.82, 0.80, and 0.79.

One of the most widely used multidimensional measures of quality of life in oncology and AIDS research is the FACIT (Cella, 1997). The FACIT is a modular instrument that incorporates a general questionnaire, designed to be used with patients across different types of illness as well as a series of disease- and treatment-specific modules, which provide information about concerns that are unique to particular types of illness or treatment. Recently, a module that assesses spiritual well-being was added to the instrument (Rush Spiritual Belief Module). A large international study of patients with cancer and HIV infection (N= 1,120) demonstrated high internal consistency for the module (alpha= .87; Fitchett, Peterson, & Cella, 1996). Principle components factor analysis yielded two factors: (1) Faith and Assurance (e.g., "I find comfort in my faith or spiritual beliefs" and (2) Meaning and Purpose (e.g., "I feel peaceful"). Moderate correlations with the total quality-of-life scores and with the separate Emotional, Functional, Social, and Physical Well-being scales suggested that the Spiritual Well-being scale was reliably related to other aspects of quality of life, but offered unique information. Compared with the Faith and Assurance factor, the Meaning and Purpose factors was more strongly associated with other dimensions of quality of life. Scores on the total Spiritual Well-being scale were influenced by gender, marital status, ethnicity, religious affiliation, and more weakly, by age. Patients with no symptoms or functional disability obtained higher scores that those with more extensive symptoms or disability.

In subsequent research with cancer and HIV-infected patients (N=131), the Spiritual well-Being Scale demonstrated significant, moderate correlations with measures of organizational religiosity (r = .34), non-organizational religiosity (r = .31), and intrinsic religiosity (r = .41; Peterman, 2000). These findings offer support for the convergent validity of the scale. The instrument showed a small but significant correlation with social desirability (Peterman, Fitchett, Brady, & Cella, 2000). As expected, spiritual well-being was associated with adjustment to cancer (Cotton, Levine, Fitzpatrick, Dold, & Tang, 1999). As yet, however, little information has been presented regarding its association with other measures of well-being, life satisfaction, or existential meaning (aside from other FACIT scores).

Jhamb, Liang, Steel, Dew, Shah, and Unruh (2013) conducted a study to examine prevalence and correlates of fatigue in chronic kidney disease and end-stage renal disease. The main objective was to examine are sleep disorders a key to understanding fatigue? They used FACIT-F scores. They found that patients with chronic kidney disease and end state renal disease experience profound fatigue. Also they found that the depression symptoms, sleepiness, restless leg syndrome provided important targets to improve fatigue in those patients with advance chronic kidney syndrome.

Spirituality Index of Well-being

This scale was developed by Daaleman and Frey (2004). This scale consisted of 12 items with five point Likert-rating scales ranging from *Strongly Agree* to *Strongly Disagree*. This scale measures spiritual quality of an individual's life. The internal consistency reliability calculated by Cronbach alpha was found to be .91 for the total scale and .86 and .89 for the subscale namely, self-efficacy and life scheme respectively. Hence the scale demonstrated good reliability and validity (confirmatory factor analysis, convergent and discriminant validation).

Spirituality Assessment Inventory (SAI)

This inventory was developed by Hall and Edwards (2002). This inventory consists of 49 items of self-report type on five point Likert rating scale where 1 indicates *Not At All True of Me* and 5 indicate *Very True of me* ((Hall & Edwards, 1996, p. 233). All the items are of SAI are positively worded. The scale comprises of five sub-scale and they measures two dimensions of spiritual development: (1) Quality of relationship with God which is measured by four subscales, namely: (i) Instability in Relationship with God (9 items) (ii) Grandiosity in Relationship to God (7items) (iii) Realistic Acceptance of God (7 items), and (iv) Disappointment in Relationship with God (7 items). (2) Awareness of God which is second dimension measured by one sub-scale, namely: (i) Awareness of God (19 items). The SAl also includes an experimental Impression Management sub-scale (5 items) for the purpose of identifying the subject's test-takingapproach and to identify illusory spiritual health (Hall & Edwards, 2002, p.342). Each sub-scale of SAI has good internal consistency reliability ranging from .73-.95 (Slater et al., 2001, p. 13).

Ghani and Singh (2014) conducted a study to assess spirituality and well-being among youth by using Spirituality Assessment Inventory (Hall & Edwards, 2002) and PGI General Well-being Scale (Verma & Verma, 1989). The result of their study revealed significant difference on the subscales of SAI namely, Awareness of God, Disappointment towards God, and Realistic Acceptance among youth belonging to different communities (Hindu, Muslim, Sikh, & Christian youths). However, no significant difference was found among youths of different community on the other scales of SAI namely, instability, grandiosity, and impression management.

Spiritual Fitness and Wellness Measures

In simple and plain terminology spiritual fitness implies fitness or wellness of soul. Spiritual fitness is fitness of soul contributing to physical fitness. Young and Martin (2013) cited the definition of spiritual fitness proposed by United State Air force as "the ability to adhere to beliefs, principles, or values needed to persevere and prevail in accomplishing mission" (p.5). Spiritual fitness does not necessarily demand an individual's affiliation to a particular religion but an atheist can also be spiritually fit. However, religion can be an additive factor. There are a number of sources other than religion that can make an individual spiritually fit or healthy namely, meaning and purpose in life, self-transcendent, value-laden behaviour, sense of altruism, spiritual practices, and belief system of an individual. Young and Martin (2013) have identified four essential construct to spiritual fitness: (1) Spiritual Worldview, (2) Personal religious or spiritual practices and rituals, (3) Support from spiritual community, and (4) Spiritual coping.

Global Assessment Tool (GAT)

Global Assessment Tool is intended to assess Army Soldiers across several psychological domains, including spiritual fitness. The spiritual fitness component of the GAT primarily measures soldiers' meaning and purpose in life without intending to specifically reference or promote religiousness.

Perhaps because of its ambiguous language, the GAT has been criticized as pronouncing soldiers to be spiritually unfit unless they indicate religiousness or spiritually unfit unless they indicate religiousness or spiritual beliefs in some form (Leopold, 2011). Currently, the GAT does not provide a way to link spiritual fitness with key well-being outcomes, such as mental health. Although administering the GAT to a sample of approximately 8000 soldiers suggested initial reliability and validity. Peterson and colleagues (2011) noted that research using a shortened version to associate GAT scores with concrete indicators of well-being is still in progress.

Spiritual Fitness Inventory (SFI)

The spiritual fitness inventory was developed by U. S. Public Health Command to assess the spiritual fitness of the soldiers to tap their readiness and resilience. The conceptual understanding behind the development of this inventory is the role of spirituality behind good physical and psychological health. The SFI consists of 10 questions on 10 point rating scale. Item no. 1-3 measures an individual involvement in spiritual practices in private as well as in public. Item no. 4-6 measures the spiritual beliefs or values that provide meaning, hope, purpose and direction to an individual. Item no.7 measures the extent to which individuals' core values or beliefs provide them self-awareness. Item no. 8-9 measures transcendence the extent to which an individual benefit others over self. Item no. 10 measures the exceptional experience of an individual that has changed his or her life.

Spiritual Fitness Assessment

The spiritual Fitness Assessment (SFA) was developed by Fletcher to examine the connection between faith and health based on his research and personal beliefs in Biblical truth. It is a 40-item questionnaire assessing 18 spiritual beliefs, attitude, and practices called spiritual exercises. The 18 spiritual exercises are broken into three categories. The first category, called Beliefs and Attitudes, include the exercises Believe in God, Believe God forgives You, and Believe God's Spirit Lives in You. The second category, labeled Your Relationship with God, encompasses the exercises Read and Study the Bible, Believe In and Receive God's Love, Love God, Pray, and Mediate, Obey God, Cry Out to God, Surrender to God/Let Go, Abide in God's Presence, Have Faith, and Trust in God. The third category, named Hoe You Practice Your Faith, includes the exercises Confess Your Sins, Forgive, Attend Church/Worship with Others, Be in Community with Others, Love and Serve Others, and Think Spiritual Thoughts/Renew Your Mind (Fletcher nd). Of the 40 items (i.e., the last two on the test) are for evaluating Practice of Faith. The two remaining items (i.e., the last two on the test) are not designed to measure the spiritual exercises but rather are used to get information on religious membership and to determine if the respondent is interested in talking with professional about how to improve their spiritual health. For all items belonging Beliefs and Attitudes and Relationship with God categories, a seven-point response scale ranging from Strongly Disagree to Strongly Agree is used. For items in the Practice of faith category, eight of the items are rated using the same seven-point scale. Six of the items are rated using a seven-point scale asking about frequency of behaviour (ranging from Never to More than once a week). The last three items are rated using a different seven-point behavioural frequency scale (ranging from Never to More than once a day).

Spiritual Wellness Inventory

Spiritual Wellness Inventory was developed by Ingersoll (1995). There are 55 items in this inventory with eight point Likert rating scale ranging from *Strongly Agree* to *Strongly Disagree* measuring manifestation of spiritual wellness in daily practicing life. There are ten different dimensions obtained through factor analysis namely: (1) Conception of the Absolute/Divine (2) Meaning (3) Connectedness (4) Mystery (5) Spiritual Freedom (6) Experience/Ritual (7) Forgiveness (8) Hope (9) Knowledge/Learning, and (10) Present-centeredness.

This scale is used for the counselling of the client with particular emphasis on dimensions having low score. The high scored dimension shows client sporty system that is driven up by the counsellor through counselling relationship. On the basis of scores of client on the overall scale and dimension wise counsellor may form a case summary also.

Spiritual Intelligence Measures

The intelligence and mastery over the potentials of soul is spiritual intelligence. Soul has the capacity to bloom, it has self-actualizing potentials, and a spiritually intelligent person is able to hear the call of his soul. In more concrete terminology spiritual intelligence is the ability of transcendence: The ability to attain wisdom, unity and peace; ability to enquire and comprehend metaphysical issues of life such as life after death, connecting with God; producing and understanding the mission of life from different sources such as one's relationship with others, affiliation to an institution, altruistic feelings and helping tendency. Safara and Bhatia (2013) gave a running commentary on spiritual intelligence as a connecting force from personal to transpersonal and the self to spirit, self-awareness, awareness of transcendental relationship (p.412). An individual is born with spirituality and spiritual intelligence is the way to attain that spirituality. Assessment of spiritual intelligence is important because it is not something static but can be in developed and grow with training (Zohar & Marshall, 2000).

(a) Spiritual Intelligence Self Report Inventory (SISRI)

This inventory was developed by King (2008). There are 24 items with five point Likert rating scales (0-4) ranging from *Not At All True of Me* to *Completely True of Me.* The inventory consists of four factors or sub-scales namely: (1) *Critical Existential Thinking (CET).* It measures the ability of an individual to critically contemplate or self-interrogation of meaning in life, the purpose one have in his or her life, query of metaphysical issues such as the afterlife, death etc. (King & DeCicco, 2009) (2) *Personal Meaning Production (PMP).* This factor measures the ability of an individual to derive meaning from everyday experiences. Many scholars have identified this factor as an important aspect of spirituality (King, Speck, & Thomas, 2001; Koenig, McCullough, & Larson, 2000; Sinnott, 2002; Wink & Dillon, 2002; Worthington & Sandage, 2001) (3) *Transcendental Awareness (TA)*This factor measures the ability of an individual to transcend from physical world to the metaphysical world (King & DeCicco, 2009). The transcendent is commonplace in definitions of spirituality (e.g., King, Speck, & Thomas, 2001; Koenig, McCullough, & Larson, 2000; Martsolf & Mickley, 1998; Sinnott, 2002). (4) *Conscious State Expansion (CSE)*This factor measures the spiritual ability of an individual to identify cosmic oneness and to expand the consciousness to a level where one can identify spiritual power such as love, unity, wisdom etc. The inventory has good psychometric property as the internal consistency reliability measure by Cronbach's Alpha was found to be .95 and the split half reliability as .94. The reliability of each factor are: CET=.88, PMP=.87, TA=.89 and CSE=.94. The Factorial validity of the scale was calculated by Exploratory Factor Analysis with moderate-strong range inter-subscale correlation. This scale is mainly use for academic, research, and educational purposes.

Parveen and Feroz (2014) conducted a study to assess spiritual intelligence among university teachers consisted of three groups i.e. Professor, Readers, and Lecturers by using *Spiritual Intelligence Self Report Inventory* (King, 2008). Findings of their study revealed that professor have more critical thinking as compared to Readers and Lecturers. Furthermore, Readers were found to be high on existential thinking as compared to Lecturers. They conclude the effect of age on Professors as having high ability of critical thinking. On the *Personal Meaning Production (PMP)* subscale significant difference was found among the three groups, where Professors scored high on the PMP subscale. On the other subscale that is *Transcendental Awareness (TA)*, significant difference among the university teachers was reported.

Spiritual Experiences Measures

Spiritual Experience Index

This scale was developed by Genia (1991). There are 38 items with 6-point Likert rating scale ranging from Strongly Disagree to Strongly Agree. This scale measures spiritual maturity among people belonging to different religion and with different faith. The scale is based on developmental perspective of spirituality that how spiritual maturity unfolds with different developmental stages. Quoted by Sperry (2012) the scale correlate with five-stage model of spiritual maturity or faith, namely: (1) Egocentric faith, dominated by splitting; (2) Dogmatic faith, fairness and clearly defines obligations, defensive and utilitarian use of doctrine; (3) Transitional faith, religious searching, and doubting; (4) Reconstructed internalized faith, characterized as a more internal differentiated, and personally integrated religious system; and (5) Transcendent faith.

Spiritual Experience Index-Revised (SEI-R)

The SEI-R developed by Genia (1997) consisted of 23-items that measures faith and spiritual journey, aiming to not impose any particular faith as part of the questions. The questionnaire is a revised version of the Spiritual Experience Index. Mainly the original has been shortened, and, through factor analysis, been revised into two subscales: Spiritual Support (13 questions) and Spiritual Openness (10 questions).

Index of Core Spiritual Experience (INSPIRIT)

The INSPIRIT (Kass, Friedman, Leserman, Zuttermeister, & Benson, 1991) was designed to assess core spiritual experience, defined as (1) a distinct spiritual event that resulted in a personal conviction of the existence of God or a Higher Power and (2) which evoked feeling of closeness to God and the perception that God dwell within. The INSPIRIT contains & items (though the 7th item is actually a checklist of 12 items, with scoring based on the highest response to any of those items). Psychometric properties were examined in a sample of 83 outpatients with a variety of medical conditions who were participating in a relaxation/mediation training program. A principle-component factors analysis suggested a single underlying factor. The instrument demonstrated high internal consistency (alpha=.90). Construct validity was demonstrated by significant associations with a measure of intrinsic religiosity and with length of time participants had been practicing meditation. Moreover, responses were significantly associated with increase in a measure of Life purpose and Satisfaction (Kass, Friedman, Leserman, Zuttermeister, & Benson, 1991) and with decrease in frequency of medical symptoms over the course of the meditation programme. Women scored higher than men.

A subsequent study evaluated the instrument in a sample of 247 ambulatory cancer patients and a sample of 124 family members recruited from a surgical waiting room (VandeCreek, Ayres, & Bassham, 1995). Estimates of internal consistency were high in both settings (alphas= .79-.85). The questionnaire was consistent with that obtained by Kass, Friedman, Leserman, Zuttermeister, and Benson (1991). However, VandeCreek and colleagues advocated a different approach to scoring the final item on the instrument; they suggest that each of the questions on this 12-part checklist should be scored, not only the one with the highest score. This type of scoring resulted in high internal consistency but a different factor structure and grater discrimination among group.

Holland and colleagues (1998) found that the INSPIRIT was highly correlated with intrinsic religiosity (Religious Orientation Inventory; Allport & Ross, 1967) in medically healthy individuals (N=301), providing further support for the instrument's construct validity (using the original scoring). Other investigators have reported significant relationships with pain and health ratings among patients treated in a family practice clinic (McBride, Arthur, Brooks, & Pilkington, 1998). As yet however, we are not aware of any data concerning social desirability response bias (divergent validity) or associations with more diverse measures of religious or spiritual involvement (convergent validity). Moreover, despite the broad appeal of a measure of "spiritual experience." The references to God in this scale may limit its applicability to individuals from theistic traditions.

Daily Spiritual Experience Scale (DSES)

The DSES was developed by Underwood and Teresi (2002). This scale measures ordinary transcendent experience in daily living such as mercy, the feeling of interconnectedness, awe, gratitude etc. The prime motive of this scale is to gain understanding of qualities of spiritual life in the form of spiritual feelings and sensation rather than the cognitive articulation related to specific belief system of an individual. According to Underwood (2011) "For many people these experiences may have a highly charged emotional tone, for other, the sensation may seem less specifically direct sensation or awareness" (p.31). Thus the scale is meant keeping in view to tap the spiritual experiences of both religious group and also for those who are not comfortable with theistic view. There are 16 items of self-report type. DSES has been translated in twenty different languages which show its wider applicability.

The construct of *Daily Spiritual Experience Scale (DSES)* has been defined as the individual's perception of God or the transcendent and the perception of support or involvement of the transcendent in his or her daily life (Underwood, 1999). The spiritual experience domain is made up of various concepts, including a personal connection with God; the perception of a supportive interaction with the Transcendent; the perception that life consists of more than physical states; a sense of wholeness and internal integration or inner harmony; gratitude, compassion, and acceptance of other; and a spiritual longing or desire to be close to God (Underwood & Teresi, 2002).

Firdous and Aleem (2014) conducted a study to assess spirituality and forgiveness among college students by using *Daily Spiritual Experience Scale* (Underwood & Teresi, 2002) and *Forgiveness Scale* (Wade, 1989). Findings of their study revealed that both male and female did not differ significantly on their daily spiritual experience and forgiveness, the reason being that both may have similar family environment, beliefs, education, and training.

Sharma, Haroon, Siddqui, and Khatoon (2014) conducted a study for measuring the impact of religious practices on spirituality among Hindus and Muslims by using Daily Spiritual Experience Scale (Underwood & Terresi, 2002) and Daily Religious Practices Checklist (DRPC). Findings of their study revealed significant difference between Muslims and Hindus on daily spiritual experience. Muslims scored significantly higher than Hindus. Significant difference was not found between the mean score females as well as between the males of the two groups. While comparing the two religious practices *Jaap* and *Tasbih* recitation it was found that *Tasbih* reciters are significantly higher on spiritual experience than *Jaap* reciters. They also found non-significant relationship between daily religious rituals and daily spiritual experience showing no impact of daily religious rituals and daily spiritual experience, attributing to the fact that people perform rituals as a religious obligation without understanding the core essence.

Majid, Khan, and Dixit (2014) conducted a study to examine daily spiritual experience and subjective well-being among Hindu and Muslim youths by using *Daily Spiritual Experience Scale* (Underwood & Teresi, 2002) *and Subjective Well-being Scale* (Sell & Nagpal, 1992). Their findings revealed that Muslim youths scored higher on daily spiritual experience scale as compared to Hindi youths. They also reported that Hindu youth scoring higher on spiritual well-being as compared to Muslim youths.

Use: The scale can be used in the area of health studies, longitudinal studies of change in spiritual experiences over time, evaluation of particular spiritual programme. It can also be used in counselling, religious organization, and treatment of addiction (Underwood, 2011).

Spiritual Transcendent Measures

Spiritual transcendence is the person's perceived transcendental experiences such as realizing relationship with God, feeling of connectedness to all human being, connecting oneself with the environment and acting for its protection, transcending oneself from mere physical world to the metaphysical world, search for Wisdom, thinking about cosmic unity, peace and perception of beauty. According to Narimani, Babolan, and Ariapooran (2011) "Spiritual transcendence refers to the ability of individuals to view life from a larger, more objective perspective and find a deeper sense of meaning" (p.136). Further they view the capacity to transcendence as suppressing own need for the welfare of other or the larger group.

Spiritual Transcendent Scale (STS)

This scale was developed by Reker (2003) with the aim to fill void and to provide a reliable and valid operational measure of spirituality. The STS is a multidimensional scale consisting of 60 items representing three dimensions: Inner- connectedness, Human Compassion, and Connectedness with nature. Response are based on a 7-point Liker rating scale ranging from "Strongly Agree" to "Strongly Disagree". A high score reflects higher level of spiritual transcendence. The original questionnaire contained 32 items that assessed components of inner connectedness (e.g., self-identity, harmony, peace, comfort, fulfillment, spiritual coping) but only a very small number of items measured connectedness with nature and human compassion. Using a rational, logical approach to test development, the scale was extended by the addition of items thought to measure the human compassion and connectedness with nature component of spiritual transcendence.

Narimani, Babolan, and Ariapooran (2011) conducted a study to examine the role of spiritual transcendence on predictives of competitive anxiety and self-confidence in among athletes by using *Spiritual Transcendence Scale* and Competitive State Anxiety inventory-2 (Martens, Burton, Vealey, Bump, & Smith, 1990). Findings of their study revealed that somatic anxiety was positively associated with self-transcendence among athletes. Furthermore, they found that the two dimensions of spiritual transcendence namely *Prayer Fulfillment* and *Universality* were found to be positively predicting self-confidence among athletes. But another dimension of spiritual transcendence namely connectedness did not predict self-confidence in athletes. Conclusively the increase in the spiritual transcendence have an incremental effect on athletes' self-confidence.

Assessment of Spirituality and Religious Sentiments (ASPIRES)

This inventory was developed by Piedmont (2010). The inventory consists of 35 items measuring two dimensions: (1) Spiritual Transcendence: The motivational capacity to create a broad sense of personal meaning for one's life, and (2) Religious Sentiments: The extent to which an individual is involved in and committed to the precepts, teachings, and practices of specific religious tradition. Spiritual transcendence is measured by three correlated facets scales: (i) Prayer Fulfilment (PF): The ability to create a personal space that enables one to feel a positive connection to some larger reality (ii) Universality (UN): The belief in a larger meaning and purpose to life; and Connectedness (CN): Feelings of belongingness and responsibility to larger human reality that cuts across generations and groups. Religious Sentiments consist of two correlated dimensions: (i) Religious Involvement (RI): Which reflects how actively involved a person is in performing various religious rituals and activities, and (ii) religious Crisis (RC): Which examines whether a person may be experiencing problems, difficulties, or conflicts with God of their understanding.

Piedmont (2010) presented information on the reliability and validity of this scale. Alpha reliabilities for the self-report scales ranged from .60 (CN) to .95 (PF) with a mean alpha of .82. Structurally, the Spiritual Transcendence Scale (STS) consists of three correlated dimensions respectively defined by the items of the PF, UN, and CN subscales. The Religious Sentiments dimension was shown to have two subscales, which consisted of the items of the RI and RC scales. Scores on these scales shown to predict significantly a range of psychological outcomes (e.g., well-being, self-esteem, prosocial behaviour, social support, and sexual attitudes), even after the predictive effects of personality were removed. Support for the structural, predictive, and incremental validity of the ASPIRES has been demonstrated across religious faiths, culture, and language (Piedmont, 2007; Piedmont & Leach, 2002; Piedmont, Werdel, & Fernando, 2009; Rican & Janosova, 2010).

Bano and Hasnain (2014) conducted a study on spiritual orientation among believers and non-believers across gender by using *ASPIRES* and *Spiritual Assessment Scale.* The findings of their study did not show significant difference between male and female non-believers. Moreover, religious orientation was not found to have influence on spiritual orientation. Both believers and non-believers were found to have same level of spiritual orientation. They concluded that the personal value system and practices seem to affect the concern for the welfare of others, tendency of forgiveness, and tolerance, which take the spiritual orientation over religious beliefs and gender.

Brief Multidimensional Measure of Religiousness and Spirituality (BMMRS)

The BMMRS (Fetzer Institute & The national Institute on Aging Working group, 1999) was developed as a health research tool for exploring the relation between multi religiousness/spirituality dimensions and health. In addition to the popular use of the BMMRS in adult research, its use with younger population including adolescents and college students has been supported

(Harris, Sherritt, Holder, Kulig, Shier, & Knight, 2008; Masters et al., 2009) and has increased in recent years (Desrosiers & Miller, 2007; Dew, Daniel, Goldston, & Koenig, 2008). The instrument consists of 40 items and ask respondents to rate their level of agreement to statements related to various aspects of religiosity/spirituality, using a 4-, 6-, or 8-point Likert scale. The BMMRS manual reports similar patterns with reliability coefficient a little higher, ranging from .54 for Negative Religious Coping to .91 for Daily Spiritual Experience. Although some subscales seem to need psychometric improvements, the BMMRS is one of the most widely accepted and used measure in the field of religion and spirituality research at the present times.

Johnstone, Yoon, Cohen, Schopp. McCormack, Campbell, and Smith (2012) conducted a study to examine the relationship between spirituality, religious practices, personality factors, and health for five different faith traditions including Buddhists, Catholics, Jews, Muslims, and Protestants by using Brief Multidimensional Measure of Religiousness/Spirituality (Fetzer Institute & The national Institute on Aging Working group, 1999) and NEO-FFI (Costa & McCrae, 1992). Findings of their study revealed that individuals with different faith traditions did not differ in terms of physical or mental health. Individuals with different faith tradition were found to have different level of spirituality and religiosity as well as different personality characteristics.

Spirituality Assessment Scale (SAS)

The SAS (Howden, 1992) is a 28item scale constructed to measure spirituality. Spirituality is conceptualized by four attributes: purpose and meaning in life, innerness or inner resourcefulness, unifying interconnectedness and transcendence. The SAS has 6-point Likert rating scale with responses ranging from *Strongly disagree* to *Strongly agree* to statements such as, "I have a general sense of belongingness". A high score on each subscale indicates greater spirituality. The alpha coefficient of the four subscales, Purpose and Meaning in Life, Inner Resourcefulness, Unifying Interconnectedness, and Transcendence are reported to be .91, .79, .80, and .71 respectively. The composite SAS demonstrated good internal consistency with Cronbach's Alpha of .92 (Howden, 1992).

Azmi and Fatima (2014) conducted a study to examine spirituality as a determinant of achievement motivation among adolescents by using Spirituality

Assessment Inventory (Howden, 1992) and Achievement Motivation Scale (Beena, 1986). Findings of their study revealed that high spirituality is related to higher achievement motivation among adolescents.

Another study was conducted by Fatma and Rizvi (2014) to assess academic performance as a function of spirituality among science and arts stream students by using *Spirituality Assessment Scale* (Howden, 1992). The findings of their study revealed no difference between the two groups in their level of spirituality. Showing that educational stream does not make any difference in the level of spirituality of individuals. However the effect of spirituality on academic performance was found to be significant.

Jahan and Aleem (2014) studied spirituality and values among BPO by using Spirituality Assessment Scale (Howden, 1992) and Schwartz Value inventory (Schwartz, 1992, 1994). No significant gender difference was found among the BPOs on the subscales of *Spirituality Assessment scale* namely Purpose in Life, Inner Resources, Unifying Interconnectedness, and Transcendence. Furthermore on Values Inventory significant gender difference was found on the values namely power and security. They also carried out correlational analysis to find out the relationship betweenspirituality and values. Significant positive relationship was found between the between the dimension of spirituality namely, purpose in life and values tradition, inner resources and benevolence and unifying connectedness among male employees. Among female employees significant positive correlation was found between unifying connectedness and tradition, transcendence and benevolence, purpose in life and universalism, transcendence and achievement, and between purpose in life and security.

Khatoon, Siddiqui, and Akhtar (2014) studied spirituality among adolescents belonging to Muslim and Hindu community by using *Spirituality Assessment Scale* (Howden, 1992). They found significant difference between Muslim and Hindu adolescents on their spirituality where Muslim adolescents scored higher on spirituality as compared to Hindu adolescents. They also found significant gender difference on spirituality where females scored higher than male adolescents.

Hilal, Saeeduzzafar, Siddiqui, and Hameed (2014) conducted a study to examine depression among students having different degree of spirituality by using *Spirituality Assessment Scale* (Howden, 1992) and Beck Depression Inventory-II (Beck & Brown, 1996). They categorized the sample into high, moderate, and low spirituality groups. Findings of their study revealed that there was no significant difference between high spirituality group and moderate spirituality group on depression. However, significant difference was found between the high and low spirituality group on depression. Furthermore, significant difference was found between the moderate and low spirituality group on depression.

Spirituality Attitude Scale

The scale was developed by Husain, Jahan, Nishat, Siddique, and Akram (2011). The SAS consisted of 31 items designed to measure sense of purpose and spiritual discipline. Respondents answer each question using a 5-point Likert rating scale ranging from *Strongly Disagree* to *Strongly Agree.* The reliability of the sub-scale were found to be .84 (sense of purpose factor) and 0.72 (spiritual discipline factor).

Fazli, Khan, and Husain (2014) conducted a correlational study to examine attitude towards spirituality and self-efficacy among nursing and medical students by using Spirituality Attitude Scale (Husain, Jahan, Nishat, Siddiqui, & Akram, 2011). They found significant positive correlation between spirituality attitude and self-efficacy among both the groups. They also reported significant positive relation between sense of purpose and general self-efficacy, sense of purpose and specific self-efficacy, and maintenance of discipline and specific self-efficacy among students pursuing MBBS. Significant correlation was found between maintenance of discipline and self-efficacy among both nursing and MBBS students.

Spiritual Orientation Measures

Spiritual Orientation Inventory (SOI)

The inventory was developed by Elkins, Hedstrom, Hughes, Leaf and Sanders (1988) comprised of 85 items which are unequally divided into nine subscales. The subscales consist of the following: *Transcendent dimension, Meaning and Purpose in Life, Mission in Life, Sacredness in Life, Material Values, Altruism, Idealism, Awareness of the tragic and fruits of Spirituality.* The subscale, in turn embodies the major features of spirituality identified by the test authors through their content analysis relevant literature.

Spiritual Orientation Inventory (SOI)

It was developed by Parvez (2001) designed to assess the extent of spiritual orientation among the people who pay visit to holy shrines. The SOI has 24 items. Each item was responded as 'Yes' or 'No', and scored as Yes=1 and No=0. There were five negatively keyed items- 3, 10, 19, 22 and 27, for which the scoring was done in reverse direction. That is, score 1 was assigned to 'No' answer and 0 was assigned to 'Yes' answer. The split-half reliability was found to be 0.89.

Spiritual Orientation Questionnaire (SOQ)

This questionnaire was developed by Husain, Hashim, and Rosli (2008) contained six questions concerning the assessment of spiritual orientation among people. The six questions could be referred to as the measurement of spiritual beliefs, importance, and practice.

Spiritual Meaning Scale (SMS)

This scale was developed by Pargament and Mahoney (2001). The SMS comprised of 20 item on 5-point Likert rating scale ranging from Strongly Agree to Strongly Disagree and it has two dimensions: (i) Theistic (SMS-T), and (ii) Non- Theistic (SMS-NT). An example of theistic item is, "The goals of my understanding of God". An example item that measure the non-theistic component is "My spiritual beliefs giving meaning to my life's joys and sorrows." A high score on each subscale indicates high spiritual meaning. In the current study, the alpha coefficient of the theistic and non-theistic subscales were found to be .98 and .94 respectively.

Spiritual Personality Measures

Ummatic Personality Inventory

This inventory was developed by Othman (2010). It is a measurement tool consisting of items which were constructed based on the values adapted from the Qur'an and *Surrah*. The term *Ummatic Personality* refers to the characteristics of an individual which is in accordance with the Islamic spirituality as described in the Qur'an and Sunnah. In the Qur'an (Al-Isra': 85). The findings revealed that with the use of PCA, *Ibadah* construct produced 5 significant factors, *Amanah* construct generated 5 factors and *Ilm* construct produced 2 factors.

Spiritual Personality Inventory (SPI)

The SPI was developed by Husain, Luqman, and Jahan (2012) was used to assess spiritual personality. The SPI consisted of 32 items with a 5-point Likert format. The SPI assesses two dimensions of spiritual personality, namely, 'noble attitude toward others' and 'moral rectitude'. The split-half correlation 0.82 was found for the whole sample. The Cronbach's coefficient alpha for the whole sample was found to be 0.86. The Cronbach's alpha for the two factors, namely, *noble attitude toward others* and *moral rectitude* were found to be 0.84 and 0.74 respectively. The noble attitude toward others factor was found to be highly correlated with moral rectitude factor (r=0.70).

Anas (2014) conducted a study to assess spiritual personality among students pursuing social work and psychology as the streams of their study by using *Spiritual Personality Inventory (*Husain, Luqman, & Jahan, 2012). Findings of his study revealed that students pursuing psychology course scored higher on the two sub-scales of *Spiritual Personality Inventory,* namely, *Nobel Attitude towards Others* and *Moral Rectitude* showing that more spiritual inclination of personality among students studying psychology than those studying social work.

Spiritual Belief Measures

Spiritual Belief Scale (SBS)

The scale was developed by Schaler (1996) which measures spiritual thinking. Spiritual thinking basically refers to belief in metaphysical power that influences personal experience. The scale consists of 8 items with two subscales namely: (1) *Release-gratitude humility-* This dimension consists of six items e.g. "I know that all the best things in my life have come to me through God". The reliability of this factor was found to be alpha .95 ((Schaler, 1996) and (2) *Tolerance-* This dimension consists of two items e.g. "I believe there are many ways to know God and that my way". The alpha for this factor was found to be .53. The items have to be responded on five-point Likert rating scale ranging from *Strongly Disagree*=1 to *Strongly Agree*=5, where higher score indicate stronger spiritual belief. The internal consistency reliability reported as alpha .92 for standardized items (Schaler, 1996).

Spiritual Maturity Scale

Spiritual maturity was measured with four items, altered from the forced choice Faith Development Scale (Leak, Loucks, & Bowlin, 1999). For each item, participants were asked to choose their relative preference of one statement over another using a bipolar, 7-point scale (e.g., "It is very important for me to critically examine my religious beliefs and values" vs. "It is very important for me to accept the religious beliefs and values of my church"). This construct is meant to assess the degree to which an individual displays open-mindedness, questioning, and complexity in regard to their faith. Finally, identification as a spiritual exemplar was measured with two items: "I serve as a model for others in my congregation for how to live a spiritual life" and "I provide a good example of how to live a spiritual life."

Structured Interview

The Royal Free interview for Religious and Spiritual Beliefs (King, Speck, & Thomas, 1995) is a structured interview that provides quantitative data concerning medical patient's religious beliefs and their perceptions about their illness. This interview differentiates among respondents who express (1) a "religious" world view (i.e., affiliation with a faith tradition), (2) a "spiritual" world view (i.e., belief in a power beyond oneself, in the absence of a specific religion), and (3) a "philosophical" view (i.e., a search for existential meaning without reference to a power beyond oneself). Separate scales provide scores for Spiritual Beliefs and for Philosophical Beliefs; in addition, individual item assess participants' beliefs about the cause and the meaning of their illness. Research with hospital staff and patients from a general medical practice suggested good internal consistency for the Spiritual Scale (alpha = .81) but poor reliability for the Philosophical scale (alpha = .60; King, Speck, & Thomas, 1995; Seybold, 1999). Test- retest reliability, assessed among hospital staff, was good for both scales and for each of the individual items. A group of highly religious respondents (e.g. chaplain, ministers) obtained higher score on the spiritual scale than did staff and patients. There is no additional information about validity.

Spiritual Values Scale (SAS)

The Spiritual Values Scale (SAS) was developed by Nazam, Husain, and Khan (2015). The scale comprised of 27 items on six points Likert rating scale ranging from *Strongly Agree* to *Strongly Disagree.* There are five factors consisting of varied number of items, namely, *Altruistic Values, Humanistic Values, Personal Values, Divine Values, and Affective Values.* The SVS is scored in the direction of high spiritual values i.e. higher the score higher the subject possess spiritual values along with the dimension described. The internal consistency reliability of the scale is 0.911 and factorial validity of the scale was also found to be high with inter factorial validity more than .40 showing that all the factors are measuring the same construct (Nazam, Husain, & Khan, 2015).

Other Assessment Measures

Spiritual Strivings

Goal measures offer a promising avenue for exploring religious involvement. Using open-ended questions and self-rating, methodologies have been developed to assess how motivational variables, variously constructed as personal strivings (Emmons, 1999). Life tasks (Cantor, 1990), or personal projects (Little, 1989), are expressed in everyday life. More recently, this approach to assessing personal goals has been used to explore spiritual or existential striving (e.g., attempts to "deepen my relationship with God" "be more forgiving"; Emmons, 1999). This methodology provides both idiographic and nomothetic data.

Projective Assessment

The Spiritual Themes and Religious Response Test (STARR; Saur & Saur, 1993; Brokaw, 1999) illustrated the adaptation of projective techniques for assessment of spirituality. The test includes 11 stimulus cards modelled on the Thematic Apperception Test (TAT). Respondents are invited to tell a story about the people depicted in the black and white photographs; alternatively, a number of other instructions and inquiries can be used. Several scoring system have been developed. Inter-rater reliability ranged from .46 to .88 for the 12 scoring dimensions developed by Misner (1995, cited in Brokaw, 1999), who also reported evidence of concurrent validity.

Measurement-related Issues

Measurement itself is a barren, the key to good measurement is the sophisticated and fertility of the theories and ideas within which the measuring instruments are grounded. A long-lasting concern in the psychology of spirituality is that its empirical study has lacked coherence as a result of an absence of guiding theoretical framework or models. Sometimes our object of the study especially spirituality is not clearly defined, including the literature that involves measurement development. Kapuscianski and Masters (2010) found tremendous diversity and lack of operational agreement among the 24 recent measures (19 of which were published after 1999) of spirituality they reviewed. Among many concerns listed, they emphasized three in particular: (1) the lack of emphasis on behavioral elements of spirituality despite the importance of behaviour to the holistic understanding of psychological makeup; (2) the lack of consensus regarding language associated with traditional religious beliefs and behaviour (they found that only about 33% of the measures included religious elements in their definition of spirituality, but 65% had individual items that contained traditional religious language), including in many studies an apparent disregard or even lack of awareness of the importance of this issue to their conceptualization of spirituality; and (3) the lack of clearly defined psychologically based transcendent element.

Measures of spirituality sometimes lack sensitivity to cultural variables (Chatters, Taylor, & Lincoln, 2002), a deficiency clearly related to the problem of adequate sample representation. Of course, differences in religious and spiritual perspective, affiliations, and practices are often related to cultural factors.

Future Agenda and Conclusion

Assessment instruments should avoid obscuring important differences among the spiritual belief, spiritual experiences, and spiritual dimensions for example, by combining them arbitrary into a total score.

Spirituality assessment is multifaceted and covers new dimensions. Hence standardization of instruments and ethical standards need to be maintained in many spiritual practices and experiences dimensions.

In order to validate theoretical constructs as suggested by Husain (2011, 2015) should be tested in the immense variety of prospective empirical studies. An in-depth knowledge of an individual's belief and experiences cannot rely on psychological tests, but need also to integrate qualitative information to mere quantitative measures.

Spirituality models of man as proposed by Husain (2013) includes bodily, mental, and emotional states. There are three states which deal with response associated with your life and helps you to interact in the outside world. The trinity states of spirituality may be the best resource for the development of personality of an individual in a spiritual direction.

References

Allport, G. W., & Ross, J. M. (1967). Personal religious orientation and prejudice. *Journal of Personality and Social Psychology, 5*, 432-443.

Amrita, S., Haroon, S. N., Siddiqui, R., & Khatoon, N. (2014). Impact of religious practices on spirituality among Hindus and Muslims. In A. Husain, S. Kaneez, & M. Jahan. (Eds.). *Studies in spiritual psychology* (pp.74-84), New Delhi: Research India Press.

Anas, M. (2014). Assessment of spiritual personality among students of social work and psychology. In A. Husain, S. Kaneez, & M. Jahan. (Eds.). *Studies in spiritual psychology* (pp.177-182), New Delhi: Research India Press.

Azmi, S., & Fatima, M. (2014). Spirituality as a determinant of achievement motivation among adolescents. In A. Husain, S. Kaneez, & M. Jahan. (Eds.). *Studies in spiritual psychology* (pp.85-94), New Delhi: Research India Press.

Bano, S., & Hasnain, N. (2014). Spiritual orientation among believers and Non-believers across the gender. In A. Husain, S. Kaneez, & M. Jahan. (Eds.). *Studies in spiritual psychology* (pp.14-25), New Delhi: Research India Press.

Beck, A. T., & Steer, R. A., & Brown, G. K. (1996). *BDI-II, Beck Depression Inventory: Manual (2nd)*. Boston: Harcourt Brace & Company.

Beck, A. T., Kovacs, M., & Weissman, A. (1979). Assessment of suicidal intension: The scale for suicidal ideation. *Journal of Counseling and Clinical Psychology, 44*, 343-352.

Beena, S. (1986). Manual of achievement motivation scale. Agra: *Agra Psychological Research Cell.*

Between Spirituality and Eysenck's Personality Dimensions. *Personality and*

Brady, M. J., Peterman, A. H., Fitchett, G., Mo, M., & Cella, D. (1999). A case for including spirituality in quality of life measurement in oncology. *Psycho-Oncology, 8*, 417-428.

Brokaw, R. K. (1999). Spiritual themes and religious response tests. In P. C. Hill & R. W. Hood, Jr. (Eds.), *Measures of religiosity* (pp.371-374). Birmingham, AL: Religious Education Press.

Bufford, R. K., Paloutzian, R. F., & Ellison, C. W. (1991). Norms for the Spiritual Well-being Scale. *Journal of Psychology and Theology, 19*, 56-70.

Cantor, N. (1990). From thought to behavior: "Having" and "Doing" in the study of personality and cognition. *American Psychologist, 45*, 735-750.

Cella, D. F. (1997). *Functional Assessment of Chronic Illness Therapy Manual*, Version 4. Evanston, IL: Evanston Northwestern Healthcare, Centre on Outcomes Research and Education.

Chatters, L. M., Taylor, R. J., & Lincoln, K. D. (2002). Advances in the measurement of religiosity among older African Americans: Implications for health and mental health researchers. In J. H. Skinner & J. A. Teresi (Eds.), *Multicultural measurement in older populations* (pp.199-220). New York: Springer.

Cohen, S. R., Mount, B. M., Bruera, E., Provost, M. Rowe, J., & Tong, K. (1997). Validity of the McGill Quality of Life Questionnaire in the palliative care setting: A multi-centre Canadian study demonstrating the importance of the existential domain. *Palliative Medicine, 11*, 3-20.

Costa, P. T., & McCrae, R. R. (1992). Revised NEO personality inventory (NEO PI-R) and the NEO five factor inventory (NEO-FFI) professional manual. Odessa, FL: Psychological Assessment Resources.

Cotton, S. P., Levine, E. G., Fitzpatrick, C. M., Dold, K. H., & Tang, E. (1999). Exploring the relationship among spiritual well-being, quality of life, and psychological adjustment in women with breast cancer. *Psycho-Oncology, 8*, 429-438.

Daaleman, T. P., & Frey, B. B. (2004). The Spirituality Index of Well-Being: A new instrument for health-related quality of life research. *Annals of Family Medicine, 2*, 499-503.

Desbiens, J., & Fillion, L. (2007). Coping strategies, emotional outcomes and spiritual quality of life in palliative nursing. *International Journal of Palliative Nursing,13*, 291-300.

Desrosiers, A., & Miller, L. (2007). Relational spirituality and depression, and in adolescent girl. *Journal of Clinical Psychology, 63*, 1021-1037. doi:10.1002/jclp.20409

Dew, R. E., Daniel, S., Goldston, D., & Koenig, H. (2008). Religion, spirituality, and depression in adolescent psychiatric outpatients. *Journal of Nervous and Mental Disease, 196*, 247-251.doi.10.1097/NMD.0b013e3181663002

Elkins, D. N., Hedstrom, L. J., Hughes, L. L., Leaf, J. A., & Saunders, C. (1988). Toward a humanistic-phenomenological spirituality. *Journal of Humanist Psychology, 28*, 5–18

Ellison, C. G., & Levin, J. S. (1998). The religion-health connection: Evidence, theory, and future directions. *Health Education and Behaviour, 25*, 700-720.

Emmons, R.A. (1999). *The psychology of ultimate concerns: Motivation and spirituality in personality.* New York: The Guilford Press.

Fatma, N., & Rizvi, K. (2014). Academic performance as a function of spirituality among science and arts stream students. In A. Husain, S. Kaneez, & M. Jahan. (Eds.). *Studies in spiritual psychology* (pp.110-115), New Delhi: Research India Press.

Fazli, M, R., Khan, M. I., & Husain, A. (2014). Attitude towards spirituality and self-efficacy among nursing and medical students. In A. Husain, S. Kaneez, & M. Jahan. (Eds.). *Studies in spiritual psychology* (pp.130-134), New Delhi: Research India Press.

Fetzer Institute & National Institute on Aging Working group. (1999). *Multidimensional measurement of religiousness/spirituality for use in health research: A report of the Fetzer Institute on Aging Working Group.* Kalmazoo, MI: Fetzer Institute. Retrieved from https;//www.gem-beta.org/Public/DownloadMeasure.aspx?mid=1155

Firdous, S., & Aleem, S. (2014). Spiritual orientation among believers and Non-believers across the gender. In A. Husain, S. Kaneez, & M. Jahan. (Eds.). *Studies in spiritual psychology* (pp.41-47), New Delhi: Research India Press.

Firoz, I., & Parveen, A. (2014). Spiritual intelligence among university teachers. In A. Husain, S. Kaneez, & M. Jahan. (Eds.). *Studies in spiritual psychology* (pp.61-73), New Delhi: Research India Press.

Fitchett, G., Peterman, A. H., & Cella, D. F. (1996). *Spiritual beliefs and quality of life in cancer and HIV patients.* Paper presented at the meeting of the Society for the Scientific Study of Religion, Nashville, TN.

Fletcher, D. (2007a). Spiritual fitness assessment. Retrieved from http://www.faithandhealthConnection. org/wpcontent/uploads/2007/11/spiritual_fitness_assessment_____4_8_071.pdf.

Fletcher, D. (2007b). An introduction to spiritual exercises for a healthier life. Faith and Fitness Magazine. Retrieved from http://www.faithandfitness.net/files/pdf/Faith%20and%Health.pdf.

Fletcher, D. (2007c). Measuring your spiritual fitness. Faith and Fitness Magazine. Retrieved fromhttp://www.faithandfitness.net/files/pdf/measuring%20your%20spirituali%20Fitness.pdf. Journal of Religion Health 123

Fletcher, D. (nd). Spiritual fitness & health assessment. Retrieved September 2, 2009 from http://www.faith andhealthconnection.org/the_connection/what-your-can-do/spiritual-exercises-spiritual-fitness-assessment/

Genia, V. (1991). The spiritual experience index: A measure of spiritual maturity. *Journal of Religion and Health, 30*, 337-347.

Genia, V. (1997). The spiritual experience index: Revision and reformulation. *Review of Religious Research, 38*, 344-361.

Ghnai, S., & Singh, B. (2014). Spirituality and well-being in youth. In A. Husain, S. Kaneez, & M. Jahan. (Eds.). *Studies in spiritual psychology* (pp.26-40), New Delhi: Research India Press.

Gorsuch, R. L., & Miller, W. R. (1999). Assessing spirituality. In W. R. Miller (Ed.), *Integrating spirituality into treatment: Resources for practitioners* (pp. 47-64). Washington, DC: American Psychological Association.

Hall, T. W.,& Edwards, K. J. (1996). The initial development of and factor analysis of the Spiritual Assessment Inventory. *Journal of Psychology and Theology, 24*, 233-246.

Hall, T. W., & Edwards, K. J. (2002). The spiritual Assessment Inventory: A theistic model and measure for assessing spiritual development. *Journal for the Scientific Study of Religion, 41*, 341-357.

Harris, S. K., Sherritt, L. R., Holder, D. W., Kulig, J., Shier, L. A., & Knight, J. R. (2008). Reliability and validity of the brief multidimensional measure of religiousness/spirituality among adolescents. *Journal of Religion and Health, 47*, 438-457. doi:10.1007/s10943-007-9154-x

Hatch, R. L., Burg, M. A., Naberhaus, D. S., & Hellmich, L. K. (1998). The spiritual involvement and beliefs scale: Development and testing of a new instrument. *The Journal of Family Practice, 46*(6), 476–486.

Hilal, H., Saeeduzzafar, Siddiqui, Z. U., & Hameed, S. (2014). Depression among students having different degree of spirituality. In A. Husain, S. Kaneez, & M. Jahan. (Eds.). *Studies in spiritual psychology* (pp.193-201), New Delhi: Research India Press.

Holland, J. C., Kash, K. M., Passik, S., Gronert, M. K., Sison, A., Lederberg, M., Russak, S. M., Baider, L., & Fox, B. (1998). A brief spiritual beliefs inventory for use in quality of life research in life-threatening illness. *Psycho-oncology, 7*, 460-469.

Howden, J. W. (1992). *Development and psychometric characteristics of the spirituality assessment scale.* Ann Arbor: Texas Woman's University, UMI Dissertation Services.

Husain, A. (2011). *Spirituality and holistic health: A psychological perspective.* New Delhi: Prasad Psycho Corporation.

Husain, A. (2013). Trinity states of spirituality: Bodily, mental and emotional. In N. Sanyal (Ed.) *Spirituality and Positive Psychology* (pp. 199-215). Kolkata: Ramakrishna Mission Institute of Culture.

Husain, A. (2015). A new approach to defining applied spirituality. In N. Sanyal (Ed.) *Spirituality and Positive Psychology* (2nd Edition). Kolkata: Ramakrishna Mission Institute of Culture.

Husain, A., Hashim, O., & Rosli, N. A. (2008). Spiritual orientation among Malaysians. In A. Husain, S., Jamaluddin, O. Hahim, L. S. Cheong, M. Md. Nor, & H. Sulaiman (Eds.), *Horizons of Spiritual Psychology*(pp.263-272). New Delhi: Global Vision Publishing House.

Husain, A., Jahna, M., Nishat, A., Siddique, R. N., & Akram, M. (2011). *Development of spirituality attitude scale.* New Delhi: Prasad Psycho Corporation.

Husain, A., Luqman, N., & Jahan, M. (2012). *Spiritual personality inventory manual.* New Delhi: Prasad Psycho Corporation.

Ingersoll, R. E. (1995). Construction and initial validation of the spiritual wellness inventory. Unpublished doctoral dissertation. Kent State University.

Jaan, U., & Aleem, S. (2014). Spirituality and values among BPO employees. In A. Husain, S. Kaneez, & M. Jahan. (Eds.). *Studies in spiritual psychology* (pp.166-176), New Delhi: Research India Press.

Jhamb, M., Liang, K., Steel, J., Dew, J. L., Shah, M. A., & Unruh, M. (2013). Prevalence and correlates of fatigue in chronic kidney disease and end-stage renal disease: are sleep disorders a key to understanding fatigue? *American Journal of Nephrology, 38*(6), 489-95. doi: 10.1159/000356939.

Johnstone, B., Yoon, D. I., Cohen, D., Schopp. L. H., McCormack, G., Campbell, J., & Smith, M. (2012). Relationships among spirituality, religious practices, personality factors, and health for five different faith traditions. *Journal of Religion and Health, 51*(4), 9615-8. DOI 10.1007/s10943-012-9615-8SS

Kapuscinski, A. N., & Masters, K. S. (2010). The current status of measures of spirituality: A critical review of scale development. *Psychology of Religion and Spirituality, 2,* 191-205.

Kass, J. D., Friedman, R., Leserman, J., Zuttermeister, P. C., & Benson, H. (1991). Health outcomes and a new index of spiritual experience. *Journal of the Scientific Study of Religion, 30,* 203-211.

Khatoon, N. J., Siddiqui, Z. U., & Akhtar, Z. (2014). Spirituality among Hindu and Muslim adolescents. In A. Husain, S. Kaneez, & M. Jahan. (Eds.), *Studies in spiritual psychology* (pp.183-190), New Delhi: Research India Press.

King, D. B. (2008). *Rethinking claims of spiritual intelligence: A definition, model, and measure.* Unpublished Master's Thesis, Trent University, Peterborough, Ontario, Canada.

King, D. B., & DeCicco, T. L. (2009). A viable model and self-report measure of spiritual intelligence. *International Journal of Transpersonal Studies, 28,* 68-85.

King, M., Speck, P., & Thomas, A. (1995). The Royal Free Interview for Religious and Spiritual Beliefs: Development and Standardization. *Psychological Medicine, 25,* 1125-1134.

King, M., Speck, P., & Thomas, A. (2001). The royal free interview for spiritual and religious beliefs: Development and validation of a self-report version. *Psychological Medicine, 31,* 1015-1023.

Kirschling, J. M., & Pittman, J. F. (1989). Measurement of Spiritual well-being: A hospice caregiver sample. *Hospice Journal, 5,* 1-11.

Koenig, H. G. (2008). Religion, spirituality, and health: Research and clinical application. Paper presented in NACSW Convention, Orlando, FL.

Koenig, H. G., McCullough, M., & Larson, D. B. (2000). *Handbook of religion and health.* New York, NY: Oxford University Press.

Leak, G. K., Loucks, A. A., & Bowlin, P. (1999). Development and initial validation of an objective measure of faith development. *International Journal of Psychology of Religion, 9,* 105-124.doi:10.1207/s15327582ijpr0902_2

Ledbetter, M. S., Smith, L. A., Vosler-Hunter, W. L., & Fischer, J. D. (1991). An evaluation of the research and clinical usefulness of the Spiritual Well-being Scale. *Journal of Psychology and Theology, 19*, 49-55.

Leopold, J. (2011). Army's Spiritual Fitness Test Comes Under Fire, Truth out programme.

Little, B. R. (1989). Personal projects analysis: Trivial pursuits, magnificent obsessions, and the search for coherence In D. Buss & N. Cantor (Eds.). *Personality psychology: Recent trends and emerging directions* (pp. 15-31). New York: Springer-Verlag.

Majid, N., Khan, M. S., & Dixit, P. (2014). Daily spiritual experience and subjective well-being: A study of Hindu and Muslim youths. In A. Husain, S. Kaneez, & M. Jahan. (Eds.). *Studies in spiritual psychology* (pp.95-109), New Delhi: Research India Press.

Martens, R., Burton, D., Vealey, R. S., Bump, L. A., & Smith, D. E. (1990). Development and validation of the Competitive State Anxiety Inventory-2. In R. Martens, R. S. Vealey, &D. Burton (Eds.), *Competitive anxiety in sport* (pp. 117–190). Champaign, IL: Human Kinetics.

Martsolf. D., & Mickley J. (1998). The concept of spirituality in nursing theories: Differing world-views and extent of focus. *Journal of Advanced Nursing, 27*, 294–303.

Masters, K. S., Carey, K. B., Maisto, S. A., Caldwell, P. E., Wolfe, T. V., Hackney, H.,...Himawan, L. (2009). Psychometric examination of the brief multidimensional measure of religiousness/spirituality among college students. *International Journal of the Psychology of Religion, 19*, 106-120. doi.10.1097/00004583-200202000-00015.

McBride, J. L., Arthur, G., Brooks, R., & Pilkington, L. (1998). The relationship between a patient's spirituality and health experiences. *Family Medicine, 30*, 122-126.

Mickley, J. R. & Soeken, K. (1993). Religiousness and hope in Hispanic and Anglo American women with breast cancer. *Oncology Nursing Forum, 20*, 1171-1177.

Mickley, J. R., Soeken, K., & Belcher, A. (1992). Spiritual well-being, religiousness and hope among women with breast cancer. *Image: Journal of Nursing Scholarship, 24*, 267-272.

Moberg, D. O. (2005). Research in spirituality, religion, and aging. *Journal of Individual Differences, 3*(2), 187–192.

Narimani, M., Babolan, A. Z., & Ariapooran, S. (2011). The role of spiritual transcendence on predictives of competitive anxiety and self-confidence in athletes. *World Applied Sciences Journal, 15*(1), 136-141.

Nazam, F., & Husain, A. (2014). Conceptual definition and standardization of spiritual values scale. *Indian Journal of Positive Psychology, 5*(4), 411-414.

Nazam, F., Husain, A., & Khan, S. M. (2015). *Spiritual values scale.* Agra: National Psychological Corporation.

Norraini Othman (2010). The development and validation of the Ummatic personality inventory using principle component analysis. In A. Husain, A. K. Al-Palaniappan, M. M. Nor, S. Jamaluddin, L. S. Cheong and A. Khan (Eds.) *Studies in Applied Psychology: Asian Perspective.* New Delhi: Research India Press.

Paloutzian, R. F., & Ellison, C.W. (1982). Loneliness, spiritual well-being, and quality of life. In L. A. Peplau& D. Perlman (Eds.), *Loneliness: A sourcebook of current theory, research and therapy* (pp.224-237). New York: Wiley.

Paloutzian, R. F., & Ellison, C.W. (1982). Loneliness, spiritual well-being, and quality of life. In L. A. Peplau & D. Perlman (Eds.), *Loneliness: A sourcebook of current theory, research and therapy*, (pp.224-237). New York: Wiley.

Pargament, K., & Mahoney, A. M. (2001). Spiritual meaning scale. Unpublished manuscript

Pervez, N. (2001). Impact of psychological factors on subjective well-being in solace seeking from visit to holy shrine. Unpublished Ph. D Thesis, Aligarh Muslim University, Aligarh (India).

Peterman, A. H. (2000). Spirituality and quality of life among cancer patients: The role of ethnicity. Paper presented at the annual meeting of the American Psychosomatics Society, GA.

Peterman, A. H., Fitchett, G., Brady, M. J., & Cell, D. (2000). Psychometric validation of the FACIT spiritual well-being scale. Manuscript in preparation.

Peterman, A. H., Fitchett, G., Brady, M. J., Hernandez, L., & Cella, D. (2002). Measuring spiritual well-being in people with cancer: The functional Assessment of Chronic Illness Therapy- Spiritual Well-being Scale (FACIT-Sp). *Annals of Behavioural Medicines, 24*, 49-58.

Peterson, C., Nansook, P., & Castro, C.A. (2011). Assessment for the U.S. Army Comprehensive Soldier Fitness Program: The Global Assessment Tool. *American Psychologist, 66*(1), 10–18.

Piedmont, R. L. (2007). Cross-cultural generalizability of the Spiritual Transcendence Scale to the Philippines: Spirituality as a human universal. *Mental Health, Religion, & Culture, 10*, 89-107. doi:10.1080/13694670500275494.

Piedmont, R. L. (2010). *Assessment of Spirituality and Religious Sentiments (ASPIRES): Technical manual* (2nd ed.). Timonium, MD: Author.

Piedmont, R. L., & Leach, M. M. (2002). Cross-cultural generalizability of the Spiritual Transcendence Scale in India: Spirituality as a universal aspect of human experience. *American Behavioural Scientist, 45*, 1886-1899. doi:10.1177/0002764202045120ll

Piedmont, R. L., Werdel, M. B., & Fernando, M. (2009). The utility of the Assessment of Spirituality and Religious Sentiments (ASPIRES) scale with Christians and

Buddhist in Sri Lanka. *Research in the Social Scientific Study of Religion, 20*, 131-143. doi:10.1163/ej.9789004175624.i-334.42

Reker, G. T. (2003). *Spiritual transcendent scale.* Peterborough, Ontario, Canada: Psychological Press.

Rican, P., & Janosova, P. (2010). Spirituality as a basic aspect of personality: A cross-cultural verification of Piedmont's model. *The International Journal for the Psychology of Religion, 20*, 2-13. doi:10.1080/10508610903418053

Rosenberg, M. (1965). *Society and the adolescent self-image.* Princeton, NJ: Princeton University Press.

Safara, M., & Bhatia, M. S. (2013). Spiritual intelligence. *Delhi Psychiatry Journal, 16*(2), 412-423.

Safi, H., & Naseer, N. (2014). Self-esteem and spiritual well-being: A comparative study of physically challenged and normal adults. In A. Husain, S. Kaneez, & M. Jahan. (Eds.). *Studies in spiritual psychology* (pp.135-147), New Delhi: Research India Press.

Saur, M. S., & Saur, W. G. (1993). Psychological adjustment and religiousness: The multivariate belief-motivational theory of religiousness. *Journal for the Scientific Study of Religion, 30*, 448-461.

Schaler, J. (1996). Spiritual thinking in addiction treatment providers. The Spiritual Belief Scale. *Alcoholism Treatment Quarterly, 14*, 7-33.

Schwartz, S. H. (1992). Universals in the content and structure of values: Theory and empirical tests in 20 countries. In M. Zanna (Ed.), Advances in experimental social psychology (Vol. 25) (pp. 1-65). New York: Academic Press.

Schwartz, S. H. (1994). Are three universal aspects in the structure and content of human values? *Journal of Social Issues, 50*, 19-45.

Scott, E. L., Agresti, A. A., & George, F. (1998). Factor analysis of the 'Spiritual Well-Being Scale' and its clinical utility with psychiatric inpatients. *Journal for the Scientific Study of Religion, 37*(2), 314–321.

Sell, H., & Nagpal, R. (1992). Assessment of subjective well-being: The subjective well-being inventory (SWI). *Regional Health Paper SESRO No.24.* New Delhi: WHO.

Seybold, K. S. (1999). The RoyalFree Interview for Religious and Spiritual Beliefs. In P.C. Hill & R. W. Hood, Jr. (Eds.), *Measures of religiosity* (pp.351-357). Birmingham, AL: Religious Education Press.

Shaheen, H., Jahan, M., Shaheen, F., & Shaheen, S. (2014). Impact of spirituality on suicidal ideation among university students. In A. Husain, S. Kaneez, & M. Jahan. (Eds.). *Studies in spiritual psychology* (pp.202-221), New Delhi: Research India Press.

Sinnott, J. D. (2002). Introductionto special issues on spirituality and adult development, Part III. *Journal of Adult Development, 9*(2), 199-200.

Slater, W., Hall, T. W., & Edwards, K.J. (2001). Measuring religion and spirituality: Where are we and where are we going? *Journal of Psychology and Theology, 29*(1), 4-21.

Sperry, L. (2012). *Spirituality in clinical practice: Theory and practice of spiritually oriented psychotherapy* (2nded.). NewYork: Routledge/Taylor & Francis Group.

U. S. Public Health Command (2012). *Spiritual fitness inventory user guide.* USAPHC TG No. 360.

Underwood, L. G. (1999). Daily Spiritual Experiences. Kalamazoo, MI: Fetzer Institute. Retrieved from http://www.fetzer.org/images/stories/pdf/MultidiemnsionalBooklet.pdf?phpmAdmin=1

Underwood, L. G. (2011). The daily spiritual experience scale: Overview and results. *Religion, 2*, 29-50, doi:10.3390/rel2010029.

Underwood, L. G., & Teresi, J. A. (2002). The Daily Spiritual Experiences Scale: development, theoretical description, reliability, exploratory factor analysis, and preliminary construct validity using health-related data. *Annals of Behavioural Medicine, 24*, 22-33. doi:10.1207/S15324796ABM2401_04.

VandeCreek, L., Ayrse, S., & Bassham, M. (1995). Using the INSPIRIT to conduct spiritual assessment. *Journal of Pastoral Care, 49*, 83-89.

Verma, S. K., & Verma, A. (1989). *Manual for PGI General Well-being Measure.* Ankur Psychological Agency: Lucknow.

Wade, S. H. (1989). The development of a scale to measure forgiveness. Dissertation Abstract International, *50*(11), 5338B. (UMI No. 9008539).

Wasner, M., Longaker, C., Fegg. M. J., & Borasio, G. D. (2005). Effects of spiritual care training for palliative care professional. *Palliative Medicine, 19*, 99-104.

Wink, P., & Dillon, M. (2002). Spiritual development across the adult life course: Findings from alongitudinal study. *Journal of Adult Development, 9*, 79–94.

Worthington, E. L., & Sandage, S. J. (2001). Religion and spirituality. *Psychotherapy, 38*, 473-478.

Zohar, D. & Marshall, I. (2000). *Spiritual intelligence: The ultimate intelligence.* New York: Bloomsbury.

Mindfulness and its relationship with emotion and health

Satchit Prasun Mandal, Yogesh Kumar Arya and Rakesh Pandey
Department of Psychology
Banaras Hindu University
Varanasi (UP), INDIA

Abstract: Mindfulness has occupied a central position in the contemporary scientific psychology and has been most widely studied in relation to alleviation of mental distress and promoting health and well-being. However, there exists wide variation in its conceptualization and connotations. Further despite its well documented beneficial health effects, the literature is still inconclusive regarding the routes through which its impact human health and well-being. Taking the said issues into account, the present chapter makes an attempt to present an overview of the different conceptualizations and connotations of mindfulness followed by a review of the link of mindfulness with emotions and health/well-being. Based on the aforesaid review, we hypothesize that emotion may be a route through which mindfulness may influence human health and well-being. We have reviewed the most prevalent view that emotion is a mediating link between mindfulness – health relationship followed by an alternative theorization that emotion may be an antecedent factor that determines the level of mindfulness which in turn determines the mental health/well-being. The former view though has received more empirical support, our own empirical findings based on structural equation modeling (yet to be published), provide support to the alternative theorization. The present review supports the notion that mindfulness has a beneficial impact on health and well-being and provides a new insight into the potential role of emotions in understanding this relationship.

1. Introduction

Mindfulness has received considerable attention in the area of health and clinical psychology as a health protective and health promotional construct. However, it has been conceptualized in different ways – some researchers have treated it as a meditation practice while others as the meditative state of mind and still others as disposition or trait. Further, as a tool of psychotherapy and stress reduction strategy, the mindfulness practice has been clinically modified to suit the different clinical situations. Despite the different connotations and usage, the mindfulness has been found to have a beneficial effect of on human health and well-being. However, the processes and mechanisms through which mindfulness exerts beneficial effects on health and well-being are still a matter of inquiry. Though several psychophysiological constructs have been explicated to explain the mindfulness-health relationship, emotion and emotion related constructs have received much attention of the researchers during last few decades. Most of the empirical studies suggest the possibility that mindfulness leads to a better emotionally regulated state of mind which in turn leads to better health and well-being (Mandal, Arya & Pandey, 2012). Contrary to this notion that emotion plays a mediational role in the mindfulness-health relationship, recently some researchers have presented the theoretical possibility that emotionally regulated state of mind is an antecedent and prerequisite attaining the state of mindfulness. Accordingly, an alternative theoretical proposition can be extended to explain the interrelationship among mindfulness, emotion and health/well-being in which mindfulness is considered as a mediational link between emotion and health relationship.

In view of the above issues related to mindfulness literature, this chapter presents a brief review of the different conceptualization of mindfulness and its relationship with health and well-being. It also reviews the empirical evidences linking mindfulness and emotion to health and well-being as well as the relationship between mindfulness and emotion. In addition, an attempt has also been made to uncover the mediational psychological constructs to explain the mindfulness-health relationship.

2. Concept of mindfulness: An overview

The concept of mindfulness has gained widespread popularity in the modern psychological research and practice because of its well documented beneficial psycho-physiological impact on human personality, health and well-being. However, the term has different connotations (e.g., a state of consciousness, a technique of meditation, as a meditative style, a trait like disposition characterized by non-judgmental awareness of and attention to inner and outer experiences etc.) and has been used in different ways. The mindfulness practice has been used as a technique to attain a higher state of consciousness on one hand and as a therapeutic tool to manage stress and promote health and wellbeing on the other. This section briefly reviews the evolution of the concept of mindfulness in the Buddhist tradition and its different conceptualization.

2.1 Mindfulness in Buddhist Tradition

Mindfulness has its historical origin in contemplative traditions of oriental Buddhist culture that can be traced back to ancient India. The conceptual underpinnings of mindfulness are embodied in the teaching of Buddha himself, who developed his doctrine in response to omnipresent sufferings of humankind and suggested the ways to go beyond these sufferings (Smith, 1986). The Buddha supposedly discovered four essentials of human existence, termed as the four noble truths –there is suffering, there is an origin of suffering, there is the cessation of suffering, and there is the way leading to cessation of suffering (Sumedho, 1992).

These four noble truths of Buddhist philosophy focus on the reality of interminable human sufferings and cite the automatic tendency of the humans to attach themselves to transitory phenomenal world as the reasons of these sufferings (Cardaciotto, 2005). Buddha in his teachings delineated the ways of liberation (Nirvana in Pali terminology) from the vicious cycle of sufferings through practices of the righteous conducts related to view, intention, speech, action, effort, contemplation and meditation. These said ways of liberation are commonly known as The Eightfold Path that sharpens cognitive faculties, yields to perfect realization of the transience of phenomena and allows individuals to cherish the life experiences up to the full, nonetheless with an attitude of impeccable detachment (Kumar, 2002).

The influence of the Buddhist doctrine became influential in the Asian lands long after the demise of Lord Buddha. Specifically at the reign of the great emperor, Asoka of Mauryan dynasty in the 3rd century B.C., Buddhism was started to be spread to south-east Asian countries (Cardaciotto, 2005). As the Buddhist philosophy and way of life drew the attention of the people over a larger geographical area, two distinct traditions of interpreting Buddha's teaching - Theravada and Mahayana emerged with time (Rahula, 1996).

Among the whole system of Buddhist doctrine, the concept of mindfulness appealed to the scholars most, as it alone represented the essence of Buddhist understanding of reality. As Bhikkhu Sujato perfectly stated "On the plane of wisdom, mindfulness extends the continuity of awareness from ordinary consciousness to samadhi and beyond, staying with the mind in all of its permutations and transformations and thus, supplying the fuel for understanding impermanence and causality. And finally on the plane of liberation, perfected mindfulness is an inalienable quality of the realized sage, who lives ever mindful" (Sujato, 2005). The detail description of mindfulness can be found in satipatthana sutra, the chief scripture of Theravada tradition (Sujato, 2005).

The English word Mindfulness is derived from a Pali word 'sati' which means memory or calling back to mind. According to Hanh (1976), "The Pali word sati (Sanskrit: smriti) means to stop, and to maintain awareness of the object", Hanh (1976). Hanh explained that mindfulness arousing meditation is to "dissolve the boundary between the subject who observes and the object being observed" (Hanh, 1976). In its traditional sense i.e. memory, mindfulness refers to active remembrance and recollection of learned virtues, lucid intellectual understanding of reality and repeated recollection of awareness to the present actions in order to make them appropriate and flawless (Sujato, 2005).

Besides its trans-scientific and religious significance, mindfulness has been substantiated as a heightened state of cognitive functioning, a sharp and active presence to reality and a major tool to eradicate human sufferings (Mandal, Arya, Pandey, 2011, 2012). It would be interesting to know how and in what way the construct mindfulness has been incorporated and defined in the arena of modern psychology.

2.2 Mindfulness as a psychological construct

Western scholars became interested in mindfulness and relevant Buddhist constructs when Zen Buddhism was gaining its popularity during the last half of 20th century. During 1960 and on onwards, Americans started to be adventurists in enquiring the depth of consciousness using mind altering drugs, hypnosis and meditations as well (Cardaciotto, 2005). So, they readily accepted mindfulness inducing meditation as it could bring out qualitative changes in the cognitive and emotive functioning as a whole (Tart, 1972). As people began to engage in mindfulness based meditations, the fruitfulness of such meditations came to fore in terms of less habituation to distractions, full awareness of environment (Kasamatsu & Hirai, 1966), increased positivity and detachment (Cardaciotto, 2005). Thus eventually, mindfulness and related meditation practices took firm ground in the psychological research arena, independent of its religious origin. Rigorous empirical researches started in social and clinical psychology as well.

According to social psychologist Langer (1989), "Mindfulness is a flexible state of mind—an openness to novelty, a process of actively drawing novel distinctions, sensitivity to context and perspective and orientation to present experiences". She described the state of mindfulness as a "Limber state of mind", (Langer, 1989).

Cardaciotto (2005) in his massive work on mindfulness listed three different categories of definitions of mindfulness- Clinical, Social Psychological and philosophical definitions. The Clinical conceptualizations of mindfulness are in accordance with ancient Buddhist philosophy. Modern western clinical ideas of mindfulness are generally similar to the ancient Buddhist tradition (Bishop, 2002). According to Baer (2003) "Mindfulness is the non-judgmental observation of the on-going stream of internal and external stimuli as they arise". Jon Kabat-Zinn (2003) mainly focused on present-oriented consciousness and defined mindfulness as an "Awareness that emerges through paying attention on purpose, in the present-moment, and nonjudgmental to the unfolding of experience moment by moment." Robins (2002) very efficiently put it as "Nonjudgmental awareness of one's experience as it unfolds moment by moment." Apart from the aforementioned definitions, Epstein (1995) equated it precisely to the process of vigilance. He defined it as "Paying precise attention, moment by moment, to exactly what you are experiencing, right now, separating out your reactions from the raw sensory events", Epstein (1995).

In sum, Clinical conceptualizations of mindfulness emphasize on the flexible awareness of and attention to the present life experiences, non-judgmental registration of events, non-reactivity to inner experiences, process of vigilance and enhancement of wellbeing.

The non-clinical conceptualizations of mindfulness (social psychological and philosophical views) share some similarities with the clinical definitions as they also focus on certain quality of consciousness such as having greater awareness of and attention to the present moment by moment experiences. However, some serious differences also exist between clinical and non-clinical conceptualizations. Unlike clinical conceptualizations, non-clinical perspectives do not hold the view that mindfulness is similar to vigilance or sustained attention process. The concept of vigilance or sustained attention refers to stable focus or concentration on a particular stimulus or idea but in case of mindfulness stimulus field is actively varied (Langer 2002). The social-psychological perspective of mindfulness puts emphasis on the cognitive processing of external stimuli, not on the processing of internal stimuli. Most importantly the social-psychological concept of mindfulness doesn't incorporate the concepts of non-judgmental registration of information or non-reactivity which are the core features of clinical conceptualizations of mindfulness. According to social-psychological perspective, mindfulness generates reflexive consciousness which denotes active cognitive operations on perceptual inputs from the external environment (Brown & Ryan, 2003).

Braza (1997) philosophically defined mindfulness as "A technique that teaches intent alertness. It means becoming fully aware of each moment and of your activity in that moment." Horowitz (2002) stated that mindfulness involves "Attention to the experienced qualities of the self in the present moment and space rather than being preoccupied with what happened in the past or fantasies in the distant futures."

So far it is clear that despite several differences in the conceptualization of mindfulness, all the definitions are in agreement on the grounds that mindfulness is a qualitatively enhanced state of consciousness, characterized by greater attention to and awareness of the present life-experiences. It promotes greater regulation of emotions and acceptance (Kabat-Zinn, 1994), reduces pain and sufferings (Sumedho, 1992) and increases well-being (e.g., Brown & Ryan, 2003). It increases the efficacy of human being by making him free from habits and traditional mindsets (Deci & Ryan, 2000). Mindful people are flexible and more open to new experiences. They can utilize and appreciate the vitality and hidden beauty of each moment.

2.3 Different connotations of mindfulness

There is a lack of consensus among academic community about the exact nature and definition of mindfulness. The terms such as mindfulness, mindfulness meditation, and mindfulness based interventions are some of the most frequently appearing terms in the existing research literature. However, these terms are often used in an interchangeable manner that consequently creates improper elucidation of the construct and posits substantial confusion in understanding of mindfulness (Cardaciotto, 2005). Further, the term mindfulness itself has been used to connote different things. For instance, it has been used to connote a specific type of Buddhist meditation practice, a higher mental state (or state of consciousness) resulting from meditation practice as well as trait like disposition characterized by highly focussed non-judgmental awareness of the internal and external experiences. This section reviews these different overlapping conceptualizations of mindfulness.

Mindfulness in its traditional sense is a state of individual's awareness, purposeful choice and capacity to be fully aware to the present life experiences (Nyanaponika Thera, 1972; Hanh, 1976). As Bhikkhu Sujato stated, "It repeatedly re-collects awareness into the present, remembering oneself so that one's actions are purposeful and appropriate, grounded in time and place" (Sujato, 2005). Buddhist tradition specifically Theravada Buddhism provides detail account of meditative practices that cultivate the virtue of mindfulness. In the words of V.H. Gunaratana, it runs "Theravada Buddhism presents us with an effective system for exploring the deeper levels of the mind, down to the very root of consciousness itself" (Gunaratana, 2011). The Theravada meditation tradition of cultivating mindfulness is chiefly identical to Vipassana or insightful meditation, documented and supported in Satipatthana Sutra (Sujato, 2005). Vipassana meditation is mainly practiced for eliminating intelligential defilements, cultivating insight over the impermanence and developing qualities of mindfulness (Sujato, 2005). Nevertheless, mindfulness in itself is different from Vipassana meditation as the second one is a practice that nurtures mindfulness related attributes and develop a watcher self (Cardaciotto, 2005; Deatherage, 1975).

Observing the beneficial effects of mindfulness meditation, psychologists started to use it in psychotherapy by 1970. Soon, it became popular in combating with wide-ranging chronic clinical symptoms and daily stresses. These newly formed therapeutic techniques, known as "third wave of behavioral therapy", combined the principles of mindfulness meditation such as present-orientation, acceptance and awareness with traditional behavioral therapy (Breslin, Zack, & McMain, 2002). The preceding generations of behavioral therapy involved the applications of experimental analysis of human behavior into clinical settings (First wave) and the extended emphasis on cognitive-behavioral changes in eliminating maladaptive behaviors (Second wave), (Cardacitto, 2005).

Among the mindfulness based therapeutic techniques, the most famous and frequently used one is Mindfulness-Based Stress Reduction (MBSR). MBSR is a group based therapy, developed as a counterpart to traditional medical systems for treating individuals with chronic health symptoms and stress (Kabat-Zinn, 1982). This technique comprises an eight-week course in which participants are instructed by an expert therapist to perform some diminutive forms of mindfulness meditations such as walking meditation, body scan therapy sitting meditation for two and half hours per week (Ekblad, 2009). MBSR practices have been proved to be beneficial in alleviating the symptoms and sufferings of chronic pain (Kabat-Zinn, 1982; Kabat-Zinn, Lipworth, & Burney, 1985), generalized anxiety and panic disorders (Kabat-Zinn, Massion, Kristeller, & Peterson, 1992), fibromyalgia (Kaplan, Goldenberg, & Galvin-Nadeau, 1993), cancer (Speca, Carlson, Goodey, & Angen, 2000) and so on.

Another important therapeutic technique is Mindfulness- based Cognitive Therapy (MBCT; Teasdale, Segal, & Williams, 1995), is basically adapted from MBSR in order to prevent relapse/recurrence of depression (Segal, Williams, & Teasdale, 2002). Like, MBSR, it is also an eight-week program that combines detachment, acceptance and awareness like mindful attributes with traditional cognitive therapy. Earlier studies showed that MBCT can successfully decrease the relapse of depressive episodes in individuals having more than three episodes previously (Teasdale et al., 1995).

Two more important mindfulness-based techniques, which do not include mindfulness meditation in itself but focus on the mindfulness attributes as the major constituents, are Acceptance and commitment therapy (ACT) and Dialectical behavior therapy (DBT), (Cardaciotto, 2005). Acceptance and commitment therapy (ACT) is grounded philosophy of functional contextualism (Biglan & Hayes, 1996; Hayes, 1993; Hayes & Brownstein, 1986; Hayes, Hayes, & Reese, 1988) which is a distinct form of contextualism that analyses psychological activities as the product of the interplay between historically and situationally defined context of the individual. According to this view psychopathological symptoms appear when individual effort fully tries to curb or suppress his negative thoughts and emotions. Training in ACT promotes the attitude of accepting all kinds of negative thoughts and emotions with a vigorous detachment which reduces experiential avoidance (Hayes, Strosahl, & Wilson, 1999). Hayes mentioned six fundamental processes of ACT that gradually induce psychological flexibility and immunity. Those fundamental processes of avoiding psychopathology are acceptance, cognitive defusion, being present, self as context, values and committed action (Hayes, Luomaa, Bondb, Masudaa, & Lillisa, 2006).

Dialectical behavioral therapy (DBT), on the other hand, was precisely designed to handle the problems of the individuals with borderline personality disorder (BPD; Linehan, 1993). It integrates Zen practices with cognitive-behavioral therapies to combat with borderline personality disorder and emphasizes the role of emotional dysregulation along with the inability to manage negative emotions as the root cause of maladaptive behaviors (Linehan, 2003). Mindfulness meditation is used in DBT to foster acceptance tendency, non-judgment and non-evaluation which reduces fear responses and involuntary experiential avoidance (Linehan, 1993). For changing dysfunctional behaviors DBT strategies use behavioral analysis of dysfunctional behavior along with several problem solving techniques like cognitive modification, exposure based strategies, skill training etcetera (Dimef & Linehan, 2001).

Apart from all the above mentioned meditation techniques and therapeutic strategies mindfulness was also conceptualized as a cognitive ability, personality trait and cognitive style (Sternberg, 2000). Sternberg viewed cognitive ability as a dormant source of cognitive skill and as a source of individual differences in such skills. Cognitive abilities are generally reflected by (a) the existence of systematic differences in individual capacities usually through factor analysis or related techniques, or (b) the identification of a unique processing component that is responsible for the individual differences on various tasks or task variants (Sternberg, 1977). He highlighted the correspondence of mindfulness to some cognitive abilities by citing the massive factor analytic study to find out latent cognitive abilities, conducted by Carrol (1993). Carrol in that study found out a class of mental abilities amongst overall 10 sets of identified cognitive abilities, which he named as concentration and attention abilities (Sternberg 2000). In further analysis Carrol extracted total 21 factors from concentration and attention abilities. These factors most possibly resemble the attributes of mindfulness (Sternberg, 2000). From the present reasoning, provided by Sternberg, mindfulness can also be viewed as cognitive ability. However, very little research has been done yet to explore this possibility.

Mindfulness has also been conceptualized as a form of cognitive style by Sternberg. Cognitive style refers to one's preferred mode of utilizing cognitive capacities (Sternberg, 1997). Cognitive style in itself is not a cognitive ability rather it is the way of using one's capacities in day to day life. The mindfulness/ mindlessness continuum is a quiet well fit to the idea of cognitive style as these two represents two different styles of information processing with specific features related to each of them (Sternberg, 2000). The mindful and mindless behaviors are qualitatively distinct, having advantages and disadvantages in both of them. However, Langer argued that mindfulness cannot be conceptualized as a cognitive style as cognitive style remains unchanged with the time and circumstances while mindfulness changes (Langer & Moldoveanu, 2000).

Mindfulness has been defined as a psychological trait by so many researchers (e.g. Raweewan, Pothongkom Jitphaisarnwattana, Samart & Tonmanee, 2012). Specifically, the cognitive theories of mindfulness explained it as an attentional state (Bishop et al., 2004) and trait variable (Frewen, Evans, Maraj, Dozois & Partridge, 2007). Initially, Langer (1992), in her social-cognitive theory of mindfulness conceptualized it as a trait, comprising the attributes like awareness, openness to novelty, abilities to draw novel distinction etcetera. According to Buddhism, mindfulness is a post meditative consistent state, having certain attributes, achieved through specified insightful techniques. The attributes that essentially define mindfulness, like acceptance, non-judgment, non-elaborative awareness, non-evaluation, can be found as psychological traits in the non-meditators also (Baer, Smith, Hopkins, Krietemeyer & Toney, 2006). If the attributes that constitute mindfulness, can be found in general people, then mindfulness can also be conceptualized as a psychometric trait. Thompson and Waltz (2007) defined trait/everyday mindfulness as a semi-consistent trait/tendency which is present across varying life situations, related explicitly to personality traits and comprises the several qualities like openness, acceptance and present-focused attention. Several psychometric conceptualization of trait mindfulness emerged accordingly which are now being frequently used in empirical researches.

3. Mindfulness and its link with health and well-being

Buddhist theory especially the four noble truths highlight the reasons of human sufferings and show the ways to get liberated from sufferings. Buddhist view pointed out that the tendency of human beings to evaluate life experiences as good/bad and eventual striving for good as well as being attached to it and avoiding bad experiences, is the root cause of sufferings (Sumedho, 1992). Along with the discomforts of bad experiences, the attachment to desired experiences also consequently results in despairs as it always creates the apprehension of losing the attachment objects/things/experiences (Nyklíček, 2011). Buddhist tradition prescribed that non-judgmental awareness and acceptance of the experiences without evaluation may act as the remedy to this habitual attachment and longing for desired experiences as well as discarding negative experiences (Epstain, 1995). It reasonably clarifies that attributes of mindfulness such as non-judgment of experiences leads to permanent happiness and well-being (Soma Thera, 2010).

Apart from the religious concepts, modern psychological theories also throw light on the relationship between mindfulness and health/well-being. For example, the relationship between mindfulness and well-being can be best described in the light of Self-determination theory (SDT) of Ryan and Deci (Deci & Ryan, 1985). Initially Deci and Ryan researched on intrinsic motivation i.e. pursuit of behaviours, driven by internal gratification and interest (Deci and Ryan, 1980), along with the process of internalizing extrinsic goals as the assimilated personal values of the self (Ryan, Huta & Deci 2006). They found that fulfillment of three basic psychological needs namely the needs for autonomy, competence and relatedness foster intrinsically driven behaviours as well as internalization process and these conditions are unanimously required for growth, integrity, personal and relational well-being (Ryan, Huta & Deci 2008).

In a nutshell, self-determination theory holds the view that well-being and vitality of the individuals depend on the societal support for the gratification of autonomy, competence and relatedness needs (Ryan, Stiller, & Lynch, 1994). Here autonomy denotes the freedom of choosing and engaging in such activities which can be pursued for the gratification of intrinsic interests (Ryan, 1995). Competence refers to the tendency to control one's situation which is supported by the availability of optimal challenges and getting positive feedback (Csikszentmihalyi, 1975). Relatedness is the need to be connected and accepted by other members of the society (Baumeister & Leary, 1995; Deci & Ryan, 1985). Self-determination theory suggests that the gratification of the said needs generates motivation and induces well-being (Deci, Ryan, Gagne, Leone, Usunov & Kornazheva, 2001). Brown and Ryan (2003) studied mindfulness and emphasized its role in promoting self-regulatory behaviors, greater autonomy and vitality. As defined earlier mindfulness is characterized by greater awareness, present-centered attention, non-judgment and non-reactivity to the experiences which sufficiently fulfils the mentioned three conditions for self-growth and well-being. Deci (1980) showed that people deviate from the autonomous and self-determining behaviors when they adapt a habitual inflexible behavioral pattern and become incapable of flexibly using information (Özyeşil, 2012). Mindfulness is an antidote to such habituated and inflexible behavioral pattern as it induces a flexible state of mind, an open awareness to novel information, enhances the capacity of actively drawing novel distinctions, makes people sensitive to context and perspectives of the stimuli (Langer, 1989). Therefore, it can be inferred that SDT congregate very well with the mindful perspective of regulating behaviours (Ryan & Brown, 2003). Moreover, mindfulness leads to myriad factors that enhances interpersonal relatedness and belongingness such as positive affect, positive self-esteem, satisfaction with life and decreases the potential hindrances of effective interpersonal relationships like negative affect, anger, neuroticism, stress-reactions etcetera (Brown & Ryan, 2003; Epstein & Baucom, 2002). Mindfulness promotes attentional self-regulation and present moment awareness (Bishop, Lau, Shapiro, Carlson & Anderson, 2004) that produces autonomous and well integrated behavioral patterns (Ryan, 1995). Thus, mindfulness enhances well-being through inducing self-regulated functioning (Brown & Ryan, 2003).

The aforementioned discussion makes it explicit that the attributes of mindfulness like amplified awareness, present-cantered attention, context sensitivity, flexibility of information processing enables a person of choosing those activities for themselves which are in congruence with the intrinsic needs and values (Deci & Ryan, 2000). The enhanced awareness also assists in identifying the basic needs and helps people to engage in authentic self-regulated pursuit of behaviours that lead to satisfaction of those needs (Brown & Ryan, 2003). So it is clear that mindfulness creates favourable conditions for psychological growth, self-regulation and satisfaction of basic psychological needs which are pre-requisites of better health and well-being.

Frederickson (2000) has associated her famous broaden-and-build theory to the practice of mindfulness. Broaden-and-build theory essentially proposes two hypotheses. The first one states that positive emotions expand the repertoire of cognitive capacities like thinking and attention (Fredrickson, Cohn, Coffey, Pek, & Finkel, 2008). This has been empirically confirmed that positive emotions broadens the range of visual attention (Fredrickson & Branigan, 2005) and widen the array of desired action (Fredrickson & Branigan, 2005). The second part holds the view that positive emotions entail a course of development and build psychological resources. Frederickson (2000) conceptualized that mindfulness meditations promote more awareness and increased experiences of positive emotions (Ekblad, 2009) which in turn broaden an individual's though-action repertoire and increase psychological recourses and well-being.

The relationship between mindfulness and well-being can also be described with the "positivity bias" (Ekbald, 2009). Positivity bias refers to the propensity of the people to attend and process positive stimuli only and to interpret neutral stimuli in the positive manner. Ekbald (2009) stated that mindfulness most possibly leads to positivity bias as mindful people are more capable of cognitively manipulating the information and construe positive interpretation out of it.

This proposition was supported by Arch and Craske (2006), who compared a mindful breathing exercise group, an unfocussed attention exercise group and a worry exercise group on their response patterns to positively, negative and neutrally valenced set of pictures (International Affective Picture System: Lang, Bradley, & Cuthbert, 1999). Result demonstrated that mindful breathing exercise group responded positively to neutrally valenced pictures and experienced lesser negative affect while observing negative pictures in comparison to unfocussed attention and worry exercise groups. Mindful breathing exercise group also showed greater enthusiasm to observe negative pictures than other two groups. According to Ekbald (2009), the findings suggest that mindfulness exercise lessens the negative affect and increases tolerance as well as acceptance to negative stimuli by inducing a positive appraisal of the neutral or negative stimuli which he labeled as positivity bias.

Issacowitz (2005) described this process as like observing the world with a "rose colored glasses." The further explanation of the relationship among mindfulness, positivity bias and well-being can be found in the Socio-Emotional Selectivity theory (SEST), given by Carstensen, Isaacowitz, and Charles (1999). SEST states that when a person focuses more on present experiences than on future expectations, he is more likely to attend positive stimuli and perceive neutral stimuli in a positive way i.e. positivity bias occurs. According to this theory, positivity bias can be found in older persons who perceive that their deaths are near and this perception makes them more oriented to present experiences (Carstensen et al, 1999). Similarly, mindfulness promotes positivity bias as it enhances awareness of present reality and lessens the load of future prospects. This increased positivity bias enhances well-being by enabling an individual to perceive positive emotional cues and disregard the negative ones. So it can be inferred from the socio-emotional selectivity theory that mindfulness may promote well-being by inducing positivity bias (Ekblad, 2009).

Another important theoretical perspective regarding the relationship between mindfulness and its positive health outcomes was proposed by Shapiro, Carlson, Astin and Freedman (2006). Shapiro et al (2006) analyzed the intentional, attentional and attitudinal components of mindfulness and put forward a model that describes the mechanism of mindfulness which suggests that intentionally attending to the life experiences with an attitude of openness and non-judgmentalness leads to a substantial change in the perspective which they termed as reperceiving. They described reperceiving as the ability to disidentify from the thought and emotional processes and observe the ongoing experiences objectively without getting into it. Reperceiving is very close to other constructs like decentering (Safran & Segal, 1990), de-automatization (Deikman, 1982; Safran & Segal, 1990) and detachment (Bohart, 1983). Moreover, reperceiving leads to some additional mechanisms such as self-regulation, cognitive and affective flexibility, value clarification and exposure which in turn results in enhanced health/well-being (Shapiro et al, 2006). In sum, the beneficial effects of mindfulness are mediated through two steps. At the first step, continuous practice of mindfulness meditation gradually develops an observing self (Deikman, 1982) and ability of reperceiving which consequently increases some additional variables like self-regulation, cognitive and affective flexibility, value clarification and exposure to internal stimuli. At the second step, the mentioned additional variables lead to betterment of health and well-being.

Unlike Shapiro et al (2006), Chambers, Gullone and Allen (2009) focused on the emotional labyrinth that underlie mindfulness practices and elucidated its role in explaining the relationship between mindfulness and psychological well-being. To clarify the said relationship they highlighted some important processes related to emotion regulation such as relaxation and metacognitive insight. Relaxation comes from getting rid of the disturbing thoughts and emotional reactions through mindfulness practices whereas metacognitive insight reflects the awareness and ability to disidentify from the negative thought and emotional processes (Nyklíček, 2011).

Nyklíček (2011) mentioned some other interconnected processes such as contact with reality and harmony while clarifying the intermediate paths between mindfulness and psychological well-being and proposed a new model, known as the RICH model of mindfulness. Here contact with reality refers to being in touch with internal bodily mechanism as well as with external experiences whereas harmony reflects the sense of positive attunement with ongoing moment to moment experiences and mind-body system (Nyklíček, 2011).

The RICH model of mindfulness is a hierarchical network that comprises interrelated higher order factors like relaxation (R), meta-cognitive insight (I), contact with reality (C) and harmony (H). All these four main intermediate factors influence second order factors i.e. reduction of perseverative thinking and experiential avoidance as well as enhancement of reappraisal. The factors of the second level in turn promote self-regulation, value clarification, compassion and valued action. At last, all these mentioned sequence of processes result in increased psychological well-being.

All the aforesaid theoretical speculations make it explicit that the relationship of mindfulness with health/well-being is mediated thorough some cognitive and affective intermediate variables. However, the affective pathways of mindfulness to health/well-being are relatively less explored as compared to cognitive variables. Moreover, Frederickson's (2000) broaden and build theory, Carstensen, Isaacowitz, and Charles's (1999) socio-emotional selectivity theory and RICH model of mindfulness (Nyklíček, 2011) heavily emphasize on some emotional processes and variables which may potentially explain mindfulness-health relationship. To further delineate this theoretical possibility in a more clear way the relationships between mindfulness and emotional constructs as well as emotional constructs and mindfulness are required to be discussed in existing theoretical framework. In the next section the relationship of mindfulness with emotion related variables are prudently presented.

4. Mindfulness and emotion: Understanding the link

In Buddhist literature there is no separate word for emotion as such, which reveals that the emotions were not conceptualized in Buddhist philosophy as isolated mental processes rather they were intertwined with cognitive categories (Ekman, Davidson, Ricard & Wallace, 2005). Modern scientific idea also echoes the same language of Buddhism that every area of brain that produces emotions, are also responsible for some aspects of cognition (Davidson & Irwin, 1999). Therefore, mindfulness as a sophisticated mode of cognitive processing is also highly intermingled with emotional processes.

Langer (1989) in her book, 'Mindfulness' explained that mindfulness enhances sensitivity and control over the context of the emotional stimuli. Mindfulness also reduces the habitual pattern of thinking and automatic submission to learned maladaptive information processing (Kang, Gruber & Gray, 2013), decreases learned emotional responses to specific stimuli (Chanowitz & Langer, 1981) and enhances cognitive control and insight over the context of information. So people, who are high on mindfulness, also enjoy greater control over context and higher emotional management (Langer, 1989).

As per the theory of mindfulness, emotions and the 'thoughts related to emotions' are regarded as the temporary mental events that do not correspond to the actual reality (Blackledge & Hayes, 2001). Further, improper understanding and mal-adaptive attempts to regulate emotional experiences posit serious threat to well-being (Nyklíček, 2011). Thus, instead of forceful behavioral modulation of emotions, mindfulness based approach promotes acceptance of emotional experiences which leads to immediate relaxation (Nyklíček, 2011). The mindfulness approach of dealing with emotions was best described in the words of Blackledge and Hayes (2001) which run as "To feel feelings as feelings, to think thoughts as thoughts, fully and without defense, and get on with the business of living". Therefore, mindfulness essentially contradicts with habitual suppression of emotion and incorporates dispassionate acceptance (Chambers et al., 2009). Thus, mindfulness practices develop emotional balance, lessens habitual suppressive tendencies and judgment of emotional valence (Kabat-Zinn, 1990). Moreover, mindfulness promotes clarity of feelings, mood repairing ability, cognitive flexibility and healthy regulation of emotions (Hayes & Feldman, 2005). Thus on this ground, it is expected that mindfulness is associated with adaptive emotion regulation capacities and emotional well-being.

Another way of explaining the relationship of emotion regulation with mindfulness is through emotional differentiation ability. Emotional differentiation is the ability to experience emotions in specific or distinctive ways (also termed "granularity" by Barrett, Gross, Christensen & Benvenuto, 2001). More specifically it is a form of emotional complexity that leads to a number of emotional-cognitive traits like the ability to analyze emotional experiences; to explain subjective feeling; the capacity to remember experience of many emotions at once, (Lindquist & Barret, 2008). People, who have highly developed emotion discrimination skills, are potent in regulating their emotions as the emotion differentiation involves the ability to be aware of the subtle distinction within emotional category (Kang & Shaver, 2004). Emotion discriminatory abilities provide huge information regarding the emotional behaviors which are cognitively accessible to a person that places him at an advantageous position to have a lucid awareness over own emotional categories and to exercise more control over emotional behaviors (Barret, Gross, Christensen & Benvenuto, 2001).

Thus, acquiring the skills to deal with emotions i.e. emotion regulation and complex and differentiated emotional system have been come out as the important emotional consequents of mindfulness practices.

5. Emotion and health/well-being

The relationship between emotion and health has been always under the focus of attention of scholars, philosophers and modern researchers.

Hippocrates, the father of clinical medicine was the first to link emotional states with health. He thought that imbalances in four bodily fluids namely black bile, phlegm, blood and yellow bile lead to health related problems (Salovey, Rothman, Detweiler & Steward, 2000).

Like Hippocrates, modern researches also confirmed the role of emotional experiences in determining physical health of the individuals (Cohen & Rodriguez, 1995; Herbert & Cohen, 1993). Generally negative emotional states are assumed to cause maladaptive physiological functioning whereas positive emotional states are related with improved cardiovascular activity and immune system (e.g., Booth-Kewley & Friedman, 1987; Herbert & Cohen, 1993). Moreover, emotional states provide rich information about situational necessities (Schwarz & Clore, 1996) which guide behavioral decisions of the individuals that in turn affect physical health and well-being (Salovey, Rothman, Detweiler & Steward, 2000).

Salovey et al, (2000) also explained that positive emotions increase psychological resilience that enables individuals to confront the threats of health problems and thus promote adaptive health behaviors. Similarly, Fredrickson (2000) thought that positive emotional experiences increase personal resources that promote creativity and broaden though thought-action repertoire (Isen, 1987). Further, positive emotional states make people more future oriented and optimistic whereas negative emotional states make people situationally bounded (Frijda, 1986).

Hitherto, it is clear that emotions have great influence on human health and well-being. Thus, regulation of emotion is of great importance in relation to human health and well-being. This idea dates back to the time of Freud who stressed that psychological health and well-being is greatly determined by how well the affective impulses are regulated (Freud, 1923/1961). Later on, the followers of psychodynamic tradition focused on effects of emotion regulatory styles on health outcomes (e.g., Vaillant & Drake, 1985). Even modern theories also highlighted that affect impulses should be properly regulated to improve psychological health (Gross, 1998).

Emotion regulation has also been regarded as important for psychological well-being (Tamir & Mauss, 2011). Absence of adaptive regulation of emotion or emotion dysregulation often leads to several forms of psychopathology, ranging from affective disorder to personality disorder (Gross & Muñoz, 1995). Observing the beneficial effects of emotion regulation on health, psychological intervention techniques like cognitive behavioral therapy (CBT), dialectical behavioral therapy (DBT), emphasize on improving emotion regulation to enhance health and reduce various psychological symptoms (Hofmann & Asmundson, 2008; Linehan, 1993).

Among the major emotion regulation strategies, expressive suppression is a response focused strategy, widely used in instances of human interaction (Gross, 1998) and is related with decreased positive emotions (Gross & Levenson, 1997), interpersonal functioning (Butler et al., 2003), and well-being (Gross & John, 2003), and increased rumination about negative mood (Gross & John, 2003). Moreover, it is also found to be associated with increased activity of sympathetic nervous system during stressful situation which in turn elevates cardiovascular risks (Butler et al., 2003; Mauss & Gross, 2004).

One more chief emotion regulation strategy is cognitive reappraisal which involves systematic alteration in the interpretation of the emotional cues that consecutively modify adverse emotion experiences and induce positive ones (Gross, 1998). Cognitive reappraisal is associated with lower blood pressure and activation of prefrontal and anterior cingulate gyrus of the brain, which are generally involved in adaptive emotion regulation (Ochsner et al., 2004). Unlike expressive suppression cognitive reappraisal leads to psychological well-being and greater interpersonal sensitivity as well as reduced negative affect (Gross & John, 2003) without the activation of sympathetic system (Butler et al., 2003; Ochsner et al., 2004).

Besides emotion regulation, adaptive perception of emotions, proper understanding of emotions, cognitive control over emotions promote mental and physical well-ness (Schutte, Malouff, Thorsteinsson, Bhullar & Rooke, 2007). These mentioned qualities reduce the probability of developing maladaptive emotional states related to mood and anxiety disorders (Matthews, Zeidner, & Roberts, 2002). Even researches also showed that people who are high on emotional understanding, control and management tend to be more able to repair their negative mood states and less vulnerable to negative symptoms (Schutte, Malouff, Simunek, Hollander, & McKenley, 2002). On the other hand defused emotional awareness and emotional dysregulation make people susceptible to the symptoms of personality disorders and impulse control disorders (Matthews et al., 2002).

In sum, the mentioned discussion brings out the fact that the emotional constructs like regulation of emotions, emotional awareness and understanding as well as adaptive management have significant impacts on human health and well-being. Moreover, emotion regulating strategies like cognitive reappraisal has positive effect on health whereas expressive suppression influences it adversely.

It is also explicit from the preceding discussion that mindfulness as a trait as well as practice is associated with better health and well-being. However, the mechanism or process through which mindfulness brings positive health outcomes is under curious concerns of the researchers. The present conceptual analyses suggest the possibility that that mindfulness may give beneficial effect on health and well-being through positively modifying the emotion regulatory mechanisms. In a recent review Nyklíček (2011) also mentioned possible role of emotion regulation in mediating the positive effects of mindfulness on well-being. However, he also proposed a new elaborated theoretical model suggesting that mindfulness influences well-being through some of its direct outcomes such as relaxation, insight, contact, and harmony. These direct outcomes of mindfulness exert their beneficial effects on a number of lower-level intermediate factors (that includes non-volitional emotion regulation), which finally influence psychological well-being.

Further, the conceptual synthesis of the definitions of mindfulness with empirical findings also indicates the emotion regulatory factors may mediate the relationship of mindfulness with health/well-being. As per Baer et al (2006), mindfulness incorporates five dimensions such as observation of emotional states, its description, action with awareness, not judging emotions in terms of its valences and non-reactivity to inner experiences. These mindfulness dimensions produces high self-regulatory emotional states by making individuals cognitively distanced from the emotion turmoil (Hayes, Strosahl, & Wilson, 1999), which consecutively may promote better health and well-being. Nevertheless, such inferences are loaded with the chances of oversimplification and generalization. Rigorous empirical investigations are needed to explore such possibilities.

6. Mindfulness, emotion and health/wellbeing: Searching the hyphen

The preceding review brings to fore that mindfulness either as a meditation/ therapy technique or personality disposition is linked with better health and well-being on the one hand and a well regulated emotional life on the other. Further, it is also evident that emotionally regulated state of mind leads to better health and well-being. Given this tripartite relationship among mindfulness and health/well-being there are two possibilities- 1) the emotion and emotion regulation may play a hyphenated role between mindfulness-health relationship, and 2) mindfulness may be considered as a hyphen between emotion-health relationship. This section briefly reviews the empirical evidences and theoretical contention in support of the aforesaid possibilities.

A growing body of research explored the possible link through which mindfulness is associated human health/well-being. For example Shapiro, Carlson, Astin and Freedman (2006), mentioned the role of reperceiving for the said purpose. According to their view reperceiving is a meta-mechanism that controls several other sub-ordinate mechanisms like emotional self-regulation, values clarification, cognitive and behavioral flexibility, and exposure (Shaprio et al, 2006). Reperceiving refers to the capacity to make fundamental shift in the perspective which Shaprio et al. (2006) described as the ability to "disidentify from the contents of consciousness (i.e. one's thoughts) and view his or her moment-by-moment experience with greater clarity and objectivity". Nyklíček (2011) went one step further and stated that "reperceiving and mindfulness are virtually identical concepts, implying the process of disidentification or cognitive defusion". He argued that reperceiving reflects mindfulness based nonjudgmental awareness of the experiences which denotes disidentification because without disidentifying from any specific thought and affect one cannot become nonjudgmental and accepting (Krishnamurti, 1987). Carmody, Baer, Lykins and Olendzki (2009) empirically tested the above mentioned theoretical model that mindfulness training leads to changes in perspective (i.e. reperceiving) which further promotes four related processes i.e. self-regulation, values clarification, cognitive and behavioral flexibility, and exposure; and these four processes consequently lead to betterment of human health in a sample of 473 adults. Participants took part in an eight week mindfulness based stress reduction program (MBSR). Pre and post test measures of the said constructs revealed that scores on all the measures significantly increased after MBSR training. However, any significant mediating role of reperceiving was not found, Authors attributed this to the considerable overlap between mindfulness and reperceiving. Therefore they used combined score of mindfulness and reperceiving and found that all four mentioned processes i.e. self-regulation, values clarification, cognitive and behavioral flexibility, and exposure partially mediated the relationship of composite mindfulness with salutogenic outcomes.

Nyklíček (2011) proposed a new elaborated theoretical model (RICH model) suggesting that mindfulness elevates the status of human health/well-being by manipulating some direct outcomes such as relaxation, insight, contact, and harmony. These direct outcomes of mindfulness modify some lower-level intermediate factors (that includes nonvolitional emotion regulation), which finally induces psychological well-being.

Apart from abovementioned cognitive and personality variables, mindfulness is also linked with health and well-being through affective pathways. However, very few studies have explored the mediating role of emotion related variables in mindfulness-health/well-being relationship as compared to cognitive and personality factors (Nyklíček, 2011). In such a study, Mandal, Arya and Pandey (2012) attempted to explore the role of positive and negative affectivity in explaining the relationship of mindfulness with mental illness in a sample of 100 university students. Analyses showed that mindfulness was associated positively with positive affectivity and negatively with negative affectivity and different symptoms of mental illness. Moreover, positive affectivity was found to be associated negatively with the mental illness symptoms whereas negative affectivity was associated positively with the same. The result of mediation analysis showed that only negative affectivity significantly mediated the relationship of mindfulness with mental illness symptoms. It can be inferred from this study that mindfulness reduces the symptoms of mental illness by decreasing the frequency of negative affective experiences.

Studies also showed that some affect related capacities and traits like self-regulation (Howell, Digdon & Buro, 2010), emotional intelligence (Schutte & Malouff, 2011), self-compassion (Hollis-Walker & Colosimo, 2011) and emotion regulation (Hill & Updegraff, 2012) play a crucial role in associating mindfulness with health/well-being. Wachs and Cardova (2007) came up with a similar finding in their study on 33 married couples. They found that control of anger; emotion identification and communicative ability statistically mediate the relationship between mindfulness and marital quality. This result suggests that mindfulness improves marital quality through control of anger, ability to identify emotions and communicative ability.

All the aforesaid theoretical speculations make it explicit that the relationship of mindfulness with health/well-being is mediated thorough some cognitive and affective intermediate variables. However, the affective pathways of mindfulness to health/well-being are relatively less explored as compared to cognitive variables. Frederickson's (2000) broaden and build theory, Carstensen, Isaacowitz, and Charles's (1999) socio-emotional selectivity theory and RICH model of mindfulness (Nyklíček, 2011) heavily emphasize on some emotional processes and variables which may potentially explain mindfulness-health relationship.

In sum, all the mentioned studies indicate that mindfulness trait and interventions/mediation invariably improve human health/well-being both directly and through different mediating mechanisms which particularly involve emotional variables. Interestingly, an alternative anecdote can be found in traditional Buddhist texts. According to Pali scriptures like Satipatthana sutra (Arousing of Mindfulness), the qualities of mindfulness arise through complete transfiguration of mind by contemplating on body, feelings and consciousness (Soma Thera, 2010). Mindfulness based interventions programs like acceptance and commitment therapy (ACT) and dialectic behavioral therapy (DBT) chiefly focus on modifying some emotional traits such as emotional self-regulation, emotional acceptance, observing feelings without judgment and effective modulation of affect for cultivating mindfulness and inducing its related benefits (Cardaciotto, 2005; Linehan, 1993). These practices mainly prioritize the role of emotional awareness, acceptance and regulation in cultivating mindfulness and alleviating sufferings as well as increasing well-being. So, there is also an alternative possibility that some emotion related traits such as adaptive emotion regulation may act as the prerequisite for developing mindfulness which further leads to better health/well-being. In other words, mindfulness may act as the mediator in emotion regulation and well-being relationship. But this possibility has not been empirically exhausted yet.

7. Conclusions

The chapter highlights the evolution of the construct of mindfulness in the classical Buddhist tradition and argues that it represents the essence of Buddhist understanding of reality. The etymology of the term 'mindfulness' and its different connotations and meanings have also been discussed in this chapter.

Despite certain variations in conceptualization of the construct mindfulness in Buddhist philosophical tradition and contemporary psychological literature, theorist and researchers agree that it involves maintaining a non-judgmental and continuous awareness of the inner and external experiences in a way that the boundary between the observer and the observed is dissolved. Further, the preceding discussion also suggests that cultivation of such non-judgmental awareness and attention to each and every aspects of human existence has a beneficial effect on human health and well-being. This benefit of mindfulness on human health and well-being has been noted irrespective of the way it is attained. In other words, whether mindfulness is present as a trait like disposition or is cultivated and developed through certain meditative or therapeutic practice, it exerts a beneficial effect on health and well-being.

As far as the mechanism and routes through which mindfulness influences health and well-being is concerned the literature is inconclusive. We have hypothesized that emotion may play a hyphenated role in the relationship of mindfulness – health relationship. The affective pathways linking mindfulness to health and well-being highlights the role of such emotional constructs as emotions regulation, emotional differentiation, emotional awareness, adaptive emotion management etc. This speculation gets support from some direct empirical evidences as well as from indirect evidences which demonstrate that such emotional constructs are linked with mindfulness as well as health and well-being. The review suggests that mindfulness and mindfulness based techniques promote adaptive emotion regulation strategies, enhance emotion differentiation ability, and encourage non-judgmental awareness to the emotional experiences and these positive emotional outcomes in turn promote mental health and well-being.

The speculation that beneficial effect of mindfulness on health and well-being is mediated by emotional processes though gets support from empirical studies, an alternative possibility that emotion may be an antecedent to mindfulness has also been discussed. According to this view, the emotions are required to be dealt with prior to mindfulness and thus a well regulated and balances emotional state is a prerequisite of mindfulness. The emotion in this model is assumed to play a role of facilitator which helps to attain a deeper state of mindfulness which in turn promotes health and well-being. This speculation is based on classical Buddhist literature and has got some empirical support from our own research findings. However, our empirical test of the relative supremacy of the two alternative possibilities revealed that both the models yielded almost equally high and satisfactory model fit. Thus the issue remains whether emotions play a hyphenated role in the mindfulness-health relationship or they are the object of the mindfulness practice itself and needs to be dealt with prior to attaining the state of mindfulness. Further, the lack of observed superiority of the one model (emotion as mediator of mindfulness-health relationship) over the other (emotion as an antecedent of mindfulness) suggests yet another possibility that emotions may have a bidirectional link with mindfulness and thus forming an undesigning cyclical relationship – better regulated emotions leading to mindfulness which in turn resulting in better regulation of emotion. However, this speculation has been presented with a risk of overgeneralization and needs further empirical and theoretical support.

Overall, the present review though provide support to the notion that mindfulness is linked with better health and well-being and this link may be explained in terms of such emotional constructs as emotion regulation and emotional differentiation, the nature of role of emotion in the tripartite relationship of mindfulness, emotion and health/wellbeing is not yet clear. Further research is needed to understand this tripartite relationship and to develop mindfulness and emotion based models of human health and well-being.

References

Arch, J. J. & Craske, M. G. (2006). Mechanisms of mindfulness: Emotion regulation following a focused breathing induction. *Behavior Research and Therapy, 44*, 1849-1858

Baer, R. A. (2003). Mindfulness training as a clinical intervention: A conceptual and empirical review. *Clinical Psychology: Science and Practice, 10,* 125-143.

Baer, R., Smith, G., Hopkins, J., Krietemeyer, J., & Toney, L. (2006). Using self-report assessment methods to explore facets of mindfulness. *Assessment, 13*(1), 27-45. doi:10.1177/1073191105283504

Barrett, L. F., Gross, J., Christensen, T. C., & Benvenuto, M. (2001). Knowing what you're feeling and knowing what to do about it: Mapping the relation between emotion differentiation and emotion regulation. *Cognition & Emotion, 15*, 713–724.

Baumeister, R. F. & Leary, M. R. (1995). The need to belong: Desire for interpersonal attachments as a fundamental human motivation. *Psychological Bulletin, 117*, 497-529. *behavior.*

Biglan, A., & Hayes, S. C. (1996). Should the behavioral sciences become more pragmatic? The case for functional contextualism in research on human behavior. *Applied and Preventive Psychology: Current Scientific Perspectives, 5*, 47-57.

Bishop, S. R. (2002). What do we really know about Mindfulness-Based Stress Reduction? *Psychosomatic Medicine, 64*, 71-83.

Bishop, S. R., Lau, M., Shapiro, S. L., Carlson L., Anderson, N. D., Carmody, J., Segal, Z. V., Abbey, S., Speca, M., Velting, D. & Devins, G. (2004). *Mindfulness: A proposed operational definition. Clinical Psychology, Science and Practice, 11*, 230-241.

Blackledge, J. T., & Hayes, S. C. (2001). Emotion regulation in acceptance and commitment therapy. *Journal of Clinical Psychology, 57*, 243-255.

Bohart, A. (1983). Detachment: a variable common to many psychotherapies? Paper presented at the 63rd Annual Convention of the Western Psychological Association, San Francisco, CA.

Booth-Kewley, S. & Friedman, H. S. (1987). Psychological predictors of heart disease: A quantitative review. *Psychological Bulletin, 101*, 343-362.

Braza, J. (1997). *Moment by Moment: the Art and Practice of Mindfulness.* Boston: Charles Tuttle.

Breslin, F. C., Zack, M., & McMain, S. (2002). An information-processing analysis of mindfulness: Implications for relapse prevention in the treatment of substance abuse. *Clinical Psychology-Science & Practice, 9,* 275-299.

Brown, K. W., & Ryan, R. M. (2003). The benefits of being present: Mindfulness and its role in psychological well-being. *Journal of Personality and Social Psychology, 84,* 822-848.

Butler, E. A., Egloff, B., Wilhelm, F. H., Smith, N. C., Erickson, E. A., & Gross, J. J. (2003). The social consequences of expressive suppression. *Emotion, 3,* 48-67.

Cardaciotto, L. A. (2005). Assessing mindfulness: The development of a bi-dimensional measure of awareness and acceptance. Unpublished doctoral dissertation, Drexel University, Philadelphia.

Carmody, J., Baer, R. A., Lykins, L. E. B., & Olendzki, N. (2009). An empirical study of the mechanisms of mindfulness in a mindfulness-based stress reduction program. *Journal of Clinical Psychology, 65,* 613-626.

Carroll, J. B. (1993), *Human cognitive abilities: A survey of factor-analytic studies,* Cambridge University Press, New York, NY, USA

Carstensen, L. L., Isaacowitz, D. M., & Charles, S. T. (1999). Taking time seriously: A theory of socio-emotional selectivity. *American Psychologist, 54,* 165-181.

Chambers, R., Gullone, E., & Allen, N. B. (2009). Mindful emotion regulation: An integrative review. *Clinical Psychology Review, 29,* 560-572.

Chanowitz, B., & Langer, E. (1981). Premature cognitive commitment. *Journal of Personality and Social Psychology,41,* 1051-1063.

Cohen, S., & Rodriguez, M. S. (1995). Pathways linking affective disturbances and physical disorders. *Health Psychology, 14,* 374-380.

Csikszentmihalyi, M. (1975). *Beyond boredom and anxiety.* San Francisco: Jossey-Bass.

Davidson, R. J., Irwin, W. (1999). The functional neuroanatomy of emotion and affective style. *Trends in Cognitive Sciences, 3,* 11–21.

Deatherage, G. (1975). The clinical use of "mindfulness" meditation techniques in short-term psychotherapy. *Journal of Transpersonal Psychology, 7,* 133-143.

Deci, E. L., & Ryan, R. M. (1980). The empirical exploration of intrinsic motivational processes. In L. Berkowitz (Ed.), *Advances in experimental social psychology* (Vol. 13, pp. 39–80). New York: Academic.

Deci, E. L., & Ryan, R. M. (1985). *Intrinsic motivation and self-determination in human.* New York: Plenum.

Deci, E. L., & Ryan, R. M. (2000). The "what" and "why" of goal pursuits: Human needs and the self-determination of behavior. *Psychological Inquiry, 11,* 227–268.

Deci, E. L., Ryan, R. M., Gagné, M., Leone, D. R., Usunov, J., & Kornazheva, B. P. (2001). Need satisfaction, motivation, and well-being in the work organizations of a former Eastern Bloc country. *Personality and Social Psychology Bulletin,27,* 930-942.

Deci, E. L. (1980). *The psychology of self-determination.* Lexington, MA: D. C. Heath (Lexington Books). Japanese Edition, Tokyo: Seishin Shobo, 1985.

Deikman, A. J. (1982). The observing self. Boston: Beacon Press.

Dimeff, L., & Linehan, M. M. (2001). Dialectical behavior therapy in a nutshell. *The California Psychologist*, 34, 10-13.

Ekblad, G. A. (2009). *Effects of mindfulness training on emotion regulation and attention.* Dissertation submitted in partial fulfillment of the requirements for the degree of Doctor of Philosophy in the Department of Psychology & Neuroscience in the Graduate School of Duke University.

Ekman, P., Davidson, R. J., Ricard, M., & Wallace, B. A. (2005). Buddhist and psychological perspectives on emotions and well-being. *Current Directions in Psychological Science, 14*, 59-63.

Epstein, M. (1995). *Thoughts without a thinker: Psychotherapy from a Buddhist perspective.* New York: Basic Books.

Epstein, N. B., & Baucom, D. H. (2002). *Enhanced cognitive-behavioral therapy for couples: A contextual approach.* Washington, DC: American Psychological Association.

Fredrickson, B. L. & Branigan, C. (2005). Positive emotions broaden the scope of attention and thought-action repertoires. *Cognition and Emotion, 19*, 313-332.

Fredrickson, B. L. (2000). Cultivating positive emotions to optimize health and well-being. *Prevention and Treatment, 3,* Article 1. Available on the World Wide Web:http://journals.apa.org/prevention/volume3/pre0030001a.html.

Fredrickson, B. L., Cohn, M. A., Coffey, K., Pek, J., & Finkel, S. M. (2008). Open hearts build lives: Positive emotions, induced through meditation, build consequential personal resources. *Journal of Personality and Social Psychology, 95,* 1045–1062.

Freud, S. (1961). *The ego and the id.* In J. Strachey (Ed. and Trans.), *The standard edition of the complete psychological works of Sigmund Freud* (Vol. 19, pp. 3 - 66). London: Hogarth Press. (Original work published 1923)

Frewen, P. A., Evans, E. M., Maraj, M., Dozois, D. J. A., & Partridge, K. (2008). Letting Go: Mindfulness and negative automatic thinking. *Cogn Ther Res, 32,* 758–774.

Frijda, N. H. (1986). *The Emotions.* Cambridge University Press, Cambridge, UK.

Gross, J. J. (1998). Antecedent- and response-focused emotion regulation: Divergent consequences for experience, expression, and physiology. *Journal of Personality and Social Psychology, 74*, 224–237.

Gross, J. J., & John, O. P. (2003). Individual differences in two emotion regulation processes: Implications for affect, relationships, and well-being. *Journal of Personality and Social Psychology, 85*, 348-362.

Gross, J. J., & Levenson, R. W. (1997). Hiding feelings: The acute effects of inhibiting negative and positive emotion. *Journal of Abnormal Psychology, 106*, 95-103.

Gross, J.J. (1998). The Emerging Field of Emotion Regulation: An Integrative Review. *Review of General Psychology, 2,* 271-299.

Gross, J. J., & Munoz, R. F. (1995). Emotion regulation and mental health. *Clinical Psychology :Science and Practice, 2*, 151–164.

Gunaratana, V. H. (1991). *Mindfulness in plain English.* Boston: Wisdom Publications.

Hanh, T. N. (1976). *The miracle of mindfulness.* Boston: Beacon Press.

Hayes, A. M., & Feldman, G. C. (2005). Clarifying the construct of mindfulness in the context of emotion regulation and the process of change in therapy. *Clinical Psychology: Science and Practice, 11,* 255–262.

Hayes, S. C. (1993). Analytic goals and the varieties of scientific contextualism. In S. C. Hayes, L. J. Hayes, H. W. Reese, & T. R. Sarbin (Eds.), *Varieties of scientific contextualism* (pp. 11-27). Reno, NV: Context Press.

Hayes, S. C. Strosahl, K., & Wilson, K. G. (1999). *Acceptance and Commitment Therapy.* New York: Guilford Press.

Hayes, S. C., & Brownstein, A. J. (1986). Mentalism, behavior-behavior relations, and a behavior-analytic view of the purposes of science. *The Behavior Analyst, 9*(2), 175-190.

Hayes, S. C., Hayes, L. J., & Reese, H. W. (1988). Finding the philosophical core: A review of Stephen C. Pepper's World Hypotheses. *Journal of the Experimental Analysis of Behavior, 50,* 97-111.

Hayes, S. C., Luoma, J., Bond, F., Masuda, A., & Lillis, J. (2006). Acceptance and Commitment Therapy: Model, processes, and outcomes. *Behaviour Research and Therapy, 44*(1), 1-25.

Hayes, S. C., Strosahl, K. & Wilson, K. G. (1999). *Acceptance and Commitment Therapy: An experiential approach to behavior change.* New York: Guilford Press.

Herbert, T. B., & Cohen, S. (1993). Stress and immunity in humans: A meta-analytic review. *Psychosomatic Medicine, 55,* 364–379.

Hill, C. L., & Updegraff, J. A. (2012). Mindfulness and its relationship to emotional regulation. *Emotion, 21,* 81-90

Hofmann, S. G., & Asmundson, G. J. G. (2008). Acceptance and mindfulness-based therapy: New wave or old hat? *Clinical Psychology Review, 28,* 1-16.

Hollis-Walker, L., & Colosimo, K. (2011). Mindfulness, self-compassion, and happiness in non-meditators: A theoretical and empirical examination. *Personality and Individual Differences,* 222-227.

Horowitz, M. J. (2002). Self- and relational observation. *Journal of Psychotherapy Integration, 12,* 115-127.

Howell, A. J., Digdon, N. A., & Buro, K. (2010). Mindfulness predicts sleep-related self-regulation and well-being. *Personality and Individual Differences, 48,* 419-424.

Isaacowitz, D. M. (2005). An attentional perspective on successful socioemotional aging: Theory and preliminary evidence. *Research in Human Development, 2,* 115-132.

Isen, A. M. (1987). Positive affect, cognitive processes, and social behavior. In L. Berkowitz (Ed.), *Advances in experimental social psychology* (Vol. 20, pp. 203–253). New York: Academic.

Kabat-Zinn, J. (1982). An outpatient program in behavioral medicine for chronic pain patients based on the practice of mindfulness meditation: Theoretical considerations and preliminary results. *General Hospital Psychiatry, 4,* 33-47.

Kabat-Zinn, J. (1990). *Full catastrophe living: Using the wisdom of your body and mind to face stress, pain and illness. New York: Delacorte.*

Kabat-Zinn, J. (1994). *Wherever you go, there you are: Mindfulness meditation in everyday life.* NY: Hyperion.

Kabat-Zinn, J. (2003). Mindfulness-based interventions in context: Past, present, and future. *Clinical Psychology: Science & Practice, 10,* 144-156.

Kabat-Zinn, J., Lipsorth, L., Burney, R. (1985). The clinical use of mindfulness meditation for the self-regulation of chronic pain. *Journal of Behavioral Medicine,* 8 (2), 163-190.

Kabat-Zinn, J., Massion, A., Kristeller, J., Peterson, L. (1992). Effectiveness of a meditation based stress reduction program in the treatment of anxiety disorders. *American Journal of Psychiatry, 149,* 936-943.

Kang, S., & Shaver, P. R. (2004). Individual differences in well-differentiated emotional experience: Their possible psychological implications. *Journal of Personality, 72,* 687-726.

Kang, Y., Gruber, J., & Gray, J. R. (2013). Mindfulness and de-automatization. *Emotion Review, 5,* 192–201. doi:10.1177/1754073912451629

Kaplan, K., Goldenberg, D., Galvin-Nadeau, M. (1993). The impact of a meditation Based stress reduction program on fibromyalgia. *General Hospital Psychiatry, 15,* 284-289.

Kasamatsu, A., & Hirai, T. (1966). An electroencephalographic study on the Zen meditation (Zazen). *Psychologia, 12,* 205-225.

Kumar, S. M. (2002). An introduction to Buddhism for the cognitive-behavioural therapist. *Cognitive and Behavioural Practice, 9,* 40–43.

Krishnamurti, J. (1987). *The awakening of intelligence.* San Francisco: Harper.

Lang, P. J., Bradley, M. M., & Cuthbert, B. N. (1999). *International affective picture system (IAPS): Instruction manual and affective ratings (Tech. Rep. No. A-4).* Emotion and motivation I 297Gainesville, FL: University of Florida, The Center for Research in Psychophysiology.

Langer, E. (2002). Well-being: Mindfulness versus positive evaluation. In C. R. Snyder & S. J. Lopez (Eds.), *Handbook of positive psychology,* (pp. 214-230). London: Oxford University Press.

Langer, E. J. (1989). Minding matters: The consequences of mindlessness-mindfulness. In L. Berkowitz (Ed.), *Advances in experimental social psychology, (Vol. 22,* pp. 137-173). New York: Academic Press.

Langer, E. J. (1992). Matters of the mind: Mindfulness/Mindlessness in perspective. *Consciousness and Cognition, 1,* 289-305.

Langer, E. J., & Moldoveanu, M. (2000). The construct of mindfulness. *Journal of Social Issues, 56,* 1-10. http://dx.doi.org/10.1111/0022-4537.00148

Lindquist, K.A., & Barrett, L. F. (2008). Emotional complexity. In M. Lewis, J. M. Haviland-Jones, & L.F. Barrett (Eds.), *The handbook of emotion* (3rd ed.). New York: Guilford Press.

Linehan, M. M. (1993). *Cognitive-behavioral treatment of borderline personality disorder.* New York: Guilford Press.

Linehan, M. M. (2003). *From Suffering to Freedom: Practicing reality acceptance.* Seattle, WA: Behavioral Tech

Mandal, S. P., Arya, Y. K., & Pandey, R. (2011). Mindfulness, emotion regulation, and subjective well-being: An overview of pathways to positive mental health. *Indian Journal of Social Science Researches, 8,* 159-167.

Mandal, S. P., Arya, Y. K., & Pandey, R. (2012). Mental health and mindfulness: Mediational role of positive and negative affect. *SIS Journal of Projective Psychology and Mental Health, 19,* 150-159.

Matthews, G., Zeidner, M., & Roberts, R. D. (2002). *Emotional Intelligence: Science and Myth.* Cambridge, MA: MIT Press.

Mauss, I. B., & Gross, J. J. (2004). Emotion suppression and cardiovascular disease: Is hiding feelings bad for your heart? In I. Nyklíček, L. Temoshok & A. J. Vingerhoets (Eds.), *Emotional expression and health: Advances in theory, assessment and clinical applications* (pp. 61-81). Hove, UK: Brunner-Routledge.

Nyklíček, I., (2011). Mindfulness, emotion regulation, and health. In: I. Nyklíček, A. Vingerhoets, & M. Zeelenberg, *Emotion regulation and well-being (pp. 101-118).* New York: Springer.

Ochsner, K. N., Ray, R. D., Cooper, J. C., Robertson, E. R., Chopra, S., Gabrieli, J. D., & Gross, J. J. (2004). For better or for worse: neural systems supporting the cognitive down- and up-regulation of negative emotion. *Neuroimage, 23,* 483-499.

Özyeşil, Z. (2012). Mindfulness and Psychological Needs: A Cross-Cultural Comparison. İlköğretim Online, 11(1), 151-160, 2012. http://ilkogretim-online.org.tr

Rahula, W. (1986). *What the Buddha taught.* New York: Grove Press.

Raweewan, M., Pothongkom; S., Jitphaisarnwattana, M., Samart, J., & Tonmanee, J. (2012). The relationship between personality trait and mindfulness dimensions in primary schools in Thailand. In *Proceedings of the 1st Mae Fah Luang University*

International Conference 2012 (1st MFUIC2012) [CD-ROM], 29 November-1 December 2012, Chiang Rai, Thailand.

Robins, C. J. (2002). Zen principles and mindfulness practice in Dialectical Behavior Therapy. *Cognitive and Behavioral Practice, 9,* 50-57.

Ryan, R. (1995). Psychological needs and the facilitation in integrative process. *Journal of Personality, 63, 397-427.*

Ryan, R. M., & Brown, K. W. (2003). Why we don't need self esteem: Basic needs, mindfulness, and the authentic self. *Psychological Inquiry, 14,* 71–76.

Ryan, R. M., Huta, V., & Deci, E. L. (2008). Living Well: A self-determination theory perspective on eudaimonia. *Journal of Happiness Studies, 9,* 139-170.

Ryan, R. M., Stiller, J. D., & Lynch, J. H. (1994). Representations of relationships to teachers, parents, and friends as predictors of academic motivation and self-esteem. *Journal of Early Adolescence, 14,* 226-249.

Safran, J. D., & Segal, Z. V. (1990). *Interpersonal process in cognitive therapy.* New York: Basic Books. Softcover edition, 1996, Jason Aronson, Inc.

Salovey, P., Rothman, A. J., Detweiler, J. B., & Steward, W. T. (2000). Emotional states and physical health. *American Psychologist, 55,*110–121.

Schutte, N. S., & Malouff, J. M. (2011). Emotional intelligence mediates the relationship between mindfulness and subjective well-being. *Personality and Individual Differences, 50,* 1116-1119.

Schutte, N. S., Malouff, J. M., Thorsteinsson, E. B., Bhullar, N. Rooke, S. E. (2007). A meta-analytic investigation of the relationship between emotional intelligence and health *Personality and Individual Differences, 42(6),* 921–933.

Schwarz, N., & Clore, L.G. (1996). Feelings and Phenomenal Experiences. In E. Tory Higgins and Arie W. Kruglanski (Eds.), *Social Psychology: Handbook of Basic Principles,* NewYork: Guilford (pp. 433–465).

Segal, Z. V., Williams, J. M. G., & Teasdale, J. D. (2002). *Mindfulness-based cognitive therapy for depression: A new approach to preventing relapse.* New York: Guilford Press.

Shapiro, S. L., Carlson, L. E., Astin, J. A., & Freedman, B. (2006). Mechanisms of mindfulness. *Journal of Clinical Psychology, 62,* 373-386.

Smith, J. C. (1986). *Meditation: A Sensible Guide to a Timeless Discipline.* Champaign, IL: Research Press.

Speca, M., Carlson, L. E., Goodey, E., & Angen, M. (2000). A randomized, wait-list controlled clinical trial: The effect of a mindfulness meditation-based stress reduction program on mood and symptoms of stress in cancer outpatients. *Psychosomatic Medicine, 62,* 613-622.

Sternberg, R. J. (1977). *Intelligence, information processing, and analogical reasoning: The componential analysis of human abilities.* Hillsdale, NJ: Erlbaum.

Sternberg, R. J. (1997). *Successful intelligence.* New York, USA: Plume.

Sternberg, R. J. (2000). Images of mindfulness. *Journal of Social Science Issues, 56*(1), 11–26.

Sujato. (2005). *A history of mindfulness: How insight worsted tranquility in the Satipatthana Sutta*. Taipei: The Corporate Body of the Buddha Educational Foundation.

Sumedho, A. (1992). *The Four Noble Truths*. www.buddhanet.net.

Tamir, M., & Mauss, I. B. (2011). Social cognitive factors in emotion regulation: Implications forwell-being. In A. V. I. Nyklicek, M. Zeelenberg, & J. Denollet (Eds.), *Emotion regulation and well-being*: Springer (pp. 31–47).

Tart, C. (1972). States of consciousness and state-specific sciences. *Science, 176*, 1203-1210.

Teasdale, J. D., Segal, Z., & Williams, J. M. G. (1995). How does cognitive therapy prevent depressive relapse and why should attention control (mindfulness) training help? *Behaviour Research & Therapy, 33*, 25-39.

Thera, N. (1972). *The power of mindfulness*. San Francisco, CA: Unity Press.

Thera, S. (2010). The Way of Mindfulness: The Satipatthana Sutta and Its Commentary. *Access to Insight*, http://www.accesstoinsight.org/lib/authors/soma/wayof.html

Thompson, B. L., Waltz, J. (2007). Everyday mindfulness and mindfulness meditation: Overlapping constructs or not? *Personality and Individual Differences, 43*, 1875–1885.

Vaillant, G. E., & Drake, R. E. (1985). Maturing of ego defense in relation to DSM-III axis II personality disorder. *Archives of General Psychiatry, 42*, 597–601.

Wachs, K., & Cordova, J. V. (2007). Mindful relating: Exploring mindfulness and emotion repertoires in intimate relationships. *Journal of Marital & Family Therapy, 33*, 464-481.

Meditation and Mental Health

Anurag Upadhyay

Abstract: The liaison between meditations and mental health has shown a growing interest in the integration of cognitive as well as spiritual elements in an individual's life. Meditation always improves the mental state positively either by attentional reimbursement or by boosting psychological well-being. Therefore, meditation is a valuable gizmo for positive mental health. The aim of current chapter is to review the empirical evidences related to the use of meditation to facilitate the healthy development of the body, mind, spirit and mental unwind. In old age, meditation was considered to be a pure spiritual act while in the present techno scenario; meditation has been proved to have concerns with health, consciousness, intellect and self-realization. The present review also emphasizes the role of transitory state of mind which plays a vital role in individual's mental health. Meditation has been practiced for thousands of years by many cultures in different countries and continents because it renders a sense of well-being along with positive mental health. In sum, the regular practice of yoga is related to the healthy development of the body, mind, and spirit which leads to a more fulfilling life as well as building a fully functioning person. The chapter also tender directions for upcoming researches, which might intend to highlight the importance of transitory state of mind, cognitive role of meditation, expansion of the scope of practicing mediation for fostering of positive mental health, and study the utility of meditation for achieve best quality of life.

Key words: Meditations, State, Mental health, Attention

Introduction

Since the sunrise of human civilization, man is born to perform. The performance of human race depends upon body, mind and soul which are initial components of the human being. For more than 3,000 years of chronicled history, the care, maintenance, and preservation of the human body have been taught through meditation and yoga in the East as well as in the West. Either Indian or in Western tradition, meditation has been practiced for thousands of years by various cultures. That show throughout the world meditation like as something essential to the human spirit which is not dependent on race, history, geography or any particular religion. The importance of meditation and yoga in maintaining psycho – physiological balance and achieving internal harmony has been established by a number of research studies (Dass, 1971; Benson, 1984; Mukhopadhyay & Renukadevi, 2004; Jain & Purohit, 2006; Kannapan & LaxmiBai, 2008). In traditional primordial period meditation is considered as pure spiritual aspect which is helpful to achieve an enlightened persona. But in modern technical scenario, meditation has proved to have more concerned with mental as well as physical health, wellbeing, consciousness and intellect self-realization.

What is meditation?

Meditation comes from the Latin word 'meditatio' which means 'awareness', 'cognizance', 'contemplation' or 'dhyana'. The word *meditation* is used to describe sense regulation and control between body and mind. The meditation has been conceptualized from different angles such as the immersion of the self, sinking into the inner by turning thought processes from the outer world (Jung, 1958) or retraining of attention, whether through concentration or mindfulness (Goleman, 1988) or refers to practices that self-regulate the body and mind, thereby affecting mental events by engaging a specific attentional set regulation of attention, is the central commonality across the many divergent methods (Cahn & Polich, 2006). In language of cognition meditation involves the selection of goal-relevant information from the array of inputs that bombard our sensory systems (Slagter, Lutz, Greischar, Francis, Nieuwenhuis, Davis, & Davidson, 2007). Various thinkers have defined meditation in different ways but there remains no universal definition for meditation formed within the modern scientific community. However, in popular usage, the word "meditation" and the phrase "meditative practice" are often used interchangeably.

Meditation and Cognition

Meditation improves our cognitive capabilities because it is directly related to mind. Ample of researches confirmed that similar to attentional process, during meditation alpha or theta wave EEG activity showed modest increment (Banquet, 1973; Hebert & Lehmann, 1977; Pagano & Warrenburg, 1983; Jacobs & Lubar, 1989; Pan, Zhang, & Xia, 1994; Aftanas & Golocheikine, 2001; Aftanas & Golocheikine, 2002; Lutz, Lawrence, Greischar, Rawlings, Davidson & Antoine, 2004; Chang & Lo, 2005). On the basis of attentional budget meditation is classified in two broad categories: concentrative or focused attention (FA) meditation *which focuses intensively on one particular object* and mindfulness or open monitoring (OM) meditation refers to *non-reactive monitoring of the content of experience from moment to moment.* (Koshikawa & Ichii, 1996; Naranjo & Ornstein, 1971; Bond, et. al. 2009; Lutz, Slagter, Dunne & Davidson, 2008). Besides these in the mid-1950s Maharishi Mahesh Yogi (1918–2008) coined the term transcendental meditation (TM). TM is also a unique type of meditation which refers to a specific form of *mantra meditation* where sound or mantras are used. By using these meditational techniques an individual achieves the state of positive mental traits like acceptance of self, self-confidence, self reliance, self actualization along with strong cognitive capabilities like vigilance (Brown, Forte, & Dysart, 1984; Jha, Krompinger, & Baime, 2007), mental imagery (Kozhevnikov, Louchakova, Josipovic, & Motes, 2009) etc. However, meditation improves concentration (Moore & Malinowski, 2009), short-term attention switching (Chambers, Lo, Allen, & Allen, 2008), memory (Ray et. al., 2001) whereas it also decreases interference (Moore & Malinowski, 2009) and attentional-blink refractory period (Slagter et al., 2007). Lots of empirical evidences from neuro-imaging studies suggest that the categories of meditation, defined by how they direct attention, appear to generate different brainwave patterns (Lutz, et al, 2008; Lehmann, Faber, Achermann, Jeanmonod, Lorena, Gianotti, & Pizzagalli; 2001). Many recent behavioral, electroencephalographic and neuro-imaging studies had also revealed the importance of investigating states and traits related to meditation in order to achieve an increased understanding of cognitive and affective neuroplasticity, attention and self-awareness (Cahn & Polich, 2006; Lutz, Slagter, Dunne, & Davidson, 2008). In current psychological researches, meditation has been defined and characterized in a variety of ways like role of attention (Goleman, 1988; Roger & Shauna, 2006; Cahn & Polich, 2006; Jevning, Wallace & Beidebach, 1992) concentration maker (Moore & Malinowski, 2009), short-term attention switching (Chambers, Lo, Allen, & Allen, 2008), memory (Ray et. al., 2001) etc. Moreover, meditation engenders a sense of well-being. Meditation always improves the mental state positively either by attentional reimbursement or by boost psychological well-being. Therefore meditation is a valuable gizmo for positive mental health.

Mental Health and Meditation

Mental Health is an initial component of the *health*. Often when the concept of health is employed in the domain of mind, it is referred to as *mental health*. Mental health *is* defined as the absence of the qualities of mental ill-health which includes almost all the disorders of behaviour which are caused by faulty perception, emotion, thinking and attitude. So, mental health is a state of maintaining harmony or balance between the needs, desires, aspirations and attitudes of the individual with respect to the prevailing conditions in the external environment. According to World Health Organization, mental health is a state of well-being in which the individual realizes his or her own abilities, can cope with the normal stresses of life, can work productively and fruitfully, and is able to make a contribution to his or her community" (WHO, 2001). Therefore mental health is an integrative concept which has several components or dimensions. Ryff (1995), exemplified several dimensions of mental health such as self esteem, realization of one's potential, the ability to maintain fulfilling meaningful relationship and psychological well-being etc. From perspectives of the discipline of positive psychology or holism mental health may include an individual's ability to enjoy life and procure a balance between life activities and efforts to achieve psychological resilience (Singh & Upadhyay, 2014). Mental health is frequently used as a state of mental as well as spiritual wellbeing of the individual. That is why from the eastern to the western culture meditation has long been used for the maintenance of "well-being" (1). Plethora of researches has confirmed that regular practice of meditation helps in the development of the mind, and spirit which leading to a healthier and more fulfilling life (Bhole, 1983; Ray, Mukhopadhyaya, Purkayastha, Asnani, Tomer, Prashad, Thakur & Selvamurthy; 2001). So it is very clear that meditation and mental health are interrelated concepts and meditation provides direction to mental health. In our modern techno scenario meditation refers to group of techniques, such as mantra, relaxation, mindfulness, or Zen Buddhist meditation etc. Furthermore, in cognitive term meditation can be conceptualized as a family of complex emotional and attentional regulatory practices, in which mental and related somatic events are affected by engaging a specific attentional set (Raffone & Srinivasan, 2009). Thus, meditation aims to calm the mind and increases relaxation (Riley, 2004) along with positive transitory state of mind.

Mental Health, Meditation and States

In Vedic mores, meditation has been considered as one of the six orthodox systems of Indian philosophy as a basic constituent of yoga because on one hand it emphasize on cognitive boosting process while on other hand advance the psychological wellbeing which is positive outcome of wealthy mental health. The practice of meditation (concentrative) may result in a self-organization of brain processes with increased efficiency in the arousal burst mechanism, leading to enhanced mismatch negativity (MMN) amplitudes (i.e. the paradigm which is an indicator of pre-attentive processing) and change detection (Srinivasan & Baijal, 2007). In addition meditation increases the bodily relaxation along with enhancement of cognitive capabilities like pre-attentive perceptual processes (Srinivasan & Baijal, 2007) which affect the transitory state of mind. The transitory states has been dealt with *Trilogy of Mind* which divides psychological functioning of stress into three domains viz. affect, conation (motivation), and cognition. Mental health depends on perfect concoction of affect, conation and cognition which nourished by meditation. So meditation plays the role of concierge of mental health that characterized by positive mental state that is subjectively experienced as being happy, contented and desired. By achieving the wealthy mental health an individual gets resilience, self realization, self-confidence and self-reliance. A positive mental health forms the understanding of one's strengths and weaknesses with his positive characteristics that outweigh the negative traits. A mentally healthy individual has the realization of personal potential of self-actualization and intrinsic motivation which encourages the person to maximize capabilities and talents. The person with positive mental health has a balance of psychic forces which is helpful for vigorous human strengths as well as developmental maturity. Thus mental health is perceived as transitory mental state that is subjectively experienced as being happy, contented and desired. When an individual doing meditation he/she try to control on senses and focused his concentration aura on a point to get state of relaxation along with cognitive dexterity. These efforts make individual self-directed, self-determine, self-controlled and independence in decision making that's why individual acts are cognitively evaluated and independently of the outside world. Additionally positive mental health make available an initial foundation to perform a task like cognitive, attentional or spiritual etc., because mentally healthy reality perception includes perception free from need distortion and views the world without distortions, apt the perception to objective cues. A mentally healthy person perceived the world that are present, and does not reject evidence because it does not fit his or her wishes or needs. So the positive mental health provides a realistic way to perceive. Hence positive mental health refers to integration at the cognitive level, which implies a unifying philosophy of life that shapes feelings and behaviours.

Plethora of experimental studies confirm that long-term training of meditation has resulted in positive changes in behavior and changes in brain activity, like increase in theta activity especially in the frontal areas (Banquet, 1973; Hebert & Lehmann, 1977; Aftanas & Golocheikine, 2002; Srinivasan & Baijal, 2007). That means meditation puts forward positive mental verve which cultivates the positive transitory state of mind as well as spiritual and affective positive resources. Moreover, meditation increases the awareness of subjective thoughts and feelings which are the crucial component of positive mental health. Nowadays, meditation is considered as a technique of stress reducing because it has been shown to positively affect a range of autonomic physiological processes, such as lowering blood pressure, impulsivity, daydreaming, depression and emotional reactivity etc. By declining in arousal impulsivity, autonomic over reactions, illogical thinking, attentional blinks or divagate and depression meditation render the collective experience of relaxation, perceptual sensitivity, mental alertness, and a sense of stronger will that produce a sense of joy and an emotional 'high', which is vital for strong positive mental health.

Positively healthy (mentally) person performed well in mundane as well as applied task; like baggage inspection at airport security checkpoints, air-traffic control (ATC), long distance driving etc. where sustained attention play vital role; due to his/her affluent cognitive, affective and conation (motivation) resources. When a person performs a task not only task specification and characteristics influence performance but performances also change the various components of person mind's transitory states. So it is very important that person maintain his positive state of mind during performing task because some time task is itself stressful and imposed a considerable degree of stress in addition to workload which are critical determinants of performance without the addition of an external stressors (Szalma, Hancock, Dember, & Warm, 2006; Davies & Parasuraman, 1982; Warm & Dember, 1998; Galinsky, Rosa, Warm, & Dember, 1993). Thus meditation is used as best remedy for stress and forming healthy positive mental state because meditation is becoming widely popular as an adjunct to conventional patches for wound of stress.

Today, meditation is used as preeminent nutrients for positive mental health because it gives an impeccable balance of psychic or instinctive forces, a unified outlook on life and resistance to stress. That is why it is extensively admired as a means of shaping the person's state of mind which is obligatory for a healthy positive mental health.

At last it is very important to understand that the higher order cognitive processes are the only factor that segregates human beings from the other species. It is also essential to note that meditation is the inner process that serves as a sharpener for our other cognitive abilities, Apart from this mediation also facilitate in maintaining a positive mental health. The increasing demand of the present externalities and pressing requirement of constant use of cognitive functions exhaust mental health. In such situations mediation serves as a major help for maintaining calm mental state. Indian mythology also puts emphasis on 'Dhyan' which in sense denotes the same connotation that is meditation.

Conclusion

The current chapter reviews the studies based on meditation and mental health. Several researches done in India and abroad conclude that regular practice of meditation helps in the development of the mind, and spirit which leads to a healthier and more fulfilling life. The major goal of the current review is to inspect the effects of meditations on mental health. Previous studies had investigated meditation being helpful for improving cognitive, spiritual as well as psychological (mental) domain of individuals. But the focus of researchers on meditation has led to neglect of other components like person's transitory 'state of mind' which may influence mental health. Meditation is essential component for individual's psyche thus it improves cognitive capabilities like attention, intelligence, memory and perceptual processes. So it is very clear that yoga as well as meditation practice should be essential to all for achieving the spiritual goal of life along with positive mental health.

Reference

Aftanas, L. I., & Golocheikine, S. A. (2001). Human anterior and frontal midline theta and EEG during meditation. *Neuroscience Letters, 330,* 143–146.

Aftanas, L.I., & Golocheikine, S. A. (2002). Non-linear dynamic complexity of the human investigation of meditation. *Neuroscience Letters, 310,* 57–60.

Banquet, J. P. (1973). Spectral analysis of the EEG in meditation. *Electroencephalography and Clinical Neurophysiology, 35,* 143–151.

Benson, H. (1984). *The relaxation response.* New York: Avon.

Bhole, M. V., (1983). Yoga and primary health care. *Yoga-Mimamsa,* 22.

Brown, D., Forte, M., & Dysart, M. (1984). Differences in visual sensitivity among mindfulness meditators and non-meditators. *Perceptual and Motor Skills, 58,* 727-733.

Cahn, B. R., Polich, J., (2006). Meditation states and traits: EEG, ERP, and neuroimaging studies. *Psychological Bulletin 132,*180–211.

Chambers, R., Lo, B. C. Y., Allen, N. B., & Allen, N. B. (2008). The impact of intensive mindfulness training on attentional control, cognitive style, and affect. Cognitive Therapy and Research, 32, 303–322.

Chang, K. M., Lo, P. C., (2005). Meditation EEG interpretation based on novel fuzzy-merging strategies and wavelet features. *Biomedical Engineering Applications, Basis & Communication, 17,* 167-175.

Dass, R. (1971). *Be Here Now.* San Cristobal, New Mexico: Lama Foundation.

Davies, D. R., & Parsuraman, R. (1982). *The psychology of vigilance.* London: Academic Press.

Galinsky, T. L., Rosa, R. R., Warm, J. S., & Dember, W. N. (1993). Psychophysical determinants of stress in sustained attention. *Human Factors, 35,* 603-614.

Goleman, D. (1988). *The meditative mind: The varieties of meditative experience.* New York: Putnam.

Hebert, R., & Lehman, D. (1977). Theta bursts: An EEG pattern in normal participants practicing the TM technique. *Electroencephalography and Clinical Neurophysiology, 42,* 397–405.

Jacobs, G. D., & Lubar, J. F. (1989). Spectral analysis of the central nervous system effects of the relaxation response elicited by autogenic training. *Behavioral Medicine, 15,* 125–132.

Jain, M., & Purohit, P. (2006). Spiritual intelligence: A contemporary concern with regard to living status of the senior citizens. *Journal of the Indian Academy of Applied Psychology, 32* (3), 227 - 233.

Jevning, R., Wallace, R. K., & Beidebach, M. (1992). The physiology of meditation: A review: A wakeful hypometabolic integrated response. *Neuroscience & Biobehavioral Reviews 16* (3): 415–424.

Jha, A. P., Krompinger, J, Baime, M. J. (2007). Mindfulness training modifies subsystems of attention. *Cognitive, Affective & Behavioral Neuroscience, 7*(2):109-119.

Jung, C. G., (1958) *The Collected Works of C. G. Jung*, vol. 11, London: Routledge.

Kannappan, R., & Bai, L. (2008). Efficacy of Yoga: Cognitive and Human Relationship Training for Correcting Maladjustment Behaviour in Deviant School Boys, Indian Journal of the Indian Academy of Applied Psychology, 34, 60-65.

Koshikawa, F., & Ichii, M. (1996) An experiment on classifications of meditation methods on procedures, goals and effects. In: Haruki, Y., Ishii, Y., Suzuki, M., (Eds.), Comparative and psychological study on meditation (pp. 213-24) Delft, Netherlands: Eburon Publishers.

Kozhevnikov, M., Louchakova, O., Josipovic, Z., & Motes, M. A. (2009). The enhancement of visuospatial processing efficiency through Buddhist deity meditation. Psychological Science, 20, 645–653.

Lehmann, D., Faber, P. L., Peter, A., Jeanmonod, D., Gianotti, L. R. R., & Pizzagalli, D., (2001). Brain sources of EEG gamma frequency during volitionally meditation-induced, altered states of consciousness, and experience of the self. *Psychiatry Research, 108* (2), 111–121.

Lutz, A., Lawrence, L., Greischar, N. B., Rawlings, Ricard, M. & Davidson, R. J. (2004). Long-term meditators self-induce high-amplitude gamma synchrony during mental practice, by in The Proceedings of the *National Academy of Sciences USA 101*(46)16369-16373

Lutz, A., Slagter, H. A., Dunne, J. D., & Davidson, R. J. (2008). Attention regulation and monitoring in meditation. Trends in Cognitive Sciences, 12, 163–169.

Lutz, A., Slagter, H. A., Rawling, B. N, Francis, D. A., Greischar. L. L, & Davidson, R. J. (2009). Mental training enhances stability of attention by reducing cortical noise. *Journal of Neuroscience, 29*, 13418–13427

Moore, A., Malinowski, P., (2009). Meditation, mindfulness and cognitive flexibility. *Conscious. Cogn.18*, 176–186.

Mukhopadhyay, B., & Renukadevi, S. (2004). Chakra meditation in achieving altered states of consciousness. In K. Joshi & M. Cornelissen (Eds.), *Consciousness, Indian psychology and yoga* (pp. 130–36). New Delhi: Centre for Studies in Civilizations.

Naranjo, C., & Ornstein, R. (1971). On the psychology of meditation. New York: The Viking Press.

Pagano, R. R., & Warrenburg, S. (1983). Meditation: In search of a unique effect. In R. J. Davidson, G. E. Schwartz, & D. Shapiro (Eds.), *Consciousness and self-regulation* (Vol. 3, pp. 152–210). New York: Plenum Press.

Pan, W., Zhang, L., & Xia, Y. (1994). The difference in EEG theta waves between concentrative and non-concentrative qigong states: Power spectrum and topographic mapping study. *Journal of Traditional Chinese Medicine, 14*, 212–218.

Raffone, A., Srinivasan, N., (2009) An adaptive workspace hypothesis about the neural correlates of consciousness: insights from neuroscience and meditation studies. In: Srinivasan N(ed) *Progress in brain research: attention*, (vol-176). Elsevier, Amster- dam, pp161–180

Ray U. S., Mukhopadhyaya, S., Purkayastha, S. S., Asnani, V., Tomer, O. S., Prashad, R., Thakur, L., et al. (2001). Effect of yogic exercises on physical and mental health of young fellowship course trainees. *Indian Journal of Physiological Pharmacology, 45*,37–53.

Riley, D. (2004). Hatha yoga and the treatment of illness. *Altern. Ther. Health Med.* 10,20–21.

Roger, W., & Shauna, L. S., (2006). The meeting of meditative disciplines and western psychology: A mutually enriching dialogue. *American Psychologist* (American Psychological Association) *61* (3), ISSN 0003-066X.

Ryff, C. D. 1995. Psychological well-being in adult life. *Current Directions in Psychological Science.* 4: 99-104.

Slagter, H. A., Lutz, A., Greischar, L. L., Francis, A. D., Nieuwenhuis, S., Davis, J. M., & Davidson, R. J. (2007). Mental training affects distribution of limited brain resources. *Plos Biology, 5*, 1228-1235.

Slagter, H.A., Lutz, A., Greischar, L.L., Francis, A.D., Nieuwenhuis, S., Davis, J.M., Davidson, R.J., 2007. PLOS Biol. 5, e138.

Srinivasan, N. and Baijal, S. (2007) Concentrative meditation enhances pre-attentive processing: a mismatch negativity study. *Neuroreport 18*, 1709–1712

Szalma, J. L., Hancock, P. A., Dember, W. N., & Warm, J. S. (2006). Training for vigilance: The effect of KR format and dispositional optimism and pessimism on performance and stress. *British Journal of Psychology, 97*, 115-135.

Tang, Yi. Y., Ma, Y., Wang, J., Fan Y., Lu, S. F. Q., Yu, Q., Sui, D., Rothbart, M. K., Fan, M., Posner M. I. (2007) Short-term meditation training improves attention and self-regulation. *Proceedings of the National Academy of Sciences, (23 October 2007), 104, No. 43*.17152-17156.

Warm, J. S., & Dember, W. N. (1998). Tests of vigilance taxonomy. In: R.R. Hoffman, M. F. Sherrick, and J. S. Warm (Eds.). *Viewing psychology as a whole: The integrative science of William N. Dember.* (pp. 87-112). Washington, DC: American.

Role of Spirituality in mental health: A Rethinking

Rejani.T.G.

Abstract: Spirituality is concerned with people finding meaning and purpose in their lives, as well as the sense of belonging, of community. The role of spirituality in general health, especially mental health received lots of attention in recent times among researchers and clinicians. This article focuses on the definition, different practices of spirituality, impact of spirituality on mental health especially alcohol and drug dependence, depression, anxiety and schizophrenia. The author concluded that more methodologically sound studies can resolve the issue of understanding spirituality in a better way and how to utilize it in the patient care.

Introduction

The role of spirituality in general health, especially mental health received lots of attention in recent times among researchers and clinicians. Spirituality and religion are not considered as same. Religion is institutionalized spirituality. Thus, there are several religions having different sets of beliefs, traditions, and doctrines. They have different types of community-based worship programs. Spirituality is the common factor in all these religions (Verghese, 2008).

Spirituality is concerned with people finding meaning and purpose in their lives, as well as the sense of belonging, of community. Because spirituality comes into focus in times of stress, suffering, physical and mental illness, loss, dying and bereavement, it is important not only in psychiatry but also throughout all of medicine (Koenig, McCullough & Larson,2001).

Spirituality has been called 'a quality that strives for inspiration, reverence, awe, meaning and purpose, even in those who do not believe in God' (Murray & Zentner, 1989). It has been described as being 'where the deeply personal meets the universal'; a sacred realm of human experience (Culliford, 2002). According to the WHO (1998), spirituality is categorized under four headings: transcendence(Connectedness to a spiritual being or force, Meaning of life, Awe, Wholeness/integration, Divine love, Inner peace/serenity/harmony, Inner strength, Death and dying, Detachment/attachment, Hope/optimism, Control over your life), personal relationships (Kindness to others/selflessness, Acceptance of others, Forgiveness), codes to live by (Freedom to practice beliefs and rituals, Faith), and specific beliefs.

Spirituality traditionally had a narrow definition centred on belief in supernatural spirits such as God. However, mental health services have become increasingly interested in addressing the "spiritual" needs of consumers in recent times, and as a result attempts have been made to redefine the term in a way that would be maximally inclusive, so as to apply to people from diverse religious backgrounds and to those with no religion (Koenig, 2008). Though there is no consensus in the definition of spirituality in the literature, many definitions focused on the meaning and purpose in life.

People practices spirituality in many different ways such as prayer, meditation, social services, and yoga. Waaijman (2000) discerns four forms of spiritual practices: (1) Somatic practices, especially deprivation and diminishment. The deprivation purifies the body. Diminishment concerns the repulsement of ego-oriented impulses. (2) Psychological practices, such as meditation. (3)Social practices such as practice of obedience. (4) Spiritual. All practices aim at purifying the ego-centeredness, and direct the abilities at the divine reality. According to Waaijman (2006), there are three elements of spirituality: a relational process between god and man, a gradual process of reciprocity, and transformation.

Many studies have focused on the role of spirituality in general health, and according to Puchalski (2001) the studies tend to fall into 3 major areas: mortality, coping, and recovery. Studies have found that people who have regular spiritual practices tend to live longer, tend to have more quality of live and positive outlook, helped to cope with diseases like cancer and HIV and faces death, able to recover from illness (Strawbridge, Cohen, Shema, & Kaplan, 1997; Roberts, Brown, Elkins, &Larson, 1997; Kaldjian, Jekel,

& Friedland, 1998). In a meta-analysis of 42 studies, McCullough, Hoyt, Larson, Koenig, & Thoresen(2000) found that people with a high religious involvement were likely to die older than their non-religious counterparts.

In addition to general health, mental health field also started understanding the importance of mental health and spirituality. There is a growing consensus that mental health and spiritual health are closely related (Barker & Buchanan-Barker, 2005). Many studies have reported positive impact of spirituality on different mental health disorders.

Alcohol and drug dependence

The studies have found spirituality predicts behavior such as honesty and responsibility helped alcohol abstinence among alcohol dependents (Tonigan, 2003). Miller, Davies, & Greenwald (2000) found that low level of religiosity was associated with substance abuse. But in a recent study, it was reported that Spiritual people were more likely than those who were neither religious nor spiritual to have ever used or be dependent on drugs, and they were also more likely to be taking psychotropic medication (King et al, 2013).

Depression

Many studies were found that spirituality act as protective factor for depression. Brown and Prudo (1981) reported that church going and active religion were protective factors to vulnerability for depression. Miller, Warner, Wickramaratne, and Weissman (1997) found that maternal religiosity and mother-child concordance in religiosity were protective against depression in the offspring. Olszewski (1994) reported that for those who find meaning or purpose in life through religion or spirituality, church attendance is often (although not always) associated with lower levels of depression and this is true for adults, children and young people. Peselow, Sarah Pi, Lopez, André Besada, and IsHak (2014) tried to find the impact of spirituality in the treatment of major depressive disorder and the findings suggested that greater spirituality is associated with less severe depression. Moreover, the degree to which the measures of depressive symptom severity, hopelessness, and cognitive distortions improved over the course of eight weeks was significantly greater for those patients who were more spiritual.

Interest continues to grow in understanding the place of spirituality in depression, but consensus has been difficult to achieve about how best to approach the intertwined emotional, existential, and spiritual dimensions of patients' depressive concerns. The framework proposed by Peteet (2012) emphasizes the need for clinicians to consider a broad range of diagnostic categories and dynamic concerns arising in depressive conditions, to recognize the existential dimension of these concerns in areas such as identity and hope that are causing emotional distress, to identify corresponding goals for an appropriately helpful spirituality, and to select interventions accordingly, so as to provide individualized, comprehensive treatment.

Anxiety

Prayer and/ or meditation and yoga were the frequently used measures to tackle anxiety in spiritual way. Many studies were also found positive outcome. Michalsen et al. (2005) found that Compared to those allocated to the waiting list control group, women who participated in the yoga-training demonstrated pronounced and significant improvements in perceived stress, state and trait anxiety, well-being, vigour, fatigue and depression. Physical well-being also increased and those subjects suffering from headache or back pain reported marked pain relief. Salivary cortisol (a measure of stress) decreased significantly after participation in a yoga class. In review, Shaw, Joseph, and Linley (2005) reported that traumatic experiences can lead to a deepening of religion or spirituality. Third, that positive religious coping, religious openness, readiness to face existential questions, religious participation, and intrinsic religiousness are typically associated with improved post-traumatic recovery.

Schizophrenia

A study in India found that schizophrenia patients who spent more time in religious activities tended to have a better prognosis at two-year and five-year follow ups (Verghese et al, 1989, 1990). According to Mohr and Huguelet (2004) religion plays a central role in the processes of reconstructing a sense of self and recovery in schizophrenia. In a review Grover, Davuluri, and Chakrabarti (2014) Available evidence suggests that for some patients, religion instills hope, purpose, and meaning in their lives, whereas for others, it induces spiritual despair. Patients with schizophrenia also exhibit religious delusions and hallucinations. Further, there is some evidence to suggest that religion influences the level of psychopathology. Religion and religious practices also influence social integration, risk of suicide attempts, and substance use. Religion and spirituality also serves as an effective method of coping with the illness. Religion also influences the treatment compliance and outcome in patients with schizophrenia.

Spirituality also can have impact on marital life such as harmonious marital relationships and better parenting skills. That in turn enhanced children's competence, self-regulation, psychosocial adjustment and school performance (Brody, 2003).

Though many studies have noted positive impact of spirituality, some studies have also noted negative impact or no effect on mental health. King et al. (2013) interviewed over 7000 people in England and the results showed that religious participants were similar to non-religious/non-spiritual ones in regards to their mental health in most respects, although the religious were less likely to have used or been dependent on drugs in the last year. Compared to people who were in the neither category, spiritual but not religious people were more likely to take psychotropic medication, to use or be dependent on recreational drugs, to have a generalised anxiety disorder, phobia, or any neurotic disorder, or to have abnormal eating attitudes. They concluded that people who are spiritual but not religious in their understanding of life are more vulnerable to mental disorders than other people.

Recommendations and future directions

Issues in definition

There is standard acceptable definition of spirituality is available, so the studies have used different definitions for the concept of spirituality which may yield conflicting results or may not give a picture of process of spirituality. Many times it may be confused with well-being or religiosity. Good mental health implies that a person has some purpose in life, is hopeful, socially connected and has peace and well-being and many researches used purpose in life, hopefulness, social connectedness, peacefulness and well-being in general for assessing spirituality (Lindeman & Aarnio,2007). Spirituality is also confused with virtues like kindness, hope which further added confusion in the interpretation of the results. There is recognition (at least theoretically) that there are differences between religion and spirituality and that either can be practiced without the necessary involvement of the other. Operationally, however, the distinction between religious practices and spirituality is often blurred, with much of the research using measures of religious practice as a proxy for spirituality (Ukst-Margetic & Margetic, 2005). The dilemma related to the definition of spirituality can be resolved by having acceptable definitions, which would be beneficial to the understanding of its impact on health, especially mental health.

Quantitative vs qualitative

Many of the available studies have used quantitative method to measure impact of spirituality on health, mental health and over all well-being. Though it is important to have quantitative measurement to understand the impact, qualitative methods are equally important to understand its process as spirituality is related to personal experiences and beliefs unique to the individual. The meaning of spirituality differs individual to individual, so it is important to understand the perception and attribution to the cause and effect. Sometimes HIV client may believe that god has punished him for his bad deeds and parents of special need children may think that the child is born as punishment to their past karma. So only using quantitate approaches may not explain the process of how it has helped them to cope in a better way or in the reduction of severity of symptoms. Moreover, studies used one or two questions to assess the spirituality which again limit the understanding of spirituality in a better way, which highlight the necessity of developing standardized tools to measure spirituality.

Mediating variables

Though many studies have proved that spirituality is beneficial in positive mental health and treating mental illness, the possibility of mediating variables are not yet addressed properly in the studies. Many studies suffer methodological issues, biased sampling and poor definition of spirituality, the finding cannot be generalized, thus emphasized the importance of mediating variables.

Conclusion

Researchers and clinicians suggest that spirituality plays an important role in client's life and it is important to give attention to it while treating them or for the enhancement of mental health. But many apprehend that it may blur the distinction between doctor and clergy. More methodologically sound studies can resolve the issue of understanding spirituality in a better way and how to utilize it in the patient care.

References

Barker, P., & Buchanan-Barker, P. (2005) *Breakthrough: Spirituality and Mental Health.* London: Whurr Books.

Brody, G.H. (2003). Religiosity and family relationships. *Journal of marriage and the family*, 4;56.

Brown, G.W., & Prudo, R. (1981). Psychiatric disorders in a rural and an urban Population: etiology of depression. *Psychological Medicine*, 11,58.

Culliford, L. (2002). Spirituality and Clinical Care. *British Medical Journal*, 325, 1434-1435

Grover, S., Davuluri, T., & Chakrabarti, S. (2014). Religion, Spirituality, and Schizophrenia: A Review. *Indian Journal of Psychological Medicine*, 36(2),119-124. doi:10.4103/0253-7176.130962

Kaldjian, L.C., Jekel, J.F., & Friedland, G. (1998). End-of-life decisions in HIV-positive patients: the role of spiritual beliefs. *AIDS*, 12,103–107.

King, M., Marston, L., McManus, S., Brugha, T., Meltzer, H., & Bebbington, P. (2013). Religion, spirituality and mental health: results from a national study of English households. *The British Journal of Psychiatry, 202*(1), 68-73. doi: 10.1192/bjp.bp.112.112003

Koenig, H. G. (2008). Concerns About Measuring "Spirituality" in Research. *The Journal of Nervous and Mental Disease, 196*(5), 349-355. doi: 310.1097/NMD.1090b1013e31816ff31796.

Koenig, H., McCullough, M., & Larson, D. (2001). *Handbook of Religion and Health.* Oxford: Oxford University Press.

Lindeman, M., & Aarnio, K. (2007). Superstitious, magical, and paranormal beliefs: An integrative model. *Journal of Research in Personality, 41*(4), 731-744. doi: 10.1016/j.jrp.2006.06.009

McCullough, M. E., Hoyt, W.T., Larson, D.B., Koenig, H.G., & Thoresen, C. (2000). Religious involvement and mortality: a meta-analytic review. *Health Psychology*, 19(3), 211-222.

Michalsen, A., Grossman, P., Acil, A., Langhorst, J., Ludtke, R., Esch, T., Stefano, G.B., & Dobos, G.J. (2005), Rapid stress reduction and anxiolysis among distressed women as a consequence of a three-month intensive yoga program: *Medical Science Monitor*, 11(12), CR555-CR561.

Miller, L., Davies, M., & Greenwald, S. (2000). Religiosity and substance abuse among adolescents in the National Comorbidity Survey. *Journal of the* American *Academy of* Child & *Adolescent Psychiatry*, 39, 1190-1197.

Miller, L., Warner, V., Wickramaratne, P., &Weissman, M. (1997). Religiosity and depression: ten-year follow-up of depressed mothers and offspring. *Journal of the American Academy of Child & Adolescent Psychiatry*,36,1416-1425.

Mohr, S., & Huguelet, P. (2004). The relationship between schizophrenia and religion and its implications for care: *Swiss Medical Weekly*, 134, 369-376.

Murray, R.B., & Zentner, J.P. (1989). *Nursing Concepts for Health Promotion*. London: Prentice Hall.

Olszewski, M. E. (1994). *The effect of religious coping on depression and anxiety in adolescents*. Valley Library: Corvallis OR.

Peselow, E., Sarah Pi, B.S., Lopez, E., Besada, A, B.S.,& IsHak, W.W. (2014). The Impact of Spirituality Before and After Treatment of Major Depressive Disorder. *Innovations* in *Clinical Neuroscience,* (3-4), 17–23.

Peteet, J.R. (2012). Spiritually Integrated Treatment of Depression: A Conceptual Framework. Depression Research and Treatment, Volume 2012 Article ID 124370. http://dx.doi.org/10.1155/2012/124370

Puchalski, C.M. (2001). The role of spirituality in health care. *Proceeding (Baylor University Medical Center),* 14(4), 352–357.

Roberts, J.A., Brown, D., Elkins, T., & Larson, D.B. (1997). Factors influencing views of patients with gynecologic cancer about end-of-life decisions. *American Journal* of *Obstetrics* and *Gynecology*,176(1),166–172.

Shaw, A., Joseph, S., & Linley, P.A. (2005), Religion, spirituality, and posttraumatic growth: a systematic review. *Mental Health, Religion & Culture*, 8(1), 1-11.

Strawbridge, W.J., Cohen, R.D., Shema, S.J., & Kaplan, G.A. (1997). Frequent attendance at religious services and mortality over 28 years. *Americn Journal of Public Health*,87,957–961.

Tonigan, J.S. (2003). Project match treatment participation and outcome by self-reported ethnicity., *Alcoholism: Clinical and Experimental Research,* 27,1347.

Ukst-Margetic, B., & Margetic, B. (2005). Religiosity and *health* outcomes: review of literature: *Collegium Antropologicum*, 29(1), 365-371.

Varghese, A. (2008). Spirituality and mental health. *Indian Journal of Psychiatry*, 50,233-237.

Verghese, A., John, J.K., Rajkumar, S., Richard, J., Sethi, B.B., & Trivedi, J.K. (1989). Factors associated with the course and outcome of schizophrenia: results of a two year follow up study. *British Journal of Psychiatry*,154,499-503.

Verghese, A., John, J.K., Rajkumar, S., Richard, J., Sethi, B.B., Trivedi, J.K. (1990). Factors associated with the course and outcome of schizophrenia: results of a five year follow up study. *British Journal of Psychiatry*,32, 211-216.

Waaijman, K. (2000). Spirituality. Forms, foundations, methods. Leuven: Peeters.

Waaijman, K. (2006). What is spirituality? *Acta Theologica Supplementum*, 8,1-18.

World Health Organization. (1998). *WHOQOL and Spirituality, Religiousness and Personal Beliefs*: *Report on WHO Consultation*. Geneva: Author.

Psychological well-being of spiritually oriented people and common people: A comparative study

Vaishali Mardhekar and NehaVartak

Abstract: The present study aimed at investigating Psychological Well-being among spiritually oriented people and common people. The term well-being originated in theology and philosophy and it described the concept of what is ultimately good for a person (Crisp, 2008). Well-being was then introduced in positive psychology as a term describing positive mental health in the absence of mental illness. Traditionally spirituality has been defined as a process of personal transformation in accordance with religious ideals. Since the 19th century spirituality is not limited to religious acts. Research has focused on role of spirituality in psychological growth of humans. The present research is an attempt to study psychological well-being among spiritually oriented people and common people. For this purpose a sample of 100 married men in the age range of 45 - 55 (50 spiritually oriented & 50 common) were selected from Pune. For selecting spiritually oriented people Spiritual intelligence self report inventory (SISRI) by King was used. Test of Psychological well-being by Ryff was administered to the sample. The test measures psychological well-being on six dimensions, namely, self-acceptance, positive relations with others, autonomy, environmental mastery, purpose in life, and personal growth. To see the differences between study groups on psychological well-being t test was used. The results showed that on all the six dimensions of psychological well-being spiritually oriented people scored higher than common people. Results of the study have been discussed in light of available research and interviews of the participants.

Psychological well-being of spiritually oriented people and common people: A comparative study.

Spirituality is a universal human experience, crossing cultural and geographical boundaries, although its substance and form may differ. Both religion and spirituality are universal and widespread phenomena, in that they are integral to numerous cultures, and influence people of all ages, socio-economic status, and educational levels. The last two decades have provided evidence from a wide range of disciplines, that human potential for psychological growth and well-being is more than what had been previously estimated. Spirituality is as much a part of human experience as any other normal form of thought and behavior, and recently a more systematic approach in investigation of the same has gained importance even in field of psychology. There is growing impetus in the field of psychology to study the effect of spirituality on psychological wellbeing. In the past decade or so, researchers across a range of disciplines have started to explore and acknowledge the positive contribution of spirituality to physical and mental health. Therefore it is most essential in present context to know and identify the spiritual orientation that determines the psychological well-being among individuals.

Psychological well-being (PWB) is a dynamic concept that includes subjective, social, psychological, and health-related behaviors (Ryff & Singer, 1998). Psychological well-being refers to the experience of growth and thriving when faced by existential challenges of life, which include pursuing meaningful goals, growing and developing as a person, and establishing and maintaining healthy relationships with others (Ryff, 1989). Ryff and Keyes (1995) presented a multidimensional approach to the measurement of psychological well-being that taps six distinct aspects of human actualization: autonomy, personal growth, self-acceptance, life purpose, mastery, and positive relations with others.

These six constructs of psychological well-being promote emotional and physical health (Ryff & Singer 1998). Attaining and maintaining higher levels of psychological well-being throughout life is considered an important aspect of healthy development (Baltes & Baltes, 1990). Psychological well-being is associated with better physical health, which improves quality of life (Liu, Shono & Kitamura, 2009). People who have higher levels of psychological well-being are better able to cope with major stressors and negative life experiences.

Spirituality is defined as the search for meaning and purpose in life, which may or may not be related to a belief in God or some higher power. The concept also relates to the notion of an intrinsically motivating life force, which involves an integration of the dimensions of mind, body and spirit. Spirituality shapes individuals' perspectives on the world and is expressed in the way that they live life. Spiritually oriented people believe that their spirituality helps them in taking decisions, their relationships with others, and the way they deal with everyday situations (Kneipp, Kelly & Cyphers, 2009). Spirituality helps people interpret their experiences and gives meaning to them (Yoon, 2006).

Spirituality has been found to be a significant predictor of psychological well-being (Sreekumar, 2008). Koenig (2010) reported that spirituality may be important for psychological well-being for numerous reasons, including fostering a positive world view, meaning and purpose in life, personal empowerment, a sense of control, and guidance for decision making.

The present study is an attempt to study spirituality and psychological well-being of people. The study purports to investigate difference between spiritually oriented people and common people on their psychological well-being.

Review of Literature

Yoon and Lee (2009) examined role of spirituality/religiousness on the subjective well-being of non-White elderly in rural areas where medical resources and financial support are deficient. The study was conducted on a rural community sample of 215 elderly (85 Caucasians, 75 African Americans, and 55 Native Americans). The results reported a significant association between dimensions of religiousness/spirituality and subjective well-being among all ethnic rural elderly groups. The results of the study suggest that health providers, social workers, and faith communities need to provide rural elderly with religious and spiritual support in order to enhance their life satisfaction and lessen their emotional distress.

Sawatzky, Ratner and Chiu (2005) conducted meta-analysis of the relationship between spirituality and quality of life. The study was designed to determine empirical support for a relationship between spirituality and quality of life, provide an estimate of the strength of this relationship, and examine potential moderating variables affecting this relationship. The research design followed accepted methods for quantitative meta-synthesis. An extensive multidisciplinary literature search resulted in 3,040 published reports that were manually screened according to pre-established selection criteria. Subsequent to the selection process, 62 primary effect sizes from 51 studies were included in the final analysis. A random effects model of the bivariate correlation between spirituality and quality of life resulted in a moderate effect size (r = 0.34, 95% CI: 0.28–0.40), thereby providing support for the theoretical framework underlying the study wherein spirituality was depicted as a unique concept that stands in relationship to quality of life. In their study on college students, Zullig, et al (2006) found that students who describe themselves as spiritual are likely to report greater self-perceived health and better life satisfaction for both men and women. Results preliminarily support the contention that life satisfaction is influenced by spirituality engagement.

In a study by Ivtzan et al (2011) a linkage between psychological well-being and levels of religious involvement as well as spirituality among people was examined. A total of 205 participants from a wide range of religious affiliations and faith groups were recruited from various religious institutions and spiritual meetings. They were assigned to one of four groups with the following characteristics: (1) a high level of religious involvement and spirituality, (2) a low level of religious involvement with a high level of spirituality, (3) a high level of religious involvement with a low level of spirituality, and (4) a low level of religious involvement and spirituality. Multiple comparisons were made between the groups on three measures of psychological well-being: levels of self-actualization, meaning in life, and personal growth initiative. As predicted, it was discovered that, aside from a few exceptions, groups (1) and (2) obtained higher scores on all three measures. As such, these results confirm the importance of spirituality on psychological well-being, regardless of whether it is experienced through religious participation.

Betton's (2004) study focused on relationship between psychological well-being and spirituality among African American college students. Participants were two hundred and sixty-two undergraduate students from a large predominately White Midwestern university. Spirituality was the strongest predictor of well-being in African American respondents. Similarly Richter conducted study on college-aged (28 males, 34 females) from a small Christian liberal arts college in the urban Midwest using convenience sampling methods. Tool used to measure spiritual well-being was Shepherd Scale and for and psychological well-being was Scale by Ryff (1989). Results indicated that Christian spiritual well-being and psychological well-being held significant positive correlation.

A study was conducted on 204 revenue & customs staff of Isfahan and Tehran cities (Abedini, Golparvar, and Mosahebi) to find relationship between spirituality and psychological well-being. The results showed that there is a positive and significant relationship between spirituality and psychological well-being. The researchers have stated the importance of spirituality for the employees' psychological well-being at the workplaces.

Aly (2010) explored spirituality and psychological well-being in the Muslim community. A convenience sample of 210 Muslim individuals (115 males and 95 females) between the ages of 18 and 71 was obtained in the present study. Results suggest that the more spiritual a Muslim individual was, the less likely he or she were to be depressed or anxious. Spirituality appeared valuable for Muslims in this study, possibly providing them with a sense of hope and resources to cope with difficult life situations.

On basis of the available research it was thus hypothesized that spiritually oriented people will score higher than common people on psychological well-being.

Method

Participants

A total of 100 married working people (50 spiritually oriented and 50 common) from Pune participated in the study. The groups of spiritually oriented and common people were matched on gender and age. Marital status and working status has been taken as control variables. Equal numbers of people from four religions (Hindu, Muslims, Christians and Jains) were taken in both groups. The age range of the participants was 40 to 50 years (Mean 44.26; SD 3.29). Purposive sampling technique was used to collect the data.

Tools

The Spiritual Intelligence Self-report Inventory (SISRI-24) by King (2008) was used as a screening test to identify spiritually oriented people. It contains 24 items to be answered on five point rating scale. Test Retest Reliability coefficient is .89. Exploratory and confirmatory factor analyses have supported the four factor model of spiritual intelligence. Construct and criterion related validity has also been supported by studies.

Psychological well-being test developed by Ryff and Keyes (1995) was used to measure psychological well-being. The test consists of 84 items to be answered to 6 point likert scale how true each statement to the respondent. The test covers 6 dimensions covered are Autonomy, environmental mastery, personal growth, positive relations with others, purpose in life, self-acceptance. Higher scores on each scale indicate greater well-being on that dimension. Test Retest reliability coefficients for the six dimensions range from .81 to .92. Factor analysis provides sufficient evidence regarding its validity.

Procedure

As per the aim of the study collecting the data of spiritually oriented people was of prime importance. Personal data sheet, Spiritual Intelligence Inventory and Psychological well-being test was given to people from spiritual oriented institutes and centers (e.g. Theosophical Society, Pathshala, Ved Bhavan). The SISRI was translated in Marathi for those participants who were comfortable to respond in Marathi. The sheets of SISRI were scored. The cumulative frequencies of the scores were computed. The scores above cumulative frequency 70 were selected as spiritually oriented people. Since the two groups were to be matched on gender, age and religion, data of common people with similar demographics was then collected from nearby residential areas of the places from where data of spiritually oriented people was collected. The people from residential areas were directly approached. The purpose of the study was explained to them. Personal data sheet, Spiritual Intelligence Inventory and Psychological well-being test was given to those who were willing to participate. The researchers administered the test as per the convenience of the participants. The tests were administered in person and ethics of test administration were followed.

Results

To see that the two groups were comparable, t test was conducted on age. The results show that the two groups were not significantly different on age ($t = .39$). To see the two groups were matched on gender, chi square was conducted and the results showed chi square value as not significant. The t test was conducted to examine significant difference of the two groups on spiritual intelligence inventory. The results revealed that spiritual oriented people (M=

72.8, SD=10.6) had significantly higher psychological well being scores than common people (M=41.8, SD=9.5) t = 15.5, p<.001. To test the hypotheses that spiritually oriented people would have a higher score on psychological well-being and all its six dimensions, separate t test was conducted. All the t values are found to be significant (Refer Table 1). The obtained results are discussed in light of available research and the content obtained from informal interviews of the spiritually oriented respondents.

Table I: Table showing Means, SDs and t values
of Study groups on PWB scales.

Variable	Groups	Mean	Std. Deviation	t
Autonomy	Spiritual oriented	62.32	12.78	8.55***
	Common people	42.48	10.29	
Environmental mastery	Spiritual oriented	64.34	10.67	8.83***
	Common people	45.28	10.90	
Personal growth	Spiritual oriented	68.42	10.84	10.08***
	Common people	44.78	12.54	
Positive relations with others	Spiritual oriented	66.72	9.69	10.85***
	Common people	43.00	12.03	
Purpose of Life	Spiritual oriented	65.34	10.94	9.41***
	Common people	43.02	12.68	
Self acceptance	Spiritual oriented	64.52	12.02	9.37***
	Common people	42.50	11.45	
Psychological Well-being	Spiritual oriented	388.92	48.54	11.58***
	Common people	261.0000	61.12	

***: Difference significant at .001 level

Discussion

In the present study, psychological well-being of spiritually oriented people and common people was compared. The results of the study confirmed the hypotheses that spiritually oriented people will score higher than common people on psychological well-being. The results of the study are consistent with other studies, which found benefits of spirituality in maintaining good psychological well-being. Results of Cherif's study (2013) indicated that spirituality was a strong predictor of psychological well-being. Yoon and Lee (2009) reported that spirituality had positive impact on the subjective well-being among all ethnic rural elderly groups.

Another reason of the finding could be that as spiritually oriented people have a background of spirituality they are able to regulate their behavior from within. As a result they may have a clear idea about their own strengths and weaknesses. Involvement in spiritual activities pushes them to analyze themselves in a more subtle way. They take the responsibility of their behavior without hesitation. For example, a respondent from Theosophical Society, Pune reported that there are a few members of the society who routinely review their daily behavior at night. The weakness or mistakes are identified and a resolution is made to avoid them. Such daily review of oneself has helped the members to act righteously in daily life.

One of the explanations for the finding of the study may be contributed to interpretation of purpose in life among people. Spiritually oriented people's perception towards purpose in life is clearer than common people. For example, one of the respondents from spiritual center reported that spirituality has helped the family to cope with life stressors effectively because for them each event in life has a definite purpose. The respondent further said each event in life has to teach one something and one should understand what life tries to teach. It is from negative events we learn to be strong another respondent expressed.

Through this study researchers have been successful in putting forth the benefits of spirituality in psychological well-being. However, the comparison of the research is limited to educated married people with a sound socioeconomic background. Further studies may investigate spirituality among people from varied backgrounds may be in terms of education, occupation or other socioeconomic aspects. Studies may also be conducted to test the reasons behind people's interest in spirituality. Certainly spirituality is deep rooted in Indian culture. There are various modes leading to the path of spirituality. For example, Karma, bhakti, dynana and yoga are ways of practicing spirituality. Further studies may investigate how these modes of spirituality contribute to psychological well-being. From the conversation with many spiritual oriented people it was observed that there are many simple things to practice to make our lives better. Through qualitative analysis it is suggested that the subtle and useful aspects of spirituality needs to be investigated which can be acceptable to any common man.

Conclusion

The main strength of the study lies in the fact that spiritually oriented people living in same conditions as that of common man have scored higher on psychological well-being. The researchers suggest that spiritual inclination is helpful in daily living and it is not necessary for anyone to live in isolation to practice spirituality. Finally a last comment, the researchers noticed from interactions with respondents that spiritual scriptures or text should not be limited for knowledge purpose but practicing spirituality in daily life is beneficial for psychological well-being.

References

Abedini, H., Golparvar, and Mosahebi, M. (2014). Explaining the relationship of meaning and spirituality at work with psychological well-being: Mediating role of positive affect. *Management and Administrative Sciences, 3*, 160-175.

Aly, H. (2010). Spirituality and psychological well-being in Muslim community: An exploratory study. *Doctoral dissertation submitted to University of La Verne*, California.

Baltes, P.B., and Baltes, M.M. (1990). Psychological perspectives on successful aging: The model of selective optimization with compensation. *In Successful Aging: Perspectives from Behavioral Sciences* (Eds. P.B. Baltes, and M.M Baltes, pp 1-43). Cambridge: Cambridge University Press.

Betton, A.C. (2004). Psychological well-being and spirituality among African American and European American college students. *Doctoral dissertation submitted to Ohio State University*, Columbus.

Cherif, N. (2013). The moderating effect of community involvement on the relationship between spirituality and well-being. *Doctoral dissertation submitted to California State University*, Sacramento.

Ivtzan, I., Chan, C.P., Gardner, H.E., and Prashar, K. (2013). Linking religion and spirituality with psychological well-being: examining self-actualization, meaning in life and personal growth initiative. *Journal of Religion and Health, 52* (3), 915-929.

King, D. B. (2008). *The Spiritual Intelligence Self-report Inventory (SISRI 24)*. Retrieved from www.davidking.net.

Kneipp, L., Kelly, E., and Cyphers, B. (2009). Feeling at peace with college: Religiousity, spiritual well-being and college adjustment. *Individual differences research, 7* (3), 188-196.

Koenig, H.G. (2010). Spirituality, mental health and well-being. *International Journal of Applied Psychoanalytic Studies, 7* (2), 116-122.

Liu, Q., Shono, M., & Kitamura, T. (2009). Psychological well-being, depression, and anxiety in Japanese university students. *Depression and Anxiety, 26*, 99-105.

Ryff, C.D. (1989). Happiness is everything, or is it? Exploration on the meaning of psychological well-being. *Journal of Personality and Social Psychology, 57*, 1069-1081.

Ryff, C.D., and Keyes, C.L. (1995). The structure of psychological well-being revisited. *Journal of Personality and Social Psychology, 69*, 719-727.

Ryff, C.D., and Singer, B.H. (1998). The Contours of Positive Psychology. *Psychological Inquiry, 9*, 1-28.

Sawatzky, R., Pamela, A.R., and Lyren. C. (2005). A meta-analysis of the relationship between spiritual and quality of life. *Social Indicators Research, 72*, 153-188.

Sreekumar, R. (2008). The pattern of association of religious factors with subjective well-being: A path analysis model. *Journal of the Indian Academy of Applied Psychology, 34,* 119-125.

Yoon, D.P. (2006). Factors affecting subjective well-being foe the rural elderly individual: the importance of spirituality, religiousness and social support. *Journal Of Religion and Spirituality in Social Work, 25*, 59-75.

Yoon, D.P., and Lee, E.O. (2004). Religiousness/spirituality and subjective well-being among rural elderly Whites, African Americans and Native Americans. *Journal of Human Behavior in the Social Environment, 10*, 191-211.

Yoga, Meditation and Happieness

P.Vijayalakshmi Anbu

Abstract: The present article highlights the dire necessity yoga that helps to improve the bliss and happiness. Health is wealth. Peace of mind is happiness, yoga shows the way. Swami vishnudevananda condensed the essence of the yoga teachings into five principles for physical and mental health as well as spiritual growth. The principles are Proper exercises (Asanas), Proper breathing (Pranayama), Proper relaxation (Shanthi asana), Proper diet (Vegetarian), Positive thinking & meditation (Vedanta & Dhayana). Swami Satyananda Saraswathi (1943) in his book,' asana pranayama mudra bandha, he explained as Yoga as the science of right living and, as such, is intended to be incorporated in daily life. It works on all aspects of the person: the physical, vital, mental, emotional, psychic and spiritual. On the basis of relevant studies and information, it is observed that yoga plays a pivotal role in promoting the positive environment and happiness.

Introduction

Yoga is the science of right living and, as such, is intended to be incorporated in daily life. It works on all aspects of the person: the physical, vital, mental, emotional, psychic and spiritual. The word yoga means 'unity' or 'oneness' and is derived from the Sanskrit word 'yui' which 'to join', bind, attach, and yoke, to direct and concentrate one's attention on, to use and apply. It also means union or communion. This unity or joining is described in Spiritual terms as the union of the individual consciousness with the universal consciousness. On a more practical level, yoga is a means of balancing and harmonising the body, mind and emotions. This is done through the practice of asana, pranayama, mudra, bandha, shatkarma and meditation and must be achieved before union can take place with the higher reality.

Iyengar in his book light on yoga (2002-page no20) the first chapter of the yoga sutra, patanjali describes yoga as 'chitta vrtti nirodhah'. This may be translated as the restraint(nirodhah) of mental (chitta) modifications (vrtti) or as suppression (nirodhah) of the fluctuations (vrtti) of consciousness(chitta).

Swami Satyananda Saraswathi (1943) in his book "Asana Pranayama Mudra Bandha", states that yoga is not an ancient myth buried in oblivion. It is the most valuable inheritance of the present. It is the essential need of today and the culture of tomorrow and also he explained Yoga as the science of right living and, as such, is intended to be incorporated in daily life. It works on all aspects of the person: the physical, vital, mental, emotional, psychic and spiritual. B.Natarajan, Sri Ramakrishna Math, (1991) in his book "thirumanthiram of thirumular", elaborates on eight limbs of yoga: yama, niyama, and asana numberless pranayama wholesome and pratyahra alike, dhrana dhyana and Samadhi to triumph. There eight are the steely limbs of yoga.

"Health is wealth. Peace of mind is happiness. Yoga shows the way". - Swami Vishnudevanada

Swami vishnudevananda condensed the essence of the yoga teachings into five principles for physical and mental health as well as spiritual growth.

Proper Exercises	-	Asanas
Proper Breathing	-	Pranayama
Proper Relaxation	-	Shanthi Asana
Proper Diet	-	Vegetarian
Positive Thinking & Meditation	-	Vedanta & Dhayana

Proper Exercise: The periodical rhythmic movements of the body are called as exercises. Proper exercise should be pleasant to the practitioner while beneficial to the body, mind and spiritual life. Yoga regards the body as a vehicle for the soul on its journey towards perfection, Yogic physical exercises are designed to develop to focus the body as well as to boom the spiritual capacities. Sage Patanjali (From 200 Bc) in his book "hatha yoga pradipika(1:17)", exposes a concise definition of yogasanas: "sthiram sukham aasanam", meaning 'that position which is comfortable and steady. Asanas are specific body poses designed to improve the awareness and muscular flexibility. They also control and regulate breathing process and open the energy channels, thus harmonizing the functioning of body, breath and mind. Yoga exercises focus on the health of the spine, its strength and flexibility. The spinal column houses the all-important nervous system, the telegraphic system of the body. By maintaining the spine's flexibility and strength through exercise, circulation is increased and the nerves are ensured their supply of nutrients and oxygen.

Proper Breathing: Yoga teaches us how to use the lungs to their maximum capacity and how to control the breath. Proper breathing should be deep, slow and rhythmical. This increases vitality and mental clarity. B.K.S. Iyengar (2002) in a book throws" light on yoga" states that pranayama is explained as prana means breath, respiration, life, vitality, wind, energy or strength. ayama means length, expansion, stretching or restraint. Pranayama is a disciplined yogic breathing practice, in which breathing process is consciously regulated. But it is important to learn under an expert guidance only. It tunes up the nervous system, improves emotional stability. It improves breathing capacity and also increases stamina and vitality.

Proper Relaxation: By relaxing deeply all the muscles the Yogi can thoroughly rejuvenate his nervous system and attain a deep sense of inner peace. When the body and the mind are constantly overworked, their natural efficiency to perform work diminishes. As long as a person identifies with the body and the mind, there will be worries, sorrows, anxieties, fear and anger. These emotions, in turn bring tension. Yogis know that unless a person can withdraw from the body/mind idea and separate himself from the ego-consciousness, there is no way of obtaining complete relaxation. Yoga-nidra is a systematic method of inducing complete physical, mental and emotional relaxation. A very special feature of Yoga-nidra is 'Sankalpa' which means a 'resolve'. The relaxed body and mind are ideal soil for making a resolve. The 'Sankalpa' is affirmation of a statement, short, positive, precise about what to achieve. The statement may be something like autosuggestion they are easy to memories and recite e.g." I am becoming happier, healthier and more relaxed".

Proper Diet: Besides being responsible for building the physical body, the foods are profoundly affecting the mind. Many people worry about whether they are getting balanced diet for our daily life. A healthy motto is: "Eat to live, not live to eat". So the greatest nutritional plan is the simple diet of natural fresh foods.

Positive Thinking & Meditation: thought correlates to the attitudes, attitudes correlate the behavior, and behavior correlates the personality. If the human being have positive and creative thoughts as these will contribute to vibrant health and a peaceful, joyful mind. A positive outlook on life can be developed by learning and practicing the teachings of the philosophy of Vedanta. The mind will be brought under perfect control by regular practice of meditation. All happiness achieved through the mind is temporary and fleeting; it is limited by nature. Human beings have on in built ability to re-establish physical and mental equilibrium through persistent meditation. Regular practice of meditation will induce deep sense of rejuvenation and relaxation. Meditation is an experience that cannot be described, just as colors cannot be described to a blind man.

Meditation is the state, complete experience of perfect concentration by calm the mind, to concentrate, go beyond the mind and turning the mind's concentration inward, upon the self. Meditation is the most powerful mental and nerve tonic. It opens the door to intuitive knowledge and realms of eternal bliss. The mind becomes calm, lasting happiness, absolute peace and steady.

Therapeutic value of yoga: according the world health organization (WHO) the state of health is defined as a state of complete physical, mental, social and spiritual well being and not merely as absence of disease or infirmity.

As per the yogic tradition and taittiriya upanishadic principles, there are five sheaths of existence of man. The sheaths are called 'kosha', which means layers of existence. The five layers (pancha kosha) are annnamaya kosha-physical body, pranamaya kosha-pranic body, manomaya kosha- mind body, vijananamaya kosha-intellect body and anandamaya kosha-bliss body. Yogic management provides various techniques to bring back the balance of each koshas. The integrated approach of yoga uses asanas, kiryaas and yogi diet that belongs to annamaya kosha, pranayama for pranamaya kosha, meditation and devotional session that belongs to manomaya kosha, notional correction to get the right understanding of the purpose and priorities at vijanamaya kosha, working in relaxation and living the life in fullness and bliss under all circumstances at the anandamaya kosha level. Using of all these practices is essential to bring about the strength of total life span period.

Modern society faces problems, which affect all these aspects. Today's lifestyle with its technological wonders is a mixed blessing. Convenience and speed is obtained at some cost to physical health. Labour savings devices physical exertion, resulting in stiffness and muscular weakness. A sedentary life causes backache, neck problems, heaviness in the limbs, and difficulty in walking. The extensive use of visual media leads to headaches and eyestrain. The mental anxieties of a competitive world deplete inner resources, inviting stress- related problems such as insomnia and digestive, respiratory and nervous disorders. If pressure is not balanced with time for quiet reflection, the quality of life is impaired. Modern trends of thought are a melting pot of old and new ideas. Artificial values stemming from acquisitiveness and self-interest lead to alternation from the spiritual purpose of life the loss of our lives can bring a sense of loss of one's own true identity.

Yoga helps in all these problems. Yogic practices integrate the body, mind and spirit. They bring harmony; develop a restful and positive attitude towards life. It helps to build immunity, inner strength, to have correct posture flexibility of spine improves their breathing capacity, and to manage stresses improve control over body and emotions. In short it is the best preventive and curative therapy. At physical level, it gives relief countless aliments. The practice of the postures strengthens the body and creates a feeling of well being. From the psychological viewpoint, yoga sharpens the intellect and aids concentration. It steadies the emotions and encourages a caring concern for others. Above all, it gives hope. The practice of breathing techniques calms the mind. Its philosophy sets life in perspective. In the realm of the spiritual, yoga brings awareness and the ability to be still. Through meditation, inner peace is experienced. 'Accept life as it is.' Put in the best efforts wherever it is possible and then let the positive spirits overtake. Yoga always emphasizes the mind which makes or breaks a situation.

In this respect, yoga is far from simply being physical exercises; rather, it is an aid to establishing a new way of life, which embraces both inner and outer realities. However, this way of life is an experience, which cannot be understood intellectually and will only become living knowledge through practice and experience.

Conclusion

To conclude, it may be stated that yoga plays a pivotal role in promoting the positive environment and happiness.

Reference

B.K.S.Iyenkar- Light on Yoga Sutras of Patanjali (Haper Collins Publications India Pvt. Ltd. New Delhi)

lindia Brannon and et al (2007) health psychology – an introduction to behaviour and health, sixth edition, printed in the united states of America, 10-11.

Nagendra HR. yoga research and applications (vivekannda Kendra yoga prakashana, bengalore)

B.Natarajan: Thirumantiram (Atamil Scriptural Classic) (Sri Ramakrishna Math, Madras.)

Porkodi, K.Subramaniam, S. and Kanaka, T.S (1979) effects of yoga and meditation health and diseases, proc, first national conference on yoga science and society, banaras hindu university, pp.104-106.

N.Ramakrishnan, Manivasakar Pathippakam (2003), –enrumnalvudharum thirumularin panniru yogangal.

Ram Nath Sharma and et al (2004),- Advanced Applied Psychology, I edition, nice printing press, New Delhi, 451-457, 475-477.

Robinso B. Natarajan, sri rmakrishna math (1991), – thirumantiram of thirumular.

Swaminathan, V.D. and Kaliappan, K.V. (1997), Psychology for Effective Living-Behaviour Modification, Guidance, Counselling and Yoga Chennai: The Madras Psychology Society Publication.

Sage Patanjali (200 bc), - Sri Pathanjali Yoga Suthiram.

Swami Sivananda: Practice of Yoga (The Divine Life Society, Shivananda Nagar, P.O., U.P.Himalayas, India)

Swami satyananada saraswati (2002), – asana pranayama mudra bandha. India edition; second edition, (India: Yoga Publications Trust, Munger, Bihar)

Udupa, K.N., Singh, R.H., Shettiwar, R.M., (1975) studies on the effect of some yogic breathing exercises (pranayama) in normal persons, zind.f.med.res., 1975,63(8): 1062-1065.

Vivekananada Kendra Yoga Research Foundation (2000), –Yoga Research And Applications.

A Nurturing Approach towards Your Own Physical and Mental Well Being

Aanchal Sharda and Subhash Meena

Abstract: This qualitative study was done to examine the strength of Qi-gong: a traditional Chinese practice, which involves our life energy and makes it easy to flow in order to gift us with a complete wellbeing. Clients with Depression (n=16); Anxiety (n=10); Eating Disorder (n=2); Kundalini Syndrome (n=1), Insomia (n=1), and Obsessive compulsive Disorder (n=1) were introduced with Qi-gong training method of "Eight Brocade" which is a static training method and later with the assurance of them becoming mindful of their own qi circulations, they were introduced to "meditative training". From the content analysis of what the clients said in the pre and post condition we find a change in the statements made by the patients, i.e. I can't talk until I scratch my arm to I can talk and open up my mouth; I start my day in distress so I am unhealthy to I can keep a control on situations; and from I hate food to I love food, etc. Thus we can say that qi-gong is appropriate technique to bring back the smile on the faces that were low, deprived of positivity and bliss of life. And physically it help Indian population from being less dependent on medication and it also helps in fighting obesity, which means the major problem which our psychiatric patient are facing can be healthily taken care of, and this in turn makes people more approachable to seek help when in need.

Keyword: Qi-gong, Depression, Anxiety, Eating disorder, OCD.

INTRODUCTION

Mindfulness is English translation of the "PALI" word sati. Pali was a language of Buddhist psychology 2500 years ago and mindfulness is the core teaching of this tradition. Sati connotes awareness, attention and remembering. Mindfulness is to be attentive towards the task you are into and it`s also about recognizing the present moment with a friendly attitude. It`s a skill which allow us to be less reactive to what is happening in the moment or simply it allow us to relate to the experience in the fullest, thus when we are mindful about the moment we are not entangled in the past or future and neither we are rejected or clinging to what is happening in the moment, i.e. we are present in the open-hearted way, and such a attention generates energy, clearheaded-ness and joy. Fortunately, it`s a skill which can be cultivated by anyone. As it has the property of making one aware about the importance of living in present, this technique seems to very useful in the psychotherapy as most of the problem occurs when one is either worried about the future or when one is clinged to their past. As this practice makes you wise enough to deal with the situations that are you learn to relate with positive or negative or neutral situations, this results in physical, mental, and emotional wellbeing. Thus educating patients with Eight Brocade gives them the opportunity to relive their life`s in a more healthy and lively manner.

Now before we try to understand what is Qigong, let`s first understand what does this Qi means? Qi (Chi) means energy. Qi is more specifically the vital energy that exists before we are born, remains in the body during our life, and persists after our lives end (Trieschmann, 1999). Qi energy is polar: it possesses a positive and negative side (Omura, 1990). In Tao philosophy all positive forces in the universe have a negative force. These opposing forces act to balance one another out. When the Qi of the body is out of balance, the body gets sick. Maintaining a balanced Qi will insure health, and in order to restore health from sickness, the Qi must be brought back to a balanced state (Trieschmann, 1999). Qi Gong is a way to balance Qi and heal and ward off illness.

Qigong is a Chinese method of healing. Traditionally it was viewed as a practice to cultivate and balance qi (chi) or the "intrinsic life energy". Qigong or chi gong; literally means "Life Energy Cultivation". Typically a qigong practice involves rhythmic breathing coordinated with slow stylized repetition of fluid movement, a calm mindful state, and visualization of guiding qi through the body. A few consider it to be some sort of exercise, though for others it's a type of alternative medicine or meditative practice. From a philosophical perspective qigong is believed to help develop human potential, allow access to higher realms of awareness, and awaken one's "true nature".

METHODS

In this experimental study we used Qi-gong (independent variable) with the patients in order to assess its` impact on symptomatology of the disorder (dependent variable).

A total sample of 31 was recruited from Kochhar Psychiatry centre, where mean age of sample was 32 years, participants were resident of Delhi. With the help of a psychiatrist we had (16 DEP+ 10 ANX+ 1 OCD+1 KS+1 OCD), all the participants were outpatients.

Here we took an informal interview of the participant's and they were asked to introduce themselves and they were motivated to share about their problems and symptoms. And there responses were noted down. After the interview was over they were engaged in the eight brocades practices for 30-45 minutes, and were ask to review depending upon their condition but time lapse was not kept more than 48 hours. A few other relaxation techniques from Neuro Linguistic Programming were used, to enhance self-love, and also to relax them whenever they are experiencing uneasiness due to their symptoms.

Procedure

We took informal interview of clients and their verbatim were recorded. In order to convince them to follow up with Qi-gong exercises they were informed that its an part of the treatment, and medicine will help you only when you help yourself. Later they were taught Eight- Brocades of mindfulness, they were described with meaning and benefits of each step they were following. After they taken the session they were asked to report how they felt and their verbatim were recorded. Patients were asked to maintain this practice when at home or whenever they are experiencing uneasiness.

Analysis

Patients who followed up came up with the response either verbally or in written, so their responses were noted and written verbatim were collected. From the responses obtained content analysis was done and on the basis of the response we compared their pre and post verbatim.

Result

From the content analysis of the patients we could find three themes: a) Physical change, b) Mental Change, c) Emotional Change

Physical Changes: Most of the patients reported that they feel more energetic and there body also seems to be lighter.

Mrs. X reported of pain in her shoulder and after following Eight-Brocade she felt that her pain is reducing and her neck pain was negligible. Similarly a girl before starting the Qi-gong was reporting of pain in abdomen and after she was forced to get involved, she herself experienced a change within her physicality i.e. she reported of the feeling floating i.e. her muscles were relaxed. Thus we can say that on doing it for the first time people could experience a change in their energy level, body temperature, calmness, stiffness, and amount of pains. This means that patients paid attention to learn the moments of exercise correctly.

Emotional Changes: As soon as patient have absorb the Eight Brocade practice, they experienced a sense of happiness, they could sense a giggle or simply they were excited and they feel a fresh, there is a blast of energy. Though a few reported of being nervous in the beginning and other felt that it`s not possible for them to balance their bodies, but sooner after the exercise they become relaxed, calm and were at peace.

Mental Changes: As initially patients were distracted with their unhealthy thoughts, they were not able to concentrate neither were they able to pay attention to what were taught to them. But soon after they have followed Eight- Brocades they were able to experience a change in their concentration and were able to focus in a better way as now the mind is calm and at peace.

Discussion

A qualitative design seemed most appropriate for this study because examining the effects of Qi-gong as a mindfulness practice is a somewhat new area of research. By using a qualitative design, we were able to look for all possible effects rather than limiting the responses we would find. This open-ended approach proved useful in eliciting a wide variety of responses from patients. The results of this study indicate Qi-gong is indeed a practice with immediate effects. Physical, emotional, and mental changes emerged from the accounts of their initial exposure to the Qi-gong practice. As from the verbatim we can understand that it shows an immediate effect whether the population is suffering from physiological problems or psychological problems. As in our study we have employed it on psychiatric patients, who are totally dependent upon psychotropic drugs, and have also lost their hope, interest and self-esteem. Though psychotherapies are available but no one is ready to opt for that option, because of stigma and also because of the availability of psychotropic drugs.

A related but distinct conceptualization of mindfulness emphasizes attention rather than thought and has been defined as a sustained, receptive attention to present events and experience. Although this form of mindfulness has been considered a natural propensity of human organism (Brown & Ryan, 2003; Goldstein, 2002; Kabat-Zinn, 2003), there is considerable agreement that it can be enhanced through training.

Sometimes it`s necessary to opt for medicine first, and then to take psychotherapies to enhance the well-being; but still there are people who relapse? Why? It`s simply because we aren`t working on the root cause, until the root is removed or resolved happiness can`t be experienced. If a psychologist follows CBT in order to bring physical, mental, spiritual and emotional changes, then it will be a lengthy process, secondly no patient can afford to come for such a longer time. With help of such technique one learns to deal with situations and event which occur in our day to day life, and after one has learned this art they won`t be facing any uneasiness. Thus in our study we have found that this Eight Brocade have started circulating it`s warmth. When it was taught to the depression patient`s, who earlier reported of the feeling of worthlessness were later feeling better, excited and were also ready to take up the initiative to work. Similarly people suffering from GAD were able to handle their anxieties in a very healthy manner. Though patients with eating disorder reported that after "I have experience a session of Eight Brocades, I have started feeling hungry and I want to have something to eat". For such patients whose self-image is destructive NLP was also used i.e. participant was asked to command themselves in front of the mirror every morning "I love you" and "I am the best person ever". Thus aim of our study is successfully accomplished, as participants feel better after a session. Such technique are better option than psychiatric drugs as such drugs are very harmful to human body and they majorly leads to obesity and other problems like Thyroid or hormonal imbalances etc. Though number of people with depression are increasing now a days, so it won`t take a much time when obesity will be nations next matter of concern. Thus following such a healthy practice in their life routinely and timely will make them feel energetic, confident, and will also keep them motivated to work with a hint of smile and will also keep other problems like cancer and heart diseases at a bay. Living in present the Buddhist thought is the virtue to modern life atrocities. Be like a baby and enjoy every moment, or simply take a sip every moment and try to absorb it as it is. Don't be judgemental, if god or the supreme energy doesn`t judge anyone, than why are you bothered to judge.

Conclusion

These findings can`t be generalized as our sample size was small. In order to refine our aim we can draw a sample of 100- 50 normal individuals and 50 psychiatric patients. From this pilot study we have found that Qi-gong is the opportunity for people. So a further research can be framed from this where we can do a comparable study between normal and psychiatric patients. In this research we can first take in the interview in pre-session phase and fill in Mindful Attention Awareness scale by Carlson and Brown, and later we can use SHS happiness scale, on the basis of their responses, number`s will be assigned and we will be able to see difference between awareness and attention of a normal and a patient. And second interview will be conducted post-session, and similarly interviews will be taken regarding how they felt and how it is changing. From such a data comparison can be drawn and we will be able to know how useful such a technique is for a normal person as well as the person who is suffering, i.e. whether it generates same amount of happiness or anxiety in both or it`s different.

References

Brown, K. W., West, A. M., Loverich, T. M., & Biegel, G. M. (2011). Assessing Adolescent Mindfulness: Validation of an Adapted Mindful Attention Awareness Scale in Adolescent Normative and Psychiatric Populations. Psychological Assessment. Advance online publication. doi: 10.1037/a0021338.

Goldstein, J. (2002). *One dharma: The emerging western Buddhism.* New York, NY: Harper San Francisco.

Kabat-Zinn, J. (2003). Mindfulness-based interventions in context: Past, present, and future. *Clinical Psychology: Science and Practice, 10,* 144–156. doi:10.1093/clipsy/bpg016

Omura, Y. (1990). Storing of Qi Gong energy in various materials and drugs (Qi Gongnization): Its clinical application for treatment of pain, circulatory disturbance, bacterial or viral infections, heavy metal deposits, and related intractable medical problems by selectively enhancing circulation and drug uptake. *Acupuncture Electrotherapy Research.* 15(2): 137-57

Ryan R.M and Brown K.W (2003). Why we don't need Self Esteem: On Fundamental needs, Contingent love and Mindfulness. *Psychological Inquiry,* Vol.14, 27-82.

Trieschmann, R. B. (1999). Energy medicine for long-term disabilities. *Diability and Rehabilitation.* 21(5/6): 269-276.

To Study the Effects of Spiritual Practices on General Well-Being of the Disciples of the Spiritual Organization

Anita Chauhan

Abstract: India is pre-eminently a sacred land, an abode of deities, religious organizations and organizations with thousands of devotees following one or the other religion. The Radha Soami Satsang Beas has become a transnational movement in the recent years. This organization emphasizes on personal interaction, transcendence and trust that endows with traditional resolutions to the spiritual and moral religious problems that are in many ways unique to the Indian culture. The present study was aimed at studying the effect of the initiation (*Nam* is given to the disciples by the spiritual head to be enchanted during meditation), experience (duration of time spent as followers of the spiritual organization) and gender on the general well being of the disciples. An unselected sample of 120 members was selected for the study. The PGI General Well-being measure was utilized for measuring the general well being of the disciples. The three way independent measure analysis of variance was employed 2 (Initiated Vs Non-initiated) x 2 (long experience Vs short experience) x 2 (Males Vs Females) on General well-being scores. The results revealed that the main effects of initiation [$F(1,112) = 1.25$, $P < .01$], experience [$F(1,112) = 20.56$, $P < .01$] and gender [$F(1,112) = 4.02$, $P < .05$] on general well-being of the subjects were significant. Thus it may be concluded that the spiritual practices enhances general well-being of the people.

Introduction

The genesis of Indian Psychology can be traced back to the ancient periods of Vedas and Upanishads. India is pre-eminently a sacred land, an abode of deities, religious organizations and organizations with thousands of devotees following one or the other religion. Religion plays an important role in enhancing the mental health of the people by eradicating the root causes of sufferings, and improving the quality of life (Goleman, 1978; James, 1902; Kapur, 2001; Konopack & McAuley, 2012; McCullough & Willoughby, 2009; Sinha, 1985; 1986). The people in the third World countries like India adhere to the religious beliefs and practices in being cured of their sufferings. McCullough and Willoughby (2009) defined religion as cognition, affect, and behavior that arise from awareness of, or perceived interaction with, supernatural entities that are presumed to play an important role in human affairs. They delineated psychological components of religion as (i) beliefs about the existence of gods and their involvement in human life, (ii) level or quality of engagement in activities that are traditionally motivated by the awareness of supernatural forces, (iii) strength of commitment to a particular religious belief system. The ancient scriptures of philosophy, religion, and folklores of India are rich sources of analysis of behavior, interpersonal interaction, and personality; and takes into consideration the holistic view of health and regards 'oneness' of the mind, body and soul in the curing the ailments (Kapur, 2001; Sinha, 1985; 1986). Indian Model of psychotherapy rests on guru and chela relationship where in guru is regarded as the supreme being capable of eradicating their suffering. Goleman (1978) propounded that Eastern countries have only one school of psychology: transpersonal school, wherein, meditation is the only technique, to explore the self that acts as a therapy in eradicating the cause of sufferings. The incorporation of the traditional patterns of dealing with psychiatric problems keeping in view the peoples cultural, and illness and their needs and requirements and the development of our own tools and methods of treating psychiatric problems is advocated by various researchers (Durganand Sinha, 1965; 1986; Kapur, 2001; Neki 1977, 1984; Hoch, 1997; Kakar, 1996; Dalal, 2001; Berry, Mishra, & Tripathi, 2003).

The present study was aimed at studying the effect of the duration of time spent as followers of the spiritual organization on the general well being of the disciples. For the present study, the disciples of the Radha Soami Satsang Beas were chosen. In the present study, Shimla Centre of Radha Soami Organization was studied. The organization's headquarter is situated beside the bank of river Beas. It is popularly known as Dera Baba Jaimal Singh in the State of Punjab.

This Radha Soami movement can be regarded as the reminiscent of the *Bhakti movement* of the medieval period. This organization represents an amalgamation of the medieval *bhakti* teachings, Sikh tradition, and the *Vaisnava bhakti* (Juergensmeyer, 1978). The Radha Soami Satsang Beas has become a transnational movement in the recent years. The popularity of this organization can be ascribed to remarkable interest in guru bhakti or devotion to a spiritual master by the people (both illiterate and educated); its relation to other religions (Hinduism, Buddhism, Jainism, Sikhism and so on); its efficient, progressive and international leadership; and its beliefs and spiritual practices that are mysterious and esoteric (Juergensmeyer, 1978; 1991). The teaching of Radha Soami masters are offered to all irrespective of their religion, caste, gender, age, nationality and so on; it demands no conversion; and aims at providing additional light to the existing knowledge of the seekers and basically emphasizes on following the path of God-realization from within us (Singh, 2001). Shiv Dayal Singh laid the foundation stone of the Radha Soami organization at Agra with its headquarters at Dayalbagh. Radha Soami Satsang Beas has flourished in North India by Jaimal Singh one of the most devoted disciples of Soami Shiv Dayal Singh. He led the foundation of Radha Soami Satsang in the state of Punjab at the banks of river Beas in 1891 and held satsang for eleven years (Singh, 2001). He has been succeeded by five gurus. Currently the spiritual head or guru of this organization is Gurinder Singh.

The Radha Soami organization can be regarded as "modern religion" of the scientific era, since it acknowledges modern tastes, and emphasizes on personal interaction, transcendence and trust that endows with traditional resolutions to the spiritual and moral religious problems that are in many ways unique to Indian culture (Juergensmeyer, 1991). This may be the reason for its increasing popularity throughout the world. The preaching of the Radha Soami Organization rests on the following features: the *living Guru*, the *Shabd*, the concept of *Nam*, norms, the experiential method, *Satsang* or spiritual discourses, and *Seva* or service to humanity (Singh, 1997). The living guru or spiritual head is believed to have reached the highest realm of spiritualism. The concept of "Nam' is the foundation stone of the organization. The living guru tells the name of God i.e. "Nam" to the disciples thereby initiating them into the path of spiritualism. *Nam* is believed to be the "sovereign remedy for all diseases"; provides motion and speed to the spiritual life, immunity from the fear of death; and helps in self-realization (Singh, 1997). Dubin (2004) elucidated that the teachings and methods of the organization rests on four basic principles: following a vegetarian diet; abstinence from alcohol and other intoxicants; living a moral and honest life; and devoting one-tenth of daily time to meditation to experience the higher realms of consciousness or self-actualization (Singh, 1999). Satsang is referred to as a spiritual college, where the devotees are taught and explained the meaning and the path of spiritualism (Singh, 2002).

Sample

The members of Radha Soami organization (Beas) from its Shimla centre were studied. There were about 2500 devotees in the Shimla centre of Radha Soami organization in 2005. Out of which 120 members were selected for the study. The devotees who were bestowed with Nam (the holy name of God) which was to be enchanted during meditation were said to be initiated into the path of spirituality. Equal number of initiated as well as non-initiated members was selected for the study. Experience was defined as the number of years spent as a member of this spiritual organization. Those subjects who had more than 20 years of membership comprised the long experience group and those who had spent 0-5years as a member formed the short experience group. There were equal numbers of females and males in the sample.

Design

The present study employed the factorial design, having two levels of initiation (initiated vs. non-Initiated), two levels of experience (long experience vs. short experience) and two levels of gender (males vs. females) (table 1). An independent measure, three-way analysis of variance was used to analyze the scores on the dependent measure of general well being. The three independent variables: initiation, experience and gender had two levels for each independent variable, and thus there were eight groups of subjects. For each group, 15 subjects were selected from the devotees' population in the town of Shimla. The selection was not random and was constrained by the availability of the devotees for the study. The dependent measure was general well-being.

Table 1

Independent measures three-factor factorial design with two levels of Initiation, experience and gender

Initiation	Experience	Males	Females
Initiated	Long experience (>20 yrs)	15	15
	Short experience (>5 yrs)	15	15
Non-Initiated	Long experience (>20 yrs)	15	15
	Short experience (>5 yrs)	15	15

Materials

The objectives of the present study were to study the effects of initiation, experience and gender on general well-being of the devotees of the spiritual organization. For this purpose, PGI General Well-being Measure developed by Verma and Verma (1989) was used to measure the general well being of the disciples. It is considered suitable to assess the positive mental health or general well-being of the Indian population. It consists of 20 items measuring various aspects such as freedom from health concern, worry, distress, emotional and behavioral control, relaxation, satisfaction, etc. It has high reliability and validity. The score on this questionnaire depicts the general well being of the people. The scoring is done by adding the number of responses (ticks) given by the subject. It ranges from 0-20. The higher the score better is the well-being.

Procedure

The data were collected from 14 July 2005 to 30 August 2005. The investigator was herself the member of the Radha Soami community. Therefore, she did not face any major problem during her conduction of the study as she was well acquainted with the members of this organization. The investigator collected data in the *satsang ghar*, residences and occupational spots of the devotees. The subjects were explained the purpose of the study and their consent was obtained for participation in the study. PGI general well-being measure was administered. The participants were asked to write their personal characteristics, such as name, age, gender and address in the provided space. Their task was to tick against the items, which were applicable to there. It took about five minutes for each participant to complete the task. The high score indicated better well-being of the disciples. In addition to the above mentioned psychological tests, the investigator observed and collected qualitative data through an unstructured interview schedule.

Results

The investigator employed the three way independent measure analysis of variance 2 (Initiated Vs Non-initiated) x 2 (long experience vs. short experience) x 2 (Males Vs Females) on General well-being scores as the dependent variable. The results of the ANOVA are given in table 2 and table 3. The main effect of initiation on general well-being of the subjects was significant [F (1,112) $=1.25$, $P<.01$]. The general well-being of the initiated members ($M=15.07\pm4.98$) was better than the non-initiated members ($M=12.42\pm5.80$). The effect of experience on the devotees' general well-being was significant [F (1,112) $=20.56$, $P<.01$]. The general well-being of the devotees with long experience in the organization ($M=15.83\pm4.12$) was better than the devotees with short experience in the organization ($M=11.65\pm6.02$). The effect of gender on the devotees' general well-being was significant [F (1,112) $=4.02$, $P<.05$]. It has been found that general well-being of male devotees ($M=14.67\pm5.27$) was better than the female devotees ($M=12.82\pm5.70$). Furthermore, it was found that there were no significant interaction effects: initiation and experience; experience and gender; initiation and gender and initiation, experience and gender.

Table 2

Summary of 2x2x2 independent measure analysis of variance on general well being scores

Source of variance	SS	DF	MS	F	Significance
Initiation	210.67	1	210.67	8.25**	.01
Experience	525.01	1	525.01	20.56**	.01
Gender	102. 67	1	102. 67	4.02*	.05
Initiation x Experience	21.68	1	21.68	<1	NS

Experience x Gender	0.08	1	0.08	<1	NS
Initiation x Gender	0.08	1	0.08	<1	NS
Initiation x Experience x Gender	0	1	0	<1	NS
Error	8558.8	112	25.53		
Total	3718.99	119			

$F_{.01}$ (1,112)= 6.87; $F_{.05}$ (1,112)= 3.93

Table 3

Mean and S.D. of general well-being scores

Variable	group	N	mean	S.D.
Initiation	Initiated	60	15.07	4.98
	Non-initiated	60	12.42	5.80
Experience	Long experience	60	15.83	4.12
	Short experience	60	11.65	6.02
Gender	Males	60	14.67	5.27
	Females	60	12.82	5.70

Discussion

The following section deals with the discussion of the results in the light of various studies corroborating the present study. This section is divided into two parts. In the first part, result obtained of the present study on general well-being is discussed in the light of various studies. In the second part, the Radha Soami Organization is discussed as a Community Mental Health Institution.

General well-being

The objective of the present study was to study effect of initiation, experience and, gender on General well-being of the devotees of a spiritual organization. Initiation means that privileged devotee is instigated into the path of spiritualism by telling him/her the name of the god or "Nam" which needs to be chanted during meditation. The general well-being may be enhanced through meditation practices as corroborated by various studies. The practices of yoga or meditation have been found to be effective in treating physical and mental ailments, and in promoting general well-being of the people (Vahia, 1984). Researchers reveal that people who practice transcendental meditation techniques were found to be more sociable, less aggressive, less nervous and less irritable, more confident, more emotionally stable and more self-reliant than those who did not practice meditation (Janid, Vyas, & Shukla, 1988). The practice of yoga and asanas contribute to the health and vigor of the body (Rao, 2000). It also helps in overcoming tensions and restlessness; reduced anxiety, psychosomatic complaints, facilitating charge and formation of new and desirable patterns. Thus, it enhances general well-being of the people and may lead to positive mental health or increased general well-being. Religious and yogic practices have been found to be effective, curative, and preventive measures against several chronic and serious diseases (Bhushan, 2004). The effectiveness of the yogic practices can be attributed to their psycho-somato-spiritual approach. It helps in alleviating the root cause of the sufferings through mental modifications that create problems and makes the mind disturbed. It emphasizes on non-attachment, as the path to enjoy lasting happiness and peace without being involved and disturbed by the attachment to the Worldly affairs. The yogic practices are based on the body-mind-spirit interaction model, thus, it provides basis for enhancement of general well-being of the people.

The main effect of experience on the devotees' general well-being was significant. The variable Experience in this study meant duration of time spent in the organization. The devotees of the organization had to follow certain norms: following a vegetarian diet; abstinence from alcohol and other intoxicants; leading a moral and honest life; and devoting one-tenth of one's daily time to meditation; attending satsang (spiritual discourses and congregations); service to community, guru and humanity; and reading spiritual literature (Dubin,

2004). As the devotes in this study differed in their experience in terms of years spent in the organization, the devotees with long experience might have been following the path or norms on regular basis. They might have become accustomed to and internalized the norms that might have led to positive mental health or general well-being. The devotees reported that they had firm belief in their guru, and regarded him the supreme power, capable of eradicating their sorrow and grief. Their firm faith in their spiritual master might have enhanced their positive mental health. Kakar (1982) elucidated that major psychotherapeutic factor in the healing by the guru wherein the seeker or disciple (maybe regarded as a patient) builds an emotional relationship with the guru. He said the disciples identifies with the guru and internalizes his idealized image that he feels as genuine and valuable additions to their own personalities. Thus, the disciple looks upon himself, his problems, views the World with the new outlook, and becomes capable of dealing efficiently with the miseries of life. This in turn enhances his general well-being. Lysne and Walchholtz (2011) in their review on religion, spirituality and mental health revealed that there was a positive relationship between religious beliefs and practices and greater life satisfaction, personal devotion produced the strongest positive correlations. Spiritual well being was a unique predictor of quality of life around three core domains, physical, social/family and emotional. The religious beliefs and practices may provide meaning and purpose to life thereby reducing anxiety and depression. It has been reported by various researches that the spiritual practices helps in gaining a broader and enhanced perspectives about life thereby contributing to general well being of the people (Oner-Ozakan, 2007), and also promotes self-control or self-regulation (McCullough & Boker, 2007; McCullough & Willoughby, 2009).

The devotees of this organization attended satsang twice a week. The word satsang implies to be in the company of good people. When the people attended satsang, they came closer to one another and shared their feelings, needs and aspirations, which might have worked as a factor in the enhancement of their well-being. Gable, Reis, Impett, and Asher (2004) examined intrapersonal and interpersonal correlates of sharing positive events with the others, that is, capitalization. They conducted four studies and found that communicating personal positive events affect well-being more than any other daily life events. They concluded that general well-being of the people may be enhanced and provide perspectives on our understanding of how people cope when things go wrong, in the sense that the intrapersonal benefits of capitalization may help build a firm interpersonal foundation for coping with the inevitable stressors and conflicts of life. Bhushan (2004) said that in a community life, satsang, devotion songs (kirtan) and dance based on bhakti yoga serve as useful tools in transforming the cognition to promote positive attitudes and emotions stressed patients have lower level of melatonin discharge which is generally increased by meditation practice resulting in feelings of well-being. Spiritual practices have also been found to enhance general well being and mental health of the individuals (Konopack & McAuley, 2012).

It may be concluded that experience in the organization play a significant role in enhancing general well-being of the individuals. It helped in self-realization, and increasing self-efficacy of the devotees that might have led to positive mental health or general well-being. The disciple looked upon himself, and his problems with the new outlook. He/she became capable of dealing efficiently with the miseries of life that changed his general outlook. They were involved in the practice of yoga or meditation. Yoga is believed to consider a holistic concept of health and well-being that include body, mind and spirit as integral and interdependent parts.

Radha Soami as a Community Mental Health Institution

The Radha Soami Organization is working at the grass root level to improve the quality of life of the people via spiritual discourses, social service and meditation. It incorporates eastern perspectives of human nature, behavior and sufferings, and traditional spiritual techniques, and western therapeutic approach that emphasizes on personal and group interaction, transcendence and provides educational, rehabilitation and employment facilities.

The Radha Soami Centre in Shimla is situated at Ram Chandra Chowk. The spiritual gatherings take place in the Satsang Ghar or Community Hall. The main features of this organization are satsang, seva, and meditation. The meaning of satsang is being in a good company. The organization seems to work on this principle. Spiritual discourses are disseminated twice a week that thrusts upon imbibing super human qualities, being in the company of good people, leading a moral and honest life, and on self-realization. Kakar (1982) said that in the spiritual discourses the perception of the real world and the unbearable painful life experiences is emphasized. He further explained that mystical withdrawal is suggested as a solution of the individual psychic needs and life problems. A system of psychological and physiological practices is offered by which a person can deliberately and voluntarily seek detachment from every day, external world and replace it with a heightened understanding of inner reality. There is thawed convection that this inner world possesses a much greater reality than the outer one. Juergensmeyer (1978) delineated distinctive features of this organization that might have contributed to its increasing membership. These features are separate tradition, science as a model for spiritual knowledge, the spiritual character of a body, a spiritual family, social service and a spiritual socialism. The separate tradition is marked by insistence on the authority of the living Guru. This organization represents a blend of various sources, including devotion to a personal Guru and devotion to a concept of the sacred without attributes and forms. The Radha Soami teachings lay emphasis on self-realization and advocate the practice of meditation. It is believed that the Guru and one's own personal experience form the basis of scientific modal to gain spiritual knowledge as the latter validates the formers and the human body can be regarded as a "spiritual laboratory". The spiritual character of the body is based on the commonly held Indian belief regarding the quality of mind and soul, and linking the soul with the sound current within. The concept of spiritual family and socialism has been emphasized by the organization. The members of the community regard the Guru as a father and other member as their family member, which provide them with the character of home.

The ancient scriptures of philosophy, religion and folklores of India are rich sources of analysis of human behavior, interpersonal interaction and personality, and takes into consideration the holistic view of health and regards "oneness" of mind, body and soul in curing the ailments (Sinha, 1986; Kapur, 2001). The Radha Soami Organization has incorporated various religious theories of human nature, behavior and sufferings, traditional spiritual techniques and foreign ideas of science, managerial organization and developmental progress (Juergensmeyer, 1978). It is the conglomeration of Eastern conservative elements and the modern thoughts, and emphasizes on personal interaction, transcendence, and trust which provide with more conservative solution to the spiritual and moral dilemmas of modern life (Juergensmeyer, 1991). The importance of incorporation of traditional mode of therapy with Western therapeutic approach is found to be more effective in the third world countries where most of the people are illiterate, poor, lack scientific knowledge, and are mostly dwelling in the rural areas (Sinha, 1986; Hoch,1977).

The Radha Soami Organization is working at the grass root level to improve the quality of life of the people. In the spiritual discourses, the ways of enhancing total growth and well-being of the people are described. The super human-being goals such as attainment of contentment, humility, peace, benevolence, generosity, tranquility, happiness etc are emphasized. Ullman and Krasner (1976) suggested social action that fosters "positive deviance" must be adopted. The teachings of this organization take out consideration the cultural factors, needs, and expectations of the people. It considers the relevance of ecological, social, inter-relationship of personality, psychopathology, and culture. It aims at reducing and mitigating the root causes of sufferings: mental, physical, social, and spiritual. The mental and spiritual health can be achieved by the experiential method described by the organization. The promotion of physical health has been enunciated in its norms. The norms of this organization are following a vegetarian diet, abstinence from alcohol and other intoxicants, leading a moral and honest life and devoting one-tenth of one's time in meditation (Dubin, 2004). The personal, social, interpersonal, and ecological interaction can be enhanced by coming in contact with the other members, sharing their feelings, attitudes, causes of suffering, and aspiring for super human goals. The members of this organization are often involved in community services for the betterment of their counter parts and people in general.

Kakar (1982) said the key factor in the attraction of thousands of people in the organization from the 'perspective of healing' lies in their aspiration to receive mental peace and direction to the flow of life. Hoch (1977) said that people are best treated with humble spirit of true human care and concern by respecting the dignity of the individual as a whole with its present, past and future. The devotees in this organization are cured of their ailments in accordance with their needs and expectations. The teachings of this organization are offered to all irrespective of their religion, caste, gender, nationality etc. There is no intention of conversion and aims at providing additional light to the existing knowledge of the seekers (Singh, 2001). In this organization, Guru-Chela relationship has been emphasized. In this relationship, dependence is fostered where guru is perceived as a divine power and is believed to be capable of eradicating the sufferings of a person, whereas the patient himself plays a passive role of a recipient or victim on whom the various practices are performed (Neki, 1977, 1984; Hoch, 1977). It has been revealed by various studies that devotion and obedience to the divine power provides with huge and incredible strength and constant source of spiritual, moral and emotional energy to deal with the adversities and resisting destructive attacks of the environment as well as social and mental disruption thereby leading to enhanced general well being (Kay, Gaucher, McGregor, & Nash, 2010; McCullough & Willoughby, 2009; Pajević, Sinanović, & Hasanović, 2005)

The Radha Soami centers can be considered a kind of community therapeutic centers, wherein the people meet others of their kind. They share their beliefs, values, and experiences with one another. Brammer and Shostrom (1977) believed that the people in the way achieve higher levels of functioning and awareness, and humanness, and further to actualizing oneself or one's potentials. Kakar (1982) said that the members of the Radha Soami organization exhibit two kinds of psychological mechanisms viz. idealization and identification. The members along with the experiential methods of unification with God or self-realization are engaged in an unconscious struggle to deepen the process of idealization and identification. He said that the process of idealization and identification is propelled to its culminating point by the guru, the senior disciples, and in the spiritual discourses of the organization. He said that the idealization and internalization of the guru gives the disciple assurance and security that He would protect them from all kind of fears and anxieties. According to James (1902), two kinds of people exist in the World, one who needs to be born only once, called healthy minded, and the others are of sick souls who needs to be born twice to attain happiness. The world is viewed, as a "double-storied mystery" in the religion of twice born in which the person has two kinds of lives one is natural and the other is spiritual. He said the character and structure of twice born is incomplete in terms of moral and intellectual constitutions. These people are believed to be suffering from anxieties related to sin, guilt, predestination and regrets of the past, due to their inconsistent and excessive passions and impulses. Their inner constitution is imbalanced, in comparison to the healthy minded people. The devotees in the Radha Soami Organization inculcate the belief (via spiritual discourses and from the senior devotees) that their Guru can provide them with ultimate source of happiness. He in their view might be considered as a healthy minded person, capable of rendering them free of miseries and hardships of life. The devotees surrender themselves to the will of the Guru. They instill a belief that by the grace of their Guru they would not be worried and remain unperturbed during adversities and hardships of life.

Conclusion

It may be concluded that experience in the organization play a significant role in enhancing general well-being of the individuals. The spiritual practices such as meditation, service to humanity, following a vegetarian diet and leading a moral life enhances general well-being of the people. It also helps in self-realization, and increasing self-efficacy of the devotees that might have led to positive mental health. The Spiritual Organization work at the grass root level to improve the quality of life of the people thus may be regarded as community mental health institutions.

References

Berry, I.W, Mishra, R.C., & Tripathi R.C. (2003). *Psychology in Human and social Development: Lesson from Diverse Culture: A Festschrift for Durganand Sinha.* New Delhi: Sage Publications

Bhogle, S., & Prakash, I.I. (1995). Development of the Psychological Well-Being (PWB) questionnaire. *Journal of Personality and clinical studies.*11, 5-9.

Bhushan, L.I. (2004). Yoga: An Instrument of Community Psychological transformation. *Indian Journal of Community Psychology,* 1, 11-24.

Brammer, L.M., & Shostrom, E.L. (1977). *Group principles and methods, therapeutic psychology: Fundamentals of Counseling and Psychotherapy.* New Jersey: Prentice-Hall.

Chauhan, P. (2000). *Eternal Health: The Essence of Ayurveda.* Faridabad: Jiva Institute.

Daftuar, C.N. & Sharma, R. (1997). Beyond Maslow – An Indian Perspective of Need-Hierarchy. *Journal of the Indian Academy of Applied Psychology,* 24, 1-8.

Dalal, A.K. (2001). Health Psychology. In J. Pandey (Eds.), *Psychology in India revisited Developments in the Discipline.* Vol.2: Personality and health Psychology. New Delhi: Sage Publication.

Dubin, H.E. (2004). *Living Meditation: A journey beyond body and mind.* First edition. New Delhi: Baba Barkha Nath Printers. Radha Soami Satsang Beas.

Gable, S.L., Reis, H.T., Impett, E.A., & Asher, E.R. (2004). What do you do when things go right? The intrapersonal and interpersonal benefits of sharing positive events. *Journal of Personality and Social Psychology,* 87, 228-245.

Goleman, D. (1978). The Impact of the new religions on Psychology. In J. Needleman & G. Baker (Eds.), *Understanding the New Religions* (pp. 113-12). New York: The Seabury Press.

Hoch, E.N. (1977). Psychotherapy for the illiterate. In S.B. Arieti & S.B Chrzanowski (Eds), *New Dimensions in Psychiatry: A worldview* (pp. 75-92). New York: John Wiley.

James, W. (1902). *The varieties of Religious Experience: A study in Human Nature.* New York: The modern library.

Jangid, R.K. Vyas, J.N, & Shukla, T.R. (1988). The effect of the transcendental meditation Programme on the normal individuals. *Journal of Personality & Clinical studies,* 4, 145-149.

Juergensmeyer, M. (1978). Radhasoami as a transnational movement. In J. Needleman & G. Baker (Eds.), *Understanding the new Religions* (pp. 190-200). New York: The Seabury Press.

Juergensmeyer, M. (1991). *Radha Soami Reality: The logic of a Modern Faith.* New Jersey: Princeton University Press.

Kakar, S. (1982). *Shamans, Mystics and doctors: A Psychological enquiry In India and its Healing Traditions*. New Delhi: Oxford University Press.

Kakar, S. (1996). *The Indian Psyche*. Delhi: Oxford University Press.

Kapur M. (2001). Mental Health, Illness and Therapy. *Psychology in India revisited Developments in the Discipline.* Vol.2: Personality and health Psychology. New Delhi: Sage Publication.

Kay, A.C., Gaucher, D., Mcgregor, I., & Nash, K. (2010). Religious belief as compensatory control. *Personality and Social Psychology Review, 14*, 37-48.

Konopack, J.F., & McAuley, E. (2012). Efficacy-mediated effects of spirituality and physical activity on quality of life: a path analysis. *Health and quality of life outcomes, 10*.

Lysne, C.J., & Wachholtz, A.B. (2011). Pain, Spirituality, and meaning making: what can we learn from the literature? *Religions, 2*, 1-16.

McCullough, M.E., & Boker, S.M. (2007). Dynamic modeling for studying self-regulatory processes: An example from the study of religious development over the life span. In A. D. Ong & M.V. Dulmen (Eds.), *Handbook of methods in positive psychology* (pp. 380-394). New York: Oxford University Press.

McCullough, M.E., & Willoughby, B.L.B. (2009). Religion, self-regulation, and self-control: Associations, explanations, and implications. *Psychological Bulletin, 135*, 69-93.

Neki, J.S. (1984). Psychotherapy in India: Traditions & Trends. In A.K. Desousa & D.A. Desousa (Eds.), *Psychiatry in India* (pp. 333-356). Bombay: Bhalani book Depot.

Neki, J.S. (1977). Dependence: Cross-cultural consideration of Dynamics. In S. Arieti & G. Chrzanowski (Eds.), *New Dimensions in Psychiatry: A world View* (Vol 2, pp. 93-112). New York: Wiley & Sons/ A Wiley-Interscience Publication.

Oner-Ozkan, B. (2007). Future time orientation and religion. *Social Behavior and Personality, 35*, 51-62.

Pajević, I., Sinanović, O., & Hasanović, M. (2005). Religiosity and mental health. *Psychiatria Danubina, 17*, 84-89.

Rama, S. (1985). *Perennial Psychology of the Bhagavad-Gita.* Pennsylvania: The Himalayan Institute of yoga Science and Philosophy of the U.S.A.

Rao, P.V.K. (2000). Yogasanas in Psychotherapy. *Journal of the Indian Academy of Applied Psychology*, 26, 73-75.

Sinha, D. (1986). *Psychology in a third World Country: The Indian Experience.* New Delhi: Sage Publications.

Sinha, J. (1985). *Indian Psychology: Cognition.* Vol.I. Delhi: Motilal Banarsidas.

Singh, K.S. (2000). Psychological Intervention for facilitating Mental Health in a village: An experimental report. *Journal of Research and Application in Clinical Psychology, 3*, 28-32.

Singh, C. (1999). *Die to Live.* New Delhi: Baba Barkha Nath Printers. Radha Soami Satsang Beas.

Singh, S. (1997). *The Philosophy of masters: The Lord and His name.* Vol.4. New Delhi: Baba Barkha Nath Printers. Radha Soami Satsang Beas.

Singh, S. (2002). *The Philosophy of the Masters: Gurmat Sidhant.* Vol.1. New Delhi: Baba Barkha Nath Printers. Radha Soami Satsang Beas.

Singh, S.S. (2001). *Sar Bachan: An Abstract of the Teachings of Soami Ji Maharaj, the founder of the Radha Soami System of Philosophy and Spiritual Science: The yoga of the sound Curren*t. New Delhi: Baba Barkha Nath Printers. Radha Soami Satsang Beas.

Ullman, L.P., & Krasner, L. (1975). *A Psychological approach to abnormal behavior.* Second edition. New Jersey: Prentice-Hall/Englewood Cliffs.

Vahia, N.S. (1984). Yoga as Therapy. In A.K. Desousa & D.A. Desousa (Eds.), *Psychiatry in India* (pp. 377-386). Bombay: Bhalani Book Depot.

Verma, S.K., Nehra, A., & Puri, A. (1998). Quality and Quantity of Mental Health. *Journal of the Indian Academy of Applied Psychology*, 24, 59-62.

Verma, S.K. & Verma, A. (1989). *Manual for PGI General well- being measure.* Lucknow: Ankur Psychological Agency.

To Study Self- Esteem and Body-Esteem among Students studying in Professional and Non-Professional courses

Nadeem Luqman, Supriya Srivastava and Amita Puri

Abstract: Self esteem is an important aspect of personality which determines our perception of ourselves and the way we think people think about us. This concept is also related to body esteem which also reflects the way we perceive ourselves and determine the way we think, act and behave., most people care about how other people see them. Unfortunately, many people judge others by things like the clothes they wear, the shape of their body, if a person feels like he or she looks different than others, then body-image and self-esteem may be affected negatively. The present study is an attempt to know about the self esteem and body esteem of boys and girls, professionals and non professionals and how do they differ in their perception in this regard. The results are interesting their implications have been discussed.

Keywords: self esteem, body esteem, professionals

Introduction

Self-esteem reflects a person's overall evaluation or appraisal of his or her own worth. Psychologists usually regard self-esteem as an enduring personality characteristic. It has become the third most frequently occurring theme in the psychological literature. Self-esteem has been defined as the "level of global regard one has for self"(Harter,1993), or how well a person "prizes, value, approves, or likes" him or herself (Blascovish & Tomaka,1991). Self-esteem is all about how much people value them, the pride they feel in themselves, and how worth while they feel. This concept is important because feeling good about yourself can affect how you act.

Similarly, body image reflects how close a person's actual shape is to their ideal shape (Furnham, Badim, & Snead, 2002). It refers to the similarity between actual and perceived ideal body shape. Everyone has body-esteem and it has strong emotional overtones based on his experience in life. Body-esteem is a multidimensional self-attitude toward one's body, particularly its size, shape and aesthetics. It refers to person's evaluations and affective experiences regarding their physical attributes, as well as their investments in appearance as a domain for self-evaluation.

Body-esteem evaluation and emotions derive in part from self perceived discrepancies from internalized physical ideals. Body-esteem investment includes the extent of attentional self focus on one's appearance, its importance or how we perceive and relate to our own physical aesthetics. Body-esteem" is closely linked to our self-esteem and is sometimes referred to as "body-image". It's very similar to self-esteem, except it relates to how we feel about our body and how we care for it. It is also the mental image we have of our bodies, and how we believe we appear to others.

We tend to relate self-esteem to body-image for several reasons. First of all, most people care about how other people see them. Unfortunately, many people judge others by things like the clothes they wear, the shape of their body. If a person feels like he or she looks different than others, then body-image and self-esteem may be affected negatively.

Concerns about weight and shape are associated with women. Fallon and Rozin (1985) reported that women wanted to be thinner than they thought they were. Tiggmann and Pennington (1990) also reported body dissatisfaction in women. In contrast man's body satisfaction appears to be high but they also show body dissatisfaction (Cash &Winstead, 1986; Ridgeway & Tylka, 2005). Concern with body image have been linked to a decrease in self-esteem and increase in dieting among young women (Tiggeman & Pennington, 1990; Hill &Rogers, 1992; Abel & Richards, 1996. Young girls with heavier actual weight perception of being over weight were particularly vulnerable to developing low self-esteem (Tiggemann, 2005). Review of literature reflect that there is hardly any study which is conducted on self-esteem and body-esteem among students studying in professional and non-professional courses. Hence the motivation to conduct the same.

METHOD

Sample

The total sample consisted of 120 students, out of which 60 were from professional courses and 60 from non-professional courses; these two groups were further divided according to gender, i.e. each group consisted of 30 males and 30 females. Further, these participants were taken from J.N Medical College and from Faculty of Social Sciences, A.M.U, Aligarh.

Tools

Self-esteem was measured by Rosenberg self esteem scale (Rosenberg, 1965). It is one of the most widely used inventories for self esteem. There is total number of 10 statements.

Body-esteem was measured by Body-esteem Scale (Franzoi & Shields, 1984). This scale consists of 35 items, each has substantial loading in at least one of the three factors for women and men. It has five response categories ranging from strong negative feeling to strong positive feeling with scores from 1 to 5.

Procedure

In order to collect the data, purposive random sampling technique was used. Respondents were contacted by the researcher individually. The data was collected in two stages. First from students studying in professional courses and then from students studying in non-professional courses. Questionnaires were distributed to the individuals and they were instructed how to fill the questionnaires. All the respondents were assured that the information collected from them will remain confidential.

Results

Table 1: Table showing comparision of self-esteem between male students studying in professional and non-professional courses.

Gender	MEAN	SD	t-value
Males (professional courses)	21.25	3.95	3.52**
Males (non professional courses)	17.92	2.77	

* Significant at .05 level

** Significant at .01 level

Above table shows mean comparison of self-esteem among males studying in professional and non-professional courses. For males studying in professional courses the mean score is 21.25, which is higher, as compared to those studying in non-professional courses which is 17.92, t score is 3.52** which is significant at .01 level. These results indicate that males in professional courses had high self-esteem as compared to those in non-professional courses.

Table 2: Table showing comparision of body-esteem between male students studying in professional and non-professional courses.

Domains of body esteem scale For males.	MEAN	SD	t-value
Physical attractiveness (professionals courses) physical attractiveness (non-professionals courses)	44.48 39.62	6.08 6.07	2.46**
Upper body strength(professionals courses) Upper body strength(non-professionals courses)	33.40 29.25	4.97 4.24	3.26**
Physical condition(professionals courses) Physical condition(non professional courses)	50.92 46.91	6.80 6.99	2.31**

*Significant at .05 level

** Significant at .01 level

A look at the table 2 shows that on the dimension of "physical attractiveness" it was 44.48 for males in professional courses while for those in non- professional courses it was 39.62, and t was 2.46**. This shows that males in professional courses had higher significant scores as compared to those in non professional courses.

If we have look at the second dimension "upper body strength", here males in professional courses had a score of 33.40 and those in non professional courses it was 29.25, and t value was3.26**, on third and last dimension i.e., "physical condition" males in professional courses had a score of 50.92, while for those in non professional courses it was 46.91, and t value came to be 2.31** which is significant at .01 level. In all, it was seen that males in professional courses had higher scores on all dimensions as compared to those in non professional courses.

Table 3: Table showing comparison of self-esteem between female students studying in professional and non professional courses.

Gender	MEAN	SD	t-value
Females (professional courses)	20.92	4.94	1.14
Females (non-professional courses)	19.74	2.19	

Above table shows mean comparison of self-esteem among female students studying in professional and non professional courses. For female students studying in professional courses the mean score was 20.92, which is higher, as compared to those studying in non professional courses which was 19.74, t score value was 1.14 which is non significant.

Table 4: Table showing comparision of body esteem between female students studying in professional and non-professional courses.

Dimensions of body esteem scale For Females	MEAN	SD	t-value
Sexual attractiveness(professionals courses)	39.40	9.16	1.38
Sexual attractiveness (non-professionals courses)	43.03	8.17	
Weight concern (professionals courses)	35.25	6.38	.357
Weight concern(non-professionals courses)	35.92	9.52	
Physical condition (professionals courses)	46.37	8.19	.632
Physical condition (non professional courses)	47.55	7.52	

On "sexual attractiveness" it was 39.40 for females in professional courses while for those in non professional courses it was 43.03, and t value for both was 1.38, while on second dimension "weight concern" females in professional courses had a score of 35.25 and those in non professional courses it was 35.92, with t value of .35. On third and the last dimension i.e., "physical condition" females in professional courses had a score of 46.37, while for those in non professional courses it was 47.55, and t value came to be .63. All the t values were non significant.

Discussion

The way one feels about oneself is determined by self esteem. It determines and impacts the way we see, think, feel, respond and act which also relates to the happiness level. If we feel that we can face a particular situation, we will be able to feel less stress and on the contrary if we feel we will be unable to handle a particular situation, we tend to see it as a threat. It's the self esteem we have of ourselves which determine our perception of a particular situation – whether we see a situation as a threat or as a challenge which we feel capable to handle. Among many things which has a major impact on a person's self esteem is their self talk. A thinking style which is generally negative tends to make one perceive the negative side of things and cause many heartaches and problems in one's life. Body esteem related to our self perception of our body image also has the potency to make or mar one's life. How males and females differ in terms of their self esteem also have a significant impact on their self esteem.

In the present context, the results show that males had high self-esteem and positive attitude towards body esteem as compared to females. Males in professional courses had high self esteem and positive attitude towards body esteem as compared to those in non professional courses. The findings suggest that on the whole males had high self esteem and positive attitude towards body esteem.

Ah-Kion(2006) in his study found significant differences in both body-image and self-esteem, with adolescent girls having lower body-image and self-esteem than their male counterparts. Now the important question stands that why do adolescent females tends to have low self-esteem and negative attitude towards body-esteem or image? Maybe the answer lies in the fact that girls are usually more concerned with their appearance than boys as they have been socialized to overemphasize their appearance. It is seen that when women cannot attain the cultural ideal beauty standards, negative self-image may occur since self-esteem in women is positively related to attractiveness.

Thus, it can be concluded from the study that building self esteem will eventually lead to self improvement if we start to become responsible for who we are, what we have, and what we do. I'ts like a flame that should gradually spread like a brush fire from inside and out. When we develop self esteem, we take control of our mission, values and discipline. Self esteem brings about self improvement, true assessment, and determination, irrespective of the fact whether we are professionals or non professionals and belonging to either gender.

REFERENCES

Abel, S.C., & Richards, M.H. (1996). The relationship between body shape satisfaction and self esteem: An investigation of gender and class differences. Journal of youth and Adolescence, 25, 61-703.

Hill, A.J., & Rogers, P.J. (1992). Eating in the adult world: The rise of dieting in childhood and adolescence. British journal of Clinical psychology, 31, 95-105.

Fallon, A.E, Rozin, P. (1985). Sex differences in perceptions of desirable body shape. Journal of abnormal psychology, 94,102-105.

Tiggeman, M., & Pennington, B. (1990). The development of gender differences in body-size dissatisfaction, Australian psychologist, 25,306-313.

Cash, H. & Winstead, N. (1986). The great American shape up. Psychology today, 12, 30-37.

Jennifer, Kion, A.H. (2006). Body image and self esteem: A study of gender differences among mid adolescents, Gender and behaviour, 4(1), 534-549.

Franzoi, S and Shields.M. (1984). The body-esteem scale: Multidimensional structure and sex differences in a college population, Journal of personality assessment, 48,173-178.

Rosenberg. M. (1965). Society and adolescent self image Princeton, N.J: Princeton University press.

Tiggeman, M. (2005). Body dissatisfaction and adolescent self esteem: Prospective findings, School of psychology, Flinders University, GPO box 2100, Adelaide, SA 5001, Australia.

Harter, S. (1993). Causes and consequences of low self-esteem in children and adolescents. In R.F.Baumeister (Ed), Self-esteem: The puzzle of low self regard. New York: Plenum.

Blascovich, J., & Tomaka, J. (1991). Measures of self esteem. In J.P.Robinson, P.R. Shaver, & L.S. Wrightman (Eds.), Measures of personality and social psychological attitudes. Volume 1 of Measures of social psychological attitude (pp. 115-160). San Diego, CA:Academics.

Furnham, A., Badmin, N., & Sneade, I. (2002). Body image dissatisfaction: Gender differences in eating attitudes, and reasons for exercise. The journal of psychology, 136,581-596.

Mruk, C. (1995). *Self-Esteem: Research, Theory, and Practice*. Springer.

Guindon, M. H. (2002). Toward Accountability in the Use of the Self-Esteem Construct. *Journal of Counseling & Development, 80(2)*, 204-214.

Robins, R.W., Trzesniewski, K.H., Tracy, J.L., Gosling, S.D., & Potter, J. (2002). Global self-esteem across the lifespan. *Psychology and Aging*, 17, 423-434.

Rosenberg, M. (1976). *Beyond Self-Esteem: The Neglected Issues in Self-concept Research.* Paper presented at the annual meetings of the ASA.

Rosenberg, M. (1979). *Conceiving the Self.* Basic Books.
Rosenberg, M., & Owens, T.J. (2001). Low self-esteem people: A collective portrait. In T.J. Owens. S. Stryker, & N. Goodmanm (Eds.), *Extending self-esteem theory and research* (pp. 400-436). New York: Cambridge University Press.
Silverstone, P. H., & Salsali, M. (2003). Low self-esteem and psychiatric patients: Part I–The relationship between low self-esteem and psychiatric diagnosis. *Annals of General Psychiatry, 2(1)*, 2.
Viktor, G. (1982). The Self-Concept. *Annual Review of Sociology*, 8:1–33.

Perceptual shifting in Yoga Practitioners: Motivating Factors

Debjani Mukherjee

Abstract: Yoga in ancient days was a science of personal discovery and self inquiry. This definition has gone a perceptual change and in modern days considered to be a regime for physical fitness as well as mental hygiene. Healthy body is an essential ingredient for a healthy mind. Young executives are getting pulled into yoga as a means of releasing their corporate stress. In this study an attempt has been made to map the changes in perceptions of yoga practitioners as they travel though the years doing so. The perceptions are regarding the changes in their motive of continuing yoga and what makes them sustain doing this activity.

Introduction

Yoga means "joined together." The word comes from the ancient Sanskrit root word yug, which means "to unify." Graham Ledgerwood says a yogi is one who consciously unifies body, mind, emotions, and spirit so that they work together very well. From that stems the direct experience of one self that is beyond the false identities. Another modern adaptation of this principle is the word holistic, meaning to become whole, or to realize your underlying completeness and wholeness.

Yoga is considered to be a treasure house of the discipline of health science. Surreal and mystical unknown perceptions has been associated with yoga that was very subjective and nobody unearthed the scientific basis of yoga for thousands of years. At the outset and initial stage people only preferred to practice the physical aspect of yoga because the body felt good, light, vibrant, healthy and energetic. That is how asana and pranayama in yoga practice became popular, and even today most people only know this physical aspect of yoga.

Deepak Chopra defined yoga, "Traditionally, yoga is the science of the Self. Yoga seeks to help us understand our inner world through various techniques that include meditation, asanas, breathing, focused awareness, and certain rules of behavior and conduct. If by religion we mean the religious experience of transcendence, the loss of fear of death, and the emergence of platonic qualities such as truth, beauty, goodness, harmony, and evolution, then yes, yoga can give us a religious experience. It is not religion in the form of ideology, dogma, belief systems, or compliance; it's a spiritual experience that gives us access to a universal domain of reality."

Generally yoga, though not a religion in the traditional and orthodox sense, was adopted and utilized by every religious tradition that emerged from Vedic India, including Buddhism and Hinduism. Yoga lays out the means to overcome suffering and achieve self-realization and mental tranquility and physical relaxations.

Yoga also recommends meditation on, and inculcation of lovingness, cultivation of compassion, goodwill and acceptance, as well as non-violence, truthfulness, training the senses, non-possessiveness, beautification of both mind and body and other such virtues. It inculcates discipline in the thought processes. Introspection and looking inward dispassionately at one's own self is facilitated by yogic dhyana and yoga nidra. Religions also recommend cultivating such virtues. However, it is self-evident that cultivating these ways of being are not themselves religion. When these are practiced in Yoga, the subtler, finer, truer aspects of our being are revealed, and this may or may not be seen in the context of religion. That choice rests with each individual person and every person develops it in his own way.

Spirituality is natural instinct of humanity. The only stimulus required is to blossom spirituality in human beings by developing divine nature of inner Self. Initially there may struggle to for our spiritual nature to bloom, just like the planted seed in the earth before it becomes a tree and bears fruit. Wikipedia defines Spirituality as a process of personal transformation, either in accordance with traditional religious ideals, or, increasingly, oriented on subjective experience and psychological growth independently of any specific religious context. In a more general sense, it may refer to almost any kind of meaningful activity or blissful experience. According to Waaijman, the traditional meaning of spirituality is a process of re-formation which "aims to recover the original shape of man, the image of God. Gender differences may be there in the ushering of spiritualism. Queries that strike the mind are:

- Why the working people who practice yoga on a daily basis don't feel good if they miss out on it, even for a day.
- What makes them get initiated into this regime and make them sustain this activity?
- Is there a perceptual change regarding yoga over the years?
- Is it the religious or spiritual factor that keeps them going?
- Are there any differences in perceptions of males and females regarding yoga?
- What is the feel good factor in the whole process that makes them take time off to partake in yoga?

In the present study the respondents are working in various professions like the public sector, academics and the corporate sector and practice yogic asanas on a daily basis. An attempt has been made to study the perceptions of these yoga practitioners regarding the exercises that they do every day.

Sample: 90 professionals were asked about their impressions regarding yoga. Respondents were categorized in three groups in terms of years of practice:

0-2 years (category 1),
2-6 years (category 2),
6 and above (category 3).

Age of the respondents varied from 25 years to 40 years. Both males and females participated in this research. All are employed in a lucrative job in the industry or academics or their own business. Most of the respondents practice yoga on a daily basis.

Pre Testing Lecture: Before the data collection was done explanation regarding religion and spirituality was given to the respondents. Differences between religion and spiritualism were made clear. Fuller and Millers explanations were used to make the concept clear. Robert Fuller describes the words religious and spiritual as generally used to describe all the various aspects of the concept of religion. Gradually, the word spiritual came to be associated with the private realm of thought and experience while the word religious came to be connected with the public realm of membership in a religious institution with official denominational doctrines. Miller points out that one possible differentiation among the constructs religion and spirituality is to view religion as primarily a social phenomenon while understanding spirituality on an individual level.

A study of the differences between those self-identified as spiritual and those self-identified as religious found that the former have a loving, forgiving while those identifying themselves as religious see their god as more judgmental. Religion is an institution established by man for various reasons and is organized and structured. Spirituality is born in a person and develops in the person. Spirituality extends to all facets of a person's life. Bryant (2007) defined spirituality as: the process of seeking personal authenticity, genuineness, and wholeness.

Characteristics Distinguishing Religion and Spirituality (Fuller 2001)

Religion	Spirituality
Society and community-focused	Personal
Observable, measurable, objective	Less visible and measurable, more subjective
Formal, orthodox, organized	Less formal, less orthodox, less sympathetic
Behavior-oriented, outward practices	Emotion-oriented, inward-directed
Authoritarian in terms of behaviors	Not authoritarian, little accountability
Doctrine separating good from evil	Unifying, not doctrine-oriented

Interpolated Activity: Sometime was given to the respondents to introspect after the discourse on religion and spirituality, before they took the test. Thereafter they were asked to mark their choices regarding the areas given below. 1 score was assigned to 'Yes' response and 0 was assigned to 'No' response.

Items	Yes - 1	No – 0
Yoga is a religion –A		
Yoga is spiritual-B		
Yoga is obsession for you-C		
Yoga is a body healing process-D		
Yoga is a cleansing process of mind and body-E		

Table 1: Female (Category 1)

Female	A	B	C	D	E
Mean	0.58	0.33	0.33	1.00	1.00
Standard Error	0.15	0.14	0.14	0.00	0.00
Median	1.00	0.00	0.00	1.00	1.00
Mode	1.00	0.00	0.00	1.00	1.00
Standard Deviation	0.51	0.49	0.49	0.00	0.00
Count	12.00	12.00	12.00	12.00	12.00
Confidence Level (95.0%)	0.33	0.31	0.31	0.00	0.00

Table 2: Male (Category 1)

Male	A	B	C	D	E
Mean	0.06	0.06	0.11	0.94	0.61
Standard Error	0.06	0.06	0.08	0.06	0.12
Median	0.00	0.00	0.00	1.00	1.00
Mode	0.00	0.00	0.00	1.00	1.00
Standard Deviation	0.24	0.24	0.32	0.24	0.50
Sum	1.00	1.00	2.00	17.00	11.00
Count	18.00	18.00	18.00	18.00	18.00
Confidence Level(95.0%)	0.12	0.12	0.16	0.12	0.25

Category 1 respondents were people who have been in practicing yoga for minimum of few months to a maximum of 2 years. Comparing males with females of this category it was found that the females had different perceptions as compared to males. 58% females agreed to the religious factor -A in practicing of yoga while only 6% males felt so. Same results showed for spirituality-B in yoga, with 33% females and 6% males agreeing to it. Both males and females of this category didn't feel the obsession-C for yoga and another common factor between both the sexes is that both agreed to yoga to be a body healing therapy-D and lastly all women found it positively affecting both the mind and body-E whereas 61% men agreed with it.

Table 3: Overall Scores (Category 1)

Overall	A	B	C	D	E
Mean	0.27	0.17	0.20	0.97	0.77
Standard Error	0.08	0.07	0.07	0.03	0.08
Sum	8.00	5.00	6.00	29.00	23.00
Count	30.00	30.00	30.00	30.00	30.00
Confidence Level(95.0%)	0.17	0.14	0.15	0.07	0.16

Therefore the overall scores of this group show that the whole group unanimously agreed with item D with the confidence level 95.0% being .07. Their perception of yoga to be a religious factor or a spiritual factor was negated by their responses. 77% people agreed yoga to be a cleansing process of both mind and body.

Table 4; Female (Category 2)

Female	A	B	C	D	E
Mean	0.50	0.57	0.50	0.64	0.71
Standard Error	0.14	0.14	0.14	0.13	0.13
Sum	7.00	8.00	7.00	9.00	10.00
Count	14.00	14.00	14.00	14.00	14.00
Confidence Level(95.0%)	0.30	0.30	0.30	0.29	0.27

Table 5: Male (Category 2)

Male	A	B	C	D	E
Mean	0.31	0.38	0.56	0.75	0.81
Standard Deviation	0.52	0.51	0.52	0.5	0.47
Sum	5.00	6.00	9.00	12.00	13.00
Count	16.00	16.00	16.00	16.00	16.00
Confidence Level (95.0%)	0.26	0.27	0.27	0.24	0.21

Category 2 respondents were people who have been doing yoga regularly for 2-6 years. Comparing males with females of this category it was found that the females had different perceptions as compared to males. 50% females agreed to the religious factor -A in practicing of yoga while only 31% males felt so. Same results showed for spirituality-B in yoga, with 57% females and 38% males agreeing to it. Around 50% males and females of this category feel the obsession-C for yoga and another common factor between both the sexes is that both agreed to yoga to be a body healing therapy-D and more men found it positively affecting the mind and body together-E, as compared to females.

Table 6: Overall Scores (Category 2)

Overall	A	B	C	D	E
Mean	0.40	0.47	0.53	0.70	0.77
Standard Error	0.09	0.09	0.09	0.09	0.08
Sum	12.00	14.00	16.00	21.00	23.00
Count	30.00	30.00	30.00	30.00	30.00
Confidence Level(95.0%)	0.19	0.19	0.19	0.17	0.16

The overall scores of this group show that more than half respondents of the group agreed with item D with the confidence level 95.0% being .17. Yoga to be a religious factor and a spiritual factor was accepted by almost 40%-47% respondents. 77% people agreed yoga to be a cleansing process of both mind and body.

Table 7: Female (Category 3)

Female	A	B	C	D	E
Mean	0.60	0.67	0.47	0.40	0.93
Standard Error	0.13	0.13	0.13	0.13	0.07
Sum	9.00	10.00	7.00	6.00	14.00
Count	15.00	15.00	15.00	15.00	15.00
Confidence Level (95.0%)	0.28	0.27	0.29	0.28	0.14

Table 8: Male (Category 3)

Male	A	B	C	D	E
Mean	0.67	0.73	0.60	0.53	0.80
Standard Error	0.13	0.12	0.13	0.13	0.11
Sum	10.00	11.00	9.00	8.00	12.00
Count	15.00	15.00	15.00	15.00	15.00
Confidence Level (95.0%)	0.27	0.25	0.28	0.29	0.23

Category 3 respondents were people who have been doing yoga regularly for more than 6 years. Comparing males with females of this category it was found that both had almost similar perceptions regarding yoga. Around 60% males and females agreed to the religious factor – A in practicing of yoga. Same results showed for spirituality-B in yoga, with 67% females and 73% males agreeing to it. Almost half of the population of both males and females feel the obsession-C for yoga and less females 40% agreed to yoga to be a body healing therapy-D, as compared to males 60%. Both men and women found it positively affecting the mind and body together-E.

Table 9: Overall Scores (Category 3)

Overall	A	B	C	D	E
Mean	0.63	0.70	0.53	0.47	0.87
Standard Error	0.09	0.09	0.09	0.09	0.06
Sum	19.00	21.00	16.00	14.00	26.00
Count	30.00	30.00	30.00	30.00	30.00
Confidence Level(95.0%)	0.18	0.17	0.19	0.19	0.13

The overall scores of this group show that more than half of the group agreed with item A, B C. Whereas for item D there has been a lowering in the preference level with less than 50% of the respondent agreeing to it. 87% people agreed yoga to be a cleansing process of both mind and body.

Graph Showing Comparative Responses of Different Categories

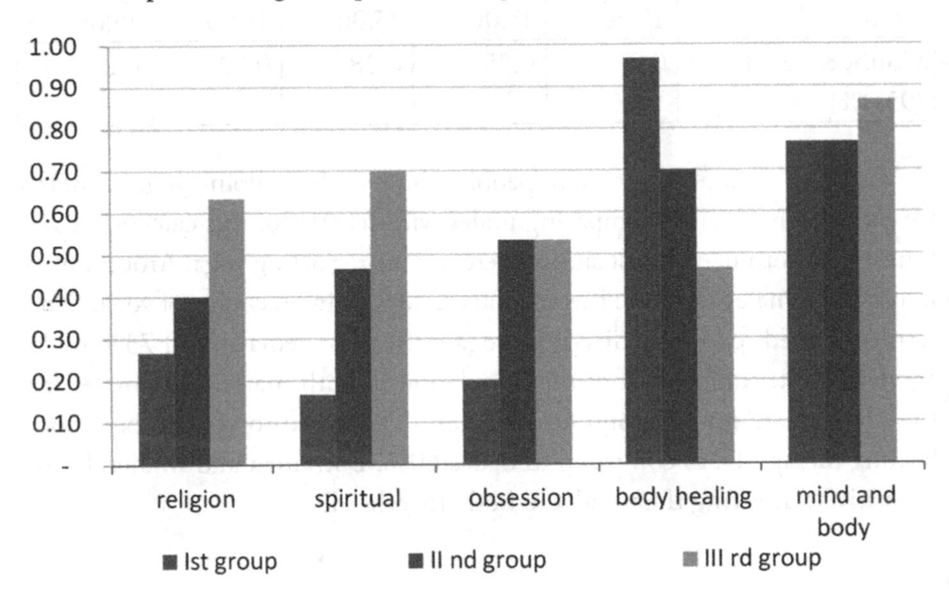

Discussion: As we can see from the graph above, there has been a perceptual shifting in all the categories of respondents.

Religious factor has been found to increase as the years of practicing yoga increased. This increase is quite significant.

Spiritual aspect in yoga also went through a perceptual change over the years. It was found to be significantly increasing as years rolled by.

Feeling of obsession regarding yoga was less in category 1, but after 2-3 years of regular practice respondents were found to be mentally hooked to it. Obsession was felt by half of the respondents of both category 2 and 3.

Amazing results were found regarding Body Healing (Item D) where significant shifting of perceptions was noticed in the respondents of all the three categories. Almost all the respondents of category A reported to find yoga a process of body fitness and healing (97%). After few years of practice, this went down to 77% in category B and only 47% of the respondents of category C reported yoga to be a body healing process.

The only consistent area was the Mind and Body Cleansing (Item E). Yoga was found to be facilitating a healthy mind as well body by respondents of all the categories.

We have seen the slow shifting in perceptions of yoga practitioners over the years. What started as a purely body fitness regime with very little religious and spiritual ingredients in it went on to become a religious and spiritual exercise with the body healing taking a backseat.

Females have been found to be having more religious and spiritual factor as compared to men. This fact has been the reported by other researchers also like Hammermeister, Flint, El-Alayli, Ridnour, & Peterson, 2005. While there may be a correlation between gender and religiousness, Simpson, Cloud, Newman, and Fuqa 2008, believe that the relationship is really between gender orientation and religiousness. In other words differences in religiousness depend on how masculine or feminine an individual is. Women are more likely to describe religion as a "relationship with God," while men more often deem it a "set of beliefs", Stokes, 1990. The alchemical processes of yoga practice affect the male and female hormonal cycles very differently, and women need to ensure that their practice supports their femininity says Felicia M. Tomasko. Bryant 2009 reports, women may experience greater social pressure to conform to the expectations of their religious friends. In adopting a spiritual persona, women may be responding to group norms with respect to internalizing and reflecting the traits that "good" women should exhibit. The pressure for men to assume socially desirable characteristics (spirituality in this case) may not be as strong in religious peer groups that potentially hold a different set of expectations for men's and women's conformity and behavior.

Religious and spiritual leanings has been reported to be positively correlated with ageing. What does change significantly is interest and vision in an inner journey. Numerous scholars have observed that middle and later life involve an experience of increasingly transcendent aspects of inner life, Alexander et al. Many people find that their attention shifts from competition toward affiliation and from self-centeredness toward generativity—care and concern for younger generations. Religious and spiritual journey is ushered as people age and gets enhanced with years of practicing yoga. This fact has been experienced in this study.

This study has mapped the shifting of perceptions of a yoga practitioner. What starts as a purely fitness regime transforms into a spiritual journey. The fairer gender are more religion oriented in their practice of yoga as compared to their male counterpart. Spiritual factor also is more in the females as compared to males. But both are affected similarly in their motive of continuing with yoga as they age. Both religion and spiritual aspect increase in them as they age.

References

Alexander, C. N. Davies, J. L. Dixon, C. A. Dillbeck, M. C. Druker, S. M. Oetzel, R. M. Muehlman, J. M. Orme-Johnson, D. W. (1990). "Growth of Higher Stages of Consciousness: Maharishi's Vedic Psychology of Human Development." In *Higher Stages of Consciousness.* Edited by C. N. Alexander and E. J. Langer. New York: Oxford University Press, 1990. Pages 286–341.

Bryant, A. N. (2007). Gender differences in spiritual development during the college years. Sex Roles, 56(11-12), 835–846. doi: 10.1007/s11199-007-9240-2

Bryant, A.N. (2009), "Gender Differences in Spiritual Development During the College Years", Springer Science + Business Media, LLC 2007

Deepak Chopra, MD, Founder of The Chopra Foundation, author, public speaker, physician, La Jolla, California

Felicia M. Tomasko, http://www.layogamagazine.com/issue18/Feature/feature.htm

Graham Ledgerwood, the author of this chapter and the book Keys to Higher Consciousness is a Guru and teacher of yoga, metaphysics, and mysticism.

Hammermeister, J., Flint, M., El-Alayli, A., Ridnour, H., & Peterson, M. (2005).

Gender and spirituality 27 differences in spiritual well-being: Are females more spiritually-well than males? American Journal of Health Studies, 20(2), 80-84. http://en.wikipedia.org/wiki/Spirituality

Fuller, R. "Spiritual But Not Religious: Understanding Unchurched America", Oxford University Press 2001, p. 5

Simpson, D. B., Cloud, D. S., Newman, J. L., & Fuqua, D. R. (2008). Sex and gender differences in religiousness and spirituality. Journal of Psychology and Theology, 36(1), 42-52.

Stokes, K. (1990). Faith development in the adult life cycle. Journal of Religious

Waaijman, Kees (2002), Spirituality: Forms, Foundations, Methods, Peeters Publisher

Miller, WR. Thoresen, CE. (January 2003). "Spirituality, religion, and health: An emerging research field". The American Psychologist 58 (1): 24–35. doi:10.1037/0003-066X.58.1.24. PMID 12674816.

Spirituality and Psychological Well-Being among Indian Women

BY

Rashmi Singh

Assistant Professor,

Department of Psychology, Mahatma Gandhi. Kashi Vidyapith University, Varanasi, U.P., India

Email- drrashmi.mgkvp@gmail.com

Abstract: *Psychological well-being is deeply related to the individual's religious beliefs. Although the positive association between spirituality and gender differences in stress, happiness and life satisfaction is well documented, theoretical and empirical controversy surround the question of how marital status and spirituality actually shape life satisfaction and effect stress and happiness. This study aims to look at daily spirituality experiences and differences in marital status tempering stress, happiness and life satisfaction among the Indian women. Results revealed that unmarried scored higher on well-being and spirituality scale than married females. Spirituality was found to be positively correlated happiness and life satisfaction and negatively correlated with stress in unmarried women, whereas positively correlated with only happiness and negatively correlated with stress in case of married women. Multiple regression analysis did not reveal any moderating effect of spirituality on the relationship between stress and wellbeing in both the cases but a direct effect of spirituality on well-being of married women only whereas stress was a stronger predictor of well-being for unmarried women. Findings of the* *present study can help students applying religion as a coping strategy against stress thus enhancing their life satisfaction and happiness.*

Happiness is the ultimate goal of human life. Much research within the field of psychology concerns well-being, in general. Feelings of well-being or life satisfaction are important mental features that healthy individuals should enjoy. Past couple of decades have viewed psychological researches adapting a holistic approach towards understanding human happiness exploring spirituality and religion as one dimension of the cognitive, emotional, behavioural, interpersonal and psychological facets that make up a human being happy. Researchers have shown that those who are more religious or spiritual, and use their spirituality to cope with life, experience many benefits to their health and well-being (e.g. Pargament & Park, 1997).

Spirituality and religion have positive associations with well-being, general psychological function, and marital satisfaction, and negative associations with suicide, delinquency, criminal behaviors, and drug/alcohol use. Especially, sense of hope and peace, love and joy, meaning and purpose in life, self-transcendence, forgiveness of self and others, awareness and acceptance of hardship and mortality, and a heightened sense of physical and emotional well-being have been indicated as consequences of spirituality in nursing literature (Coyle, 2002; Haase et al., 1992; Reed, 1986; Tanyi, 2002).

The single best predictor of human happiness is the quality of social relationships (Diener, et al., 2008; Gleen, 1988; Gilbert, 2005). Perhaps married people are happier than unmarried and single ones, because "Marriage seems to buy you a decade or more of happiness," **It's not marriage that makes you happy, it's happy marriage that makes you happy**, says Gilbert (2005). Seligman (2002) writes: "Unlike money, which has at most a small effect, marriage is robustly related to happiness it is a proven fact married people are happier than unmarried people". Married persons report higher levels of happiness and well-being than single folks (Diener, 2000, Orden et al. 1968). Other data has shown a spouse's happiness depends on the happiness of their partner (Diener, 2008). This study also found younger wives were happier than older wives. On the other hand, at least one large study in Germany found no difference in happiness between married and unmarried people (Becker, 2003). Marriage has been associated with numerous positive outcomes, including better mental health, greater overall happiness and greater physical and emotional sexual pleasure than is experienced by cohabiters (Waite & Joyner 2001; Waite & Lehrer 2003).

On the global level, spiritual experiences have been shown to buffer against the negative effects of stress on well-being, A growing body of literature suggests that people often turn to religion when coping with stressful events. However, studies on the efficacy of religious coping for people dealing with stressful situations have yielded mixed results. No published studies to date have attempted to quantitatively synthesize the research on effect of marital status, spirituality and perceived stress on happiness. The purpose of the current study was to investigate if there are any differences in happiness and life satisfaction and among married and unmarried women.

LIFE STRESS AND WELL-BEING

In order to fully establish a rationale for the present investigation, literature documenting a firm inverse association between spirituality (e.g. internal religious orientations) and negative affective symptoms (Pargament, Cole, Vandecreek, Belavich, Brant, & Perez, 1999; Duncan, 2000) must be reviewed. As reported in numerous studies, adopting any one of several personal spiritual orientations often buffers against negative affective outcomes (Simoni & Ortiz, 2003; Fabricatore, Handal, & Fenzel, 2000). Previous literature has also pointed to a link between life stress, spirituality, and affective wellbeing (e.g. Tarakeshwar, & Pargament, 2001, Peltzer, Cherian, & Cherian, 1999). Fehring, Brennan, and Keller (1987) demonstrated the positive impact of spiritual well-being, existential well-being, and spiritual outlook on negative moods in response to life stress. Spirituality can help us develop healthy behaviors and lifestyles; find psychosocial support; and effectively deal with suffering, life's problems, and negative emotions such as stress, anxiety, fears, anger, and frustration.

SPIRITUALITY AND WELLBEING

The relationship between spirituality and well-being has been well-documented in the United States. Numerous empirical findings indicating salutary effects of spirituality/religion on physical and mental health have been found in the literature in Western society. In general, spirituality and religion contribute to lowering the risk of certain diseases (e.g., heart disease, emphysema, stroke, and kidney failure, etc.) and overall mortality. Spirituality and religion have positive associations with well-being, general psychological function, and marital satisfaction, and negative associations with suicide, delinquency, criminal behaviors, and drug/alcohol use. Especially, sense of hope and peace, love and joy, meaning and purpose in life, self-transcendence, forgiveness of self and others, awareness and acceptance of hardship and mortality, and a heightened sense of physical and emotional well-being have been indicated as consequences of spirituality in nursing literature (Reed, 1986; Tanyi, 2002). Shigaraki (1983) also maintained that whether or not people attain enlightenment, religion is considered to provide a peace of mind by integrating and harmonizing various contradictions, confrontations, and confusions in a daily life by providing existential meaning and reality and the principle of life. People will have comfort and hope through the existential meaning and gain emotional support through the principle of life.

Satisfaction with life is one of the efficient factors of human promotion and evolution. This issue is particularly important amongst women. The results have shown a meaningful relation between spiritual intelligence and life satisfaction, as well as between emotional intelligence and life satisfaction. Spiritual and emotional intelligence variables are predictors of life satisfaction. Fabricatore *et al.* have found that spirituality influences general satisfaction with life. Personal spirituality is a reliable predictor of increased satisfaction with life. Starks and Hughey in a survey of the relation between spirituality and life satisfaction in African American women have shown that women who had higher religious towards spirituality enjoyed meaningful correlations with satisfaction in life. Spirituality was a variable that played a role in life satisfaction in middle aged African women despite their age, income and education levels. The results of a study by Okulicz-Kozaryn have also shown that being religious was connected to higher satisfaction with life. With due attention to the aforementioned studies and the importance of satisfaction with life and recognition of factors related to this satisfaction, this research sought to determine if a connection between spirituality, stress and well-being (happiness and life satisfaction) existed in two groups, unmarried and married females. Spiritual intelligence was defined based on individuals' adjustment abilities that consequently influenced satisfaction with life.

Given the theoretical frame work present study aims at studying the psychological well-being in terms of their perceived happiness in life and life satisfaction, perceived stress, daily spirituality experiences and differences in them caused by marital status among the Indian women. More specifically the study aimed to study the levels of spirituality, stress and well-being and their and relationships among married and unmarried women, along with studying the predictability of psychological well-being by stress and spirituality, and moderating effect, if any.

Method

Sample: Two hundred (200) urban women (104 married and 96 unmarried) age between 20-40 yrs from Varanasi, selected through random sampling method, participated in the study. Number of extraneous variables liked family structure, number of dependents, socio-economic status, caste and the like were also recorded with the objective to equate the entire groups in order to find representative sample for the study.

Tools

1. **Perceived Happiness Scale** (Singh, 2014). PHS is a 20 item scale with five point rating scale. All the twenty items are related to positive mental health, directly or indirectly. The Inter-rater reliability of .86, Test-retest reliability of .86 and alpha co-efficient of .89 and the predictive validity through significant correlation with other test and original scale support its psychometric properties.
2. **Perceived Stress scale-** (Cohen et al, 1983, Hindi adaptation by Singh et al)- PSS is a measure of the degree to which situations in one's life are appraised as stressful. It is a 10-item scale and it was developed to measure the degree to which overall transactions with the environment were appraised as stressful.
3. **The Daily Spiritual Experience Scale** (Underwood, L. G. & Teresi, J., 2002). A 16-item self-report measure of spiritual experience. It specifically aims to measure ordinary, or daily, spiritual experiences – not mystical experiences (e.g., hearing voices) – and how they are an everyday part of the individual's life. The first 15 items of the

questionnaire are measured on a 6-point Likert-type scale: many times a day, every day, most days, some days, once in a while, and never or almost never. Item 16 is measured on a 4-point scale: Not Close at All, Somewhat Close, Very Close, As Close as Possible. Greater score shows lesser spirituality. Cronbach's α in the original version was 0.89, and in the present study, it is 0.92.

4. **Satisfaction with Life Scale** (Diener, 1985) was designed to measure global cognitive judgments of one's life. SWLS consists of 5 items. Statements representing scores ranging from 1 indicating 'strong disagreement' to 7 indicating 'strong agreement' were provided. The higher the score is on this instrument, shows the higher the global life satisfaction is obtained. An example of a statement is, "In most ways my life is close to my ideal". The authors reported that, test-retest reliability of .82, internal consistency of .87 and moderate relationships of the SWLS with other measures of subjective well-being.

Procedure- Participants were contacted in convenience sampling style by the researcher at their home. After rapport building and consent taking data was collected from personally on individual basis Participants completed the study voluntarily and they were assured of their anonymity. All the behaviour measures were explained and they were told to feel free to ask questions, if any. Next day they were collected and tabulated.

Results and Discussion

The obtained data was subjected to analysis of variance and mean comparisons and Regression analysis with the help of SPSS (16.1). The results appear in Table 1-4.

Difference Level of Happiness, Life Satisfaction, Stress and Spirituality according to marital status of women

Table 1 reveals that women of both groups based on marital status differed significantly on their levels of happiness (t(198)=2.279, p<.050. It is found that unmarried women with scored significantly higher on happiness scale (M=77.89; SD= 16.39) than married women (M=72.76; SD = 15.40) and similarly unmarried women scored significantly (t (198)= 4.456, P< .01) higher on Daily Spirituality scale than unmarried women (M=23.50; SD= 7.06) than married women (M=28.79; SD = 9.46). However no significant difference was found on level of stress and life satisfaction among both groups in this study.

Table- 1: Mean, SD and t-values on the Measure of Happiness, Life Satisfaction, Stress and Spirituality as a function of marital status of women.

Variables	**Marital Status**	**N**	**Mean**	**SD**	**t**	**df**	**p**
Happiness	Married	104	72.76	15.40	2.279	198	.024
	Unmarried	96	77.89	16.39			
Life Satisfaction	Married	104	26.00	5.52	-.273	198	.785
	Unmarried	96	26.21	5.25			
Stress	Married	104	19.88	4.58	1.443	198	.151
	Unmarried	96	18.93	4.69			
Spirituality	Married	104	28.79	9.46	4.456	198	.000
	Unmarried	96	23.50	7.06			

Correlates of Variables

Table 2 proves inter correlation coefficients (r) in happiness, life satisfaction, stress and spirituality among two groups of women. Significant positive correlation were found between happiness and life satisfaction (r=.401, $p < 0.01$); happiness and spirituality (r=.309, $p < 0.01$); significant negative correlation were found between happiness and stress (r = -.230, $p < 0.05$) ; spirituality and stress (r = -.-.299, $p < 0.01$) in married groups while in case of unmarried women significant positive correlation were found between happiness and life satisfaction (r= .380, $p < 0.01$); happiness and spirituality (r=.359, $p < 0.01$); life satisfaction and spirituality (r =.232, $p < 0.05$). Significant negative correlation were found between happiness and stress (r = -.206, $p < 0.05$) ; life satisfaction and stress (r = -.363, $p < 0.01$); life spirituality and stress (r = -.250, $p < 0.05$). Correlation analyses indicated that happiness is positively correlated to satisfaction with life, and greater levels of daily spirituality in both groups.

Table- 2: Correlation coefficients (r) between Happiness, Life Satisfaction, Stress and Spirituality

	Married Female				Unmarried Female			
	1	2	3	4	1	2	3	4
Happiness	-	**.401****	**-.230***	**.309****	-	**.380****	**-.206***	**.359****
Life Satisfaction		-	-.091	.061		-	-.363**	.232*
Stress			-	-.299**			-	-.250*
Spirituality				-				-

*p < .05. **p < .01.

Prediction of psychological well being by spirituality and perceived stress

Multiple Hierarchical Regression analyses were computed in order to assess the impact of daily spirituality and perceived stress on well being of women of both groups separately. Results are presented in Table 3. It is revealed from table 3a that spirituality of married women predicted in model-1 a small but significant (13.5%) portion of variance on happiness, (R^2= .135, F=6.68, p<.002). The relationship between spirituality and happiness is positive and significant (ß=.309, p< .01), i.e. increase in spirituality is associated with increase in happiness. Stress did not predict happiness (ß=.-.151, p> .01). Model-3 revealed that all the three variables predicted about 20.4% of variance in happiness among married women and 16.8 % of variance explained in case of unmarried women, altogether.

Spirituality did not predicted significantly alone (R^2= .097, F= .857, p > .01) whereas both stress and spirituality were predicting 19.6% variance Stress and spirituality were predicting 16% variance in happiness in unmarried women. Beta coefficient of stress *(*ß= -.130, p< .05) was significant and negative revealing that increased perceived stress in unmarried women was associated with lesser happiness in life.

Table- 3a: Summary of Hierarchical Regression Analysis for Variables Predicting Happiness

	Married Women (N = 104)									Unmarried Women (N = 96)								
	Model 1			Model 2			Model 3			Model 1			Model 2			Modeal 3		
Variables	B	SEB	ß	B	SEB	ß	B	SEB	ß	B	SEB	ß	B	SEB	ß	B	SEB	ß
Spirituality	.502	.153	.309*	.429	.160	.263*	.398	.159	.245*	-.595	.120	.332	.538	.118	.300	.528	.248	.116
Perceived Stress				.-508	.329	-.151	-.436	.328	-.130				-.778	.219	-.234*	1.204	.340	.351*
Perceived Stress X Spirituality							-.062	.034	-.170							.006	.069	.009
R2		**135***			**.196***			**.204***			.097			**.164***			**-168***	

*p < .05. **p < .01.

For married women neither spirituality nor stress was found to predict life satisfaction (ß= .081, p> .01; ß=.-.120, p> .05) respectively vide table-3b, both predicting only .04% and 1.7% of variance in life satisfaction. For unmarried women perceived stress (ß= -.325, $p < .05$) explained a total of 15.3% variance in life satisfaction (R^2= .153, F = 8.406, $p<.01$). Regression analysis in model 3 capturing interaction effect did not reveal any moderating effect of spirituality on the relationship between stress and wellbeing in both the group in neither of criterion variables (vide table-3a b, unmarried SP x ST on HAP ß= 009, p>.05; unmarried SP x ST on LS, ß= -.041, p>.05); (married SP x ST on HAP ß= -.170, p>.05; married SP x ST on LS, ß= .112, p>.05). All the three variables predicted about 15.5% of variance in life satisfaction among unmarried women altogether. Therefore, Hierarchical Regression Analysis reveals that unmarried women's wellbeing (happiness and life satisfaction) is predicted in the present study by their perceived stress rather than spirituality.

Table- 3b: Summary of Hierarchical Regression Analysis for Variables Predicting Life Satisfaction

	Married Women (N = 104)									**Unmarried Women** (N = 96)								
	Model 1			**Model 2**			**Model 3**			**Model 1**			**Model 2**			**Model 3**		
Variables	**B**	**SEB**	**ß**	**B**	**SEB**	**ß**	**B**	**SEB**	**ß**	**B**	**SEB**	**ß**	**B**	**SEB**	**ß**	**B**	**SEB**	**ß**
Spirituality	.035	.058	.081	.056	.060	.096	.049	.061	.084	.034	.044	- .055	.117	.076	.151	.126	.080	.162
Perceived Stress				-.144	.124	-.120	-.161	.125	-.134				.358	.109	-.325*	-.356	.109	-.323*
Perceived Stress X Spirituality							.015	.013	.112							-.009	.022	-.041
R2		.004			.017			.029			.063			**.153***			**.155***	

*p < .05. **p < .01.

Discussion

Results reveals that women of both groups based on marital status differed significantly on their levels of happiness and Spirituality. It is found that unmarried women with scored significantly higher on happiness scale and daily Spirituality scale than married women However level of stress and life satisfaction was more or less equal among both groups. Unmarried women possessed more happiness than married women, this can be explained in terms of Kalantarkousheh et al. (2014) who also found more life satisfaction in married than in unmarried women. Seligman also regards happiness and life satisfaction to be a reflection of balance between an individual's desires and his/her present situation. In other words, no matter how much the gap between an individual's level of expectation and his/her objective is increased, there will be a decrease in satisfaction (Zaki, 1386). Ading (2012) found no difference among stress, spiritual involvement and life satisfaction but only on happiness among women.

Satisfaction with life and happiness is one of the efficient factors of human promotion and evolution. This issue is particularly important amongst women. The results have shown a meaningful relation between spiritual experiences, happiness and life satisfaction, as well as between stress and life satisfaction. spirituality in current study was found to be positively correlated with happiness and life satisfaction and negatively correlated with stress in unmarried women, where as positively correlated with only with happiness and negatively correlated with stress and no relation with life satisfaction in case of married women. Indicating that when there was a higher level of spiritual experiences, the level of happiness was found to be high and perceived stress found to be low in both groups. Loewenthal (2007) also emphasized that spirituality is closely linked with positive feelings in people. In spiritual perspective, pious people are more patient and more accepting to the fact what life that has been destined to them. Myers and Diener also found similar findings. Tloczynski, Knoll & Fitch (1997) found that high levels of spirituality were associated with healthy personality characteristics. Richter supported the hypothesis that spirituality approach to life is correlated with well-being.

Hierarchical Regression Analysis revealed that unmarried women's wellbeing (happiness and life satisfaction) was predicted in the present study by their perceived stress rather than spirituality. whereas only happiness in married women was predicted in the present study by their spirituality rather than perceived stress. Fabricatore et al. have found that spirituality influences general satisfaction with life. Personal spirituality is a reliable predictor of increased satisfaction with life. Starks and Hughey in a survey of the relation between spirituality and life satisfaction in African American women have shown that women who had higher religious towards spirituality enjoyed meaningful correlations with satisfaction in life. Spirituality was a variable that played a role in life satisfaction in middle aged African women despite their age, income and education levels. The results of a study by Okulicz-Kozaryn have also shown that being religious was connected to higher satisfaction with life.

It could be concluded in the end that direct effect of spirituality only on happiness of married women were noted in the study whereas stress was a stronger predictor of well-being (both happiness and life satisfaction) for unmarried women. It was interesting to note that in the present study unmarried women scored higher on happiness scale and had more spirituality score than their counterparts both variables were significantly positively correlated also married women scored comparatively significantly low on happiness and spirituality score than their counterparts both variables were significantly correlated also. Regression analysis revealed that their spirituality predicted their happiness scores more than stress, less spirituality led to less happiness than unmarried women. Stress scores predicted both happiness and life satisfaction in unmarried women, lesser stress and more spirituality led to greater well-being in them.

Findings of the present study emphasise the importance of spirituality and stress in predicting well-being among women. Spirituality of married women predicted their perceive happiness whereas stress was found to be important in predicting both happiness and life satisfaction of unmarried women. Findings of the study can help students applying religion as a coping strategy against stress thus enhancing their life satisfaction and happiness.

REFERENCES

Becker, A., (2003). "Marriage Is Not the Key to Happiness", *Psychology Today*, March 18, 2003.

Coyle, J. (2002) Spirituality and health: towards a framework for explaining relationship between spirituality and health. Journal of Advanced nursing, 37(6), 589-598.

Diener, E., & Suh, E. M., (2000). "Culture and subjective well-being. *Cambridge, MA: MIT Press.*

Diener, E., Emmons, R. A., Larsen, R. J., & Griffin, S. (1985). The Satisfaction with Life Scale. Journal of Personality Assessment, 49, 71-75.

Diener, M., & Diener McGavran, M. B., (2008). What makes people happy? A developmental approach to the literature on family relationships and well-being. In M. Eid & R. Larsen (Eds.). *The science of subjective well-being.* (pp. 347-375). New York: Guilford Press.

Fabricatore, A. N., Handal, P. J., & Fenzel, L. M. (2000) Personal spirituality as a moderator of the relationship between stressors and subjective well-being. Journal of Psychology and Theology, 28, 221-228.

Fehring, R. J., Brennan, P. F., & Keller, M. L. (1987). Psychological and spiritual wellbeing in college students. Research in Nursing and Health, 10, 391-398

Gilbert, D., (2005). *Stumbling on Happiness.* New York, NY: Vintage Books. ISBN 1-400-04266-6.

Glenn, N. D., Weaver, C. N., (1988). "The changing relationship of marital status to reported happiness. Journal *of Marriage and the Family* 50: 317–324. doi:10.2307/351999

Haase, J.E., Britt, T., Coward, D.D., Keidy, N.K., & Penn, P.E. (1992). Simultaneous concept analysis of spiritual perspective, hope, acceptance and self-transcendence. Journal of Nursing Scholarship, 24, (2), 141-147.

Hoppmann, C.A., Gerstorf, D., Willis, S.L., Shaie K.W., (2011). Spousal interrelations in happiness in the Seattle Longitudinal Study: Considerable similarities in levels and change over time. Developmental Psychology 47 (1): 1–8. doi:10.1037/a0020788]

Kalantarkousheh, S.M., Nickamal, N., Amanollahi, Z. & Dehghani, E., (2014). Spiritual Intelligence and Life Satisfaction among Married and Unmarried Females. *Open Journal of Social Sciences*, **2**, 172-177.

Loewenthal, K (2007). *Religion, Culture and Mental Health.* New York: Cambridge University Press.

Maselko, Naderi, F. and Roushani, K., (2011). Relation between Spiritual Intelligence, Social Intelligence and Death Anxiety. Woman and Culture.

Okulicz-Kozaryn, A. (2010). Religiosity and Life Satisfaction across Nations. *Mental Health, Religion & Culture,* **13**, 155-169. http://dx.doi.org/10.1080/13674670903273801

Orden SR, Bradburn NM. Dimensions of marriage happiness. American Journal of Sociology.1968, 73:715–731.

Orden, S.R., Bradburn, N.M., (1968). "Dimensions of Marriage Happiness". *American Journal of Sociology* 73 (6): 715–731. doi:10.1086/224565. JSTOR 2775777

Pargament, K. I, Cole, B., Vandecreek, L., Belavich, T., Brant, C., & Perez, L. (1999). The vigil: Religion and the search for control in the hospital waiting room. Journal of Health Psychology, 4, 327-341.

Pargament, K., & Hahn, J. (1986). God and the just world: Causal and coping attributions to god in health situation. *Journal for the Scientific Study of Religion,* 25, 193-207.

Pargament, K.I. & Park, C., (1995). Merely a defence? The variety of religious means and ends, *Journal of Social Issues,* 51, 13–32.

Peltzer, K., Cherian, V. I., & Cherian, L. (1999). Minor psychiatric morbidity in South African secondary school pupils. Psychological Reports, 85, 397-402.

Reed, P.G. (1986). Developmental resources and depression in the elderly. Nursing Research, 35(6), 368-374.

Seligman, M. E. P., Steen, T. A., Park, N., & Peterson, C. (2005). Positive Psychology Progress. American Psychologist, **60**, 410-421.

Seligman, Martin, E. P. (2002). Authentic Happiness: Using the New Positive Psychology to Realize Your Potential for Lasting Fulfillment. New York: Free Press. ISBN 0-7432-2297-0.

Shigaraki, T. (1983). Nenbutsu no genze riyaku:tokuni Shinran-shonin no baai [a worldly benefit of a Buddhist invocation: specifically a case of Shinran]. Jujutsu, Kito to Genze Riyaku:Taihorin-sensho. Tokyo: Daihorinkaku

Simoni, J. M, & Ortiz, M. Z. (2003). Meditational models of spirituality and depressive symptomatology among HIV-positive Puerto Rican women. Cultural Diversity and Ethnic Minority Psychology, 9, 3-15

Singh, R. (2014). Perceived Happiness and Daily Life Spirituality. Unpublished M.Phil Dissertation, Mahatama Gandhi Kashi Vidyapith, Varanasi. Spirituality and Human Psyche

Starks, S.H. and Hughey, A.W. (2003) African American Women at Midlife: The Relationship between Spirituality and Life Satisfaction. *Affilia,* 18, 133-147. http://dx.doi.org/10.1177 /0886109903018002004

Tanyi, R.A. (2002). Towards clarification of the meaning of spirituality. Journal of Advanced Nursing, 39, (5), 500-509

Tarakeshwar, N., & Pargament, K. I. (2001). Religious coping in families of children with autism. Focus on Autism & Other Developmental Disabilities, 16, 247-261.

Tloczynski, J., Knoll, C., & Fitch, A. (1997). The relationship among spirituality, religious ideology, and personality. Journal of Psychology and Theology, 25, 208-213.

Underwood, L. G. & Teresi, J., (2002). The Daily Spiritual Experience Scale: Development, Theoretical Description, Reliability, Exploratory Factor Analysis, and Preliminary Construct Validity Using Health-Related Data. *Annals of Behavioral Medicine.*24 (1).22-33.

Waite L. J., Joyner, J. (2001). Emotional satisfaction and physical pleasure in sexual unions: Time horizon, sexual behavior and sexual exclusivity, Journal of Marriage and The Family, 63,247-264.

Waite, L. & E.L., (2003). The Benefits from Marriage and Religion in the United States: A Comparative Analysis. Population and Development Review, 29(2): 255-275.

Yeganeh, T., Shaikhmahmoodi, H., (2013). Role of Religious Orientation in Predicting Marital Adjustment and Psychological Well-Being, Sociology Mind, 3(2), 131-136, http://www. scirp.org/journal/sm.

Printed in the United States
By Bookmasters